ETHICS OF TRAGEDY

Ethics of Tragedy
Dwelling, Thinking, Measuring

Ari Hirvonen

COUNTERPRESS
OXFORD

First published 2020
Counterpress, Oxford
http://counterpress.org.uk

© 2020 Ari Hirvonen

Rights to publish and sell this book in print, electronic, and all other forms and media are exclusively licensed to Counterpress Limited. An electronic version of this book is available under a Creative Commons Attribution-NonCommercial (CC-BY-NC 4.0) International license via the Counterpress website:

https://counterpress.org.uk

ISBN: 978-1-910761-09-0 (paperback)

Typeset in 11.5 on 13 pt EB Garamond.

Cover photo by Maiju Loukola.

Global print and distribution by Ingram

Acknowledgements

In order to write this book, I have had to listen closely to multiple other voices. My writing is a response to these words and sentences, sounds and rhythms, thoughts and bodies, scenes and movements.

I would like to express my deepest gratitude to Gilbert Leung for his generous comments, invaluable editorial skills, and especially for his great enthusiasm. I wish to thank Maiju Loukola for the cover picture that captures the soul of the book. Thanks also to Stephen Connelly for proofreading.

I owe heartfelt thanks to all my comrades, who have encouraged me with thinking philosophy, psychoanalysis, politics, and theatre. From Angus McDonald, I learned not only about Mark Fischer but so much when it comes to the interconnection between radical politics and critical thinking. The annual International Symposium in Phenomenology has been one of the most important spaces for me over the years. Especially, I would like to thank Cecilia Sjöholm, who introduced me to the Symposium and Jacques Taminiaux for his generous reception of my early paper on Greek tragedy that encouraged me to continue. Françoise Dastur and Sami Santanen have taught me how to pull through Hölderlin. Esa Kirkkopelto and Denis Guénoun have shown how to be a philosopher, a theatre director, and a dramaturg. Philippe van Haute and Simon Critchley have become my soulmates. Helsinki Lacan Circle has been my home base. Finally, I am indebted to the late Philippe Lacoue-Labarthe, who years ago wrote a dedication, 'One more, OK,' on my copy of the Finnish translation of his *De l'éthique: À propos d'Antigone*.

Contents

INTRODUCTION: OUR DWELLING PLACE 1
   Angels and Capitalist Discourse 4
   Paranoia. 9
   No Ethics? 12

1. MEASURING POETICALLY 18
   Sacred Names 20
   Faith 22
   Wink 24

2. WHERE NOW IS ATHENS? 27
   Death of Tragedy? 27
   Interability of Tragedies. 31
   Measuring of Justice 36

3. BEING IN EXILE 45
   Refugee Tragedies 45
   Children of Heracles 48
   Suppliants 51
   Oedipus, the Refugee 58
   Sanctuaries for Refugees 63

4. TRAGIC CATHARSIS 73
   Fear and Pity in Tragedy 75
   Cathartic Purification 77
   Phenomenological Catharsis. 79
   Desire and Catharsis 83

viii Contents

5. Tragic Conflict and Beyond 87
   Sovereignty 88
   Freedom Fighter 90
   Ethical Life 94
   Absolute Justice 102

6. Heroine: The Supplement 104
   Sexual Difference 105
   Eternal Irony 107
   Human Vulnerability 112
   Agonistic Humanism 115

7. Law and Dust 118
   Antigone—The Eternal Refugee 119
   Valid Law 122
   Certain Legality 130
   Unwritten Laws 132

8. Uncanny Stranger 138
   Dasein as Deinon 140
   Heart 144
   Ethics of Being 149

9. Unconditional Desire 156
   The Real 159
   Antigone's Desire 161
   Glimmering Crime 165
   Infidel Criminal Fidelity 149

10. Caesura 176
    Deconstructing Figures 178
    Interruptive Silence 182
    Antitheos 185
    Law of Tragedy 191
    Thinking/Measuring 199

11. SCENE 204
    Reading Tragedy 205
    Tragic Transport 209
    Material Tragedy 215
    Rhythm and Tragedy 220
    Scene as Assembly 223

12. THEATRE TRUTHS 226
    Concrete Tragic Situations 228
    Courage 233
    Justice 238
    Care 243
    Ethical Catharsis 250

CONCLUSION: CAPITALISM AND TRAGEDY 254

BIBLIOGRAPHY 259

NOTES 282

Introduction: Our Dwelling Place

In John Carpenter's 1982 film *The Thing*, a group of American researchers at Antarctic research station US Outpost 31 encounter a parasitic entity which metamorphoses and absorbs anything it contacts. By consuming and replicating living cells, the Thing is able to make perfect impressions of absorbed people into whose memories it has tapped.

Found from a block of ice in Antarctica, the Thing has a large mouth with sharp teeth, crab-like legs, and talon-like digits reminding one of a huge beetle. However, even this figure is not the true form of the Thing but an assimilated creature from another planet. Instead of any original form, the Thing has an indefinite number of various assimilations. Or more precisely, its true form is a single cell. It consists of billions of single-celled versions of itself that function in cooperation, forming complete organisms and parts. The Thing is able to choose the shape that suits its immediate needs.

The film received hostile reviews: 'boring ... impersonal,'[1] 'despairing and nihilistic,'[2] without the 'optimism of E.T.'.[3] The reviewers had got the idea. Instead of a grandiose narrative on extraterrestrials, the film reflects contemporary capitalist realism and its deterritorializing effects; as Mark Fisher writes, 'the limits of capitalism are not fixed by fiat, but defined (and re-defined) pragmatically and improvisationally' as it 'seamlessly occupies the horizon of the thinkable.'[4] For him, capitalism not so much incorporates as precorporates materials that used to have subversive potential. Capitalist economy and culture pre-emptively formats desires, hopes, aspirations, and alternatives. At the same time, it absorbs the past by transforming radical political events into reminders of the seduction of ideological fanaticism and totalitarianism, and transforming emancipatory literature, music, and art into artefacts. Practices, processes, and rituals are converted into aesthetic, consumerist, or entertainment objects. The contemporary reality is not solid and immovable, but this does not mean it is open to alternatives. Instead, we have to subordinate ourselves to 'a reality that is infinitely plastic, capable of reconfiguring itself at any moment.'⁵ Space and time, the body and the psyche, the subject and the object, a truth and a lie are governable entities. They are constantly processed and remade by an infinitely self-globalizing capitalist mode of governance. Moreover, techno-scientific capitalism has invaded bodies much more radically than industrialists. It has transformed autonomous human beings into the bodies of manual labour in order to extract from these bodies the maximum amount of surplus value. The Capitalist Thing transforms itself—through processes of production via the accumulation of money profits in financial markets for the commodification of biological processes—and back again. In this genome capitalism, the processes of production mean the synthetization of genomes and thus the building of synthetic life. As it accumulates the profits of genetic material, we might speak of the alienation of genetic ancestry. 'Unless we took those territories, somebody else would and that this would be still worse.'⁶ The Capitalist Thing is based on the growth imperative and exploitative practices that drive economic, political, and social spheres.

The Thing also presents a community in crisis. A group of Norwegian researchers chase a dog from their research station to US Outpost 31. A Norwegian shoots the dog and is subsequently shot dead by one of the Americans. The dog, adopted by the Americans, that is the Thing hidden in its dog form, fuses with the station's sledge dogs. The Americans find the Norwegian base in charred ruins. Among the frozen corpses there is a humanoid in a crippled state, which they take to their base only to find out that this injured thing ensnares the meteorologist George Bennings with its tentacles. Subsequently, the helicopter pilot RJ MacReady (Kurt Russel) burns Bennings-Thing. One by one the Americans are assimilated by the Thing, which finally destroys the station's electricity in its attempt to hibernate until a rescue mission comes, providing it with an opportunity to leave Antarctica and assimilate the rest of the world.

After two hours of crisis and paranoia, MacReady destroys the station and the Thing by triggering explosives. Childs, the station mechanic who had vanished in the snowstorm, returns out of the darkness. 'Where were you, Childs?' MacReady wonders. In the nihilistic final scene, MacReady and Childs, suspicious of each other's true identity, sit together outside the burning station with a bottle of scotch waiting to be slowly frozen to death. The film fades in black only to leave us in dread and unease.⁷ An alternative ending brings us to the next day. A dog runs away from the burned-down station. It stops to briefly look back, only to continue its run.

In 1917, Lenin believed that 'the crisis has matured' to 'a great turning-point' and 'we are on the threshold of a world proletarian revolution.'[8] Instead of being the messenger of global revolution, the turning dog is the Capitalism-Thing, which not merely causes and survives the crisis of US Outpost 31, but also benefits from it as it continues its run. The station biologist, Dr Blair, had a paranoid belief that the Thing, capable as it was of perfectly imitating any organism, would transform all life forms on Earth. Having paranoid views does not mean they are not true. The Thing's logic makes it spread across the planet. Marx anticipated this logic as he wrote in *The Communist Manifesto*, 'the need of a constantly expanding market for its products chases the bourgeoisie over the entire surface of the globe. It must nestle everywhere, settle everywhere, and establish connections everywhere.'[9] Today, only in what Jacques Rancière calls 'the imaginary radicalism,' which involves aggravating the crisis so far that it is brought to its tipping point, is there a belief that a radical break may be possible.[10]

Capitalist-democratic liberalism seems to be in constant crisis: from the financial crisis to the sovereign debt crisis, from the refugee crisis to global warming, from natural catastrophes to terrorism. In medicine, crisis (*krisis*) refers to 'the moment of resolution.'[11] The concept of crisis designates today the pathological state itself. Crisis is 'normal, at the heart of the capitalist system' and 'the pathological lexicon has become normal.'[12] Instead of being a state of exception, crisis has become a permanent state of things. It is not an exception but 'an excess in the logic of the system' and 'the extreme form of a normal operation.'[13]

The capitalist crisis policy defines the existing situation and contributes to the distribution of the sensible that sets up divisions between visible and invisible, audible and inaudible, inclusion and exclusion that 'reveals who can have a share in what is common to the community.'[14] That is to say, the crisis policy constitutes the symbolic, social, political, economic, and physical space as 'a certain way of dividing up the sensible.'[15] Instead of predicting the coming revolution, what we have is, as Leibniz would have put it, 'the best possible world'[16] in which the Capitalist Thing, the existing state of things, or the prevailing distribution of the sensible consists of intertwined single cells of apparatuses of capitalism, crisis, and security. Crises legitimize the hegemony of the security principle, which has become inherent to the normal function of political, juridical, and economic systems. A new model has the declaration of the state of exception gradually replaced by an unprecedented generalization of the security paradigm as the normal technique of government.[17]

4   Ethics of Tragedy

'The normal functioning of society is a functioning inhabited by illness,' or, as I would say, by the Thing.[18] The capitalist realism could be described as 'the dissolution of the transcendental,' the withdrawal of the political (*le politique*), the homogenization of all spheres of life, and the elimination of all alterity.[19] Capitalist realism presents itself as ontologically, politically, aesthetically, and geographically ubiquitous. This 'systemic violence of capitalism' is not attributed to concrete individuals or groups but is 'purely "objective," systemic, anonymous.'[20] Politics is identified with the effective management of capital and the security paradigm. 'Marx's once scandalous thesis that governments are simple business agents for international capital is today an obvious fact.'[21] The objective necessities of reality guarantee the legitimate governance and management. Democracy is vanishing as executive privileges are 'implied by the spreading logic' of the state of emergency.[22] Jean-Jacques Rousseau made a firm difference between the legislative power of the sovereign and the executive power of government. Today this distinction has melted away. There is 'an overwhelming domination of government and economy over popular sovereignty, which has been progressively run down in all senses.'[23] Consensual practices suppress political disagreements and struggles, which leads to 'the denial of the democratic ground of politics.'[24] Democratic politics is effaced under 'the exigencies of the limitlessness of global Capital.'[25] According to Simone Weil, for 'the possessor of force' there is nothing that would 'interpose between the impulse and the act, the tiny interval that is reflection.'[26]

Angels and Capitalist Discourse

In Paul Klee's *Angelus Novus* (see fig. 1) an angel of history hovers among the dead. His eyes are full of melancholy and despair as he sees the catastrophe, which piles wreckage upon wreckage, hurling it in front of his feet. Walter Benjamin describes the image thus:

> The angel would like to stay, awaken the dead, and make whole what has been smashed. But a storm is blowing from Paradise; it has got caught in his wings with such violence that the angel can no longer close them. This storm irresistibly propels him into the future to which his back is turned, while the pile of debris before him grows skyward. This storm is what we call progress.[27]

Fig. 1: Paul Klee, *Angelus Novus* (1920)

The infinite storm is the devouring Capitalist Thing. The wings of the angel are unable to hinder the high aspirations and great acceleration of progress. Her rhythmic scream of agony—*aiai, oimoi, aiai*—remain unheard. This unlimited progress and endless or mindless economic growth leave behind ruins. Capitalism that pervasively drives the economic, political, social, and moral spheres produces excluded and dispensable individuals from refugees and undocumented immigrants to the unemployed, poor, and homeless.[28] The angel witnesses human beings reduced to mere bare life in contemporary concentration camps; bodies excluded (or more properly: included in their exclusion) in urban ghetto hinterlands; human beings marginalized into silence and invisibility in the socio-politico-economic-aesthetic distribution of roles, positions, functions, occupation, and places; peoples colonialized and demonized all over the world.

Capitalism installs endlessly false needs that people have to satisfy, which 'shapes our experience of subjectivity.'[29] The imperative of late capitalism is that there shall be no limits for the self-management of capitalist subjects. Capitalist socio-economic and bio-material progress is excessively unlimited. Capitalism has no place for lack. Loss is merely a challenge for systemic and individual entrepreneurship. The subject can always fill its lack with chosen objects that are supposed to produce lack-less enjoyment. Ultimately, the subject's enjoyment is the enjoyment of its limitlessness. Simultaneously it has its own peculiar forms of discourse and knowledge formation.

For Jacques Lacan, the symbolic order refers to the social world of language and signification, intersubjective communication and relations, norms, conventions, and contracts. It is the pact through which language links the subject with other subjects. The practice of language is what dominates society. Lacan's concept of the-law-of-the-father refers to the law of separation that inaugurates the subjective life in language and signification that makes differences. As a result of the process of symbolic castration, the subject is, on one hand, marked with lack, and on the other hand, able to represent emptiness and negativity. The symbolic castration occurs through language, more properly, through the signifier that prohibits full enjoyment by replacing a thing with a word. The Name-of-the-Father, the paternal metaphor that creates the function of the symbolic father, introduce the child to the law, and ties law and desire, signifier and signified together. The lack marks the subject as the cornerstone of its being a speaking and desiring being. Without the law and the lack, desire would fade away. Without the symbolic father, everything falls apart.

The change of the subject's relationship to the symbolic and normative order of society started earlier. In 1972, Lacan introduced the concept of the discourse of the capitalist (*le discours du capitaliste*), which is related to the logic of consumption instead of the logic of production. The capitalist discourse had started to replace the master discourse, even though it was a mutated version of this.[30] Capitalist discourse brings the cultivation of a semblance of dissatisfaction together with the fantasy of completeness of the self-sufficient subject. In the discourse there are four elements: agent, an other, production, and truth. Crucial to the four earlier discourses is the desiring agent addressing an other (*autre*). This refers to the human tendency to create social relations with others, even though an other never receives the message as it was intended by the agent. The action upon an other has effects. The effect of such action is the product of the discourse. All actions of the agent of the discourse are based on the hidden or impossible truth, that is, what the agent of the discourse says conveys meaning that is unknown to the agent 'barred S' or '$\bar{S}$'. The agent cannot speak the truth but only in the name of truth. In the master discourse, the agent formulates a master signifier 'S1' (e.g. human dignity), which is imposed onto an other who is supposed to act by means of knowledge 'S2' (e.g. a citizen has to accept humanitarian intervention). This address rests on the repression of a subjective division of the agent '$\bar{S}$' (e.g. actually, human dignity may demand that we do not use war as a means of protection of human rights). As a product, an other is reduced to the position of an object '*a*' (e.g. a citizen is nothing but a pawn in the militarization of human rights).

In capitalist discourse, there is no connection between the agent S1 and an other S2. The divided subject $\bar{S}$, the semblance of dissatisfaction, is in the position of the agent. This means that discourse starts from the experience of subjective division, as in hysteric discourse, but instead of addressing an other, it addresses the master signifier S1. Capitalist discourse recuperates the lack and discontent of the subject within the system. The master signifier, the Market, functions as the truth for the divided subject whom it answers with promises of satisfaction. As a consequence, 'the capitalist discourse is grounded on the foreclosure of the impossibility of totalization that marks other discourses.'[31] One can circulate 'within the capitalist discourse like go-carts on a racetrack.'[32]

In capitalist discourse, the market economy tells us that we need. At the same time, it responds to the need by offering signifiers that are part of the master signifier S1, namely the Market and its various commodities and merchandise that satisfy the needs of the divided subject. The subject holds these signifiers as the truth of its discontent and remedy. Through the master signifier, the subject is able to ask for practical knowledge to produce objects for consumption. The subject is thus able to overcome its dissatisfaction and lack. This takes place through its alienation in the signifiers that promise to compensate for the lack and any flaws. Because the lack is presented not as structural but accidental, the subject may fill the lack within the market of supply and demand with commodities. Desire is transformed into demand that can be satisfied with practical solutions. For Lacan, 'the great invention of capitalist discourse is the exploitation of desire.'[33]

Capitalist discourse means the rejection (*Verwerfung*) of symbolic castration. The relation of the subject to the symbolic order is structured so that the subject considers itself a being without lack that cannot be repaired. The loss of absolute jouissance is denied and the unconscious is ignored. The subject believes it is in total charge of itself and able to freely decide the direction of its life insofar as it is free to choose objects that produce satisfaction. The powerful subject in capitalist discourse seems to be freed from its history, its genealogy, and the signification of inscriptions. In the capitalist society that functions without limits, capitalist discourse repeatedly pushes the subject towards limitless libidinal enjoyment.[34] The capitalist discourse that revolves around enjoyment turns the subject from desire and others towards the lack of enjoyment and means to satisfy it by the objects of enjoyment. The promised limitless freedom and enjoyment turns out to be the fact that the subject no longer occupies the position of an agent. The subject is not in charge; rather it is the object of enjoyment that exploits the subject.[35]

Renata Salecl relates capitalist discourse to capitalist ideology. Ideology, as Louis Althusser defines it, determines the subject's perception of the function of society, politics, and economy where this function is presented as obvious and given. It is not even necessary for subjects to believe in the ideology. It is enough that they believe that others believe in it and to pretend that they believe in it also. The ideology of the limitlessness of the subject and its freedom of choice dominates the subject's relation to the symbolic order and the law. The subject addressed by the ideology of late capitalism is 'someone for whom enjoyment is without limit.'[36] This ideology insists that the subject 'has the possibility to become a total master of his or her life.'[37] As subjects—living in the time of extreme individualism—internalize this ideology of limitlessness, they seem to be able to push the boundaries of pleasure endlessly and to satisfy their continuously expanding desires. Ultimately, capitalist discourse runs too fast and burns itself out.[38]

Paranoia

Capitalist epistemological practice is one of paranoid forms of knowing. By 'paranoid' I do not refer to any pathologizing diagnosis. It is strictly a certain position in relation to phenomena, things, and the world from which knowledge is produced.[39] Paranoid epistemic strategies are ways to access and organize 'true' knowledge. 'Paranoia is anticipatory.'[40] The imperative of paranoia is to avoid uncertainties and surprises. This means knowing what is ahead and behind. To avoid surprises, all possible risks and threats must be always already known and predicted. Crises and threats can be explained as the future is scientifically anticipated. Delusions and trust in the power of knowledge are thus linked. Paranoia is contagious and it tends to construct symmetrical epistemologies. It blocks alternative ways of understanding and alternative things to understand. Paranoid knowledge organizes the world. Its knowledge/power practices include a tendency to hegemonize itself. Paranoia is a strong theory since its truth is wide-ranging or all-encompassing and, thus, necessarily reductive. There are no fissures within paranoid knowledge. Paranoid knowledge strategies must dismiss all alternative knowledge formations and world explanations that threaten its authority. Truth is conditioned or affected neither by time and space nor subject and body. As non-situated and valid in every place, it is knowledge formed by a 'god trick.'[41] Paranoia is not merely a monopolistic strong theory but 'a strong *negative* affect theory.'[42] The crisis narrative is based on negative affects—fear, anguish, distress, terror, and anger. Paranoid knowledge is organized so that these affects and their causes are anticipated, identified, and warded off.

Paranoid knowledge strongly emphasizes the efficacy of knowledge. This knowledge is used by rational policy makers, public and private managers, planners, engineers, and financiers to construct the necessary governance and management structures of the state, economy, societies, bodies, and subjects. Paranoid knowledge reveals inevitable truths that dictate necessities to various stake holders. These unquestioned truths justify extraordinary measures and emergency state institutions and their normalization. The crisis narrative based on paranoid knowledge combines with the progress narrative of effective policies and economics. This monopolistic combination constitutes the *hubris* of capitalist knowledge/power practices.

The book *And the Weak Suffer What They Must* by Yannis Varoufakis is about the harsh austerity with which the European leaders decided to solve the sovereign debt crisis.[43] The title comes from Thucydides' *History of the Peloponnesian Wars*. Having invaded Melos in 416 BCE, the Athenians demanded that the Melians surrender and pay tribute to Athens—or be destroyed. The Melians argued that they were not the enemy of Athens but a neutral and independent city. They appealed to gods for assistance as theirs was a just cause. The Athenians could not understand their lack of realism. The powerful Athenians explained that rights are valid only between equals in power. For Athenians, 'the strong actually do what they can and the weak suffer what they must.'[44]

In Sophocles' *Antigone*, the second choral ode, called 'Ode to Man,' ventilates achievements, conquests, powers, and limitations of human beings.

> Many things are formidable, and none more formidable than man! He crosses the grey sea beneath the winter wind, passing beneath the surges that surround him; and he wears away the highest of the gods. Earth, immortal and unwearying, as his ploughs go back and forth from year to year, turning the soil with aid of the breed of horses. And he captures the tribe of thoughtless birds and the races of wild beasts and the watery brood of the sea, catching them in the woven coils of nets, man the skillful. ... And he has learned speech and wind-swift thought and the temper that rules cities. ... all resourceful; he meets nothing in the future without resource; only from Hades shall he apply no means of flight.[45]

A human being is the strangest of all (*to deinotaton*). An uncanny being (*deinon*) refers to both what is terrible (in the sense of overpowering) and fearful (of that which human beings are exposed). Wonderful but also monstrous, as Friedrich Hölderlin translates it: 'Monstrous (*Ungeheuer*) are many. But nothing / More monstrous than man.'[46] We, as monstrous and overpowering beings, have conquered nature and permanently transformed the biosphere, our ultimate dwelling place. We use power in the face of overpowering. As we respond to our own constitutional exposure with violence, we may bring disaster upon ourselves.[47]

The chorus of *Antigone* predicted the fate of the human being as a telluric force that transforms the biosphere, causes climate change, alters biochemical and element cycles, and increases carbon dioxide and reactive nitrogen levels. Immanent to 'The Ode of Man' is the alleged geological time of the Anthropocene and its predecessor, 'carboniferous capitalism,'[48] caused by the uncanny human being, the results of whose productive activities have crossed critical planetary boundaries and measures that define a safe operational space for human inhabitants with respect to the Earth system.

Still, the Capitalist Thing faces no future. Consider the one thing the wonderful human being is not able to conquer—our mortality; this ultimate limit, border, and measure. 'Death stays dark. Death he cannot doom.'[49] Today, the monstrous human being attempts to overpower death. Genome capitalism promises to extend life past its current boundaries, refusing to accept that the human being is not 'a mind with a body.'[50] Thus, capitalism is or aims at, in Hölderlin's words, 'the monstrousness, how of the God and man are paired.'[51] Martin Heidegger's words are more relevant today than ever: 'The self-assertion of technological objectification is the constant negation of death.' This death-denying objectification 'wills everywhere the constancy of produced objects,' finance instruments, bodies, and beings.[52] According to Françoise Dastur, the mortal being, the *Dasein* (*existentia, being-there, to-be-being*), cannot make itself finite because it is not the origin of its own being and is thrown into the midst of beings. Hence, 'it is *always-already finite*.'[53] It is this 'always-already' that limitless progress attempts to cross over. If what makes us human is being in time, being that is characterized by finitude—being towards death—then surpassing our temporal character does not merely lead to inauthentic being but to the loss of our ownmost way of being. Capitalism has already gone beyond Rainer Maria Rilke's view of *der grosse Tod*: 'The great Death that each within himself has, / that is the fruit around which everything revolves.'[54]

Immanent to our being is a double bind of being powerful as the inventor of language and thought and being powerless to set limits for ourselves. The latter is the essence of capitalism, which it does not see as a lack but a precondition for its progression beyond limits. The Greeks had a name for this, *hubris*. An arrogance that offends gods and brings about *nemesis*, the downfall of the perpetrator of *hubris*. Phaethon, which means 'shining one,' seeks assurance from his mother that his father was the sun god Helios. His mother told him to turn to Helios to find proof of his relationship to the sun. Helios promised to give to Phaethon whatever he wished and so he demanded to drive the fiery hot chariot of the sun to prove his divine birth. As he was placed in charge of the chariot, he was unable to control the fire-breathing horses. The horses scorched the ground and incinerated all upon the earth.[55] Earth cried and Zeus had to strike down the chariot with a lightning bolt. Like a falling star, Phaethon plunged into a river.

In its *hubris*, capitalism is unable to even imagine that it could be struck down by a lightning bolt, by the storm blowing from the biospheric Paradise bringing with it the ultimate *miasma* (pollution). In Greek composer and sound artist Yannis Kyriakides' 'Ode to Man,' written for the vocal group Silbersee for their production *Homo Instrumentalis*, four female voices move from articulation of the choral odes to raw vocality. Throughout the composition, the text of the ode is dismantled into phonemes as electronic sound overpowers and unbalances human voices. Is this the *hubris* of capitalism or the noise of the final tempest?

I have sketched out our dwelling place. This is the world we share and must share. Our home. There is no other world. It is naïve idealism to believe otherwise, which does not mean that an alternative world is not possible. Is there immanent to the capitalist immanency of our dwelling place the possibility of transcendence, this world transcendence? It is from this question that thinking must begin.

No Ethics?

Is there any time and space in the contemporary world for measures and limits? Do we have time to set limits? How can we rethink the concept of the limit freed from capitalist arrogance and its alleged necessities? What could be the future meaning of measure and measuring? These questions come back to the question of the possibility of a dissensual ethics, one that has a force of resistance and includes a transformative power.

The Greek word *ethōs* denotes custom and character. It is tradition that is rooted in the life of the community. For the Greeks, the ethics of the good referred to a good way of being and a correct course of action. Ethics 'organizes practical existence around the representation of the Good.'[56] Aristotle's *Nicomachean Ethics* 'is properly speaking the first book to be organized around the problem of an ethics ... [that] focus primarily on the problem of pleasure' and on the 'enigmatic problem of the relation of pleasure to the final good (*le bien dernier*).'[57] What does Aristotle then say about ethics? Practical or ethical wisdom (*phronesis*) rules over moral virtue or excellence (*ēthikē aretē*) of a character. The disposition (*hexis*) to exercise virtues arises from upbringing, action, and habit. The highest good is *eudaimonia* (consisting of *eu* 'good' and *daimōn*, 'spirit'), happiness, or more properly, human flourishing or prosperity. *Aretē* and *eudaimonia* are interrelated, since the virtues and their exercise is the essential constituent in *eudaimonia*, even though external goods like health and beauty also effect it.

Lacan sees the function of the master (*maître*) to be at the centre of Aristotle's ethics. Intemperance and fault are revealed to be relative to 'the essential virtue of the one whom Aristotle is addressing, the knowledge of the master (*savoir le maître*).'[58] The master is a human ideal in the plenitude of its presence. However, for Lacan, this universal ethics is localized and limited to a certain social type and class. The master is a privileged representative of contemplative life (*bios theoretikos*)—a man of leisure—who avoids work to be able to 'concentrate on a contemplative ideal without which the ethics doesn't achieve its proper aim.'[59] The proper place for contemplation is *schole* (school), which refers to free time (Latin: *otium*) that is not subjected to the subject's own passions or those posited by some other (Latin: *negotium*, 'time not free').[60] In G. W. F. Hegel's master-slave dialectic, the position of the Aristotelian master is extremely devalorized and utilitarian ethics—the maximum satisfaction of all—finally marks 'the radical decline of the function of the master.'[61]

Instead of the subject of virtue and the good, Kantian ethics speaks of the subject of duty, that is, the subject of the fact of reason (*das Faktum der Vernunft*) that freely approves it. The ethical is the combination of two things. First, the subject is solely motivated by respect for the moral law. One does not act merely in accordance with the law but from the moral law. Ethics is autonomy. If we are not the source of the law, the law is not considered ethical. We, sovereign self-legislators, act because of the moral law that we give freely to ourselves. Second, the subject has the power of choice (*Willkür*) and can freely adopt maxims that are universalizable in accordance with the categorical imperative, '*I ought never to act except in such a way that I could also will that my maxim should become a universal law.*'[62] If we do not will our maxim to be universally valid, it is wrong and unethical. Kant's ethics turns around followability, that is, the reason to act for me, as an autonomous subject, is the reason to act for all who are autonomous subjects.[63] If for Aristotle, true ethics was reserved for the aristocracy, Kant's ethics represent the equality of reason: we are all capable of creating a moral law for ourselves. That is, rationality is immanent in the human condition.

In his 1959–60 seminar *L'Ethique de la psychanalyse* (The Ethics of Psychoanalysis), Lacan addressed the ethics of psychoanalysis which was heavily based on his reading of tragedy. Around ten years later, Lacan comes back to this seminar in his *Encore* seminar (1972–73). 'It so happened that I did not publish *The Ethics of Psychoanalysis*.'[64] This does not mean ethics was a secondary or subordinary topic. On the contrary, it concerned an essential issue, the possible historical inscription of psychoanalysis.[65]

In a 1990 lecture, Philippe Lacoue-Labarthe said that reopening the question of ethics at the beginning of 1960s required courage, because the century had ethics forbidden by Heidegger's *Letter on Humanism* and by Marxism having taken the place of morals. The path towards ethics, even towards the direction of the question of ethics, was perilous and called for a complete re-elaboration of the question of ethics. According to Lacoue-Labarthe, Lacan knows that after Kant, tragedy is the decisive test for philosophy. In the interpretation of tragedy, the possibility of philosophy is played out or an access to another thought beyond philosophy is opened. Lacoue-Labarthe calls Lacan's re-elaboration of ethics as arche-ethics (*archi-éthique*), which is the only ethics truly able to respond to the age of the immemorial death of the god.[66] Ethics understood in this way may be the best response to today's limitless world of capitalism. It may force us to rethink the limits which seem to have disappeared, without returning to divine beings or fixed moral norms.

Arkhē of arche-ethics refers to two different but interconnected views. First, it concerns Freud's concern for the origin of ethics. On the one hand, the origin of analysis has an ethical character, because Freud started out with an ethical intuition. The Freudian experience as an ethics makes ethics the most essential level of psychoanalysis.[67] On the other hand, in Freud's metapsychology there are traces that reflect ethical thinking. Moreover, his anthropological texts deal exclusively with ethics.

Second, *archē* means to search for a more original ethics than philosophical ethics—the ethics of the good—that dominates ethical thinking. One must cross the line (*franchir la ligne*)[68] The line to be crossed is 'the barrier erected by the structure of the world of the good.'[69] It must be crossed because the sphere of the good erects a wall across the path of our desire, which is the enemy of the good and pleasure. The movement of desire itself has to cross the line of the pleasure principle as Freud discovers the death drive. Moreover, the world of the good as a historical line is revealed as the world of evil, where the reign of happiness turns into a murderous politics, where beyond death as pure suffering dominates, where Kant and Sade are reversible. For Lacan, there is 'hope' (*espoir*) that the threshold can be crossed. [70] Without hope, the world of the good, pleasure, and happiness drags 'us to our destruction.' [71] Psychoanalysis as arche-ethics designates the beyond-the-line while also necessitating access to the beyond. At the same time, we may have to return to the *grands thèmes* Lacan spoke of in his first seminar. His question was whether psychoanalysis should become one of those 'fundamental dialogues on justice and courage, in the great dialectical tradition?' We are not used to approaching 'these grand themes,' since we prefer 'to resolve things in terms of conduct, of adaptation, of group morale and other twaddle.'[72] As already said, morality is always already a representation of something given. This prevents any possibility for new positive visions of the ethical. To understand ethics in a more radical way, we ought to turn from the good, code, principle, and essence, from Kant's abstract universalism to the singularity of a situation. A philosophical ethics differs from social and legal sciences, which investigate social and political problems and institutional and normative orders. I would discern five main tasks for a philosophical ethics. First, it ought to point out the urgent need for orientation towards solidarity and responsible action. Second, it has to consider a non-metaphysical essence of measure and limit; and consider the possibility of disclosing measures and limits, which can exist to experience being-in-the world. Third, it must show how and why ethical experience is not dictated by transcendental entities (onto-theology), the monology of practical reason (deontological ethics), the calculation of happiness (utilitarianism), or deliberative dialogue (discursive and procedural ethics). The possibility for this kind of ethics is based on being (*Sein*)[73] of being-there, *Dasein*, and especially on the modes of being-towards-death and being-with in a political community. Fourth, ethics attempts to bring forth the disclosure and withdrawal of the experience of attuned responsibility here on the earth. Fifth, this ethics cannot be translated into a teachable code of conduct or a cannon of commandments that would issue from it. These five tasks can be condensed into one sentence that sets the task for thinking: philosophical ethics reveals 'a nonmetaphysical description of our *ethos* as forms of a measure that exists *on earth*.'[74]

However, we 'can have no certainty that there exists some kind of good ... no certainty even about the appropriateness, the truth, the authenticity of what we have chosen to do or not to do.'[75] In the end, a series of 'perhapses' that I hope to test. Perhaps ethics has more to do with being a stranger than with being at home with familiar virtues, values, and moral norms. Perhaps ethics is not about fastening human character or behaviour to a series of substantive and fixed 'goods' (i.e. manifestations of the good) and values, which would culminate in some supreme good. Perhaps goods should be considered as signifiers, which means that no act is good in itself but only with reference to another good in the signifying chain of goods. Perhaps we are involved with goods through the way they represent us to other signifiers, that is, other goods. Perhaps ethics could be thus understood as public use of reason where singularity participates in universality by breaking through the particular order and dwelling place. Perhaps ethics is related to 'the enduring maxim of singular processes,' which concerns 'the destiny of *truths*, in the plural,' that is, singularity that immediately participates in universality.[76] Perhaps ethics requires that a singularity emerges as the universal and that the universal emerges as a singularity. Perhaps, ethics would be something that takes place between 'the singular universal' (Žižek) and 'the universal singularity' (Badiou), as I will show when we come to theatre truths.[77] 'Contrary to consensual ethics, which tries to avoid divisions,' this kind of ethics 'is always more or less militant, combative.'[78] Perhaps we should re-consider, as Alain Badiou suggests, Mao Tse-tung's words: 'if you have an idea, one will have to split into two,' that is, instead of consensual ethics, an ethics that is always splitting into two.[79] What if this lack of moral truths—all these 'perhapses'—is an essential part of any ethics or even any ethical truth, which would be a truth that, perhaps, constitutes and dissolves itself at the same time.

Lacan prefers the term ethics to morality. For him, it is 'not because I take pleasure (*plaisir*) in using a term that is less common' than morality.[80] Morality refers to acting in accordance with the established moral and juridical laws of the state. Ethics, in contrast, is beyond this kind of moral legality, and also beyond the concept of the good that would be actualized in the norms and commandments of the moral law. Lacan's ethical dimension 'overlaps with an affirmation, with the subject itself claiming for itself the structure of its desire.'[81] Hence, ethics is about 'the irreducibility of a subject that configures its own destiny.'[82]

I will also prefer the term ethics. Instead of analyzing ethical theories or constructing one, I will consider the ethical in tragedies and tragic poetry. For me, the ethical way to rethink tragedy is by thinking in interiority, that is, by being immanent to the tragedies one writes, experiences, senses, and thinks.[83] Moreover, ethics is related to *il faut* (one must), and we must keep in mind that *il faut* refers both to an obligation and a failure. Between an ethical obligation and a failure is the space of the ethical. Becket writes, *il faut continuer*, 'one must go on,' even if 'I am not able to go on, one must go on, so I will go on.'[84] Ethics hints at the possibility of a passage from Lacan's 'do not give up on your desire' to Mao's 'you are right to rebel.'[85] With this in mind, let us keep on going.

1

Measuring Poetically

Instead of asking what ethics is, I ask where and how ethical measuring may possibly take place. Ethical measuring or reflection is not limited to any designated space or practices. Everyone is always already capable of ethical action anywhere. Is there a specific space, a *topos*, where ethics—motivation, reflection, decision, action, justification, etc.—would open itself to a thinking that is neither abstract speculation and systematization nor empirical or psychological scientific research? As I said, I will concentrate on the interrelated spaces of poetry and tragedy in my search for the possibility of measuring.

In 'What are Poets For?' Heidegger speaks about destitute time by answering a question Hölderlin, whom Heidegger considered to be the quintessential modern poet, presented in 'Bread and Wine': *Wozu Dichter in dürftiger Zeit?* ('What are poets for in a destitute time?').[1] Odysseus Elytis, a poet and 1979 Nobel Prize winner for literature, answers that times have always been *dürftig*, but 'poetry has never ... missed its vocation' to accompany 'our earthly destiny ... as the only place where the power of numbers proves to be nothing.'[2]

Immanent to the question of 'our earthly destiny' is the ethical without which it would be impossible to speak about our finite being in the world with others, which is our destiny. You and I, we are as singular beings exposed to our own existence and the existence of the other. We are exposed to the existence of blackbirds and foxes, birches and granite, water and air. Our earthly destiny consists of a plurality of intersections, a multiplicity of surprising events, infinite possibilities/impossibilities in finitude, all of which includes the fundamental question: what is the ground of my singular being as it exists with and through these intersections? As Hölderlin writes, *immer bestehet ein Maß*, 'always a measure exists.'[3] And remember, in our finite human existence: 'Bread is a fruit of Earth, yet touched by the blessing of sunlight (*Lichte*).'[4]

This is an ethical question that I will consider not by grounding it in a system of moral philosophy but by thinking, like Hölderlin, how it is asked and perhaps answered in poetry. Instead of writing poetry, I will write philosophical notes on poetry, again like Hölderlin in his translations of Sophocles (and like Lacoue-Labarthe in his translation of tragedy).

'But my friend! We have come too late,' Hölderlin mourns in 'Bread and Wine.'[5] Considering what I have said about the hegemony of limitless capitalist realism, we may—perhaps should—share Hölderlin's mourning, 'because we are heartless, mere shadows.'[6] For him, the gods live in a different world and seem to care little whether we live or die. Then again, 'we think of the Heavenly who once were / Here and shall come again remember the gods thereby, those who were once / With us, and who'll come back when the time is right (*die kehren in richtiger Zeit*).'[7]

Heidegger's answer to Hölderlin, based on his reading of him, is as follows, 'To be a poet in a destitute time means: to attend, singing, to the trace of the fugitive gods. That is why the poet in time of the world's night utters the holy.'[8] Let us consider this answer step by step.

First, to be a poet in a destitute time, the destitution of time must have made 'the whole being and vocation of the poet a poetic question for him.'[9] Hölderlin's words provide a ground for thinking: 'For never the heavenly fire / Will suffer captivity.'[10]

Second, language is the ground of our being. Language speaks in a poem and gives voice to being. The poet listens to language in reminiscence of being. The original language is the language of poetry.

Third, what does the poet's poetry say? 'Its word is: the holy. This word speaks of the flight of the gods.'[11] The poet is able to confront the holy, the ether in which gods are gods in that they have the sense of the trace of the fugitive gods. Hölderlin has a divine calling: 'A different task and calling have been assigned. / The Highest, he it is whom alone we serve, / So that more closely, ever newly / Sung, he will meet with a friendly echo.'[12] For Hölderlin, the poet's vocation (*Dichterberuf*) and courage (*Dichtermuth*) is to 'contemplate divinity in the plenitude of its divinity while revealing it to mortals in that earthly semblance which their eyes are capable of contemplating.'[13]

Fourth, gods arise thunderously and human beings can endure their fullness only momentarily. Even this needs as strong a heart as the gods have. Thus, the poet takes an enormous, even fatal, risk when tracking these traces. The precondition for the song of these singers is the poet's unshielded and stubborn intransigence. As Rilke's poem goes: 'in the end, / It is our unshieldedness on which we depend.' The poet cannot calculate the risk of a direct confrontation with the heavenly sun that burns the eyes but not the gaze of the poet. The poet cannot afford to shield herself by remaining in the Platonic cave enjoying the comfortable fantasy called reality. At the time, the gods did not create the poet for fun but because they were constrained to do so; they needed the poet, 'the envoy of the flowing word,' in the same way human beings need poets.[14]

Fifth, 'all is intimate,' is one of the key verses of Hölderlin's poetry. Gods and human beings, earth and heaven are intimate—which makes it fourfold—but intimacy does not mean 'obliteration of distinctions. Intimacy names the belonging together of what is foreign, the ruling of the strange, the claim of awe.'[15]

Finally, 'Hölderlin's poetry is a destiny for us. It waits for the day when mortals will correspond to it. Correspondence leads on the path of an entry into the nearness of the gods who have fled: the region of their flight will protect us.'[16] We have to participate in poetry and to participate in conversation with it. We have to listen to Hölderlin's singer singing. Hölderlin reminds us in 'The Titans' that: *'Nicht ist es aber / Die Zeit'* ('Not yet, however, / The time').[17] The time is not yet because the attunement must be correct. We have to experience the loss of gods without any pretext or temporary help, without making godlessness a rational argument or opinion. It must be recognized as a destiny (*Geschick*). From this, a gate for the gods is opened. This gate proves that gods also stand under presence and absence and that they belong to being that prevails *over* them.[18]

Heidegger turns now to the attunement of the historical people in which the people opens itself to being. For him, 'authentic poetry does not come to light appropriately in every period.'[19] Only when this takes place, when the poetic comes into light appropriately, 'then man dwells humanly on this earth' and his life is a 'dwelling life,' as Hölderlin wrote.[20] Otherwise, we live unpoetically.

Sacred Names

Heidegger's manipulative reading of Hölderlin is annoying because, first, he understands his poetry in the proximity of the last god; second, this god yet to come reveals himself only to one people, that is, the German people; and third, he considers himself to hold the truth of the configuration of the world in destitute times.[21] The commitment of the poet and to poetry leads to the restoration of ethno-nationalist hegemony. Even if Heidegger starts from the idea that a constituent part or our existence is to be wayfarers here and now. As Lacoue-Labarthe notes, he elaborates a soothing, even religious, thematic of proximity, the nearby, dwelling, the presence of things, the earth, the sky, the remoteness of gods, which is also their presence.[22]

Heidegger seems to read Hölderlin's poetry from the perspective of 'Alemanian-Swabian rootedness in the native soil.'[23] Hölderlin does not dwell on the banks of the Danube. He lets one be touched by the flow of the river. The word carried by the river is split as it travels through the mountains and valleys; the word formed in a process of exile. The poet is able to hear merely echoes of this word. At the same time, he seems to ignore the admiration Hölderlin showed towards the French revolution. It was a purifying storm followed by fresh air. Then again, Hölderlin recognizes the chaos that the subject cannot control and integrate as a necessary part of the revolutionary process, one of whose names is *Gott der Zeit* (god of the time). Instead of seeing Hölderlin as the poet who speaks the being and/or destiny of the people or the nation, we should re-read him maintaining a distance from attachment, participation, and attunement from collective destinies and also from the metaphysics of presence. Let us try to do that.

As previously said, God is not a transcendental entity for Hölderlin. Stefan Zweig explains: 'According to Hölderlin the making of the poet is necessary to God, who is not divine but for the existence of the poet, becomes divine only through the poet's instrumentality.'[24]

In his poem '*Heimkehr*,' Hölderlin writes '*es fehlen heilige Namen*' ('sacred names are lacking'). What we have is a lack of names of divinity or heavenly beings. The lack itself is proof that there are, somewhere or nowhere, sacred names. We do not know what these names are or what they lack. Instead of there being no names for the gods, there are an arsenal of names for new gods. 'God has perhaps become everything (or nothing); perhaps he has become, potentially at least, every true question, exigency, or furthest extreme of thought.'[25] If the withdrawal of divinity, as being, essence, origin, source, sending, is immanent in our thinking, we are stuck with onto-theology, be it negative or positive.

In 'What is god?', Hölderlin answers that the divine is the face of the sky/heaven (*Angesicht des Himmels*). Heidegger understands this as divinity retaining its invisibility and unknowability being made manifest (*offenbar*) by the sky/heaven dispatching itself in the appearing of the world. Here we must pause for a while. What Heidegger does is attempt to ontologize, perhaps even onto-theologize, Hölderlin's poem. Does Hölderlin really say that the gods have withdrawn *and* are yet to come?

Jean-Luc Nancy criticizes Heidegger's interpretation as based on the logic of absence and presence, manifestation and concealment. Nancy's interpretation is that the poem does not say that god is revealed by means of the sky/heaven. Instead, it suggests that the god 'is' only 'as manifest as the heavens.'[26] The sky/heaven is not merely a screen or surface for gods, whose presence is somewhere else. Nancy considers that the invisible divine lets itself be by resting itself upon the face of sky/heaven, 'or woven into it, sent or destined therein, but as another face that lets itself be seen *here, without "here" serving as a mediation for it.*'[27] The divine is im-mediate. The 'im' refers to a relation, Hent de Vries explains, that has 'absolved itself from that of both mediacy *and* immediacy, and concerns man alone. The "im-mediate" gives a hint man can follow up on, or not.'[28] The sky/heaven and the god have no common measure but 'the sovereign interplay of darkness and radiance, of radiance withdrawn into darkness and of darkness as manifest as radiance.'[29] The conclusion is that revelation is neither presentation of the god or representation of a message but only the evidence of the possibility, which is never a necessity, of being-unto-god. 'Or more exactly, it becomes manifest that such a being-unto-god is possible.'[30] In his poem, Hölderlin addresses nothing but the possibility of a possible. Once again, being-unto-god is not any kind of access to the god or giving place to the god but merely being-unto-open, which gives place to the possibility of poetry and the possible sense of the world. God does not make the poet and a poem—or beings—be. They are not produced 'and production exists only within the world of beings.'[31] We have to keep in mind that 'divinity is *not* God. In a sense it is nothing.'[32]

The poet brings forth in his poetry divine names that are not proper to the divine. They are lacking names. The lack in these names makes it possible to not represent the true essence of the divinity but to bring to light the possibility of divinity. The poet waits without a specific horizon of expectation.[33] He is not oriented towards any place. Thus, his mood is pure openness. Poeticizing is positioned in front of the unsayable. Language calls the poet and the call is near and distant or 'neither in the ear nor far from the ear.'[34] The name of the god names the trace of a singular event that renders poetry possible.

Faith

The practice of the poet is faith. However, it is not the poet's faith that is subjected to a god as the supreme being. It is not faith practised in any church or prayers. The death of god does not equate with the death of faith. Hölderlin, the poet, is necessary for creating acts of faithful listening to the opening of the world. 'There remains for us neither cult nor prayer, but the exercise—strict and severe, sober and yet joyous—of what is called thought.'[35] These words by Nancy precisely describe Hölderlin's poetry as an exercise of listening, thought, and saying. His poems sense the opening of the sense of the world. The precondition for this is that the poet as a self is rendered inadequate. His poetry is an excessive practice, a triangle of faith, thinking, and action; each word 'a singular address to a singular god.'[36]

We have to learn to listen to the poet—defined by Hölderlin as 'the voice of the gods,' 'the herald of the hero,' and 'the tongue of the people'—who in the language of poetry is exposed to beings and world, and which in turn open themselves to the poet.[37] Through the saying of poetry we may have to participate and attach ourselves to the holy. This ought to be understood as a universal call for a singular being sharing the world with other singularities.

For Hölderlin, the speaking subject is split between the idealistic poet of divine youth, who is close to the voice of the god that has *Ahnung*, and the poet of saying (*sagen*), an articulation in which thinking takes place. Hölderlin does not simply bring into language the voice of the god but attempts, in his poetry, to get along with the overpowering voice that threatens to destroy the speaking subject, as he would be dissolved into the gods. The relation is one of *Auseinandersetzung*, the identification of the self and the other *and* the difference between the self and the other. The most blind of the god's sons are rivers to which the poet has a connection, but at the same time he walks his own way with open eyes. The voice of the people is connected to rivers and gods. Hence, the poet respects it. In his poetry, he presents a definite distance from the voice of the god and a warning to the people in the name of the god *and* the people. Hölderlin does not speak in the name of the god or the people but in the name of 'and,' that is, in the name of difference between gods and human beings. 'And' is the limit and border that cannot be crossed. The voice of the god can never be taken as the voice of the mortals. The voice of the people is not the voice of the god but is compared to it in their difference.[38] The same goes for the voice of the poet and the voice of the people. There is a triple connection and difference—the voice of the god, the voice of the people, and the voice of the poet. Hölderlin's poetry is a warning against the mixing of these three voices which nevertheless raises a connection.

His poetry is a limit between these voices, between three words. The god and the people need the word of the poet. The word of a poet is a human gift to the god, which confirms the human relation to gods as a separation. The poet, who speaks, is thrown outside of gods and gods are thrown outside the word.

Wink

For Nancy, being is not the god, Supreme Being, or any mortal that necessarily has a proper place. Being has no place. 'Being is simple the being of beings, what is,' the fact that beings are.[39] We ought to take one more step away from the god, or the place of gods, since they do have a place, even if their place is in their retreat or absence. The absence means that the lack of gods does not refer to the possibility of their being held in reserve, that is, today we have to face the no-return of the gods.

A better name for the god in its sky/heaven manifestation is, as Nancy proposes, *Wink*, the divine nod, which signifies nothing in particular, nothing that exists down on the earth or the heavens above. *Wink* signals without signifying any*thing*. In this sense, divine glory is 'open, offered, dazzling like that of heavens and effaced like them.'[40] Giving a nod or a sign that evokes a gesture of naming 'is perhaps always—divine.'[41] The poet is open not towards the god, or any divine being or essence, but towards the *Wink*. Consequently, the poet's way of being is to be unto-the-*Wink*.

Instead of returning to the metaphysics of presence (of the proper, gods), the unto-the-*Wink* should be understood as opening out onto the non-proper as the condition of the poet. This is the precondition for the poet bringing into language the measure and the limits. The ethical in the poem is not the representation of the gods or eternal ideas that would be present, rather it is unknown to us or in retreat from our everyday existence. The ethical as presence of limits and measures is not something that would fill the lack of gods or absolute values or become the presence of the proper that would purify the impropriety of our being. Moreover, the ethical cannot offer a basis for identitarian and auto-conceptual thinking. The ethical takes place in the space of a poem, which presents the ethical as the poet open unto-the-*Wink*.

Lacoue-Labarthe, who has a definite reticence towards any theological inflection of philosophy, would bring here god and language together to demystify or de-theologize what I have attempted to elaborate here. The remedy for the onto-theological reading of poetry is not simply to challenge the notion of transcendence. For Lacoue-Labarthe, the transcendence of alterity is, 'the thought of the intimate, a paradoxical way of thinking the intimate,' an extimacy.[42] This intimacy he relates to Hölderlin's *Innigkeit* and St. Augustine's formula, 'a God more internal than my own intimacy.' This intimate God is nothing but the event of language. 'There is language' is the origin of our being, the abyss of that origin within us.[43] Because of this origin—which means also admitting that there is no defined human nature—we are all actors, playing roles in language, existing in the process of imitation and identification, that is, subjects of mimesis, which is not imitation of something given but originary mimesis. As a consequence, as mimetic subjects—already hollowed out and undermined by an unassignable gap or hiatus that cannot be closed—we are not bound to our given roles but free to imitate.[44]

Another time and place, another poet who is unto-the-*Wink*. Liu Xiaobo, the Chinese poet and human rights activist, confronted the 1989 massacre of Tiananmen Square by commemorating it every year in a poem. His poems show the poet's intransigence. Instead of 'staying asleep,' he chose to 'exist without companions' reminding us in his fearless and bold poems of the destitute time of injustice. The anniversary of the massacre is 'a fatal virus / no one's willing to approach' and because of this 'a nation is unable to breathe freely.'[45] At the same time, his poems tracked a sign of the presence of justice and its eventual return, 'which we / May appreciate in our human fashion, as we used to.'[46] In his poems, we are able to hear the stubborn innocence as he pursues the coming gods of justice. Liu criticized those critical writers who avoided direct engagement with politics: 'They've matured without experiencing innocence; they've given up without experiencing the pursuit.' Liu was incarcerated four times after the Tiananmen protests and only granted medical parole about two weeks before his death in July 2017. Most of the poems were thus written in confinement. He was awarded the Nobel Peace Prize in 2010 but was not permitted to attend the ceremony. If Liu's poetry answers the question of what poets are for, the empty chair shows why the songs of the singers are needed in these times of destitution.

As we suffer political, ethical, economic, and social destitution today, our possibility may lie in the preparation of a readiness for the appearance or absence of the holy, which should not be understand in terms of ontical transcendence, that is, as some divine being or the Christian God that transcends beings on earth. The holy refers to gods, earth, heaven, or justice in whose truth the human being stands, and which may be understood in relation to Heidegger's fundamental ontological transcendence in that *Dasein* understands being and stands in the truth of being, which secures its freedom. We need, as Liu shows, thinking, poeticizing, and political action. His poetry is a way to transform '*Nicht ist es aber / Die Zeit*' into 'now it is the time.' How must one now understand the measure and measuring? By listening to poetry that exposes us to justice. Since gods and justice are mute, 'the poet speaks in their name and in their spirit.'[47]

The poet is open towards this divine nod and as such the heralding of this non-signifying sign. It is the poem—the writing, the reading, the citation, the thinking, the sensing, the deliberation, the discourse—that is crucial in the nod. The poem is touched by the nod. And the poem, on its behalf, touches all those who touches the poem or are touched by the poem.

My overly short answer to Hölderlin's question about the vocation of the poet is as follows. Poetry starts from the acceptance of the withdrawal of gods. What the poet must confront is a world lacking transcendental truths or any other exterior grounds. A sense is circulating within this world and through the exposure of human and non-human beings. The sense that touches the poet through her listening and which she turns into singing/writing/speech is not transcendent or immanent. There is no reserve of meaning over there or here that would lay the ground or foundation for this sense. Sense is coextensive with the shared world and with its sharing. The vocation of the poet: to be touched by the ethical that slides through the sharing of the world.

Another answer, an ancient slapstick comedy. In Aristophanes' *Frogs*, Aeschylus and Euripides discuss in Hades about the vocation of a dramatic poet:

> Aeschylus: Come, tell me, what are the points for which a noble poet our praise obtains.
>
> Euripides: For his ready wit, and his counsels sage, and because the people he trains to be better citizens and worthier men.[48]
>
> *Enter Hölderlin.*
>
> Hölderlin: The poets vocation? The poet likes to join with others / Whether it is early or late, always a measure exists. / Lets the child even taste this vine.

2

Where Now Is Athens?

In 'The Archipelago,' Hölderlin asks, '*Sage, wo ist Athen?*' ('Tell me, where now is Athens?').[1] If we turn our gaze in the direction Hölderlin points at, towards Athens, we cannot avoid confronting tragedy. 'Here, on your shores ... your city.'[2] Perhaps, ancient Greek tragic poets still speak on our shores and cities. Perhaps dramatic poetry still speaks to us as a site of the measurer and measuring. Perhaps it is an answer to the question about the vocation of the poets. Perhaps tragedies hint at the sense of our being and limits in the late capitalist world. 'Or, does a trace (*Zeichen*) remain, so much that a sailor / Passing by, will mention her name and recall her?'[3]

Then again, what if ancient tragedy has 'utterly crumbled to ashes.'[4] Is its fate the same as in Hölderlin's lament for Diotima. 'Once, how different it was. O youth, will no prayer bring you back, then, / Never again?'[5] There will never again be a path back to ancient tragedy. I will take up three possible answers, a negation, a refusal and an affirmation.

Death of Tragedy?

In 1955 Albert Camus wondered if modern tragedy were possible.[6] His point was that the great periods of tragedy occurred at exceptional moments when there was a dramatic turning point in the history of culture. Camus saw only two periods when tragedy flourished. The first was in ancient Greece. The second was born from Elizabethan theatre, continued in the golden age of Spanish theatre, and ended in the formal perfection of French 17th Century theatre. During these periods a transition occurred from divine forces to rational concepts, and 'the final triumph of individual reason ... dries up tragic production.'[7] Given this, are we living today an exceptional moment where a position of finitude and a sense of limits is transitioning to unlimited powers and yet to come catastrophe? If so and even if we agree with Camus, we can still affirm the possibility of tragedy.

George Steiner is more definite. In his *The Death Tragedy*, Steiner posits that the rationalism of the Enlightenment and the optimism of Romanticism made tragedy impossible. John Milton (1608–74) is 'the last major poet to assume the total relevance of classic and Christian mythology.'[8] A poet and civil servant under Cromwell's Commonwealth, Milton wrote his poetry in extraordinary times, a time of political upheaval and religious flux. As magic, miracle, collective myths, extreme figures, and dreadful gods disappeared, tragedy was transformed into a modern drama of mourning.

The precondition for tragedy is a tragic situation, the irresolvable ethical, political, or social conflict. If tragic conflicts are overcome by turning them into manageable political, legal, or economic problems, tragedy turns into bureaucracy. Hegel once said that when tragedy overcomes the tragic conflict it is dissolved into comedy. Nietzsche did not deny this. For him, the dissolution of tragedy happens in a process that leads out of the ethical experience of tragic conflicts into an aesthetic comedy, where the ethical withers away permanently. At the end, we have merely waves of uncontainable laughter.[9]

The process of dissolving tragedy may take place as tragic conflict. Here ethical experience is also dissolved into a post-tragical experience of rational self-consciousness, hence moving beyond tragic ethics. Conflicting tragic duties are considered nothing but a comic spectacle when thought prioritizes progress, security, and consensus,. The ethics of tragedy is not overcome through inclusion but reduced to the capitalist post-tragic morality of effectivity and limitlessness.

Another route to dissolution is to refuse the return of/to tragedy, even if it would be possible: 'we live as did the ancients when their world was not yet disenchanted of its gods and demons.'[10] However, today there is a risk that old gods are rising from their graves and may strive again to gain power over our lives and resume their eternal struggle. Tragedy is considered a negative-mythical position and the tragic-mythic world would be the end of modernity and its rational logic and bureaucratic governance.

The opposite view would be to affirm the eternal return of tragedy. In the context of the original Greek tragedies and their reception over centuries, what is a correct reception, understanding, reading and rereading, interpretation, rewriting, and restaging of an ancient tragedy? We could avoid the question by promising fidelity to the 'true' and 'pure' original. This I would call the nostalgia of tragedy.

Suffering in exile and longing for a homecoming determines the relation to a Greece lost in a bygone past. Winckelmann, who detested baroque, rococo, and realism, trusted that the moderns could raise themselves to the glory of the ancients if they imitated them. Nostalgia offers a possibility for restoration. An ancient tragedy is to be confronted, understood, and staged in a more or less authentic form. This naïve nostalgia turns against tragedy, which becomes a farce or spectacle that has nothing whatsoever to do with tragic conflicts, ethical acts and errors, pain and terror, wonderment and critical reflection, unavoidable fates and possible futures. A nostalgic good soul—be it a poet, director, or actor, a classicist or philosopher—calls: 'tragedy come forth!'

A. E. Stallings writes: 'Nothing is more permanent than temporary / Sometimes when I'm feeling weepy, you propose a theory: / Nostalgia and tear gas has the same acrid smell.'[11] Nostalgia and tear gas are connected. The acrid smell makes her weep. Weeping disturbs the sense of what is going on around a weeping being. The task of tear gas is to control the masses, prevent political action, and stop demonstrations. Nostalgia has the same function. The acrid smell distorts the past, the present, and the future. The nostalgic mood takes control and forces the subject towards the past in a desperate dream of golden times and knowledge that this past is foregone. The radical potential of the past for today and the days to come are lost in weeping and tears. As tear gas paralyzes demonstrators or forces them to flee, nostalgia paralyzes those who dream of returning to the origins that have never been present. The nostalgia paralyzes our possibility to think the ethical in tragedy. The attraction of tragedy lies not in the remembrance of the original and not only in its 'savage and troubling beauty' but also, and more importantly, in its 'massive and unacknowledged relevance to the contemporary physical and political situation.'[12]

A more dangerous version of this nostalgia of tragedy can be found in the various aesthetic and political fantasies that dream of a return to the mythical origins, which may serve as a model for a nationalist nostalgia and mythology. Since the modern world lacks gods, myths, and grounds, they say we ought to re-find the mythology of founding moments and fathers that laid the ground for concepts such as divinity, race, blood, soil, or ethnicity. In other words, a totally self-fulling idea that explains the history of the people as a consistent process that discloses by its movement the mythical origin.[13]

Both naïve and racist nostalgia are ideological formations based on indisputable feelings, logic, and practices that ignore gaps and remainders, insecurities and discontinuities. The immediate antidote for naïve or racist nostalgia—and it is politically, though not aesthetically, important to keep these separated—is to realize that truth in Greek tragedy is not in the mystery cult of Dionysus, the god of intoxication, and in the disappearance of limits between oneself and others. As we read tragic poetry, we cannot jump in to any original textual meaning of Greek tragedies without taking into consideration the genealogy of its translations, performances, and interpretations. Moreover, we do not know exactly how the Athenians experienced the performance of tragedies. Finally, nostalgia that has no critical distance justifies the criticism against the long philosophical tradition that suffers from the disease of the 'tragic-heroic paradigm.'[14]

Eduard Devrient's performance as Haemon in Sophocles' *Antigone* at the Potsdam Court Theatre in 1841, reminds us of the awareness of the historic distance between Athens and Potsdam. The play was commissioned by the Prussian King Friedrich Wilhelm IV.[15] Devrient commented on the performance: it did 'not aspire to an archaeological imitation of what scholars thought they knew about the performances in Athens ... it was and had to be an experiment in modern acting as it would be impossible to return to ancient conventions.'[16]

This illustrates that tragedy may be used to serve state interests. It is not self-evidently something that challenges the legitimate political order. We should be aware of this. However, the way Devrient understood the play shows that the possibility of tragedy today requires us to think, sense, and realize tragedy in-between the ancient and the modern, as a phenomenon not beyond the conditions and coordinates of time and space.

It is self-evident that the point of departure for thinking Greek tragedy is Athens. As I turn towards tragedy here and now, the destination between me and tragedy is this here and now.[17] Therefore, ancient tragedy is both decontextualized and re-contextualized if we claim to have any relation to tragic poetry and plays.

'The word that makes us free is also the word that kills,' a Swedish dramaturg Lars Noren concludes.[18] Language is the site in which we experience the nostalgic pain of our separation from the supposed unity of life but also where we expose ourselves to the possibility to confront Greek tragedies in their strangeness and familiarity. We are all refugees in language, but language is our home here and now and the only possibility to be in touch with the unhomely past/present/future. Language is, in other words, our dwelling place that is always already open to other dwelling places in time and/or space. This kind of sharing in and of language is a site that cannot be without ethical dimensions.

There is no sense in attempting to restore the language of ancient tragedy. Instead, we have to listen to tragedy, the unheard and unspoken language of Greek tragedies and their lost meanings, their familiar/unfamiliar echoes, clangs, and moods of tragic experiences, including ethical conflicts. We should differentiate between the meaning of the text of tragedy and the sense of tragedy. Philology is mainly interested in the meaning of ancient texts. The philosophical, ethical, and theatrical understanding of tragedies are more interested in their sense in the coordinates of time and space.

Interability of Tragedies

The origin and source of the text of tragedy is displaced. The truth of tragedy is thus a radical 'absent presence.' Tragedy is not being there (ancient Athens) but neither is it present here (late capitalism). To understand tragedy, especially if we wish to consider the ethics of tragedy, we must first affirm this absence of presence of tragedies. Secondly, this absence is not the absence of tragedies but only the absence of their presence. That is, the possibility of the 'presence'—here and now—of tragedies lies in their repeatability, that is, in their iteration. As Jacques Derrida notes, a 'writing that is not structurally readable—iterable—beyond the death of the addressee would not be writing.'[19] Re-reading tragedies in iterated ways is not parasitic reading subjugated to a valid understanding of the true meaning of these tragedies. Tragedies sent from Greece are always already decentralized and transformed with every repetition. Moreover, context does not define the sense of tragedies because they too are indeterminate and indeterminable.

What is decisive in relation to tragedy and its ethical possibilities is to think the present, as I have done, and to think tragedy in the present, as I will do. This present I evoke is not the presence of absolute immanence, established order, immediate being in the contemporary world, or fleeting instances of decisions. I understand the present and the presence of tragedy along the same horizons as Nancy.[20] This is presence in the sense of an arrival of the past and future, an approach of the ancient tragedy thrown towards a yet-to-come. It is a presence in which tragic conflict, being, limits, measures, and measuring present themselves.

I use the term 'presentation' as I speak of the theatre performance. Presentation (German: *Darstellung*, Latin: *praesentatio*) and representation (*Vorstellung*, *re-praesentatio*) are sometimes used as synonyms even though they have different connotations. Representation refers to a repetition, since it *re*-presents what is present. It renders objects present and sets out these objects before us and in relation to us so that they can be at our disposal. It gives both a ground from which the object represented emerges and a stable identity to this object. It functions as a substitution. Presentation is, for Kant and Hegel, a sensible presentation of an idea. I will understand it more as an exposition and an exhibition. What is presented is allowed to present itself in its own terms or truth. Rather than re-presentation, substitution, or a re-production of an original thing, object, or presence, it is presencing.[21]

If the difference between these two terms are understood in this way, this means the theatre performance is not representation but presentation in which something spurts forth or erupts into presence, the coming into presence of a presence. The theatre event as a presentation is always a surprise. It leaps over 'every presented and presentable present.'[22] The theatre is a leaping presentation in a coming that articulates 'the difference between nothing and something,' which surprises itself every that it is a singular coming.[23]

Tragedy has two intertwined spheres. On the one hand, there is the content of the play: the ethical, political, or social conflict. On the other hand, there is the presentation of the tragic conflict as a text and on the stage. Tragedy is ethical and aesthetical, as Søren Kierkegaard defined it. However, for him tragedy is not either conflict/ethics or representation/aesthetics but the overlapping of the two.[24] This ethical-aesthetic sphere is the place of the appearance of what is called tragedy. Tragedy is an ethical phenomenon that takes place through the experience of the tragic and the aesthetic.[25] Tragedy is the intimate connection of the tragic and ethics, tragic conflict, and ethical obligations. I share Jean-Pierre Vernant's definition of tragedy: 'Tragedy is not only an art form; it is also a social institution which the city, by establishing competitions in tragedies, sets up alongside its political and legal institutions.'[26] The chorus plays a crucial function here. It is the projection of the civic identity of the Athenians. The 'collective and anonymous presence' of the chorus as a political community functions to express the judgments, views, feelings, hopes, and fears of the spectators.[27] It would be a grave mistake to ignore the 'collective character of ancient drama.'[28] Another mistake would be to consider various elements of tragedy as pieces gathered together and not as semi-independent parts of the tragic corpus. Instead of being a collection of bits and pieces, tragedy is a constellation consisting of an assemblage of text, plot, figures, director, actors, décor, costumes, stage, and public.[29] Tragedy must be understood in its practical and material dimensions as it gathers people together not because of any pre-given cause but to sense the possible effects of the tragic play as tribunal and to disagree or agree. Tragedy as tragedy cannot be reduced to the text.[30] I will come back to this essential issue later.

In a 1966-diary note, Philippe Lacoue-Labarthe writes that Greek tragedy is the only art anterior to metaphysics, which makes it so strange to us.[31] Simon Critchley correctly expresses 'caution about finding a tidy metaphysical essence of tragedy with clear moral consequences. I have sought to see tragedy as a kind of prebuttal of philosophy that refuses to sprinkle idealistic rosewater on reality.'[32] Instead, tragedy is 'a unique space that provides an unparalleled experience of sensory and cognitive intensity that is impossible to express purely in concepts or to abstract stratospherically to the status of an *idea*.'[33] By watching tragic figures in extreme situations,[34] 'we look into the *core*, the core of life, of aliveness, in all its burning intensity, moral ambiguity, emotional devastation, erotic doubling, and political complexity.'[35] Even though tragedy is not a metaphysical idea, it is, Aristotle affirms, 'more philosophical and more serious than history.' That is, tragic poetry tends to make universal statements and history particular ones. If history repeats factual facts, poetry reflects possibilities and a higher truth. This is why tragedy is about aliveness.

Continuing this line of thought, we could say that tragedy disrupts all the conventional epistemological realist forms of knowledge. Instead of a representational description, in tragedy we find a performative relationship to the world. Tragedy is true as far as it effectively opens the world in its being, brings forth conflicts and various ways of being together in spite of or because of such conflicts, and proposes various futures and possibilities. This is contrary to Plato, who was the first to pave the way towards philosophy's hostile view of tragedy as an imitation of an imitation removed from the sphere of ideas and provoking, in addition, various dangerous passions. It is well known that Plato excluded the tragic poet and especially tragedy even though he was, at the same time, the first philosopher to affirm its power and effectiveness. This absolute ban was adopted by Christianity, which was afraid of the dangerousness of theatre. Philippe Lacoue-Labarthe, Jean-Luc Nancy and Jean-Pierre Vernant, the director of *Théâtre National de Strasbourg*, produced a play presented in Avignon where actors performed various texts by priests, scholars, and historians who had, following Plato, unanimously condemned theatre. Theatre is illusion miming human action. This imitation provokes emotions. It is a system of indirect presentation: the actors have nothing to do with the characters they incarnate and situations in which they pretend to be; they do not speak in their own name; the tragic poet does not say directly what he has to say; no personal responsibility is taken and anything can be offered with impunity.[36]

If we listen to Hegel, we would hear him praise tragedy as the supreme form of art. For him, human speech is the proper medium for presenting spiritual life. Dramatic speech combines the subjectivity of lyrics and the objectivity of the epic. Even though material elements—bodies, sounds, and scenography—are necessary for drama, they are merely a background 'out of which the language of poetry is in its free domination asserted as the commanding central focus upon and around which all else revolves.' Tragedy for Hegel was not merely a literary genre. It was much more: an idea that brings together aesthetic, ethical, and philosophical spheres. Therefore tragedy is intimately bound with history as the progress of spirit. It presents how the incarnated spirit is divided into particular forms that are in conflict, but which is reconciled through the destruction of two one-sided ethical forces. This speculative train leads inevitably to a synthesis, even to absolute justice, *das absolute Recht*, which may shine as the truth of the tragic conflict. Hegel manages to assimilate tragedy and its core—conflict—into an essential part of his speculative system building.

According to Critchley, tragedy is more interesting than philosophy as it is able to stage moral ambiguities that cannot be easily resolved because we don't know how to judge. These ambiguities tragedy articulates constitute life in the *polis* but also in our own societies. Instead of some kind of Dionysian fusion with being, tragedy consists of rational argumentation between two opposing positions. Since this conflict remains often unsolved, tragedy is, for Critchley, more pessimistic than philosophy.[37] Taking this into consideration, we can say that tragedy is more relevant in our situation than any philosophy that attempts to solve or veil ambiguities. An ethics that confronts ambiguities does not immediately start to construct a consistent and coherent philosophical system; it returns to tragedy and opens itself to ambiguities—that may still speak to us if we listen—in tragedies. Ethics cannot be grounded on obsessional systems. The 'world needs to be understood in tragic terms in the name of realism.'[38]

At the same time, Critchley criticizes the primacy of tragedy in our recognition of our finitude and limitedness. It is too centred on the finitude of the tragic hero, which disfigures the more modest and weaker conceptions of finitude. In contrast to 'the tragic heroic paradigm,' where the hero is an ethical model, Critchley proposes 'the comic anti-heroic paradigm,' where the model is more human.[39] The limitedness of our human condition calls for comic acknowledgement and laughable identification instead of tragic affirmation and heroic authenticity. Tragedy supports the idea of a strong subject, the comedy destabilizes this kind of subject. Laughter 'arises out of a palpable sense of inability, inauthenticity, impotence and impossibility.'[40] Should a tragic hero, like Antigone, become a less heroic and sublime figure so it can appear as a modest acknowledgement of our human finitude? Humour, laughter, and comedy? Should she 'break wind on the way to her death'?[41] This comedy over tragedy view is problematic, or more precisely, Hegelian, as Mark de Kesel shows. The fart at the most tragic moment would merely laugh the joke away. Something that should be censured appears momentarily, repression confronts its limits and is not able to control the traumatic unconscious. Laughter immediately undoes the realization of my being the unconscious subject based on lack, neutralizes the threatening trauma and restores the subject in its imaginary power. The farting Antigone would be recognized as an imaginary ego and not the subject of the desire as in tragedy. Laughter functions as a Hegelian *Aufhebung*. The confrontation of our negativity, finitude, and unconscious is laughed off. Deconstruction of the subject is sublated and the subject is restored as the master of the negativity. This process fortifies the conscious subject.[42]

We could accept that there is a dissolution (*Auflösung*) of the ethical experience of tragedy into aesthetic play and thereby the dissolution of tragedy into comedy. However, dissolution does not mean total overcoming tragedy. Instead, it takes place only from the aesthetic perspective, which cannot completely replace the ethical perspective. In the process of tragedy, the ethical perspective and the experience of tragedy remains. Tragedy moves to comedy and back again. This is 'the inner law of the movement of tragedy.'[43] The strife between the ethically experienced tragic and the aesthetically experienced play is the site where tragedy may be experienced. However, this conflict is not an opposition but a mutually transformative relationship that constitutes tragedy. Tragedy is a strife between ethical and aesthetic experience.[44]

Measuring of Justice

In the Archaic period the efficacy of speech culminated in religious rituals and the pronouncement of the king, while in the Classical period speech became the most important political tool. The pre-eminence of public speech over other instruments of power cannot be overestimated. The more political-democratic thought was separated from myths, religion, and rituals, the more the human condition was subjected to critical discussion. The agora was the communal open-air space for political and ethical argumentation and disagreements, like the stadium was an open and shared space for the games.[45]

The importance of speech brings together the agora, theatre, and trial. Walter Benjamin thinks the trial, the tragedy, and the games in terms of an agonal triangle of Greek life. They take place at a designated forum, they are temporally delimited, and they are formed by a consistent action. Essential for tragedy and the trial is the word and the argumentation (*logos*) in the form of an agonistic dialogue between adversaries.[46] Benjamin's view accords with Louis Garnet's definition of the trial as a struggle (*agōn*) between equal adversary parties.[47] In a similar way, Loraux compares the structure of the trial with Aristotle's conception of tragedy. Like tragedy, the trial has a beginning (an examination of the parties before the magistrates), a middle (the parties pleading their case before the judges), and an end (the vote of the court and the verdict).

Aristotle assumes that Solon made his laws unclear, because he wanted the citizens to be the final masters of a decision (*krisis*). The judges do not merely apply the law but supply verdicts through their sovereign vote. The judgment is *1) diarein* (to divide into parts), *2) diagignōskein* (to judge between two claims) and *3) diakrisis* (to decide by choosing between the arguments and proposals of the litigants).[48] Therefore, *krinein* (to separate, to distinguish, to sever, to decide) and *krisis* (separation, selection, judgment, decision) are essential parts of the agonistic legal process. For Nicole Loraux, the *polis* thinks. The Greeks did not consider this idea as strange. For them their city was a subject with a soul (*psukhē*), which was the democratic constitution (*politeia*).[49] What does the *polis* think? It thinks itself to be 'a very tightly woven fabric.'[50] It considers that it has a centre (*meson*) that gathers together 'citizens conceived of themselves as interchangeable units within a system whose law was the balance of power and whose norm was equality.'[51] In the Athenian egalitarian community of equals (*homoi*), the principle of *isonomia* grants the citizens an equal participation in the exercise of power and a steady rotation of institutional positions and duties.

In this way, the *polis* projects itself as a figure of unity, as the One with a stable identity. What it avoids seeing is 'that at the heart of the political there is ... a conflict,' which is 'always yet to be overcome.'[52] The strife is excommunicated from the imaginary coherent self of the *polis*. This same way of thinking is seen in the Athenians' oath after the Peloponnesian War. When the oligarchy of the Thirty was smashed, the Athenians swore in a harmonious consensus to disremember the horrible past.[53] The oath re-affirmed Achilles' words for Agamemnon: 'Now, however, let it be, for it is over.'[54] They will let the strife, rage and, anger that has taken place be a thing of the past. The traumatic memory (*mēnis*) of the strife (*stasis*), which could also in future cause a rift and tear Athens apart, was excluded from the *polis*. Could we conclude that the ethical and political function of tragedy was to affirm this imaginary representation of the *polis*? The ethics of tragedy would have consisted of a re-construction of an ideological figure, which the *polis* and its citizens wished to project over their community.

This image contradicts the fact that disagreements and conflicts were 'congenital to the city' and immanent to 'the foundation of the political.'[55] A counter-memory functioned against this kind of conventional memory that relegated conflict and strife outside the *polis*. According to Loraux, a conflict 'leads to unity more surely and more solidly than any process of consensus.'[56] The *polis* also thought 'by listening to the multiplicity of voices and respecting the multilayered instances of enunciation while refraining from isolating a particular discourse.'[57] The *polis* was centred on the agora, the public square of open discussions and disagreements. The *agora* was *hestia koine*, the public heart of the political community. It made Athens 'a *polis* in every sense of the word.'[58]

Tragedy makes the *polis* think itself by negating the forgetting and denial of past conflicts and disagreements. Perhaps Athenians consumed tragic conflicts and the conflictual mythical past in the safety of theatre. Theatrical remembrance would have helped to forget contemporary conflictual politics. Tragedy would be the affirmation of the unity of the political community.

However, tragedy was not a representation of the myths and mythical past but a presentation of the contemporary issues in the form of a critical rethinking of the myths. It is more convincing to consider that the mythical conflictual past functioned as a remembrance of the political and ethical conflicts that were an essential part of the democratic *polis*. The Athenians shared common democratic convictions in the name of which the mythological world was deconstructed. The tragedy functioned as a mirror for the spectators. Perhaps tragedy was the imitation of the established values and ideas of justice. This is a simplified picture. Such a tragic performance would merely mirror the citizens' given identity and their community. In the tragic play, there must be something strange and unfamiliar, something that surprised the spectators. The tragedy included interruptive cuts and an internal strangeness that brought forth something that was not yet present.

Tragedy served as a reminder that political, juridical, and civic practices necessarily include conflicts. The conflict in tragedy, 'is not between themes or contents but rather between the very elements constituting tragedy as a theatrical form and as discourse endowed with meaning.'[59] Hence, the tragedy is the presentation of the disagreement (*diaphora*), a deconstruction—or if we use a Greek term, *luē* (unbinding)—of the alleged unity of the political community. The tragic conflict disentangles or unties (*dialuō*) the intertwined political and ethical convictions.

Dialuō has a double meaning. It refers also to a re-weaving of what has come undone, a reconciling and unbinding of what dissociates. The Greeks did not differentiate between *dialuein*, to unbind by separating, and *sullein*, to unbind together, 'since it is the dividing force at work in the city that is finally unbound.'[60] *Dialuō* consists of division and community, disagreement and togetherness, conflict and commonality. What is held in common and shared together is disagreement, discord, and strife. This double meaning constituted the *polis* and what it aimed to repress. The tragedy disclosed this through the presentation of the tragic conflict. One more reason for Plato—who considered discord, disagreement and conflict as nothing but a separation and a degradation of the *polis*—to condemn tragedy.

Another crucial concept is *harmonia*, which refers to the joining of dissimilar parts. Harmony includes both the principle and actualization of a well-fitting joining. For Empedocles, harmony was another name for Aphrodite, who seals the reconciliation of subjects. The tragedy joins the opposing figures, forces, and principles together. Then again, we cannot but consider a non-tragic play a tragedy that would result in a peaceful harmony. Tragedy does not end in the cemented consensus of a political community, the excommunication of conflicts, and the assimilation of disagreements where everyone has a designated role, status, and place in the organic whole. Such harmony would achieve 'the tight joint that eliminates the gap through which we can discern the world ... absolute darkness, blacker than night.'[61] A failed tragedy, indeed. Heraclitus says 'what opposes unites,' but adds that 'all things come about by strife.'[62] Harmony is necessarily in relation to strife and discord, to tensions caused by movements coming apart and together. The joining always already includes difference, splitting, and severing. The conflict among Antigone's brothers presents 'the social bond as a compound of heterogeneous elements, of separate parts, of classes.'[63] Tragedy presents harmony as a confrontation between concord and discord, since harmony itself is, as previously noted, a conflictual concept and functions as such in tragedy. The struggle (*eris*) we have to keep in mind is inseparable from justice (*dikē*): 'all things come to be through strife and are so ordained.'[64] Therefore, the tragic conflict is a play of harmony and discord, strife and justice.

Theatre was a laboratory of measuring. It was a democratic environment where justice was measured through spectators' experience of social attachment, disagreement, oppositional discourse and conflicts. Theatre addressed and created the spectators as equal political subjects capable of thinking, political argumentation, and ethical deliberation. What I am going to do is to reiterate ancient tragedies. Instead of a nostalgic longing, I will understand our relation to tragedy through a creative discovery of the Greek world that might have never been. My context is not only here and now. Tragedies are reiterated in the context of the tradition of theatre and philosophical thinking. The risk is that this ends in estrangement in repetition and unforgivable betrayal. Paradoxically, this may be the only way to show fidelity to ancient tragedy.

To be loyal we have to understand that Greek tragedies did not display psychological complexes and conflicts of characters. There is no hesitation or deferral. Their measure is a destiny, a decision, an action, as they affirm and take destiny upon themselves, making it *their* fate. Nancy wonders

> what Derrida might do if we asked him ... [when will you write an ethics?] Let us imagine that he might answer: Write an ethics? But what does it mean *to write* the law? Is it a matter of copying out its pure and transcendent utterance, or is it rather in writing that the law might be said to trace itself? Could writing legislate? And if so, how?'[65]

What I see taking place in tragedy is ethics tracing itself in its writing. Thinking tragedy philosophically, or writing philosophical notes on the margins of tragedies, to tease out ethical conflicts and questions, may be even considered an empirical study. This may sound paradoxical, but if we hear in the Greek term *empeiria* the meaning of 'taking a risk,' this is not such a strange idea. For Aristotle, *empeiria* meant confronting something that confronts us. Focusing on tragedies as they focus on us does not aim at forcing out the truth out of the object of thinking and research. Instead, it makes visible (*exponere*) the opening of confronted/confronting tragedies. The thinking of the ethical immanent in tragedy opens itself towards tragedy as a process of *ex-perientia*, a voyage without return, as an ethical, political, and aesthetic empirical experiment that draws us within it as it lets itself be experienced. In other words, what I am attempting is to find paths and traces, figures and imitations, words and vibrations, purification and sense—what Marcel Duchamp calls *inframince*—to think and sense the ethics of tragedy.

Ancient tragedy is always already a dislocation of a myth without a definite origin—or the anonymous myth itself is constructed through various dislocations of the mythical narrative whose origin is effaced. The origin of tragedy is an originary displacement. Thus, there is not only a split between myth and theatre, between the 'original' meaning of the story and the experience of spectators of the play in democratic Athens, there is also the split between myth and tragedy. After all, tragedies undergo multiple transformations as they are deployed in different situations, contexts, and discourses in so far as the so-called original tragedy is necessarily a 'speculative hypostasis of later citations.'[66]

This does not give us carte blanche to rewrite Greek tragedies—lyrically or prosaically, dramaturgically or philosophically—as vehicles for our political, philosophical, aesthetic or artistic aims. We have no other possibility to confront tragedy than to show fidelity to the text of the tragic play. It is not bad to start from J. W. Goethe's letter, dated 6 June 1824, to Chancellor Müller. Goethe writes, 'All tragedy depends on an insoluble conflict. As soon as harmony is obtained, or becomes a possibility, tragedy vanishes.'[67]

'The word that makes us free is also the word that kills,' writes Noren.[68] Language is the site in which we experience the nostalgic pain of our separation from the supposed unity of life but also where we expose ourselves to the possibility of confronting Greek tragedies in their strangeness and familiarity. We all are refugees in language, but language is our home here and now and the only possibility to be in touch with the unhomely past/present/future. Language is, in other words, our dwelling place that is always already open to other dwelling places in time and/or space. This kind of sharing in and of language is a site that cannot be without ethical dimensions. There is no sense in attempting to restore the language of ancient tragedy. Instead, we have to listen to the unheard and unspoken language of the Greek tragedies and their lost meanings, their familiar/unfamiliar echoes, clangs and moods of tragic experiences, including ethical conflicts—responsible actions turned into loss and sorrow, so well-trodden and strange for us.

The Greek tragedies institute a time and space that permits the aforesaid continuous re-enactment of these tragedies. The Greek mask has its eyes and mouth open. The mask does not give up seeing and speaking in the same and different way time and again. In Aeschylus' *Agamemnon*, the chorus signs 'Zeus whoever you are.'[69] Our open eyes and mouths are open for this 'whoever you are,' that is, whatever comes to us as aesthetic and ethical possibility. This is a radically open question about which kinds of chains of signifiers relate to the lone signifier 'Zeus' and how they may carry the ethics of tragedy to us.

At the same time, we should understand the difference between us and the Greeks, a difference that is not merely a separation. Even though there is a difference between what the modern Hölderlin speaks of and our late-modern capitalist, Hölderlin's considerations are still valuable. In a letter to Casimir Ulrich Böhlendorf, Hölderlin tells that he is convinced the Germans will stop commenting on previous poets and begin to sing patriotically (*vaterländsich*), naturally (*natürlich*), and truly originally (*eigentlich originell*) as first ones after the Greeks.[70] However, in a previous letter to Böhlendorff dated 4 December 1801, he writes that 'nothing is more difficult to learn than to freely use the national (*Nationelle*).'[71] (Today the nationalist terminology may upset us, but Hölderlin understood it in the context of the vocabulary of the French Revolution he admired). This means that every culture is able to found and return to itself, to learn on one's own, only if it has gone through the other and the strange. That is, the native trait does not become authentically one's own before it is tested by the face of the ungraspable and incomprehensible. Because of this, difference is original.[72]

For Heidegger, the Germans should encounter what is foreign to them. To freely utilize their ownmost to conflict with 'the foreign' is necessary. The soul must voyage to a foreign place. It does this not to lose itself and to forget its native land but to become strong and ready for its own in the foreign. 'What the Germans ... must become experienced with in the foreign land, is the fire of heaven. Through the shock of being struck by this fire, they will be compelled to appropriate and to need and use their own proper character.'[73]

Hölderlin considers that for the Greeks, native elements are a sacred pathos and fire of heaven, which describes their heroic relationship to the *phusis*, gods, and forces of nature. This is the Oriental Greece of a wild, aorgic,[74] counter-organic world, which implies the inclination towards the transgression of finitude and fusion with the One-Whole. To protect themselves from this fire and immediacy, the Greeks distance themselves from *phusis*. In their art, the Greeks adopt clarity and sobriety. The eccentric enthusiasm and passionate excess of the sacred fire is the natural element of the Greek spirit, their native element, but it was harder to use their own (*Eigene*) than excel in representation that was a foreign element (*Fremde*). To excel in the native trait, they had to gain the mastery of the foreign. The art is for them a foreign element, but in it they become masterly. Only through art they would be able to become what they are.

For Hölderlin, the task of culture and art (*tekhnē*) is to surpass nature (*phusis*) and native by bringing to completion what nature cannot achieve. Therefore, art opposes and imitates nature, distances itself from the native and reveals its essence in the turn-round. In its lucidity, sobriety, and clarity of exposition, Greek art goes beyond the ecstatic, passionate, and aorgic nature of the Greeks to return to their native elements. When culture reaches its highest point, it ought to return to the essence of nature through a patriotic, 'native or national turn or reversal (*vaterländische Umkehr*).'[75] However, the more they distance themselves from their own, to take in and affirm what is their own, the less they arrive at their own.

For Aeschylus, the limit and the border between humans and the gods remains demarcated after the border crime that exceeds this limit. However, in Sophocles' tragedies, the limit itself as the limit and the border itself as the border are in question. The Kantian law is presented as the categorical imperative devoid of divinity. Instead of being a divine law or vision of the gods, it is already the retreat of the divine: 'The law is the most proper document of such a retreat.'[76] And Sophocles' tragic is 'the most essential document of this categorical retreat (*détournement catégorique*) of divine.'[77] Henceforth, Sophocles' tragedies are about the retreat and distancing of the divine. This is a double retreat since Antigone as *atheos* turns away from the divine and expresses herself in the forgetting form of infidelity. At the same time, because of the combination of transgression and turn around, she commits her criminal act in a holy manner, that is, as a tragic hero.

The human being forgets himself because he is entirely at the present moment. God forgets himself because he is nothing but time, which means that they are nothing but the Kantian conditions of time and space. The gods are unfaithful, because time turns categorically 'and the beginning and the end no longer rhyme at all; the human being because within this moment he must follow the categorical turn, and thus cannot at all equal the beginning in what follows.'[78] As Antigone proceeds to the pedestal of Dike and commits a border crime, she, first, encounters the gods and the time, second, in this encounter she is faced with the pure and empty form of time and law. Fusion and inclusion with Dike and the infinite law is impossible because of the categorical withdrawal of the gods.[79] No traces of their laws are left behind.

At this moment, Antigone is the witness and guardian of the infidelity of the gods. She becomes the exponent of their infidelity. However, she needs the absence of the infidel gods. That is, she exists entirely at the moment of her transgressive act through which she becomes disloyal to the gods. To complete the withdrawal of the gods, Antigone has to turn away from the gods and their laws. In her categorical reversal and revolution, she turns away from, on the one hand, divine laws, and on the other hand, established human laws, customs and opinions. The categorical turn springs from her rebellious ethical act.

For Hölderlin, *Umkehr* does not mean merely reversal but also a revolution, which includes, on the one hand, a democratic-republican revolution, and on the other hand, a longing for an ethico-political community beyond the state.[80]

For the moderns, what Hölderlin calls Hesperian, things are inverted. The modern art has to return knowingly from the ecstatic art back to the sober and composed native way of being.[81] For the moderns, native/natal and proper is 'the Junonian sobriety' (*die Junonishe Nüchternheit*) and 'the clarity of presentation' (*die Klarheit der Darstellung*).[82] For the moderns, the transgression has become impossible and the lot of moderns is the affirmation of finitude. They are captivated by the 'ability to grasp, the designing of projects, the erection of frameworks and enclosures, the construction of boundaries and divisions, dividing and classifying.'[83] The lack of fate, the distance from nature is peculiar to the moderns. Even death is a silent exile. They are masters of pathos and desire for the infinite and limitlessness, which are foreign elements to them. The paradox remains the same; how to adopt one's own by distancing from one's own.

What is evident, is that we the moderns cannot follow the Greeks in our native being and we should not abstract 'the rules of art merely from the excellence of the Greeks,' Hölderlin writes to his friend.[84] However, he continues, 'the Greeks are for us irreplaceable,' because we have to learn what is our own but also what is foreign (*Fremde*).[85] 'Greece as such, Greece *itself*, does not exist, that is, at least it is a double, divided—even torn,' Lacoue-Labarthe writes.[86] Since the Greeks did not assimilate its utmost own, we can never return to the original Greece, which never took place. What we are able to reach is their art and through it a glimpse of ancient Greece. This does not mean that we can imitate Greek art, because it is art and its sobriety is native to us. We cannot imitate Greek tragedy but we must get Greek art or text to say what it was unable to fully say.

Greek tragedy still has weight. Their words weigh on us by calling us to experience the ethical in tragedy and the sense of the tragic. Instead of answering *what* is the ethics of tragedy, which would necessarily lead us to an ontological discourse or a speculative process of grounding tragedy and ethics in factual or normative universal foundations (or in a divine being), the foundational explanation of the ethics of tragedy is rejected. The ethics of tragedy is not an onto-theology of tragedy, which is what tragedy as I have sensed it interrupts. My more mundane and less transcendent-oriented question that has passed and will pass through this treatise focuses on *how* the ethics of tragedy functions.

Tragedy is 'conceived as form in which conflict exists, comes to expression.'[87] Let us see how we can understand this.

3

Being in Exile

'Our existence is our currency, it's all we have, in other words, we have nothing,' says a refugee in Elfriede Jelinek's re-writing of Aeschylus' tragedy *The Suppliants*.[1] In her *Schutzbefohlenen*, Jelinek's analyses the plight of refugees fleeing 'monstrous killers back home' to Vienna where they occupy the Votiv-Kirche at the historic core of the city.[2] 'Our words, only sighs, squeezed from the depth of the heart.'[3] At the same time, 'we don't stop talking ... point[ing] out problems and solutions,' even if no one wants to hear it.[4] What is our political and ethical obligation 'the suffering people [who] are falling like water off the cliff' impose on us?[5] Their multiple voices ask this question again and again. The dead no longer ask anything—'All dead. All dead. Equal in value, but dead'—but I, alive turned into a supplicant, 'have no position here, so you could easily point me to an opening, a place I may settle down.'[6] What would be 'the first step in creating a way for all of us' to be together?[7] The multiplicity of refugees' voices tells us 'that's solidarity for you, readiness is all, for action, naturally, because that is anything but natural, not a gift of nature.'[8]

Refugee Tragedies

In Greek tragedies, we confront the figure of the refugee. Even if the concept of the refugee in the modern sense was elaborated during the 20th Century, the ancient Greeks had recognized refugees and suppliants. A refugee, *phugas*, was one who flees civic strife, political persecution, terror and war or is exiled by legal sentence. In Aeschylus' tragedy *Suppliants* (or, *Suppliant Maidens*) a company of maidens, who have fled from the land of Zeus, 'whose pastures border upon Syria,' and have just landed on the shores of Argos calls themselves *phugades* (refugees): 'Our band that has fled from the haze-shrouded land.'[9] Ancient Greek vocabulary had multiple categories and names for forced migrants. In addition to *phugas*, *hiketa* and *hiketeuontes* referred to suppliants, *ekpiptontes* or *ekpesontes* to displaced people, *ekballomenoi* or *ekblethentes* to those forcible exiled and *planomenoi* to helpless wanderers. Even if in tragedies refugees are often mythical figures, the best (*aristoi*) and the few (*hoi oligoi*) with aristocratic or upper-class backgrounds—sometimes followed by ordinary women, men, and children—they came mostly from more modest conditions. The 'particular origins and character of the suppliants are irrelevant,' since everyone had an equal claim to compassionate aid.[10]

The foreigners in Athens consisted of voluntary migrants, former male and female slaves manumitted by their owners, refugees, and evacuated women and children. Most of the foreigners were Greeks from other city-states but there were also non-Greek (*barbaros*) migrants. A term that designated non-*politai* was *metoikos*, an immigrant and a resident alien. In Aeschylus's tragedy, *Persians*, the concept of *metoikos* comes from a combination of *meta*, indicating change, and *oikos*, a dwelling place, home. *Metoikos*, a metic, is someone outside of one's community, a person in movement, an immigrant, a person in exile granted refuge in the polis. Solon offered Athenian citizenship to those non-Athenians who would relocate to the city to practice their craft. After the citizenship laws of Pericles, a metic became a legal concept designating foreign residents in Athens who did not have citizens' rights.

At the start of the Peloponnesian War in 431 BCE, around a third of the population were metics who had fled persecution and violence or sought economic opportunities. The majority were from other Greek cities but there were also immigrants from places like Thrace and Lydia. Former slaves who were exclusively from non-Greek areas were also considered metics. Citizenship was inherited, so the second-generation immigrants born in Athens did not get citizenship unless it was given to them as a gift.

From the moment a foreigner received the title of a resident alien he was protected by Athens. But refugees also had rights. For an adult Greek male refugee, it would have been a disgrace to be in a helpless position of dependence on their hosts. Consequently, the Athenians attempted to grant refugees at least relative freedom and independence as subjects even if they would have not been fully assimilated in the political community. Refugees were not considered bare lives or depoliticized victims in need. Cleisthenes 'enrolled in the tribes many foreigners and alien slaves.'[11] Foreigners were integrated into the political community to participate in civic rights. Some of the metics had important roles in social, cultural, scholarly, or economic life, but they were excluded from politics. The Akarnanians did not have citizenship but they had an unrestricted right to buy houses and to participate fully in the courts. They also had the full support of the officials and an exemption from metoikion, the tax on resident foreigners.¹² The dialogue in Plato's *Republic* takes place in the house of a metic. Citizens and metics are equal in this dialogue since Plato does not differentiate between them. Everyone is capable of discussing and expressing their ideas in speech. The speaker's status is secondary to his thoughts and arguments.

Athens was proud of keeping its doors open to refugees from other parts of Greece. Herodotus tells of how Athenians referred to myths of how Athens offered protection to displaced Greeks. Pericles, in his funeral oration, praises the readiness of the Athenians to help destitute people and those in need. The relative open-door immigration policy benefitted Athens. 'The impact and importance of these non-*politai* was enormous.'¹³ Among them were also builders, musicians, artisans such as the playwrights Alexis and Philemon, three of the ten canonical law court orators Lysias, Isaios, and Deinarkhos, and of course Aristotle.

Various Athenian tragedies tell of non-*politai* human beings, refugees, and immigrants. Tragedies bring the fate of people in exile to the centre of the Athenian public space: their success and their despair, their wandering and their reception, the borders they confront and the temple altars that offer protection.

I call refugee tragedies those tragedies that present the destiny of exiles who are displaced through war, civil strife, persecution, or other causes. The refugee tragedies ask how Athenian democracy confronted exiles and how they considered asylum and hospitality. Even though the ancient Greeks had no general legal principles or consistent policy to guide decisions on refugees, they shared ethical ideas regarding a compassionate concern for all fellow human beings by virtue of their humanity. The most relevant circle of care, solidarity and compassion were the family and the city-state, but concern towards vulnerable exiles went beyond the borders of the *polis*, even beyond the Greek people. In Sophocles' *Tereus*, the chorus of the Thracian women declares universal equality: 'There is one race of human beings, a single day produced us all from a father and mother; no one was born superior to another.'¹⁴ Some of us are 'nurtured by fate of misfortune, other by prosperity,' but yet we all are equal beings sharing the world equally due to our common progenitors, Deucalion and Pyrrha.¹⁵

Children of Heracles

The most important refugee tragedy surprisingly seldom produced, and mostly neglected by philosophers is Euripides' *Children of Heracles* (430 BCE). The tragedy is about the plight of the refugees, the children of Heracles known as *Herakleidai*, in exile. After the death of Heracles, who attempted to seize the absolute power of Peloponnesus, his children were left without a protecting father or a home. Old Iolaus, the comrade-in-arms of Heracles, looked after them. King Eurystheus of Argos vowed to kill all the descendants of Heracles. The children, helpless in the face of persecution by the Argives, had to flee.

As refugees, together with Iolaus, they wandered throughout Greece to find a safe haven. Iolaus says, 'We wander now in exile, / fleeing from one town's boundaries to another's.'[16]

No city granted them protection, for Eurystheus had threatened to attack with his powerful Argive army those who give them protection. Those suppliants who requested help were repeatedly extradited and debarred from cities. 'With no place of our own in all of Greece.'[17] Eurystheus demanded they return to face their death sentence and justified his position as one that he had inherited. The herald warned them, 'There's no one on earth who'll choose / your useless llypowers in preference to Eurystheus.'[18] In exile, they were abandoned to sovereign violence and exposed to death. The *Herakleidai* remind us of the figure of homo sacer, even though the concept is one from Roman law, a sacred and accursed human being who is banned and may be killed without punishment.[19] Moreover, whoever offered them protection would be also killed without punishment.

Finally, they arrive at the altar on the front of the temple of Zeus at Marathon, where they take refuge as suppliants. The temple sites were chosen carefully. The appropriateness to the god, the beauty of the place, and the visibility of the temple were decisive factors. For example, the Temple of Poseidon near Athens, built in 444 BCE at the same time as the Parthenon, was constructed with local marble; its slender Doric columns gleaming white were discernible from a long distance from the sea giving comfort to sailors coming back home. The same comfort it gave to those suppliants wandering in exile longing for a place of a refuge.

Temples and altars were considered inviolable spaces that offered safety and protection to those persecuted. An asylum in a sacred place was considered unconditional and open to everyone. Sometimes, as in the play, the citizens would scrutinize the case to make a decision on the asylum application.[20] The asylum application could be rejected only if it was in compliance with the will of gods. When the Thirty condemned the moderate oligarch Theramenes to death without trial, he sprang to no avail towards an altar for sanctuary. 'And I, sirs, beg only bare justice ... these Thirty are not only the most unjust toward men, but also the most impious toward the gods.'[21]

At the front of the temple, Iolaus begs the chorus of Elders to offer protection to them. The herald of Eurystheus has followed them and demands the chorus to extradite the suppliants. The answer of the chorus is a resounding no: 'It's impious for a city to surrender / a suppliant group of strangers.'[22]

Enter Demophon, the king of Athens and son of Theseus, together with his brother Acams. The herald claims to have right on his side, since the refugees are runaways condemned to death by the decrees of the land. The herald even threatens to return with a mighty army of Argive spearmen. Demophon, whose name means 'the voice of the people,' promises to give them protection: 'fear not: no one will drag / you or the children by force from this altar,' since the sanctuary of the gods is 'a common refuge for all.'[23] Demophon does not hesitate, even if it would be 'good to keep one's foot out of trouble,' as the herald reminds.[24]

The Argive army led by Eurystheus arrives and threatens to destroy Athens. An oracle had foretold that Athens would lose the war if noble blood is not sacrificed. The daughters are again at risk, since Demophon is not willing to sacrifice one of his own blood, which would lead 'into conflict with my citizens.'[25] Iolaus understands this, but tells of the universal fate of the refugees: 'Children, we're just like sailors who have escaped / the fury of a storm and gained grip / on land, but they are swept back out to sea / by fierce wind.'[26] For them, a seeming safety is fragile.

Macaria ('she who is blessed'), the daughter of Heracles, offers herself as the sacrifice. The chorus praises her noble death. She is not considered a suffering refugee or an apolitical woman but a speaking being; someone capable of a political speech act as she declares her voluntary commitment. The tragedy presents her as a courageous woman who, due to her deed, guarantees asylum for her siblings. Her act may have been Euripides' own invention, which suited his plot and/or his ethico-political views. If we are to believe Aristophanes, Euripides was inclined to give a voice to women and slaves. 'The mistress talked with all her might, the servant talked as much,' which is, Euripides says in Aristophanes' *Frogs*, his 'democratic way.'²⁷ In the play, Euripides tells Aeschylus he 'shoved them the scenes of common life.'²⁸

In the ensuing battle, the forces of Heracles' son, Hyllus, join the Athenians. Miraculously, old Iolaus is transformed into a powerful and heroic young man. The Athenians repel the attack. Eurystheus is captured alive and put to death. The refugees accepted as suppliants survived and later founded the dynasty of Heraclids, the Dorian rulers.

The tragedy was written during a period of instability, caused by attacks against Athens by Sparta. At the same time, as Athens was in danger, the Athenians seem to have accepted the burden of refugees. It presents the amorality of those in power, Eurystheus, and the vulnerable situation of the refugees. The refugee children remain silent throughout the play, except Macaria. It is Iolaus and Alamena, Hercules' mother, who speaks for them. However, they become visible in Athens as persecuted people who are in desperate need of protection. They are recognized as subjects. As refugees, even in Athens, they are dependent on Demophon's decision. It is up to the sovereign king of Athens to decide whether they are worthy of living. The decision of the king, the voice of the people, is based on Athenian moral and legal tradition. He also justifies it by referring to Athens as a free city and the kinship and debt he owns to Heracles. He does not calculate with benefits even though the herald says that allowing refugees into his country does not benefit the Athenians. Instead, if they are deported, the Argos would become a mighty ally of Athens. However, respect for refugees is so important for Athenians that Demophon chooses to protect those 'wandering beggars,' as Iolaus describes himself and the daughters.²⁹ 'I'll not give these people up,' Demophon confirms.³⁰

The play interpellates the spectators to recognize that refugees are not the absolute outside of the *polis* but a constitutive outside. Yes, in the play they are outside the political community, but at the same time, they define the *polis* through the way it is prepared to share its space with strangers. The limitless sovereignty of the community that closes its borders from the suppliants and other strangers ignores the ethics of sharing. The spectators consider the politics of exclusion as unethical and are not willing to identify with it.

The play presents Athens as a city of justice that has the civilizing virtue of offering protection to refugees even by force. The chorus leader affirms this: 'This country now and always has been ready / to help others in difficulties, if the cause is just.'³¹ This symbolizes the ethical courage of the Athenians. Iolaus, a refugee, who in the eyes of the herald is a 'complete nothing,' recognizes this: 'But I know the Athenians' character, their nature: / they'll be prepared to die. Among good men / honor is regarded higher than staying alive.'[32] The protection of the suppliants was also profitable for the polis. We remain here, Iolaus promises, 'sitting as suppliants for the well-being of the city.'[33]

The acceptance of suppliants and the legal, moral, religious, and military protection of refugees was very popular among the fifth-century Athenian audience. Lysias praises Athens in his funeral speech for granting a protection to the children of Heracles, which he considers as proof of the Athenians' tendency to fight for the weaker with justice instead of handing the victims of injustice over to their persecutors.[34] The Athenian aid to the refugees in The *Children of Heracles* reveals the ideal of Athens: 'Athens will be true to Hellas and all that Hellas stands for: for law, for the gods of mercy, for the belief in right rather than force.'[35] Peter Sellars, who directed the play in 2003 at the Ruhr-Triennale in Bottrop, Germany, tells that the play used to serve 'as a town meeting about refugee issues.'[36]

Suppliants

In *The Suppliants* (423 BCE), Euripides presents Athens as a democratically and responsibly governed city that respects the law and morals. The background of the play is Thebes after the civil war. After Oedipus left Thebes, his son Polynices and Eteocles fight for control of the city. Polynices goes into exile and marries the daughter of Adrastus, the king of Argos. Polynices, who has on his side the army of Argos, attacks Thebes. Polyneices and Eteocles die in the battle, which the Argive army lose. Creon, the brother-in-law of Oedipus, takes power and decrees that invaders are not to be buried.

The play takes place at the temple of Demeter at Eleusis, near Athens. Adrastus and the mothers of the Argive invaders, the chorus, are the suppliants seeking help form Theseus, the king of Athens, and his mother, Aethra. Creon refuses to bury the invaders. They beg Theseus to intervene and persuade Creon to deliver the bodies so they could be buried. Aethra takes pity on the mothers. With the consent of the Athenian people, Theseus decides to help the suppliants. Since Creon does not give up the bodies, the Athenian army takes them back by force. Theseus wins the battle and the bodies are laid to rest. It is important to notice that Theseus was seen as the founder of Athens and the protector of the suppliants. Immanent to the *polis* from its beginning are the open borders facing those in exile.

Funeral rites were the extremely important topic for Greeks. However, unburied bodies have to rest in a hostile foreign land that does not respect the law and burial traditions. Moreover, their bodies are exiled from memory and human community if left unburied, since the bodies becomes nothing but organic parts of nature. Interrupting this natural process with funeral rituals is a kind of asylum for dead bodies.

The bodies are absolutely vulnerable and have no effect on how they are treated. Thebes refuses to guarantee them protection through interruption. It is a city that does not take responsibility for those who are in need, be they dead or alive. The city that refuses to deliver the bodies to their mothers, or not even bury them, would not open its borders to asylum seekers or any other suppliants. It is a city of closure and exclusion that is based on the distinction between friend and enemy (strangers). It does not differ from the warriors of *Iliad*, who in the tumult of the battle threaten to leave the bodies of dead enemies unburied to be eaten by dogs and birds.

On the contrary, Athens grants protection and place for asylum seekers and also helps to protect those in need even if they are not Athenians. Athens acts as a just city not only because of the sentiments of its citizens—their empathy towards others in need, towards refugees, suppliants, and unburied sons—but because of the fidelity to their laws and ethics. Athens is proud of its fidelity to offer asylum to those who flee persecution and terror.

Aeschylus's *Eleusinians* has not survived but based on Plutarch we know that it is juxtaposed with *The Suppliants*. At the beginning of the play, Adrastus and Argive suppliants encounter the chorus of Eleusinian men. The chorus sends for Theseus, who hears the fate of the seven leaders of the army. The suppliants ask Theuseus to aid them in recovering the bodies. Theseus is successful in negotiations with Thebes. The conflict ends in a truce, the bodies of the Seven are putrefied beneath the Cadmea and finally buried in Eleusis. Why a peaceful solution? The trilogy of Aeschylus already contained an account of the war between the Archive army and the Thebans and he may have not wanted to repeat the battle description. A more relevant explanation seems to be that he wanted to emphasize, on the one hand, the plight of the suppliants, and on the other hand, the ethical attitude of Athens towards them. The battle would have taken too much attention from this fundamental issue about the attitude of Athens towards the suppliants.[37]

Hecuba, the wife of the king of Troy, Priam, is put on the stage in

Euripides' *Hecuba* (424 BCE). Troy has fallen. The city is sacked. Husbands are dead. The victorious Greeks have not yet departed. When the war threatened Troy, Polydorus was sent as a refugee to king Polymestor of Thrache for safekeeping. Unlike Athens, the Thracians did not show respect and fidelity to the asylum status. When Troy lost the war, the king had Polydorus murdered.

The play takes place on the coast of Thrache. The Greeks are returning home. The captive Hecuba and other surviving Trojan women are taken away as slaves. Hecuba's daughter, Polyxena, is to be killed as a sacrifice to honour Achilles. Oedipus, whose life Hecuba once saved, ignores the mother's pleas. The chorus of the captive Trojan women lament their fate living as slaves in a foreign land. Polyxena prefers to die proudly and avoid this fate. If this were not enough, Hecuba soon hears about the treacherous murder of her son. Her mood transforms from lamentation to anger. She rages against this terrible injustice and betrayal. She considers revenge as her right and asks Agamemnon's support. Agamemnon reluctantly promises to help her in her revenge. It is not an impulsive act of rage but a well planned and calculated act. As Polymestor arrives, Hecuba invites him and his sons into a tent, where she kills the sons and blinds Polymestor by stabbing his eyes. Agamemnon enters, and the argumentation turns into a trial. Polymestor defends his act as the preservation of the Greek victory. The young Polydorus would have turned into an enemy of the Greeks. Hecuba shows that his speech is mere sophistry. Agamemnon's decision is that justice has been served by the revenge.

Polymestor has violated his promise to protect the young refugee. This is the *hubris* of that barbarian thug. The fall is the price he has to pay. His actual blindness doubles his symbolic blindness in not seeing the limits of the king who had given a refuge. The Greeks, instead, show themselves as respecting the asylum status. Therefore, justice is on the side of Hecuba. At the same time, the play presents the suffering and the aftermath of the war. The women must suffer the death of their children and the fact of being violently separated from their homes and land.

Hecuba, a Refugee was staged in an ancient theatre on the uninhabited Greek island Delos in 2016. Despoina Bebedeli, starring as Hecuba, expresses the plight of the refugees as she spreads her arms and cries: 'Just one day was enough to lose everything … Respect me.' After which she falls to her knees.

Euripides' *Trojan Women* continues the story of war, conquest, displacement, and plight. Throughout the play, the Trojan women lament the loss of their native land that had reared them and their children.

Euripides was not uncritical towards Athens. *Iphigenia at Aulis* was written when it was clear that Athens would lose the Peloponnesian war against Sparta and its allies. Euripides himself is in exile having moved to relatively peaceful Macedonia. Agamemnon, the leader of the Greek coalition during the Trojan war, decides to sacrifice his daughter Iphigeneia to appease the goddess Artemis. This is the condition for his troops to be able to set sail towards Troy. After having second thoughts about offering his daughter, he has an argument on the matter with his brother Menelaus. During the discussion each changes the other's mind. Iphigenia is told that she is to marry Achilles, who does not know that this is merely a plot to sacrifice Iphigenia. When the truth is revealed, Achilles is furious and promises to protect Iphigenia. Iphigenia and her mother, Clytemnestra, try desperately to change Agamemnon's mind. However, Iphigenia finally offers herself to be sacrificed. The play is about undecidabilities and the changes of mind of Agamemnon, Menelaus, and Iphigenia. It shows Euripides' pessimistic view that Athens would no longer be the city of justice governed in a responsible way.

At the same time, we have Iphigenia who is not a fleeing refugee since she does not know her fate, that is, to die as a casualty of the war. This dimension of the tragedy was presented in a 2018 adaptation of the play at the *Volksbühne* in Berlin by a group of Syrian women. The play documented the lives of Syrian women in different phases of the Syrian war. In the presentation, the stories of displaced Syrians make them individuals who are not simply part of the mass of refugees but have their own voices.

Aeschylus's *The Suppliants* or *The Suppliant Women* (c. 470 BCE) is part of the Danaid tetralogy. The Danaids—fifty daughters of Danaus—flee with their father from a forced marriage to their Egyptian cousins, fifty sons of the king Aegyptus, the twin brother of Danaus. Finally, they reach Argos and apply for protection from the king Pelasgus. The suppliants (*hiketides*) mourn their fate as refugees (*phugades*). They have not committed any crime but had to escape the abhorrent forced marriage. They indulge their 'grief in Ionian strain' and the 'cull the flowers of grief'—it is their 'heart' (*kardia*), the seat of feeling and passion that speaks about their desperate situation.[38] It is not merely a matter of emotions and empathy. They plead to 'the cause of righteousness (*dikaios*).' *Dikaios*, an adjective derived from noun *dikē*, justice, refers also to an observance of duty to gods and men, a right and fair thing to do.[39] *Dikaion idontes* may be also understood as seeing or perceiving righteousness, a right way to behold.

They have a right behind them to ask for a shelter against harm and those who answer the call of 'those who flee' (*phugasin*) are righteous people.⁴⁰

The Danaids have performed the formal ritual of supplication to plea for hospitality from the *polis*. The king Pelasgus wishes to consult the citizens on the matter. The tragedy presents the asylum as subject to a vote by the citizens, whose will may grant the Danaids asylum.⁴¹ The Argives decide to grant safety against threats and persecution. Argos recognizes a universal duty required by Zeus, the protector of all suppliants irrespective of their particular features. Pelasgus declares himself a *prostatēs* (guardian or sponsor) who offers official protection.⁴² No one—neither Argive nor foreigner—could capture or violate them. A citizen who fails to protect the will lose his civil rights. Having the status of refugee, they were considered inviolable.

After this the Danaids may choose an accommodation that is the most pleasing to them.⁴³ Even if the Danaids could choose their dwelling place, it seems self-evident that they, as a doubly marginal group of women refugees, would be excluded from the public spaces of the *polis*. For the Athenian audience this was not as simple as that. If politics in the *polis* is studied through official institutions, this view can be justified. The Danaids had no voice in the assembly (*ekklēsia*), the council (*boulē*), the law courts, or the magistrates.

Then again, the division between politics and economy, action and work, public and private, the state and the household, men and women, citizens and migrants were not strict and static. In ancient Greece the political had a double sense. In the institutional sense, politics was conceived as organized through different institutions to which access was regulated.⁴⁴ Who is the citizen, Aristotle asks and answers, 'whoever is entitled to participate in an office involving deliberation or decision is;' and correspondingly, the *polis* is 'the multitude of such persons.'⁴⁵ This was how the *polis* structured and defined itself.

In the sense of collective practices, the political referred to the ensemble of activities that had no specific institutional substance or form. It consisted of multiple experiences and practices that were undertaken in the context of conflict and disagreement.⁴⁶ Various forms of collective practices offered much more open and wider stages for the expression of political power, arguments, and disagreement than the institutional setting.⁴⁷ If the diversity of public life in the *polis* is recognized, political, ethical, and legal discussions cannot be reduced to the aforementioned institutions and those who had a voice in them

Agora (from *ageirō*, 'to gather') was an open public space for gathering. It included public buildings, shops, booths, and work-shops, which brought together exchange, work, and civic life. Turnips and lawsuits, wine and rumours, honeycombs and arguments, lambs and disagreements came together in this open space. *Phronesis* (reflection and reasoning) is often reduced to the privilege of citizens who simultaneously practised their practical wisdom and civic rights. Isocrates shows this wrong: 'We sit around in our shops denouncing the present order and complaining that never under a democracy have we been worse governed.'[48] The agora was not only occupied by business and private things but also by *agon*, a public contest, combat and quarrel, that is, disagreements and conflicts concerning political, legal, ethical, and economic issues. Through these open spaces shopkeepers, artisans, wage labourers and peasants but also women, slaves, migrants, and refugees were included in the Athenian body politic.[49] The agora was a space where actions and labour, politics and work, necessity and freedom, fabrication and speeches were mixed. It was a space for the democratic politics that has no proper place. In other words, the agora became a political space when people carried out speech acts, gave themselves names, drew up contracts and spoke like those who had the institutional and legal right to political speech. In this way, they attributed equality to themselves as citizens.[50]

In addition, banquets, scholarly communities, cult groups, dining clubs, trading agreements, associations for work and other associations brought people with various positions and backgrounds together.[51] Aristotle confirms, 'all kinds of community (*koinonia*) are like parts of the political one.'[52] Even though Aristotle subordinates these communities to the political community, he recognizes that the diversity of various communities that deconstructs the institutional divisions is what makes the *polis*. That is, for him, the multiplicity of communities is an essential part of the political community. Discussions in these communities may have exceeded particular interests and momentary advantages, especially when the topic of disagreement concerned political and ethical issues.

The Danaids would have had possibilities to act and discuss in refugee communities and associations. Refugees found imaginative and effective ways to act and interact as citizens-in-exile by creating institutions, public activities, political spaces, and voluntary associations. These cities-in-exile, where migrants had relative autonomy and self-sufficiency, were based within and outside Athens and border regions between city-states.[53] The Plataean community in Athens had a monthly meeting at the cheese market; the refugees from Messenia forced into exile by the Spartan army settled in the city of Naupaktos; the Athenian refugees who had fled the oligarchy established a city-in-exile at Phyle on the margins of Athens' territory. These communities interacted with Athens, which also supported their establishment and security as long as they were loyal to Athens. City-states and migrant communities around Greece created social, economic, and religious associations that cut across the boundary between a citizen and a voluntary or forced migrant.[54] Ancient Greece was 'rich in self-confident, resilient and politicized refugees.'[55] Ultimately in Athens, the Danaids, who did not have legally recognized political rights, would not have been excluded from public spaces and from acting and speaking together.

Both in Aeschylus' and Euripides' *Suppliant Women* the chorus of the women is at the very centre of the play. This is an ambiguous centrality since it is socially defined as an 'inability, as women, to determine their own lives.'[56] According to John Gould, they are not empowered to decide their own lives but are in the hands of male citizens. Therefore the chorus is simultaneously central and marginal to the tragic action. The chorus is doubly marginal since, 'they are not only women but also foreigners and outsiders.'[57] The marginality of 'such groups as these ... deprives the chorus of tragic authority.'[58] Gould gets it wrong. It is true that the chorus of the suppliants express the values of 'the experience of the excluded, the oppressed, and the vulnerable.'[59] However, the chorus constructs on the stage a world where their claim for protection and status as refugees becomes valid and effective. They express their ethical demand in a situation where they are marginalized. Their collective expression is in disagreement with their exclusion from the political community. Thus, they become active actors on the stage with an undeniable tragic authority.

Immediately after the decision, a herald comes and threatens to return the Danaids to their cousins for marriage. He violently attempts to drag them away. Pelasgus intervenes. He threatens the herald with his army. He urges the Danaids to remain within the walls of Argos where they will get protection.

The play does not have a single hero, downfall, or a tragic conclusion in the sense we have learned. Thus, it was thought to be the earliest surviving play by Aeschylus. Recent evidence shows that it was written after *The Persians*, Aeschylus' second extant play. Perhaps, we could consider these non-tragic elements of the play not as archaic but consciously archaizing elements. Thus, the play would be not the most ancient but the most 'modern' tragedy, like plays with the conventions and form of the tragedy.

There is a tragic conflict between the persecutors and the refugees, those who consider they have the power and right to marry the women and the daughters who disagree with this demand and refuse to marry. Even if there is no one tragic hero, the refugees act as a collective hero. The play does not merely turn around them. They are not represented by their father, who would give a voice to the voiceless refugee women. Instead, they are given voice and visibility as the Danaids act as the chorus. As a hero, they do not fall, even if their refusal could be considered *hubris*. At the end of the play, they retreat behind the safety of the walls of Argos. The asylum in the play is so powerful that it protects the refugees from any fall. This is the non-tragic conclusion of the play. *The Suppliants* speaks powerfully about the tragic condition of those in exile around the world. The play is a meditation on the aporias and impossibilities they have to endure as suppliants.

Once again the play shows how much the asylum is appreciated in Greece tragedy. The king and the people defy demands and threats of those who would violate the Danaids, whose position is now being-protected. The Argives are even ready to go to war to protect those it has granted protection. The protection offered to refugees is thus the right thing to do. The common chorus of the Danaids and the suppliants finish the tragedy by praising 'the course of justice' (*dika dikas*).[60] Is this 'the due measure' (*metrios*) that the tragedy 'teach[es] (*didaskeis*) me,' as one of the Danaids asks.[61] We can affirmatively answer that this is an ethics of the suppliants. Keep in mind that the answer of a suppliant to the question of the nature of the moderate prayer is: 'In things of Heaven ask not too much.'[62] Perhaps, we could understand this to refer to the fact that measuring and due measures are not simply things that one can teach. One must learn to measure oneself.

Oedipus, the Refugee

As is well known, *Oedipus the King* (*Oedipus Tyrannus*) tells of how after having killed his father, Laius the king of Thebes, Oedipus marries his mother Iocasta. His father had the baby exposed on Cithaeron after he was warned by an oracle that his son would slay him. Oedipus was raised by Polybus the king of Corinth and his wife. When Oedipus visited Delphi, he learned that his fate was to kill his father and marry his mother. To avoid the fate, he decided never to return to Corinth. Instead, he travelled towards Thebes and on his way met Laius, with whom he had quarrel. When the truth became known, Iocasta committed suicide and Oedipus blinded himself.

Sigmund Freud's understanding of the myth of Oedipus, which became the fundamental myth of psychoanalysis, has so strong an effect that we are not often able to see Oedipus beyond the Oedipus-complex. Even if Freud offers a relevant way to read *Oedipus the King*, we should reconsider the true position of the figure of Oedipus. He is a human being in exile, a refugee. This is what defines his fate and his tragic voyage on the earth.

In the beginning of *Oedipus the King*, Oedipus is in exile. Thebes not only accepts this refugee as one of them but makes him the king. This is a repetition of the baby Oedipus as a refugee who was accepted into the royal family of Corinth. *Oedipus at Colonos* closes the circle of Oedipus the refugee as it presents his final wandering around Greece as a refugee living a life of the categorical turn of the gods, a life of death in postponement.[63]

Oedipus had once saved Thebes from the plague caused by the Sphinx through solving its riddle. Now the praised saviour king had himself become the cause of the pollution. In *Oedipus the King*, the last thing Oedipus's eyes confront, before he blinds himself, is the gaze of the Other, the empty gaze of the dead mother towards her child/husband. Her gaze is nothing but a terrible eye without limits, a pure and open eye. The horrible emptiness of the gaze is followed by a strange voice. Blind Oedipus hears an anonymous voice that cannot be turned into images or translated into words. In Hölderlin's translation Oedipus calls: *Weh! Weh! Weh! Weh!* ('Pain! Pain! Pain! Pain!'). He asks from the voice 'Where to an earth / Am I being carried suffering thus? / And where does the voice extend and where will it bring me? / Where are you pulling, demon?' The voice neither answers nor calls again. Susanne Gottlob attempts to listen to this voice. Whether the voice is divine, human, demonic, or a mere production of Oedipus's imagination remains unknown. The source of the voice is impossible to define. It is without origin. The voice is without melody or note, which would make it possible to listen to it and attempt to find its sense. The voice is divided into a soundless voice and a voice where all sounds are sounding inseparable at the same time. It is this experience of the nameless and placeless voice, a voice that is overpowering and momentary, beyond articulation and representation that Oedipus attempts to turn into words as he speaks with the chorus.[64] Where is the voice pulling? The chorus answers this question: 'Into the all powerful ones, unheard, unseeable.'[65]

At the moment when Oedipus's name, body, story, and fate seem to come together as his coherent identity, the voice interrupts this coming together. At the same time, the voice interrupts representation, sense, and images. Then again, this voice may be his origin, the cut or division between word and body, which precedes all signification and meaning. Simultaneously, *Weh!* is a hinge between the stage of blindness and language. The voice opens speech that speaks and brings (nothing) into speech. As it calls Oedipus, it interrupts silence and blindness. As such, it is a new promise but also a possibility of a new threat. Gottlob calls it *Klangraum*, a sound-space where the unheard and unseen appears.[66] It is simultaneously what has dropped off from speech and is immanent to speech. The voice is a dialogue between the disappearance of sight—direction, aim, horizon—and the introduction of the voice. Keeping this in mind, we could re-read Hölderlin's relation to the anonymous voice of absent divinity that the poet attempts to bring to language.

Back to Oedipus, the voice is the truth of Oedipus, not as a king or tragic hero but as a refugee, which he has been from his childhood. The call has no home or origin, no direction or aim, but it calls Oedipus, pulls him towards the unseen and unheard. It anonymously calls him to his exile. For Oedipus, it is a demonic call, the Greek *daimon* referring to the guiding spirit that divides him from his origins. It is the divider of Oedipus's lot on earth and a tutelary that calls to him.

Oedipus goes into exile (*phygē*), called by the voice. This refugee narrative is the story of *Oedipus at Colonus*. It is a tragic narrative presenting an exiled Oedipus wandering with Antigone as his guide and vision; both are stateless refugees (*phygades*).

In her insightful analysis, Cecilia Sjöholm regards *Oedipus at Colonus* as 'a tragedy of the relation between exile and political community' and sees Antigone being displaced as 'a symbol of a feminine position in society into a figure of the refugee.'[67] Oedipus himself is in the same position as he follows the daughter. Antigone follows her father into exile but becomes his guide: 'Follow, follow me this way with your unseeing steps, / father, where I lead you.'[68]

In his exile, Oedipus becomes a ghost and a shadow, a homeless and stateless being without protection of any political community. He is stripped of citizenship and legal status. He becomes a fallen stranger doomed to wandering. After Oedipus has confronted the chorus in *Oedipus the King* (or *Oedipus Tyrannus*) by saying that it asks 'for death or exile (*phugē*) from this land for me,' the chorus answers that he is *atheos*, 'given up by gods'⁶⁹ Oedipus is without (*a-*) gods (*theos*). The gods have abandoned him 'to a solitude of one,' that is a refugee 'destined for a slow and delayed death.'⁷⁰

In exile, the blind banished being becomes invisible, protected only by another refugee, Antigone. Oedipus and Antigone are exposed, excluded from legal protection and rights. They are beyond humanity. As a refugee he is between two deaths. Actual physical death will come only at the end of *Oedipus at Colonos*, but meanwhile another death has seized him, a spiritual death, which condemns him to wander in this world.

In her Arendtian reading, Sjöholm points out that Oedipus as a refugee represents unqualified naked life, *zoē*, reduced to sheer necessity. Only in a political community does life as *bios* acquire meaning and force. A political life is possible only in a community, an organized space between people that arises out of acting and speaking together. In this space of plurality and differentiation, multiple singularities create together shared perspectives. Only through public space does the world appear and its appearing to others take place. Community is where people expose themselves towards the plurality of others. 'The tragic conflict is set between naked life and political life.'⁷¹

Forced into exile, Oedipus and Antigone are not merely outside or indifferent to Theban laws but abandoned by human and divine law. They are stripped of their qualified forms of life or political life (*bios*), and their lives are reduced to the simple fact of living or life rooted in nature (*zoē*). However, their situation reminds us more of Giorgio Agamben's conception of *zoē* than Hannah Arendt's. Their lives are reduced to a bare life, but *it* is not merely a pure natural life or pre-political substance but life produced by sovereign power through abandonment, through exclusion from political community. It is the remainder of that which is left after all forms of political and civic life, *bios*, is cancelled. Oedipus and Antigone are banished from the polis, but at the same time they are defined by its laws.⁷²

Oedipus, led by Antigone, arrives at Colonus near Athens. They are refused asylum because the ground there is sacred to the Furies (*Erinyes*). Oedipus finds this strange, since in his prophecy Apollo predicted that he would die at the place sacred to the Furies and that he would be a blessing to the land in which he is buried. After learning that he is the son of Laius, the Elders are even more convinced that Oedipus must be immediately deported.

Finally, the king Theseus of Athens offers protection to Oedipus and Antigone.⁷³ Oedipus is not merely granted asylum but is honoured with citizenship. Oedipus offers Theseus the gift of his burial site, which will protect Athens and ensure victory in future conflicts with Thebes. In this way, Oedipus refers to the difference between Thebes and Athens; one is the place of tyranny and unjustified violence, the other, the model for democracy and the rule of law.

A fierce thunderstorm is a sign from Zeus that for Oedipus his end is near. He walks towards the sacred grove of Furies followed by Antigone, Ismene, and Theseus. Oedipus bids farewell to his daughters: 'Children, the end of life that was prophesied has come upon this man, and there is no way of putting it off.'[74] Antigone asks how he knows this and Oedipus answers that he recognizes and understands it. Oedipus has learned to know well (*katoida*).[75] Oedipus dissipates into the horizon. Only Theseus witnesses this without really witnessing it. He was shading his face as though some terrifying thing unbearable to see had been presented. The one who reports the events is the messenger who was not allowed to see what happened to blind Oedipus and Theseus whose eyes were momentarily blinded by the intolerable sight. His passing bestows power upon and protection over the site of the departure. By perishing, Oedipus fulfils his promise that Athens will be protected by gods as long as his burial site is kept secret. As the refugee sacrifices himself in the name of political community, he becomes the protector of Athens.

Exiled as a refugee, a suppliant granted citizenship. Finally, Oedipus has come to the point where he stops speaking, goes towards the beyond of language and symbolization, towards the Real. At the moment of his disappearance, he knows and is able to undo what he has done and knotted together in the *polis* and family, as a tyrant and father/son/husband. Remaining silent implies a duty to indicate, to point. One must show of which you must remain silent, that is, point the finger at the unsayable Real.[76] This is what Oedipus does as he points in the direction of the king of Athens. This is what his daughter/sister will later do. They point in their own way to possibilities that they, at the same time, bring forth.

In the play, the existence of Antigone and Oedipus is not rooted in the place where they would flourish. They are out of place, or more properly, their place is to be nomads in exile condemned to non-proper space under the wide-open heaven. They are exiled on the earth, separated so far from their home that their place has become that of separateness.

The Athenian audience is talking and talked about on the stage. More fundamentally, the city itself—its law, politics, religion, virtues and practices—is put on the stage, where it plays itself. According to Jean-Pierre

Vernant, tragedy 'does not reflect that reality but calls it into question.'[77] In this way, the tragedy puts itself on stage. It enacts on stage its own problems, internal contradictions, and divisions.

Sanctuaries for Refugees

For the Athenian audience, the refugee tragedies were part of a democratic discussion about refugees which took into consideration civic self-interests and universal ideals. In these tragedies there is a tension between, on the one hand, a political community, a *polis* identity, and a civic solidarity, and on the other hand, the universality of mortality, care, solidarity, and the sharing human community.

Sophocles' play *Tereus* (c. 414 BCE), survives only in fragments, tells of tragic figures who move between Thrace and Athens. Tereus, the king of Thrace, is married to Procne, who is the daughter of Pandion, the king of Athens. Procne complains to the chorus of Thracian women: 'Now, however, I am nothing on my own. But often I have regarded the whole female sex in this way—that we are nothing.'[78] As young girls, they live the most pleasant life in happy ignorance, but when they come 'to awareness' they are pushed out from their families, 'some into homes empty of joy, some into homes full of abuse.'[79]

Procne misses her sister Philomela and asks Tereus to bring her from Athens. On the homeward journey, he rapes Philomela and cuts out her tongue to prevent her from telling the truth. Tereus lies about what had happened during the journey, but the lie is undone when Philomela reveals the crime through a piece of weaving, which functions as a 'shuttle voice (*kerkidos phonē*).'[80] At this moment of recognition (*anagnorisis*), Procne is no more a silenced woman without position in the public space. She is beyond fear carried by the strength of her loyalty to the cause of the truth. She encourages an Athenian man, perhaps a herald who had accompanied the king in his journey to Athens, to confirm what had taken place.[81] 'Have no fear! If you speak the truth, you will never come to harm.'[82]

A furious Procne exacts gruesome revenge upon her husband-king by killing their son Itys. After this, she cooks his body and feeds it to an unsuspecting Tereus. The Athenian audience may have accepted Procne's action as she sacrificed her son to protect the honour of herself and her Athenian natal home violated by the treacherous Thracian barbarians. Tereus' counter-revenge, as head of the conjugal family, is cut short when an intervening god, a *deus ex machina*, turns Procne into a nightingale,

Philomena into a swallow, and Tereus into a hoopoe. As a nightingale, Procne is doomed to stay awake all night singing songs that mourn her dead son. After the metamorphosis, she is able to fly freely across all borders even though she is exiled from the human *polis*.

The refugee tragedies brings forth two interconnected reasons for Athenian hospitality.

First, Athenian hospitality was considered an essential part of Athenian virtues. The sense of obligation towards refugees was recognized both on a collective and individual level. According to Isocrates, Athens shows that it is 'ready to go to the aid of the oppressed' and those who are afraid of oppressors and 'suffer evil at their hands will come to us for refuge.'[83] Athens has 'offered the city as a common refuge,' even though Athenian universalism would be restricted to the Hellenes.[84] But 'the name "Hellenes" suggests no longer a race but an intelligence, and that the title "Hellenes" is applied rather to those who share our culture than to those who share a common blood.'[85] Athens presented itself as the city of refuge that respects the principle of universal justice that transcends the borders of a political community.[86] Xenophobia was not prized in Athens. It was considered a Spartan practice. The descendants of the exiled Plateans, who had been granted 'the right of common citizenship,' appeal to Athens' history of giving aid to them, as they have to flee the destruction of Platea like their forebears.[87]

Then again, the openness of Athenian borders was still a long way off the ideas of the Cynic philosophers Diogenes of Sinope and Crates of Thebes, both forced in exile, who attacked the particularism of city-states and their borders. They could never be exiled from their true home, the cosmopolis, an all-encompassing global *polis* that would consist of 'the citizens of the world.'[88]

Second, the tragedies show that the decision to grant asylum requires discussion about the effect refugees have on the *polis*. Various civic, political, economic, and security issues are aroused as the case of Heracles' children shows. Exclusive citizenship, the particularism of a political community and civic patriotism had an effect in the consideration of asylum applications. Immigrants were often considered as benefiting Athens financially, militarily, and politically. Isocrates and Xenophon consider migration as the enchantment of the city's prosperity.[89] The refugees offer Athens 'not only the hegemony but their own support.'[90] The 'polis of the citizens could not exist without the presence of strangers.'[91] The reciprocal obligations motivated the acceptance of refugees and evacuees from war-torn allied cities.[92] Demosthenes warned the Athenians not to restrict the rights of those refugees who had fled because of their loyalty to Athens. Their protection encouraged potentially loyal people in other cities to fight for Athens. They knew they could trust Athens if they had to flee from their native soils. Patriotism is part of Athenian hospitality. By opening its doors to refugees Athens shows its strength and virtuousness to the Athenians and other Greek city-states. These tragedies show that Athens does not fear the suppliants. It has courage to defend them against perpetrators. Therefore, Athens is morally superior to those states which refuse to offer protection for those in need. The spectators re-affirmed their identity as virtuous citizens as they reflected in themselves the image of being protectors and helpers of those in exile.

These two reason are embodied by Athena, the daughter of the mighty god, who was born with a metallic war cry. To his motherless daughter, Zeus accords his own powers. 'Zeus has given me, too, keen wisdom' (*phronēsis*).[93] Not only does the city belong to Athena but she has a personal relationship with the Athenians, whom she calls 'my citizens.'[94] In Aeschylus' *Eumenides*, she identifies herself with the *polis*, slides from the *polis* to herself and names the Athenians holders of the *polis*, a privilege usually reserved for gods.[95] The intimate relation with the goddess does not make the Athenians exclusive nationalists, which would be considered *hubris*. Due to their practical wisdom, which the Athenians receive from Zeus through his daughter, they have reason and courage to keep their borders open for the suppliants.

This is how Athena receives exiled Orestes in Aeschylus' *Eumenides*, the conclusion of the *Oresteia* trilogy. Before this, let us see how both Orestes and Electra are double refugees. After Clytemnestra had killed her husband Agamemnon, Electra, the daughter of Agamemnon and Clytemnestra, rescued her younger brother from their mother by sending him to Strophius, the king of Phocis. In exile, Orestes is under the care and protection of the king and he becomes friends with his son Pylades.

In Euripides' play, Electra is cast out of the royal place. Clytemnestra has other children with Aegisthus, which she seems to prefer to Electra. She is also afraid that when Electra is married, her children would revenge the murder of Electra's father. She is married off to a Mycenean peasant and forced to move to countryside on the borders of Argiolis. She praises her husband, who has been a healer in her misfortune: 'I hold you equal to the gods in kindness, for in my distress you have not insulted me.'[96] She wonders, 'In what city and what household do you wander about, my wretched brother?'.[97]

Sophocles' *Electra* begins when Orestes, years later, returns from exile to his 'native land' and the 'house of my fathers,' which he hopes will receive him in good fortune.[98] Because he returns in justice, he wishes not to be exiled from 'the land dishonoured.'[99] However, as Electra, Orestes has to go into exile. After having killed Clytemnestra, and her lover, Aegisthus, Orestes has to flee, even though he pleads that his vengeance was commanded by Apollo. Death is, Orestes says, a punishment 'to all who would act outside the laws.'[100] In the *The Libation Bearers*, he says 'that it was with justice that I pursued this killing.'[101] He becomes, 'a wanderer (*alētēs*), an exile (*apoxenos*) from this land, in life and death leaving this report behind.'[102] He is persecuted and driven beyond borders (*horos*) by the Erinyes. 'They hound me on, I cannot stay!'[103] The chorus sees him off with protective words, 'may the god watch over you.'[104] Even if he had committed crime, in his exile he should be granted protection from persecution.

At the end of the play, Euripides' *Electra*, Clytemnestra's brothers, Castor and Polydeuces, reassure Electra and Orestes that their mother had received a just punishment, but the matricide is so shameful an act that they must purge their souls. As their repressed affection of their mother surfaces, Electra and Orestes repent their deed, which is beyond reparation. Hate is combined with the love of the mother.

Electra has to marry Pylades and leave Argos. Orestes flees Argos pursued and tormented by the Erinyes, the chthonic goddesses of vengeance, the daughters of the never-dying Black Night who haunt and punish those who have killed their own. Advised by Apollo, Orestes seeks the protection of Athena, who calls Orestes a holy, pure, and proper suppliant and says, 'I welcome you,' ,' in Aeschylus' *Eumenides*.[105]

However, the infernal Erinyes have followed Orestes to Athens. Athena sets up a trial and lays procedural rules for it. The Erinyes function as accusers, Apollo as a defender. It will be up to the Athenian citizen-jurors to vote for where justice lies. Since the jury vote is evenly split, Athena's ballot for the acquittal decides the case. 'I was stripped bare of my homeland,' Orestes complains as he swears eternal loyalty to Athens before leaving for home.[106]

The Erinyes, who make up the chorus, curse the goddess and the citizens who have disgraced these earth-dwelling deities and trampled age-old laws. They threaten to destroy the city and the surrounding lands. Athena attempts to sooth their black wave of rage by offering them an honourable seat in Athens. They can 'live here with us ... enjoying honor justly and forever' so they can never say that they were 'driven into exile from this country.'[107] Athena raises her voice, 'if you leave here for a foreign country I warn you now you'll long just like a lover for this country you have left behind.'[108] Athena props up her flattering persuasion with a threat. She is the only god that knows where the key to the storehouse of Zeus' thunderbolts is hidden, thunderbolts that helped to defeat the chthonic deities. Instead of force, it is her practical reason that wins the case for her, which reflects the decision making in Athenian democracy.

The Erinyes' anger eases as they become convinced that Athena is not planning to imprison them in the bowels of the earth like Zeus had done to Cronus and other Titans. Happily, they accept their new role as the protectors of justice, who will keep Athena 'on the straight path of justice (*orthodikaion*).'[109] Dressed in purple robes, which the resident aliens wore in the Panathenaea, the main festival in honour of Athena, they are led 'by the dancing lights of torches' to their new abode.[110] Athena renames them *euphrones*, 'kindly ones,' who will 'Watch over Athena's city well.'[111] In Euripides' *Orestes*, they were named Eumenides.

The space of theatre can be considered as a space where the children of Athena publicly considered their moral responsibility towards refugees and other suppliants, wandering beings fleeing their native land, beings simply on the way, or beings on the way to asylum; those who are in a situation Iolaus describes in the beginning of *The Children of Heracles*: 'So we have lost our city / but kept out life.'[112] The answer of the Athenian spectators, if we base it on the events in the plays, was to be proud of the Athenian tradition of allowing refugees to find shelter in Athens. Those kings and cities, who persecuted them and forced them to flee from their native land, were considered figures of arrogant *hubris*. The same goes for those who did not lend their ears to the suppliants. We could consider Antigone as a refugee expelled to death as a punishment. In Bertolt Brecht's *Antigone*, she wonders, "Who throws me out?"[113] And as she is dragged away by the guards she addresses the Elders: "How piously you gaze upwards at the blue heavens, but you don't look me straight in the eye. ... You don't look far enough."[114]

Tragedy shows that there is responsibility—an excess of responsibility—which is not limited to the family, the neighbour, the citizens, or the *polis*. The chorus in *The Children of Heracles* sets the ethical principle, 'It is reasonable to respect the gods' suppliants ... / and not to defile the seats of the deities with violent hands. Lady Justice will not be treated so.'[115]

It is not only the sanctuaries of the gods that are a 'common refuge for all,' as king Demophon defines them. The refugees and suppliants are also protected by justice—*dikē*—herself.[116] As stated, the just city shows fidelity to its laws and customs according to which those in need should be protected, even though this would be limited to other Greeks. The chorus leader points out, 'this country now and always has been ready / to help others in difficulties, if the cause is just.'[117]

One should keep in mind that in the *Nicomachean Ethics* Aristotle defines friendship (*philia*) between strangers. 'One can see even with people on their travels how to a human being every human being is a kindred thing and an object of friendship.'[118] '"When two go forth together",' Aristotle cites *Iliad*, they are more able to notice and to act better than one.[119] Friendship, a virtue related to the virtue of justice, is present 'in members of each species towards each other, particularly in the case of the human species.'[120] The circle of potential friends includes the whole of humankind. Therefore, 'we praise those who love mankind (*philanthrōpos*),' those 'who cherish their friends (*philophilos*).'[121] This love of humankind is not some kind of humanitarian philanthropy. Neither is it an affective state or a capacity. It is, first of all, a disposition.[122] The refugee tragedies present this disposition as a friendship with the asylum seeker 'without qualification.'[123]

We cannot ignore Medea, whom many would turn away from their doors, but who claims that the Greeks are, after all, xenophobic. Euripides' tragedy *Medea* (431 BCE) presents the story of Medea, the princess of the barbarian kingdom of Colchis. She leaves her own native land and the people for her husband Jason. Love turns sour as Jason leaves her for Glauce, the daughter of Creon, king of Corinth. For Jason, the choice between a barbarian woman and a Greek royal princess is self-evident. Medea reminds him that all Greeks hate the barbarians. Jason, the misogynist, replies that he will keep Medea as his mistress. She reacts furiously and is exiled, but decides to take a revenge against the patriarchal society that has dismissed her as a woman and foreigner. She returns to convince Jason that she regrets her reaction born of anger, mourns her forced exile, and begs Jason to convince Creon that her exile should be lifted. In cold blood, she kills Glauce and Creon with her gift of poisoned robes and coronet. After this, she kills her sons with a knife. Medea flees to Athens ruled by King Aegus with the bodies of his children. There she stays—in a non-tragical way—unpunished.

The refugee tragedies may be understood as tragedies addressing the issues of mortality, vulnerability, and lament shared by all human beings.

The refugees are recognized as mortal beings whose birth is authorized by the yet to come death. In their vulnerability they reveal the truth of the human being: 'the very fact of being born is already inscribed in death. Corrosion is already there at birth ... we suffer, we endure.'[124] It is the face of the other (*le visage d'autrui*), a suppliant, in its nakedness and mortality that addresses me. The defenceless face of a refugee exposed to death, 'a source from which all meaning appears,' demands me to answer for and respond to her, to open myself to her death.[125] I am, first of all, a being for-the-other (*pour-l'autre*). Thus, I am in an ethical relation to suppliants and refugees before any legal and moral norms. In the last instance, it is the infinite and divine him-ness (il-leity) that 'signifies from the face of the other person' and commands me from the face of the other.[126]

According to George Eliot, 'there is much pain that is quite noiseless: and vibrations that make human agonies are often a mere whisper in the roar of hurrying existence.'[127] The pain of being in exile is, on the one hand, noiseless and unuttered, and on the other hand, unnoticed and unheard. We could well imagine that those in exile have experienced too many blows so they would share Simone Weil's words about those who are 'unable to cry anymore' and have 'sunk into a state of dumb and ceaseless lamentation.'[128]

The Greeks held the assumption that the sharing of suffering creates a bond between human beings as mortals.[129] Even Priam and Achilles, devoted enemies, weep together when Priam has come to ransom Hector's body. Momentarily they are joined together in grief. The Greek hostilities against the Trojans are suspended. Common finitude is shared. The ethics of mortality ties even the epic war heroes together as they recognize shared finitude.[130]

Judith Butler concludes that there is a principle by which we vow to protect others from the apprehension of a common human vulnerability. Even if it is allocated differently across the globe it is commonly shared since it emerges with life itself and precedes the formation of the self. From the beginning we are given over to others in our primary vulnerability, helplessness, and need, which are immanent to the very conception of the human. The vulnerability is perceived and recognized in an ethical encounter, but there is no guarantee that this kind of encounter will take place. The recognition of vulnerability depends on the norms of recognition that are essential to the constitution of vulnerability. Butler considers it important that 'we need and want those norms to be in place, that we struggle for their establishment, and we value their continuing and expanded operation.'[131]

In *The Inventions of Athens*, Loraux considered the public funeral oration with fixed rhetoric under Athenian democracy as a secular institution. Rather than being ritual death lamentations, these orations praise the city of Athens and its citizens. For example, death in a battle was praised as a courageous ethical act. Orations addressed the Athenian polity. In a similar way, tragedy represented and affirmed the Athenian democracy. The citizens, purged from their individual passions through catharsis, left the theatre with confirmation of their identity as citizens. Both orations and tragedies functioned as a *polis* ideology.

In *The Mourning Voice*, Loraux considers her previous view too functionalist and based on the idea a tragic education (*paidea*). Now she emphasizes tragedy as the play of lamentation, which calls the spectators to share suffering. Instead of public discourse and the mastery of meaning (*logos*), the phonological soundscape of the tragedy consists of the voices and cries of bereavement and mourning, the *aiai* (*phōnē*). The lamentation of female characters is a phonic and mimetic way to be relieved of the paralysis caused by grief. The mourning songs of Euripides' female heroes and choruses, Cassandra's cries of horror in her lamentation (*thrēnos*) for herself or Electra's for her father, the funeral song of mourning (*kommos*) in *The Trojan Women*, Antigone's final grief—these are just a few of the weeping songs. The lamenting that was banned from public spaces became a theatrical event.

The refugee tragedies signal lamentations that brings diverse spectators together and moves them to experience their commonality as mortals. The mourning differs from 'the solely political logic of civic society.'[132] The tragedy is not restricted to the *polis* ideology and identity. Instead, it is a humanist institution that calls for the spectators 'less as members of the political body than as members of that entirely apolitical body known as the human race or, to give it its tragic name, "the race of mortals".'[133] These tragedies—that 'abolish the boundaries so carefully drawn in ancient Greece to define communal and the individual spheres'—are tragic configurations of an ethics of earthly community in which we all dwell together.[134] The spectators' experience of the tragedy affirmed 'a sense of belonging to the community of mortals.'[135]

Loraux's apolitical community of mortals is not as apolitical as she would like to think. This universal community is not a consensual community but consists of different conceptions of finitude and the human condition. These differences are political issues. Moreover, contrary to Loraux, the boundaries between public and private are not stable and apolitical, but thoroughly political definitions. The tragedy that reinterprets the human condition and interrupts established borders thus concerns political issues. Loraux affirms this by saying that the tragedy 'diverts, rejects, or threatens, consciously or not, the obligations and prohibitions constituting the ideology of the city-state.'[136] This apoliticization of tragedy is the problem of this kind of 'mortalist humanism of universal voice, cry, or suffering.'[137]

Nonetheless, if we see the tragic refugees merely as vulnerable beings without political subjectivity, they are reduced to labour (the biologically determined ceaseless and immersive life of *animal laborans*) or work (*homo faber* who fabricates objects that shelter memories which have permanence and durability). They are excluded from Arendt's third element of the human condition, that is, an action, the political activity and the sense-making among equals, the principles of which are natality and freedom.[138] Yet again, I trust that I have shown that this is not necessarily what happens in the refugee tragedies, which includes a tension between exclusion and inclusion from which the ethical arises.

All in all, the refugee tragedies neither represent the mythical past nor reproduce the refugee policy of democratic Athens. The refugees have experienced apparent misfortunes and distressing oppression. Their plight is not usually their own fault. To be undeservedly forced into exile is a possibility that may befall even the citizens who are witnessing a refugee tragedy in the audience.[139] In the tragic theatre, the *polis* reflected itself and spectators were led to consider their ethical and political views. The refugee tragedies did not merely reflect reality, but called it into question and in this way they were an integral part of open and public discussion on refugees, hospitality, and borders.

Being forced to flee is a catastrophe. The Greek term *katastrophē* means a turning upside down (*kata*, 'down' + *strephein* 'turn'). The lives of refugees are turned upside down. But *katastrophē* may be also understood to mean a turning upside down of the prevailing definitions, borders, and positions. The suppliants, refugees, and strangers are turned from excluded into politically active suppliants.

The refugee tragedies presents an ethics based on mortality, which calls us to care and to share our being-in-the-world. It interpellates us to responsibility and solidarity towards suppliants, since 'pain and suffering begin with existence and end when it ends.'[140]

Refugees should not be understood merely as vulnerable victims, they are also subjects that declare wrong done to them. They bring forth the injustice they have suffered. They disagree with a narrow *polis* ideology. They refuse to remain excluded. They demand in the public discourse protection and a dwelling place that is guaranteed to them according to the law and customs but which they are denied.

The subject matter of tragedy is an ethical and political thought in the very process of elaboration. These tragedies give a voice to the pain of being forced to flee. They do have the courage to get over this passivity and mood of surrender to act one more time, to demand what belongs to them—protection, a dwelling place—even if it is denied from them time and again. The refugees and suppliants in these tragedies are not merely passive objects. Though they are victims in need of protection, they are more fundamentally tragic subjects. They are transformed into demands for protection, asylum, or the right to have rights, that is, they have become members of a political community. Tragedy presents a subject effect, that is, how victims are transformed into subjects, which they have already been even if not recognized as such by the pure force beyond the limits of law I call terror.

We can understand the refugees in these terms. They have the courage to flee the regime of terror, to wander in exile and demand asylum. They refuse courageously to internalize the law of the blood and to continue its infinite debts. Nor do they turn against it in rage. They refuse to be part of the continuous cycle of obsessive repetition. Their courage is the resolute endurance of the dreadful situation they are in and their knowledge of how to master the loss. Frustrated with being excluded and refused time and again, the impossibility of being assimilated into a new setting, they still—time and again—have the courage to face their unhomely situation and to question its meaning. The suppliants have the courage to make the impossible possible and to endure the time of the impossible exclusion, injustice, and inequality. Even if care and mortality are elemental topics of these tragedies, we should not reduce the ethics of tragedy to a humanist and humanitarian ethics of lamentation.

4

Tragic Catharsis

The exile-tragedies are not ethical lessons but theatre that brings spectators together as they are moved to experience their common finitude. What is this experience? An enjoyment of the spectacle that heals our bodies, an uncanny horror story that brings about a biological relief, a moral-religious exhibition that purifies our souls or spirits, or what?

Tragedy is presented before an audience. It is for spectators. Their mode of being is being there present, being present in the space of theatre, *theatron*. Hans-Georg Gadamer names the spectator *theoros*, those who participate in the presentation of tragedy by being there present and giving themselves to the presentation. This participation requires self-forgetfulness, being out of one's conventional place. The spectator watches the play, watches the others watching the play, and watches himself watching the play. The spectator has absolute distance from the performance. His attitude is that of 'tragic pensiveness.' This is an aesthetic or theoretical distance from the mimetic *praxis* presented as necessary for the spectator to see the play and to be absolved from direct participation in the play.[1]

One of the aims of ancient tragedy was to influence the spectator. Aristotle defines tragedy not only in its own terms but also by its effect. Tragedy is 'a presentation (*mimēsis*) of an action (*praxis*) which is worthy, complete and of a certain magnitude ... in a dramatic enactment ... and through the arousal of pity and fear brings about a catharsis (*katharsis*) of such emotions.'[2]

Tragedy is the mimesis of a complete action composed of consequent tragic events and conflicts that occur unexpectedly but not by chance. At the end of the *Poetics*, Aristotle compares epic and tragic poetry. Epic poetry is made up of several separate actions. Tragedy as a representation of a single action is more concentrated. Tragedy consists of a well-constructed plot giving rise to a formal unity where events occur necessarily or at least plausibly. In addition to all the elements of the epic, it includes spectacle and music.[3]

What is crucial here is the concept of mimesis. Leaning on Aristotle,

Lacoue-Labarthe considers that ultimately tragedy is the practice of thinking. In tragedy, thinking and learning to think are related to mimesis, which produces learning (*mathēsis*).[4] According to Aristotle, through mimesis we learn our earliest lessons. Moreover mimesis and tragic pleasure—suffering that is enjoyment—are interrelated. Human beings feel pleasure in things imitated. Things that in reality we regard as terrifying and painful, gives us joy when we see their mimetic presentation. We are delighted to contemplate them. Mimesis is central to our understanding of tragedy. Tragic poetry has sprung from two causes: from the instinct of mimesis and the instinct for harmony and rhythm.[5]

Poiētikē tekhnē is the art of mimesis (*mimesis praxeos*), the mimesis of *praxis*.[6] Tragedy transforms *praxis* into a work of art that has a beginning and an end by forming a connection between *archē* and *telos*. This is done by transforming *pragmata* (acts) into dramatic action so that the cause and the consequence are connected. This is invisible for us. What we see is physical action, movements of bodies, expressions, and voices.

In relation to Plato's view on tragedy, 'imitation' is a justified translation. However, not in the case of Aristotle. Aristotle considers human beings not merely as speaking or political animals, but also as more mimetic, *mimētikōtaton*, than other animals. Mimesis is essential for us insofar as our identity is based on mimesis.

For Aristotle, mimesis is not a mirror-like imitation but a creation of the work of art. It is not subjected to how things appear; rather, immanent to it is the possibility of producing something new. It has a relation to reality, not as a mirror but as something that brings forth universally valid truths and visions. Mimesis is not interested in particulars as it functions on a more universal level even though it may be contextual. Aristotle uses mimesis in relation to presentation, representation, expression, description, imitation, and production. It is what is characteristic for human beings and it brings together reason and pleasure while at the same time having an educative function. Those things that in reality might be disgusting or horrible feel pleasurable in the products of mimesis.

Mimesis is not merely imitation, copying, identification, following a model, or mimetic rivalry. Mimesis is about bringing forth that which would otherwise remain hidden. Thus, it is not to be reduced into the order of representation. Lacoue-Labarthe follows here Friedrich Schlegel who translated mimesis as *Darstellung*, (re)presentation, which differs from imitation and also from *Vorstellung*, an objectifying representation. Mimesis does not function in the order of representation, since rather than *re*presenting something already present, it brings forth something that otherwise would not be disclosed or presented. Therefore, mimesis is about a non-eidetic and original presentation. If representation is an objectifying re-presentation, presentation accentuates the moment of presentation, spacing, and presencing. Presentation renders present, that is, it re-presents only insofar as it brings forth. *Darstellung* emphasizes a theatrical dimension of bringing forth. It is thus a theatre presentation.[7] All in all, tragedy is a form of mimetic art.

Fear and Pity in Tragedy

Tragedy is better than an epic at achieving the goal of poetry. The audience considers the events portrayed as so convincing and plausible that they could also happen to them. In spite of this, the spectators feel tragic pleasure as they respond to the presentation of tragic events emotionally and intellectually. Pleasure is felt when, through the art of representing life in action, the tragic feelings (*pathē*) of *phobos* (fear) and *eleos* (pity) are released.[8]

Why is this so? There is 'nothing pleasurable per se about experiencing pity and fear,' but the process of catharsis provides a relief that is itself 'either pleasurable or it helps to explain the proper pleasure which is derived from tragedy.'[9] Why we do enjoy the tragic *pathos*, both a terrible event, misfortune, or deed (objective *pathos*) and a painful emotion.

Phobos is a 'pain or agitation derived from the imagination of a future destructive or painful evil.'[10] Only those evils are feared that potentially cause great suffering and pain. This possibility should be neither immediate nor in the distant future.

Like fear, *eleos* is a fundamental human feeling. It is 'a certain pain at an apparently destructive or painful evil happening to one who does not deserve it and which a person might expect himself or one of his own to suffer, and this when it seems close at hand.'[11] As a distressing affect, pity is caused by the misfortune of others. There are four requirements for pity: seriousness, similarity, deservedness, and distance. First, the seriousness requirement means that the suffering is not trivial but significant. Second, the similar possibilities requirement presumes that the situation of the subject, who experiences pity, is similar enough to the person who suffers, that is, this kind of suffering may befall the subject or someone close to him. Third, according to the just desert requirement, the suffering must not be undeserved (pity is not a mere feeling, but requires a judgment about unjust or undeserved suffering). In *Rhetoric*, Aristotle defines pity as a mark of an ethical character because it refers to the sensibility of injustice. Thus, pity is 'intimately related to justice.'[12] Fourth, pity requires distance between a suffering person and the subject who feels pity. Aristotle mentions the pharaoh Amasis. When his son was led to be executed, he did not cry because the execution inspired horror in him that drove pity out. But as his friend was begging for his life, he cried because there was a relative distance between them. Pity was not paralyzed.[13] Pity is an emotion and an ethical movement that bridges the distance between one and another, but at the same time, retains the distance. The subject is connected to the other through pity as com-passion. Since *phopos* is horror, *eleos* is not any kind of humanitarian sympathy but dreadful com-passion and co-suffering; *Mitleid*, as Freud would say. However, the humanitarian vision turns pity into the passion of the human community without differences. Tragedy purifies us from this humanist empathy of compassion.

How might one translate *eleos*? Martha Nussbaum proposes that we should avoid translating it as 'pity' because nowadays it has the negative connotation of condescension and contempt.[14] Pity brings to mind a derisive form of feeling 'sorry for someone, often directed at people who are perceived as pathetic or having brought about their own misery.'[15] It refers to a patronizing attitude that regards the suffering person as a passive object lacking autonomy, subjectivity, visibility, and voice. If we translate *eleos* as compassion, this may relate it the Augustinian concept of compassion, a co-suffering (*cum patior*) residing in our hearts, which moves us to relieve the neighbour of pain and misery. For Aristotle, the notion of pity rather involves 'a stronger, more violent emotion' than ours, which is tinged by the Christian-humanist notion of compassion, benevolence, and mercy.[16] *Eleos* ought to be kept separate from *kharis* that refers to an altruistic feeling of grace, which gratuitously moves the subject to do something for the other.[17] Then again, if we consider *eleos* as dreadful com-passion, as suffering together, a shared horror and pain, something that does not reduce the suffering other into an object of the benevolent master, then compassion would be better than pity. However, I will use 'pity.'

In *Poetics*, fear and pity are related to each other because pity is associated with fear for oneself. That which provokes a feeling of pity for another may happen to me. In *Rhetoric*, fear and pity are not necessarily connected, since if I feel great fear, I am so concentrated on my own situation that I cannot feel any pity.[18] If I consider myself to be inviolable or if have lost everything, I cannot feel pity.[19]

In addition to the temporary state of mind of a person who fears or feels pity, it must be kept in mind that ethical virtues (*aretē*) are aspects of a character. The person's continuing and habitual condition or disposition (*hexis*) is related not only to actions but also to feelings. It is 'in terms of these that we are well or badly disposed in relation to the affections.'[20] A well-disposed person has a tendency to have appropriate feelings. The subject who feels fear or pity ought to know how these feelings are regulated and how to act in situations when these arise. The pity should be felt 'at the right time, at the right things, for the right people, and for the right end.'[21] For example, if we fail to feel pity when confronted by a suffering refugee, we are 'violently or sluggishly disposed' and have inappropriate feelings.[22]

Two crucial questions concerning pity and fear are: *1)* What are the appropriate feelings of pity and fear; and *2)* What is the right action based on these feelings? In addition to ethical virtues, we have to take into consideration the other aspect of character, the practical wisdom (*phronēsis*) that guides a person's conduct. Only when ethical virtues are combined with this are they considered fully developed. Appropriate emotional responses, correct judgments, and right actions thus operate in a matrix.

Cathartic Purification

Only now can we come back to the question of the catharsis of these two tragic emotions. A clean body or a pure soul are described with the adjective *katharos*. Therefore, catharsis refers to purification rituals that expel a scapegoat—*pharmakos*, which is both a disease and the cure for this disease—from the community. As a biological process, Aristotle relates catharsis to menstruation, which he considered a 'discharge,' the expulsion of the excess female seeds that otherwise provide the matter for the child.[23] Catharsis may be understood as a medical and biological purification or purification that is metaphorically employed in political, religious, and moral spheres. Catharsis functions thus as a remedy.

Aristotle himself does not speak of catharsis as a tragic cure, but in *Politics* he speaks of cathartic melodies that excite the soul so that a listener thus influenced may experience catharsis and healing. However, this is not a pathological condition since cathartic melodies hold for anyone emotionally influenced by various events.[24] Neither does Aristotle consider catharsis as a medical purgation, a homeopathic tragedy-*pharmakon*, which would introduce tragic emotions into the body to purge the noxious emotions from the soul.

Tragic catharsis is not a purgation or purification of tragic emotions. First, tragedy neither transforms pain into pleasure nor abolishes tragic emotions. Second, the spectators respond to the tragic events with fear and pity, but these distressing emotions are also experienced as pleasurable in the context of theatre. Third, even virtuous subjects whose emotions are not impure experience catharsis at the theatre. For Aristotle, the emotional response to the tragic events are not impurities that should be purified, since they are something that a virtuous subject ought to feel.[25]

A humanist view of catharsis understands tragic pleasure more as a cognitive phenomenon than an emotional pleasure. Tragedy is a moral educator that provides a humanist master class of tragic emotions so that moral agents may experience these emotions correctly and react humanly to tragic events. Tragedy evokes feelings in the safety of the theatre so that we may learn from the experience. Through this moral education, we learn to evaluate events, act in a noble way, and develop appropriate feelings towards others. This kind of learning would include a pleasure. There may be a difference between cathartic pleasure and pleasure in understanding, but a strict difference between mimetic and cognitive pleasures ignores the fact that thinking, reasoning, and understanding are not excluded from the experience of tragedy.[26]

Catharsis is not a corrective process. It is not a training regime. Tragedy is the *mimesis* of tragic events and not a description of real-life events. It is theatre in the space where the presentation gives rise to catharsis. The appropriate emotional response to the tragic events at the theatre is not the same as proper emotional responses in situations outside the theatre. Even if the Greek audience identified with the tragic figures, they recognized the difference between tragic events on the stage and their own real-life tragedies. Tragedy cannot be reduced to the procedure of *polis*-education that would train the youth to interiorize a virtuous disposition and to react correctly to various events, situations, and characters. The organization of this is included in politics and, as Aristotle reminds us, correctness in poetry is different to correctness in politics.[27] Catharsis caused by mimesis goes beyond the limits of education, but understanding is not excluded from the cathartic experience. We should also keep in mind that the child does not derive pleasure from a mere contemplation of an object but from a mimetic production of an image. A mimetic pleasure and a cathartic pleasure are hence connected.[28]

We learn through mimetic action and viewing bodies, images, and movements, but seeing requires a network of signification and textuality which makes it possible to know what the events on the stage represents. The scenes on the stage are not a mere passive representation of what is known but an original actualization of knowledge. The stage where action takes place is a separated place, place as separable, marked by borders. Because these borders are porous, the stage remains in contact with what is outside of it. The outside that it simultaneously presupposes is the audience. In other words, 'separation *communicates* with that from which it distances itself.'[29] The learning provoked by tragedy is the communication marked by borders and separation that is neither abolute separation nor the dissolution of differences.

Phenomenological Catharsis

Werner Marx's *Gibt es auf Erden ein Mass?* can be read as a phenomenological understanding of catharsis, even if his main question is how to ground an ethics that is not preoccupied with the religious or theological import of transcendence. Marx begins his answer by referring to Walter Schultz's ethics of responsibility for whom the good is the order of social life that ought to be protected from evil, the latter being understood as the suspension of order. The task of ethics for him is the promotion of order. Marx refuses this kind of definition of ethics for two reasons. First, the ethics of order opens the door to considering totalitarian *order* as ethically good. In its eyes, all disorder and disagreement are evil. Secondly, instead of the substantive concepts of good and evil, Marx takes as the ultimate determinant of ethics the concept of measure: What measure is used to define the good as good? Marx wonders how to find an experience that would provide measures *here on earth* to distinguish between good and evil. The question of measure (*das Mass*) is determinative for ethics as it provides standards for responsible action. The essential feature of ethics is that measures are thought non-metaphysically. This does not mean that non-metaphysical ethics would be relative since it does not have stable metaphysical grounds. It is 'binding on the grounds of "absolute certainty",' even for those who do not believe or are not metaphysically oriented.[30]

Marx's non-metaphysical *Nächstenethik* sets *Nächste* (one that is near, a neighbour, a fellow being) as its subject. Marx situates his phenomenological ethics 'between tradition and another beginning.'[31] On the one hand, this ethics does not give up on an onto-theological metaphysics that leads to a belief in human faculties of reason and intellect, trust in the rationality of reality, and a focus on freedom as the essence of a human being. Ethics also includes traditional virtues of love, compassion, and recognition of the other. These are founded in the essence of human being (*menschlichen Sein*).[32] On the other hand, Marx takes as his starting point Heidegger's other thinking (*andere Denken*), which deconstructs the metaphysics of reason and light, substance, and subject. However, he also proceeds further (*Weiterdenken*).[33]

As stated, Marx claims that this ethics is grounded in absolute certainty. This ground is the fact that human beings are born mortal. Our mortality does not refer here to death as the end of life, which is beyond our experience. Instead, mortality is an awareness of being mortal. We are always already dying. Mortality constitutes the truth of our being. Another crucial element of nearness-ethics is affectivity, which is not suspended as irrational or disruptive. Edmund Husserl spoke about a pre-reflexive and pre-predicative understanding that precedes cognition. Heidegger corrected Husserl by arguing that this kind of understanding takes place only in relation to the mood one finds oneself. The pre-predicative understanding preceding volition and reflection is thus accompanied by an attunement (*Gestimmtheit*) or disposition (*Befindlichkeit*). As such, it is disclosing. It opens up the being of *Dasein* and reveals her world to her as a whole including everything within it. For Heidegger, the basic attunement of *Dasein* is anxiety. One becomes authentic when one confronts the experience of anxiety about oneself and one's being-in-the-world. Marx argues that transformation towards authenticity, which closes off other people, is not the only possibility. Transformation can also move towards traditional virtues of love, justice, and compassion, which also recognizes the fact that we are always beings-with and beings-together. This is the attunement that changes one's relations to other beings and to the world. According to Marx, the experience of our mortality has the power to open a path which leads us to love, justice, and compassion. In this transformative healing force, the capacity for compassion and love becomes operative.

The experience of one's own mortality does not by itself lead to virtue and the assuming of responsibility. These must reveal themselves in one's being. One must be willing to take this path like Heidegger's resolute *Dasein* that has the courage to face essential anxiety. When I experience my mortality, my continuous dying, my being-towards-death, the radical affect of horror strikes me. I am expelled from everyday modes of being-in-the-world and being-with others. My rational planning, fixed views, and well-trodden ideas are displaced. My feeling of security is shattered as a mere illusion. I am displaced and set beside myself. Fright surges through me as I realize that I am all alone in my being-towards-death. As a consequence, my attunement of indifference is changed into the attunement of horror, forlornness, and helplessness.

This experience of my being-towards-death and the corresponding attunement opens a path through my indifference in which my capacity for 'com-passion' becomes increasingly operative. My attunement is first transformed to that of extreme need. But others may help me in my forlornness and loneliness. In a silent or explicit way, I appeal to them, beg for their attention, call their response. As I am heard by others, I experience delight. I am nearing the other. Suddenly, I am in an elevated mood. My attunement of horror and need is transformed into the attunement of joy.

My previous day-to-day indifference or common politeness towards my 'fellow-beings' (*Mitmensch*) is transformed. To my transformed attunement they reveal themselves as 'others of myself,' as Hegel calls this relationship in *Phenomenology of Spirit*. These others share the world with me. I am liberated from the captivity of indifference and freed from limitations. I become emotionally closer to others. I see them in a transformed way and hear their call. I acknowledge them in equality: all and everyone is equal. I also realize in an intuitively rational way that, as myself, they are speaking and hearing beings that are able to see me as their fellow-being and hear my call. Like me, there are mortal beings given over to death from their birth. While they may offer to help me when I call them, their mere existence means they equally need my help in their distress and agony. I and others of myself share the same destiny as beings-in-the-world. My compassion for the other leads me from indifference to self-respect as I become aware of the truth of my being as a being-towards-death, which is the fate I share with all other beings. The experience of suffering my constant dying makes me learn and accept sharing with others what befalls them in the form of suffering.

A sphere of freedom opens for me, where I am emotionally open to a new kind of intuitive rational seeing. This change in my relationship with the fellow-being does not take place through volition but as the result of the transformation of my attunement. Encountering the other in her being that determines her as other and my capacity for com-passion are the existential possibilities of my *Dasein*, being-there. This functions as a force in my concrete relations to others. This force radiates through traditional virtues of love, acknowledgement, and sympathy giving them a new kind of intensity and dimension. At the same time, these intensified virtues determine me as a being-there and being-with that acts in a responsible way. The operative force of the capacity for com-passion is the measure that determines the virtues thoroughly.

This is related to being-with. My readiness to share my suffering with my fellow-being and all others corresponds to this fellow-being's readiness to share her suffering with me and all others. My fellow-being touched by my compassion may turn her into a compassionate being. Nearness increases and becomes more and more intimate as I and the other are nearing each other and all others as well. This phenomenon shows that in the world there is always already an attuned commonality. This readiness is anchored into being as the fact of mortality. To understand the ontological determination of being-with we must see it inspired and enlivened by being-favourably-disposed-towards. It opens a shared world of attuned encounters. We share the world in nearness as one and the other are nearest, that is, fellow-beings. This sympathetic being-with is the ground of true intersubjectivity.

The path that begins from the attunement of horror leads to the transformation of my being in the attunement accompanied by insight and compassion. As this attunement is steadied into a permanent attitude towards others and rational powers of judgement and critical faculty take over, I will continue to acknowledge others of myself enduringly on the basis of justice. However, judgment and justice do not function autonomously, since the experience of mortality and corresponding affects and attunements remain in the background. Then again, I have to experience the path, otherwise there is no transformation. I may also consciously or unconsciously oppose the possibility of transformation. Moreover, I may slip back at any time to the attunement of indifference.

Along the path of ethical transformation, there is an unaccountable healing force at work in me. There is the experience of joy of my being-there and the nearness of the other. I experience being healed from the attunement of indifference. This force as a disclosed possibility of compassion continues to heal me as a giving. It bestows healing as it gives itself in the form of love, acknowledgement, and sympathy.[34] The healing force in this form is a measure but it is neither a Kantian maxim nor an imperative, command, or standard. Instead, as a transformed being, I dwell in this measure. The measure encompasses me and determines me. At the same time, the healing force and the forms of love, acknowledgement, and sympathy have absolute certainty and universal validity. As my way of being is responsible readiness I can measure what is good and evil. This measure for the capacity of compassion is disclosed to me during the path. It is not a measure used by calculative reason but something borne by and through experience, affects, and intuitive rational seeing and hearing. The measuring being dwells in the measure that is the measure for solidarity and responsible action here and now on the earth.

This is the emotional ground of the tragical effect. The effect itself is not emotional or some kind of purification of these emotions. Instead, it is an ethical effect. The spectator responds to the call of the tragic events with more than their attention and emotions. This response is the ethical relation to the figures, and more fundamentally, to the other and others. The pity is transformed, 'purified,' into the immediacy of the other, the suppliant, who requests for immediate help, an asylum. The ethical effect opens the spectator's being into a being already on the way towards the other, the neighbour, or the stranger, the proper and the separate, being-in-common and being-with. In the space of theatre, the world is a shared world and the sense of the shared world, the world shared with others, is the ethical effect of tragedy. The ethical effect may endure only during the presentation of the play. The effect may cause a more fundamental transformation in the spectator who *was* present there. The spectator's mood may be different the morning after the play, but his attunement may change more permanently. Who knows? Anyhow, I would understand catharsis as an ethical effect on the spectator. The purification should be considered a short-term or long-term ethical transformation.

This ethical effect is not merely a private matter but open to public discussion and deliberation. The tragedies and the plots, figures, and conflicts in them were discussed in the Athenian agora. There is no reason not to consider—especially taking into consideration the principles of *isēgoria* (equality of opportunity to speak) and *parrhēsia* (the tendency of free speech)—that their ethical consequences and effects also formed part of a democratic politics in Athens. In this sense there is no strict difference between private and public, ethical and political. Instead, they are intertwined. Thus, catharsis as an ethical effect includes a potential political effect. In the space of theatre, there is no room for ethical indifference.

Desire and Catharsis

Psychoanalysis gives one more view on catharsis. Anna O.'s hysteria was considered in the light of catharsis. In the *Studies on Hysteria*, Joseph Breuer and Sigmund Freud, influenced by Aristotle's notion of catharsis in tragedy, presented a clinical-cathartic method which Breuer developed in his patient Anna O.'s case. As psychoanalysis started to take its first steps, Breuer and Freud saw catharsis as discharging those paralyzing effects related to pathogenic traumatic memories. The cathartic method consists of a discharge of these pathogenic elements through an abreaction.[35] Now we return to the technique of purification, which was already dismissed. Actually, Freud himself dismissed the cathartic cure of the Anna O.'s case. It was shown to be merely a partially effective symptomatic treatment, which may even become an obstacle to the analysis of resistance.

More fertile is Freud's understanding of *Oedipus the King*. The tragic events of the play produce not only a reaction of fear and pity that allows one to experience and purify those emotions. It affects the activation of our repressed unconscious wishes as a representation of these wishes. The mimesis of the tragic events shakes up the repressed impulses that are similarly repressed in all of us. We recognize our own repressed wishes in Oedipus because we are susceptible to the same conflict. His non-knowledge of the identity of his mother and father is the space of our unconsciousness. The spectators, instead of considering what is taking place on the stage, are gripped by the conflictual and repressed emotions. Even though this cathartic process lowers the resistance and opens a way for the repressed material to reach consciousness, some of the resistance is saved like in a psychoanalytic treatment.[36] 'Being present as in an interested spectator at a spectacle ... does for adults what play does for children, whose hesitant hopes of being able to do what grown-up people do are in that way gratified.'[37] Theatrical catharsis is about the subject and its relation to desire. As Freud considered the effect of theatre, he said that if we accept the idea of Aristotelian catharsis, we could describe the purpose of tragedy 'in rather more detail by saying that it is a question of opening up sources of pleasure or enjoyment in our emotional life, just as, in the case of intellectual activity, joking or fun open up similar sources, many of which that activity had made inaccessible.'[38]

Lacan defines the extreme point of the tragic hero: 'To have carried an analysis to its end is no more nor less than to have encountered that limit in which the problematic of desire is raised.'[39] The tragic hero does not sacrifice herself to the demands of the super-ego but runs the risk of castration. This is related to the spectators' desire that implies an overstepping the limit. Catharsis allows the spectator-subject, on the one hand, to approach, sense, and play with the limit, and on the other hand, to encounter its desire and expose itself to this desire.[40] Catharsis is not the purification of tragic emotions. Rather, it is linked to the trajectory of desire in psychoanalysis.

In tragedy, the locus of the repressed wishes is made evident in and through the spectators' cathartic reactions to the tragic emotions: 'the theatre is not so much identification and illusion as the experience of the unconscious itself.'[41] This means that in tragedy the identification goes beyond the mirror stage and the imaginary formation and beyond the emotional reception of the ego of the hero, which would merely reinforce the narcissistic experience of the unity of the imaginary ego.

Catharsis is the deconstruction of the agency of the ego and the imaginary alienation that establishes imaginary completeness and identity. An emotional attachment 'guarantees instinctual satisfaction in a disguised form by allowing him to be whatever he would like to be.'[42] After various layers and unconscious issues are unveiled, things are not same for a spectator. This unveiling is the condition for catharsis and the aesthetic pleasure. At the theatre, as in analysis, the subject may be confronted with its truth at the most intimate level of its being, which is an experience it would have rejected in another situation. For catharsis to function, there must be a distance—not too close, not too far—between the mimesis of tragic events and the experience of the spectator. In psychoanalysis, there is a similar distance, that of unconsciousness, which is also the psychical agency of repressed ideas, representations, images, and wishes as the tragic space of the signifiers of destiny and the oracle, since the unconscious consists of enigmatic knowledge. Theatre and psychoanalysis are spaces where desire is uncovered and discovered.

Catharsis 'connects the subject with the question of desire.'[43] This is why Lacan considers tragedy to be 'at the root of our experience as the key word catharsis implies.'[44] This path cannot be taken on the stage, in analysis or at the theatre without paying a price. 'The spectator has his eyes opened to the fact that even for him who goes to the end of his desire, all is not a bed of roses.'[45] Again, the eyes are opened to 'the value of prudence that stands in opposition to ... relative value of beneficial reason, attachment to pathological interest.'[46] This is what Lacan calls 'the purification of desire' that is an access to desire, which necessitates crossing fear and pity.[47] Due to this, 'the subject learns a little more about the deepest level of himself.'[48] The psychoanalytic understanding of catharsis involves the becoming-subject, which is an ethical process.

Let us give the final word on this to Aristotle, who defines mimesis as an inevitable learning process, which is related to the process of recognition, *anagnōrisis*. The learning process seems to consist of putting a thing or an event in its proper place by subsuming a particular under the general. In this case, what a spectator gets is just a reconfirmation of his identity, since he re-identifies with his position, knowledge, experience, values, and his place in the community. Theatre effect would be merely the repetition of the same and the recognition of the self-same.

Then again, Aristotle speaks of how the tragic poets 'succeed in achieving their aim through wonder (*thaumastos*).'[49] Events in a good tragedy occur unexpectedly but in intelligible connection with each other and then they are more wondrous than when they occur by chance.[50] What is wondrous Aristotle connects with the desire to understand.[51] Therefore, a tragic plot (*muthos*) must include a change, *metabasis*. Moreover, the change should be unpredictable. This kind of turn of event Aristotle calls as *peripeteia*. The unexpected interruption creates excitement. Since tragedy is not simply a continuity of spectacular changes, something else is required. *Anagnōrisis* ought to be understood as a passage from the wonder of the unexpected turn to an insight. In a great tragedy, the *peripeteia* and the *anagnōrisis* take place simultaneously.[52] Catharsis brings all these elements together, since they are the precondition for the proper functioning of the theatre effect that provokes emotional and social, political and corporeal, aesthetic and civic effects that otherwise may be ignored. Considering all this, catharsis is to be understood as ethical catharsis.

Catharsis is not all there is. We could consider the notion of *philanthrōpos*, 'loving humankind or the human being, humanity, being humane,' as a tragic effect. For Aristotle, the most untragic events are those where a wicked person passes from bad fortune to a good one. This does not 'satisfy our sense of justice (*philanthrōpos*) or arouse pity or fear.'[53] If this crook falls from good fortune to bad, our sense of justice is satisfied even though 'it arouses neither pity nor fear, since pity is felt towards a person whose misfortune is undeserved and fear is felt towards a person who is like ourselves.'[54] All in all, the aim of tragedy is 'a tragic effect which also satisfies the general sense of justice (*tragikon gar touto kai philanthrōpon*).'[55] Tragedy may be considered as a space for desire and the ethical provoked by wonder.

5

Tragic Conflict and Beyond

The war is over. The city is totally ruined. Antigone dressed in white, Creon in black. This is a scene from Oliver Py's *Antigone* (2018), created with inmates of the Avignon-Le Pontet prison. The play was first performed in the prison for inmates and the staff, then outside the prison walls at the seventy-second Avignon Theatre Festival. The prisoners were given leave to defend Antigone. In the performance, the language of tragedy puts politics both on stage and off the stage by asking how and why human dignity is above legal and social judgments. Law and dignity are not always the same. Even if Polynices is a criminal, Antigone insist that his body should be treated with dignity. Creon's decree is a double penalty, which many prisoners have experienced. It is not enough that Polynices is killed. His dignity is stripped away. Antigone has to go through this double punishment. Even if—or because—she consciously acts against the law, Antigone embodies ethics, that is, living against all odds with dignity.

The ancient Theban civil war is repeated today time and again. Only the names, ideologies, and positions of the characters change. In Sophocles' *Antigone*, the brothers Eteocles and Polynices die fighting each other. Their father Oedipus had prescribed that they rule in relays. Eteocles refuses to give up his power to Polynices. Polynices attacks Thebes with the Argive army. Creon, the new ruler of the victorious Thebes and the uncle of Oedipus's children, declares that Eteocles is to be honoured but the body of Polynices is to be left unburied on the battlefield. Antigone vows to bury his brother in defiance of Creon's edict. Her sister Ismene does not follow Antigone in her act. She buries the body and is condemned to being buried alive. Haemon, Creon's son and Antigone's fiancée, kills himself after attempting to attack his father. After hearing the news, Creon's wife Eurydice curses him and commits suicide. The bodies of Polynices and Antigone were excluded from the city, but they come back in the form of two other bodies. Haemon's body, a mark, sign, and reminder of Creon's guilt, is seen carried by his father. Eurydice's body 'is no longer hidden indoors,' the chorus sings, but is pushed on the stage resting on a mechanized wheeled platform. In the end, a devastated Creon staggers away.

Antigone, a 'volume small enough to slip into your breast pocket but containing in fine print one of the finest tragedies.' This is how George Eliot describes tragedy in her essay 'The Antigone and Its Moral' from 1856.[1] According to her, even if we no longer believe that if a brother is left unburied, he is 'condemned to wander a hundred years without repose on the banks of Styx;' even if we no longer think that neglecting funeral rites 'is to violate the claims of the infernal deities;' the motive of the play is not foreign to modern sympathies.[2] *Antigone* is relevant, Eliot continues, because the substance of the play concerns something other than these bygone beliefs. What is essential and not merely accidental is the dramatization of the conflict between Antigone and Creon, between her principles and her obedience to the state, between 'the impulse of sisterly piety' and 'the duties of citizenship,' between 'the unwritten law of God' and 'the well-being of the State.'[3]

'All tragedy depends on an insoluble conflict,' such is Goethe's definition of tragedy.[4] The tragic conflict between Antigone and Creon is almost too familiar. We know well who they are, what they represent, embody, incarnate, and stand for. Admiration and disgust, sanctification and demonization, love and hate, sublime and profane, glory and gutter, heroes and crooks, police and thieves, and so on and so forth. Creon is exasperated, Antigone hardened. Only a handful of us would be legally qualified for jury service in the case *Creon v Antigone*.

To remind you of some of the characterization of these figures, Creon stands for authority, sovereignty, government, legitimate order, valid law, unity of the *polis*, social coherence, stability, common good, conventional morality, obedience, rule of law, normative institutions and practices. He stands for social, political, and legal responsibility. His law is declared in the interest of state security. His authoritative speech is identified with the public voice and the will of the people. He is backed by the unanimous *dēmos*. His will reflects the united will of the *polis*. He speaks for the reason of the state and acts to defend the public order. His position constitutes a political necessity.

Sovereignty

The laws protect the city and everyone belonging to it. Because of this, there should be no disagreement about the validity and content of laws.

Obedience should be absolute, disobedience leads immediately to anarchy (*anarkhia*) without the ruler (*arkhē*). For Creon, there are only two alternatives: order and disorder. This view would be supported by Karlheinz Stroux's 1940 production of *Antigone* in Berlin. *Völkisher Beobachter* commented that the play 'does not correspond to the standards of the sacrosanct idea of the state.'[5] In *Berliner Börsenzeitung*'s review, Creon was considered as 'a representative of the principle of state' acting out of 'political necessity' while Antigone was seen as a character 'rebelling against the dictate of the reason of the state' in the name of 'abstract concepts.'[6]

Creon is blamed by the chorus for 'having hurled below one of those above, blasphemously lodging a living person in a tomb' and having 'kept here something belonging to gods below, a corpse deprived, unburied, unholy.'[7] Creon has thus caused a cosmic disorder that pollutes the city, that is, he himself is the reason for the disorder that he accuses Antigone of provoking. Creon must become *antididonai*, something that 'gives against' the disorder.[8] He is an antidote for the pollution he has himself caused.

Even though a tragic error is part of the human condition, it 'represents an experience and a vision of life peculiarly Greek.'[9] *Hamartia*, a flaw, a fault, a misunderstanding or a misapprehension over vital matters, identities, or situations are an elemental part of tragedy. The verb *hamartanein* means 'to miss the mark, to err, to fail.' The consequence of this is *hamartema*, a mistaken action or a crime that leads to disastrous consequences.

Peripeteia is a reversal, which is not a normal transition, but a startling change in the direction of the dramatic action. It is connected to *anagnorisis*, which is the recognition of the identity of oneself, another person, or the situation that arises from the tragic events. The tragic figure is transformed from ignorance to knowledge. When Oedipus learns his true identity, nothing remains the same.

Teiresias warns Creon about the consequences of his action. He should learn to 'bear a more sensible mind within his breast (*phrēn*) than he bears now.'[10] Only after Teiresias has gone do the words of the seer strike home. An upset Creon turns to the chorus to beg for advice. 'What must I do? Tell me, and I will obey. ... You would have me yield?'[11] Since the breast refers to the physical seat of feelings and thought, Creon's recognition is not merely an emotional issue but related to knowing. As his 'judgement takes this turn,' Creon recognizes himself as a ruler under the rule of law: 'It is best to keep the established laws (*kathestōtas nomous*) to the end of life.'[12] From a tyrant to a legitimate ruler. But it is too late. In the end the king has lost everything. The corpses of Antigone, Haemon, and Eurydice remind him of the total loss of his control.

To become an antidote, Creon has to pay an unbearable price. The suicide of his only son Haemon and his wife Eurydice. The chorus is merciless as it announces that 'here comes the king,' whose 'ruin came not from others but from his own failing.'[13]

Perhaps, Creon should have listened the king of Athens, Demophon, who refuses to sacrifice citizens' daughters against their will, since this would provoke conflict with his citizens, 'My power's not absolute, as in barbarian nations; but, if I act justly, I'll get justice in return.'[14]

Creon is unable to understand Antigone's claim. For him, she is a stubborn woman, even hysterical because of her gender, her family history, and the death of her brothers.[15]

Freedom Fighter

Enter Antigone. She appears in all her *kalos* (beauty), standing out in the brightest light, drawing Eros to herself.[16] We should remember Eros is power that releases people from the bonds of the law.[17] Antigone convinces to Ismene that 'it is honourable (*kalos*) for me to do this and die.'[18] Or more properly, she will die in the radiance of good and beauty (*kalos*). If she would act, her 'death will not be one of honour (*kalos*).'[19]

Antigone is a transgressor. She is an ineffable, singular, absolute, and unconditional being who ecstatically fights for her cause. She speaks with manifold voices repressed by the official discourse. She fixes her gaze upon the body of her brother, upon her task of fulfilling the burial rituals, upon her own death and void. Weil stands up for Antigone: 'Antigone is a perfectly pure being, perfectly innocent, perfectly heroic, who voluntarily gives herself up to death to preserve a guilty brother from an unhappy fate in the other world.'[20] The figure of Antigone equals Christ in his absolute purity. She even dies for sinful human beings. There is 'no question of a *hamartia* on the part of Antigone herself; what she did was right.'[21] With reference to the unwritten laws, Creon is mistaken about them because he is disinterested, but to be unaware of these laws is ignorance that amounts to wickedness.[22] Antigone defines herself as *kalon*, beautiful, good, auspicious, noble, honourable, glorious: *kalon moi touto poiousēi thanein*, 'I shall bury him! It would be honourable for me (be beautiful for me) to die while doing it.'[23] She transforms her ethical act into a beautiful death or her beauty in her death.

Nelson Mandela, who once played the role of Creon in a reading of *Antigone* during his time on Robben Island, said that it 'was Antigone who symbolized our struggle; she was, in her own way, a freedom fighter, for she defied the law on the ground that it was unjust.'[24] It seems that the lonely voice of Margaret Thatcher definitely would have stood behind Creon as she condemned Mandela's ANC as a typical terrorist organization.

The chorus is in disbelief as Antigone is brought before Creon. 'Surely they do not lead you captive for disobedience to the king's laws (*basileioi nomoi*).'[25] Passion stirs up conflicts and quarrels. 'You [Eros] wrench just men's minds aside from justice, doing them violence.'[26] The chorus refers to Polynices' and Eteocles' struggle but the true aim is Antigone. 'Victory goes to the visible desire that comes from the eyes of the beautiful bride, desire that has its throne in sovereignty beside those of the mighty laws.'[27] For the chorus, the ethically correct action for Antigone would have been to accept the established position of a bride. In her *hubris* she transgresses established laws and positions. The result: 'Advancing to the extreme of daring, you stumbled against the lofty altar of Justice, my child! And you are paying some torment from your father.'[28]

Creon considers Antigone to be an individual that causes anarchy and lawlessness, destroying the unity of the political community. The model for a good citizen is not even Eteocles, who fought in a duel against Polynices, but the hoplite army, where individuality must give way to the unity of the line. The dead soldier is substituted by the next in line. Creon tells Haemon that a man that is able to rule and be ruled is staunch in the storm of spears. He stands his ground and is a loyal, unflinching comrade at one's side. Insubordination destroys lives, but discipline and living by law protect cities. Whoever steps out of line calls for anarchy.[29] This is the position of Antigone. She does not remain on the line.

Antigone goes too far. She must pay for her father's incest which similarly is a crime against temporality as he fails to pass on his inheritance to the next generation.[30] Antigone is thus subjugated to the signifying chain of her incestuous family history, which depends on inheritance, traces, language, and the unconscious. Antigone is a real point of impossibility of the political, legal, and ethical order of the polis. She is a punctual breakdown of the order.

Antigone laments that she has same fate as Polynices. Her death is excluded from the city. 'No longer may I, poor creature, look upon the sacred eye of the shining sun; and my fate, unwept for, is lamented by no friend.' She does not trust Ismene would publicly lament her. She mourns her own fate. But more important than her unmourned death and disappearance without trace is her being forgotten as someone who resisted Creon's law to defend the higher idea of justice. She chose to act ethically and now there is a risk that no one will remember her refusal to give up her ethical position. Actually, Creon shares her view, since he trusts that by burying her alive outside the city walls, he is able to bury disorder and anarchy with her body.[31] This would also remove pollution from the city.

The traitors were punished even after their death by casting their bodies outside the borders of the city, into the sea or into gorges. According to laws and customs, it was legal to dishonour the body of the traitor. However, Creon's proclamation is a flawed one, since it was not sanctioned to leave the body exposed. This causes pollution.

For Bonnie Honig, Creon has democratic leanings. The ban on lamentation and his 'emphasis on the harms of individuality represent the fifth-century democratic view.'[32] In Athens and more generally in Greece, lamentation and burial rituals were not merely a private issue; they were also regulated. Solon's legislation restrained the wild and disorderly behaviour of the mourning women. In the democratic *polis*, norms regulating funerals functioned to restrict the power of aristocracy, who organized spectacular funerals, to put an end to the cycle of revenge that remembrance of the dead fed. Such norms transmogrified the mourning of an individual into glorifying the dedication of the living and the dead to the *polis*. With democracy, women's private mourning become repressed and the public funeral orations that consolidate the identity of the democratic *polis* take their place.[33]

Antigone violates the prohibition of the private mourning and lamentation in her mourning speeches, first for Polynices and then for herself, where she 'weeps in advance over her future life,' like a Homeric hero.[34] She excessively and endlessly mourns her losses, the downfall of her family, her own being between two deaths, her yet-to-come death. Creon makes an attempt to stop this. He orders her to be taken away quickly, 'I can give you no hope.'[35] Unlike Eurydice, who mourns the death of her son inside the house on the sacrificial altar, Antigone mourns openly in public.

In democratic Athens, where private mourning and lamentation practices were suppressed and forbidden, tragedy becomes a public space where it is allowed to show openly the emotions of loss, grief and mourning. Grief is not merely apolitical expressions of grief but also, as Honig notes, also fundamentally political. As a political act, it litigates or seeks redress to the wrong. Grief 'connotes mourning, resistance to injustice, rectification of wrong and vengeance for it.'[36] Hence, Antigone could be seen as incarnating the ethics of lamentation and mourning, which is both private and public, or more properly, transgresses or dissolves the borders of these spheres.

Eliot writes that we should not consider Antigone 'a blameless victim' and Creon 'a hypocritical tyrant.'[37] There is no coarse contrast. Creon, as well as Antigone, has right on his/her side. Both are, Eliot writes, 'conscious that, in following out one principle, they are laying themselves open to just blame for transgressing another.'[38] Whenever someone's intellect, consciousness, or affection brings him into opposition with the rules of society, the conflict between Antigone and Creon is renewed. Blameless revolutionists and martyrs fighting against injustices also turn out to be wrongdoers. Thus, they have to dare not only to be right but also to be wrong. Because of this, Eliot argues that 'our protest for the right should be seasoned with moderation and reverence,' a morality to which the chorus also points.[39] The conflict between Antigone and Creon represents 'the struggle between elemental tendencies and established laws by which the outer life of man is gradually and painfully being brought into harmony with his inward needs.'[40] We could solve the opposition conflict by arguing that Antigone represents the structural necessity of perversion to the law. That is, law includes its own perversion. Creon's sovereignty, authority, and law would be already invested in Antigone's perversion and violation of Creon's law. Thus, Antigone's dissent would have been always already included in Creon's position. Opposing Creon, she merely reconfirms the force and legitimacy of Creon's authority. This is not convincing. One should keep in mind that the context of the tragedies was democratic Athens. Tragedies were performed at a festival of democratic Athens. Perhaps, the experiences of tyranny and repression are transferred onto the mythical past or to non-democratic cities. Is *Antigone* a condemnation of tyranny? Is Antigone a monstrous lawbreaker exceeding all limits, a terrorist ready to destroy everything in the name of the cause? Or does she stand up for resistance, radical disagreement, and the rebellious fight against a tyrannical and violent authority? Before rushing to give a definite answer we have to stop to consider Hegel's point, that the tragic heroes are just as much innocent as guilty. That is, 'innocence, therefore, is merely non-action.'[41] Moreover, non-action does not make tragedy a play and theatre. This is how Aristotle defines the tragic figure. 'Character is the element which reveals the nature of a moral choice (*prohairesis*), in cases where it is not anyway clear what a person is choosing or avoiding.'[42] The tragic figure must exercise her will by choosing between various possibilities of conduct. This ethical commitment takes place not in a situation where the set of codified moral or legal norms would dictate the choice. The tragic figure is disclosed as a subject who has to make an ethical and political choice and commit herself to it. Ethics cannot be exhausted by codified morality for the tragedy of morality would not make any sense.

Ethical Life

In the 1790s, the philosophy of the tragic, provoked by Friedrich Schelling and the Schlegel brothers, August, and Friedrich, was distinguished from the poetics of tragedy dating back to Aristotle.[43] The Jena revolution defined tragedy as a conflict between opposing ethical forces and between freedom and necessity. Schelling sees the tragic contradiction as a mortal hero fighting against the fate that makes him a malefactor and who is punished for the crime that was the deed of destiny. Since fate is absolutely superior, the hero has to succumb. The hero 'must be *punished* for succumbing because he did not succumb *without a struggle*.'[44] That is, the tragic hero acknowledges the absolute power that threatens his freedom with annihilation but fights against it by exerting his freedom.[45] The tragic hero is an autonomous moral subject who possesses an 'absoluteness of the character' from which 'the action must always emerge.'[46]

The essence of tragedy is 'actual and objective conflict between freedom in the subject … and necessity.'[47] This conflict ends so that 'both are manifested in perfect indifference as simultaneously victorious and vanquished.'[48] Freedom and necessity, Kant's second (ethics) and first (epistemology) critique are thus reconciled in tragedy, which we could consider as Kant's third (aesthetic) critique. Schelling's tragic hero is Oedipus, who is first determined by necessity as he does not know that he commits patricide and incest. In the end, the truth is revealed. He is free because he knows who he is and what he must do. That is, he freely accepts his fate and is led from the stage by Antigone. Enter Hegel.

Sittlichkeit (ethical life), related to the Greek *ethos* (habit and custom), is put on stage in Hegel's reading of the Greek tragedy. If we move from catharsis to the tragic play itself, we cannot avoid taking Hegel as our reference point. If Freud chose Oedipus as the central figure of psychoanalysis, Hegel turned to the figure of Antigone to consider ethics, politics, family, and limits. For Hegel, Antigone embodies the ethical consciousness that is more complete than Oedipus. We confront a division that cuts through the sphere of ethics: Antigone, an ethical figure, Oedipus, the father, also an ethical figure but not so complete. The reason for this is that he does not commit his crime consciously. He breaks the law unwillingly and unconsciously. 'But the ethical consciousness is more complete, its guilt more inexcusable, if it knows *beforehand* the law and the power which it opposes, if it takes them to be violence and wrong, to be ethical merely by accident, and, like Antigone, knowingly (*wissentlich*) commits the crime (*das Vebrechen*).'[49] The difference between Oedipus and Antigone is the difference between the excusable and inexcusable. Likewise, Kierkegaard, as he reads Hegel's reading of *Antigone*, differentiates between Antigone, who knows the truth of the incestuous family history, and Oedipus, who is not conscious of his incestuous deed.

Does Hegel really mean that the more freely and willingly an offender violates the law, the more ethical a character this perpetrator is? There is no simple answer, or the answer is found from his conception of tragedy, where ethics and transgression are intimately related. Perhaps ethics is something that remains within the transgressive act based on the critical and reflective will of the tragic hero. Perhaps the tragic figure, first, consciously decides to choose the object or the purpose of the act, and second, concretely acts following or motivated by this willful decision. Perhaps the tragic subject commits a crime to act in an ethical way. These multiple 'perhaps' are what I attempt to consider by travelling through the tragic landscape as Hegel maps it.

We can start by placing Antigone, the criminal, in the place of ethical consciousness. This is crucial if we wish to understand the Hegelian tragedy of ethics. If you do not trust me, trust Hegel who affirms it beyond any doubt: 'ethical consciousness … like Antigone.' If we follow Hegel's advice and change the concept of 'ethical consciousness' to the proper name (of a character) 'Antigone,' Hegel's sentence runs like this: Antigone knows beforehand the law and the power, which she opposes and thus she knowingly commits the crime.[50] If you have any doubts about this, go back to the paragraph 470 of *Phenomenology of Spirit*. It is Hegel who writes that the more complete the ethical consciousness is, the more inexcusable the guilt. Hegel has Antigone carry the inexcusable guilt with her—like Brecht had her carry the door on her back—but Antigone refuses to take the Hegelian burden on her shoulders.

In his *Phenomenology of Spirit*, Hegel sets out infamous co-ordinates for reading *Antigone* as the embodiment of the ethical life. However, Hegel leaves Antigone unnamed most of the time, as if he would strip her of her singularity. For him, the figure of Antigone represents the principle of kinship upon which political community is founded in its purest form, since the relationship between sister and brother is without desire. The brother 'is for the sister a passive, similar being in general; the recognition of herself in him is pure and unmixed with any natural desire (*natürlicher Beziehung*).'[51] The reason for this statement is not merely the incestuous family tradition, but the fact that for Hegel, family as a natural ethical community is not based on desire for, and love of, a particular family member but on universality, that is, the ethical bond with family members generally.

The relationship between loving partners is never purely ethical and based on the knowledge of mutual recognition. Without love, or at least some feelings, partnership would be, well, quite frustrating, which Hegel must admit. What comes to the children, the products of the not-so-ethical relation, are dependent on their parents. This relationship is marked by inequality. Hegel himself deconstructs the purity of the familial ethical relationship or recognition. And he well knows this. Brothers and sisters come to rescue the idea of the ethical relationship.

Therefore Hegel is able to reject the idea that Antigone would have defied Creon's law because of her love or pity. Duty and desire are different spheres for Hegel. One should not ignore that 'the ethical principle is intrinsically universal.'[52] It would be a mistake to read Hegel through the Freudian Oedipus-complex. Then again, the insistence on the sister-brother relationship without desire hints that the spectre is haunting Hegel's *Antigone*, the spectre of Oedipus.

Moreover, it is her duty as a family member to bury the brother and an essential duty for the Greeks. Without funeral rites the individual belongs solely to nature. A pure death would remain something irrational and the rituals invest a pivotal aspect in the dead body. Something is done, as Hegel would say. The 'right of consciousness' adds to the natural process of 'the movement of consciousness,' which interrupts the work of nature.[53] The blood relationship is rescued from destruction due to the funeral rites. Polynices is transformed from a rotten corpse to a dead being. His name is preserved. In this process, he is freed from particularism, sensuous reality, and the 'accidents of life,' and turned into 'the calm of simple universality.'[54]

Things are much more complicated. Without the character of Creon there is no Antigone—and they definitely do not have 'the same *essential* nature.'⁵⁵ The ethical consciousness that is essentially a character 'is *decisively* for one of the powers.'⁵⁶ The two ethical powers (*die beiden sittlichen Mächte*) are in an antagonist relationship. Tragedy presents ethical life actualized in the state and the family as split. It is a stage, for Hegel, where these two powers dialectically oppose and even contaminate each other. Opposition and identity, division and unity, split and reconciliation are the running forces of this dialectical machine that Hegel finds or sets in tragedy. The aim of the Hegelian dialectic is the realization of subjectivity.

Spirit that advances to the consciousness of what it is immediately 'must leave behind it the beauty of ethical life' to achieve a knowledge of itself and self-consciousness in the actuality of a historical situation. The beauty of ethical life (*Sittlichkeit*), for Hegel, was represented by ancient Greece, the period of an immediate spirit. This beauty consisted of an ethic where one identified immediately with the norms of the state. Laws considered as legitimate without reflection. The ethical behaviour was grounded in laws, custom, and tradition. They were developed through imitation, inclusion, and habit in accordance with the objective laws of the community. These laws were immanent and there was no critical or reflective distance to them. The Greek society of immediate spirit was dominated by the objective will, that is, citizens did not recognize their particular interests and aims. Subjective consciousness is not yet separated from the ethical substance. The immanent substance of the ethical life consisted of valid laws, civic habits, and customs. The ethical order is always already given. There is, in other words, no critical distance to legal and social norms. Pericles' funeral oration lends support to Hegel. Pericles describes Athenian democracy as relying on an idea of civic community and the ethics of participation instead of rivalry between individuals and the ethics of competition.⁵⁷

Harmony, unity, and consensus are what make things run in Greek society. People are 'holding by the existing state of things.'⁵⁸ When subjective critical reflection of a singular being 'comes into play, the inquiry is started whether the Principles of Law cannot be improved.'⁵⁹ Now internal conviction is relied upon and subjective freedom begins. Politics, law, ethics, and customs are brought to the test of one's own conscience. The result may be the 'defiance of the existing constitution.'⁶⁰ From the perspective of the Greek objective ethical life, this kind of will of a self-conscious subject is considered a destructive element. The manifestation of disagreement is a threat to the unity of the political community and to the harmonious ethical life. The beautiful ethical synthesis without contradictions may be divided and split as a result.

In Hegel's dialectical logic, contradictions are necessary for the formation of the spirit. Enter Creon and Antigone—and with them the tragic conflict that shakes the harmonious unity of the ethical life. Tragedy presents a contradiction between the posited human law (*das menschliche Gesetz*) and immediate divine law (*das göttliche Gesetz*), between the state and the family, between the common ethical substance and the natural ethical community, between the objective freedom and the kinship relationship. On the one side, the *polis*, the government, political argumentation, the open *agora* under the sunlight; on the other darker side, the household, the unmediated power, the unconscious.

In the *Philosophy of Right*, Hegel considers this opposition to be related to an essential sexual difference: 'Man has his actual substantive life in the state, in learning ... in labour and struggle with the external world and with himself ... Woman, on the other hand, has her substantial vocation and her ethical disposition in the family.'[61] The masculine part is on the side of citizenship, political and public space; the feminine element stands for kinship, familial and natural immediacy.

For Hegel, a woman's individuality is 'not the natural pleasure' (*die natürliche der Lust*).'[62] On the contrary, the husband has 'the right of desire' (*das Recht der Begierde*).[63] Woman is excluded from the ethical community of the family and particularity, but when it comes to desire, which is for Hegel particular, she is seen as centred on universality. Man, defined as universal, suddenly has the right to the particularity of desire. Hegel attempts to save his dichotomies and binary oppositions by explaining that man is essentially divided. The self-conscious power of universality is separated from desire and because of this man has the right to desire in the sphere that is proper to it.[64] Woman, who is not able to enter the public sphere, must be protected behind close doors from an overpowering Dionysian pleasure. Hence, an otherwise particular womanhood is turned into universality the moment desire enters the house.[65] Woman is a series of exclusions: no desire, sexual passivity, the public and the political closed off. Hegel makes a strict distinction between ethical duty and desire. He himself deconstructs this by admitting that the ethical community of family includes love and desire. For Pericles, even in the public sphere of politics, ethics was related to desire. A later dictum by Pericles assures that the Athenians should not have a respect and filial love for Athens, like a child has for parents, but should instead become erotic lovers (*erastei*) of the democratic city. The political community arouse love (*eros*) and the citizens ought to desire the erotic object of the city. For Pericles, *eros* (perfectly free and committed passion) is to be considered also as a political passion that attracts citizens into civic duty.[66]

Likewise, the law is divided in a gendered way. The splitting of law does not depend on any particular legal, political, or social situation. The split is essential, since nature 'assigns one sex to one law, the other to the other law.'[67] Divine law is related to woman. It is the law of household gods and the underworld. Human law is related to man. It is manifested in the political community (the universal existence of the law), in the manhood of the community (the generally active law), and in the government (the effectively active law). Human law '*is*, *moves* and *maintains* itself.'[68] It is an existing, gathering, and effecting ethical power, which absorbs and consumes the particularism of separate families 'presided over by womankind' and prevents families from being dissolved into their fluid continuity.[69]

In the play, this gendered antagonism is embodied by the tragic figures of Creon and Antigone. These fixed characters coincide with ethical consciousness. Their action takes place in the ethical sphere, but it is not the space of harmonious unity of ethical life but a divided space. The 'action is itself this splitting into two.'[70] Tragedy offers a medium for Hegel's concepts of law, individuality, subject, and will, a means 'through which these intangible essences are allowed to come into being.'[71] When Hegel returns to Antigone in *Philosophy of Right*, he considers her an example of the difference between instinctive sentiment and political virtue. Her actions are based of the natural ethical life of the family, which consists of sentiments and feelings. On the contrary, political virtue is not a sentiment. It is a willing of thought and a known universal end.[72]

At the same time, we have to keep in mind that ethical relations both in the state and the family are universal and spiritual, which is the essence of any ethical relationship and bond.

We now come to the heart of Hegel's understanding of tragedy. It can be crystallized in three sentences, the first two of which ought to be read together, even at the same time (*Philosophy of Right* § 156 and *Phenomenology of Spirit* § 466).

> The ethical substance, as containing self-consciousness which has being for itself and is united with its concept, is the *actual spirit* of a family and a people.

> The ethical consciousness, because it is *decisively* for one of the two powers, is essentially character.

Ethical life is divided, but Hegel cannot let the two opposing domains and forces be absolutely separated. They are—have to be—in a dialectical relation. The state and the family, the universal and the particular are not mutually exclusive but interdependent. How they exist in a necessary interaction Hegel explains in the dense paragraph 460 of *Phenomenology of Spirit*. The family possesses in the political community 'its substance and enduring being.' Conversely, the community possesses in the family 'the formal element of its actual existence.' Moreover, human law possesses 'in the divine law its power and authentication.' In its living process, human law proceeds from the divine and the 'law valid on the earth' proceeds from the law of weakness and darkness, like the conscious from the unconscious and the mediate from immediate. The power of the divine and the nether law actually exists in political community and on earth. They become through conscience 'existence and activity.'[73]

Another way—immanent in the paragraph 460—to understand the dialectic of the opposites is to grasp the fact that both spheres comprise the whole substance of the spirit and the various moments of its content. The state and the family both contain universality and particularity. While the family would be purely the sphere of particularity, the ethical dimension would be possible only in the public sphere.[74]

This explains what Hegel means with the infamous definition of woman as the 'eternal irony of the community (*die ewige Ironie des Gemeinwesens*).'[75] The female principle is an inner enemy of political community. Womanhood is simultaneously suppressed and exists as essential to the community. This principle is the irony of community. It transforms the universal end of the political community into a private end, universal activity into the business of an individual, and the universal property of the state into a family possession.[76] The irony is that the family is not naturally a rebellious sphere. Political community must suppress the spirit of individuality to survive as a unity. By suppressing it the community creates this spirit. What is more, the community 'creates it by the repressive attitude towards it as a hostile principle.'[77] Hence repression turns out to be a creative force—it creates what it represses.

In his lectures on aesthetics, Hegel reconsiders the opposition between the state and kinship. As a husband, father, and uncle, Creon has and recognizes familial duties. As a member of the *polis*, Antigone has political and civic loyalties, which she does not deny. There is not merely an external conflict between Antigone and Creon but also a conflict that is internal to these opposing figures. Only after this internal struggle does Antigone defend the gods of the underworld, the guardians of the blood ties; and does Creon refer to Zeus, the power of public life and commonwealth.

However, both Antigone and Creon adamantly claim that her/his law is 'absolute valid.'[78] They are sure of their law, duty, and justification of their positions. In their 'immediate firmness of decision,' there is no room for any doubt or reflection.[79] They are subjects, who are sure what she/he must do. They are both figures of an ethical pathos, temperament, and power, which motivates their conscious acts. In their fixedness, both Antigone and Creon represent one sided ethical consciousness, one universal will, which excludes the other will. Their action is doomed to remain one-sided throughout tragedy. The tragic conflict is not accidental but necessary. It is immanent to these tragic figures. As a consequence, the division of the ethical life is played out in the play.

Now we get to the third crucial sentence, which is found in Hegel's *Aesthetics*: 'the collision has its basis in a transgression.'[80] In their one-sidedness, Antigone and Creon inevitably violate the opposing domain they should respect. They are both responsible, since Antigone should have respected the laws of the political community as she guarded the 'sacred claims of the family,' while Creon should have respected the laws of kinship as he acted as the sovereign law-giver.[81] At the same time, their ethical consciousnesses direct their acts. They will rationally and act in accordance with this will. Their expression of their wills as subjective are actions. Antigone's act is an ethical action (*die sittliche Handlung*). So is Creon's. The transgression is double sided: as the tragic hero breaks the law, she/he realizes her/himself in and through the act that corresponds to her/his purpose. It is a necessity for Antigone and Creon to act in accordance with the law they identify with. The subject of the tragic hero and what she/he wills as her/his object are inseparable. Hence, the object is not something alien to the subject. Instead, the ethical consciousness of the subject '*consciously* produces its object.'[82] Antigone and Creon are active agents that produce objects and purposes. Their acts are ethical insofar as they shape in which way they—as ethical consciousnesses—actualize themselves in nothing other than what they know. In the action, the individual is revealed. Antigone buries her brother as she had declared. Creon punishes the perpetrator as he has decreed. Consequently, her/his act takes place in the sphere of the ethical and is justified. Transgression is thus an ethical act, even though it transgresses another law. Because innocence, for Hegel, 'is merely non-action,' Antigone and Creon cannot be purely innocent, but both innocent and guilty.[83] Respecting absolutely the law (*das Gesetz*), breaking absolutely the law (*das Gesetz*)—this is what makes them tragic figures.

Absolute Justice

Finally we come to the resolution of the tragic conflict in the dialectical process from contamination to purification. This final stage consists of three concepts all related to limits and borders: guilt, fate, and justice (*Gerechtigkeit*).

1. Guilt. Even if their acts are justified and are not caused by any evil will, both Antigone and Creon are guilty as they have ignored the other law and the limits it sets. 'The ethical consciousness must, ... on account of its deed, acknowledge its opposite as its own actuality.'[84] Therefore, it 'must acknowledge the guilt.'[85] The guilt is experienced in the experience of breaking one law in and through another law. By acknowledging the guilt, the tragic hero acknowledges the opposite position, which she/he had violated, that is, she/he recognizes the split in the ethical sphere.

2. Fate. Hegel writes, 'fate drives individuality back within its limits and destroys it if these are crossed.'[86] The transgression to which the tragic hero is guilty causes her/his destruction. The tragic hero accepts the fate as her/his lot. The demise of the two culpable/legitimate figures is inevitable. Tragedy presents the fate that leads to the dissolution of the one-dimensional position and force.

3. Justice. This end of tragedy is not destruction but justice. The demise of the opposition and the division of the ethical life leads to reconciliation and the emergence of an elevated form of ethical life (*Sittlichkeit*). The dialectic of *Aufhebung* leads to the legitimate authority recognizing both the state and the family. However, in this process the universality of the state overcomes and also assimilates the particularity of the kinship and the family. Absolute justice functions in the ethical life.

Where does justice take place? This final stage does not take place on stage. The play ends in Creon's symbolic death; he is left between two deaths. With Haemon already dead, no Fortinbras will arrive to pick the pieces of the shattered state and institute a new legitimate political community.

The process of *Aufhebung* requires something beyond the stage and the play. The scene after the final scene does not take place behind the stage—like Antigone's deed or Haemon's death—but in front or around the stage. Hegel imagines this reconciliation taking place among spectators.

This takes us back to catharsis. As we understood catharsis as an ethical phenomenon this interpretation sounds reasonable.

One more possibility. Perhaps *Antigone* comes to its ultimate end inside Hegel's head or at the heart of his dialectical philosophy. Tragedy is interpreted through speculative and dialectical thought while the earliest stage of the speculative process and dialectical logic are founded on the model of tragedy.[87] Tragedy supplies a model for philosophical idealism, which in turn provides the setting for the interpretation of tragedy. In this strange movement, theatre and philosophy reciprocally or in relays found each other. In *Phenomenology of Spirit*, Hegel is, from the beginning, heading towards the final reconciliation and absolute justice. His words unwaveringly point us towards that direction. He seems to consciously create the object—absolute justice—of his action, namely writing. What if tragedy is for Hegel just a staging of his thinking and his philosophical discourse? One cannot ignore the fact that the *Phenomenology of Spirit* itself is constructed like a drama, where chapter after chapter Hegel moves us from opposition and antagonism to interrelatedness and resolution.

6

Heroine: The Supplement

Hegel started by praising Antigone, but what is the role of the feminine in this new state based on legitimate authority? Perhaps she is once again excluded from the political and sent back to her proper place in kinship relations. Hegel seems to verify this as he takes kinship to be an inner feeling and the feminine to be an intuitive awareness in the sphere of the unconscious 'exempt from an existence in the real world.'[1] Or she may function as a legitimation effect, that is, without her transgression there would exist the universality of a state authority but not the universality of a *legitimate* state authority.[2]

Lacan criticizes Hegel's view that *Antigone* represents a 'clear opposition ... between the discourse of the family and that of the state'—'things are much less clear.'[3] Let us see how unclear they really are. Antigone, Hegel's eternal irony of community, is outside the *polis*, outside political and public space. However, she is in an outside without which the *polis* could not exist. The incarnation of apolitical and pre-political kinship is thus the precondition for the possibility of the political. As Derrida writes: 'Isn't there always an element excluded from the system that assures the system's space of possibility?'[4] Apolitical kinship based on blood relations differs from the political space. At the same time, pre-political family relations precede the political community. Keep in mind that Creon's position as the sovereign is based on his kinship relations. In the public sphere, these relations are 'repeated' so that they lose their particularity and become more general relations based on the law, social customs, and civic virtues. Thus, private and public, kinship and state are separate but also necessarily related to each other.

My claim is that Antigone deconstructs the Hegelian division between state and kinship, public and private. Antigone does not remain in the private sphere which is considered as her proper place. Political authority would not care if she mourned and lamented her brother in privacy. Keep the tears inside the house. She disagrees with this boundary between home and agora. She is excluded from the political, but she intrudes into the public space and speaks there. She speaks ... .

Rhonda Katab considers Antigone's status as the defender of kinship more problematic than Hegel does. Her figure prefigures the self-conscious individual with the freedom of will and rights this entails. Antigone has a paradoxical relation to state law. Without being absorbed in law and by virtue of her claim, she challenges 'the very structure of limitation through which the political is defined.'[5]

Sexual Difference

Luce Irigaray reads *Antigone* in the Hegelian context against Hegel, rethinking sexual difference. For her, Antigone is an outsider and remains outside the political sphere. She is 'silenced in her action. Locked up, paralyzed, on the edge of the city,' which brings us back to the fate of the suppliants in exile.[6] She is neither master nor slave. This upsets the order of the Hegelian dialectic, which is 'produced by the discourse of patriarchy.'[7]

Thus, Hegel's understanding of ethical life is a part of phallogocentric Western thought based on the hierarchical structure of gendered binary oppositions. For Hegel, Antigone presents, on the one hand, the kinship and feminine principles, on the other hand, the transition from the matriarchal to patriarchal ethical order.

In this structure, Creon represents phallogocentric authority and power that is constituted by maintaining these hierarchical oppositions. No wonder Irigaray sees Creon in a radically different light from Hegel. Creon submits everyone to a 'tyrannical domination' by using 'force and terror,' 'sacrifices those who are closest to him,' 'builds his kingdom on an empty space with an abstract logic.' His 'manner of speaking is poor' and an 'abstract affirmation of himself.' He is merely an 'abstract consciousness' or even 'nothing.'[8]

Irigaray's answer to Hegelian dialectics—that has affected immensely our understanding of *Antigone* and the ethics of tragedy—is to 'negate the negation,' that is, negate Hegel's negation of feminine freedom. Antigone must be recovered from being exiled from subjectivity. This is why Irigaray defines Antigone as an anti-authoritarian figure. Her insurrectionary power defies masculine state authority. However, she remains outside the political. She incarnates concrete singularity and its ties to concrete collectivity, never expresses herself in a solely abstract manner, and cherishes home and family, gods, earth, and fellow-beings. In a word, she represents the kinship principle and is the guardian of blood-relations, which refers not so much to a blood-line than to blood as a remainder of the masculine order and normative-symbolic public space. Blood is related to the fluidity of maternal and feminine bodies, unconsciousness and fluids, which are the excluded excess of the masculine abstract—bloodless—universality. Antigone resists being reduced to ethical life based on masculine self-consciousness.

For Antigone, the blood of life consists of attention to and care for others. 'Her law—neither simply civil nor simply religious—is not abstract or empty.'[9] The law is about respect for those who are close to her. 'It is up to us to rediscover a measure, certain valid measures.'[10] For Irigaray, the measure is earth and body: 'the earth demonstrates if the gesture is good or bad, appropriate or not. And the same holds true for the body of the living.'[11] She takes Polynices 'into her own place,' that is, 'in the womb of earth.'[12]

Antigone's ethical position is to be read together with Irigaray's ethics. Even if there is no particular ethical system of norms that would have absolute validity for all of us and between us, since instead of a single origin we have different genealogies and multiple origins, she affirms that love—neither obliged nor voluntary—used to be the supreme legislator and 'the measure necessary for life.'[13] Love used to be a peaceful coexistence and natural harmony until the father, the paternal principle, imposed himself as the sole authority. Nature and family belonged together and were separated from the sphere of politics, even though the father continued to dominate over family as a private authority. The ethical alternative to the patriarchal order would be love that emerges as the love of each for the other. This would be possible due to a difference that opens a subjective exchange in which words intervene.

All in all, Irigaray's reading of Antigone may be read as a feminine operation, 'a writing of the woman' (*écriture de la femme*) that speaks woman and deconstructs the masculine order and ways of understanding tragedy to recover the freedom of Antigone, the figure of woman.[14] Doesn't Irigaray return to Hegel's logic and essentialize woman calling for feminine/matriarchal identification? In the end, Irigaray cannot avoid the hierarchical dichotomy in her *Antigone*, even though it is a reversed one.

Irigaray reminds that we have to listen to what Antigone 'has to say about government of the polis, its order and its laws.'[15] This is the precondition for continuing to understand tragedy of ethics. Let the figure and the voice of Antigone touch us to hear, see, and feel the sense of her ethical position. However, Irigaray repeats Hegel in her reading of the play. Antigone's insurrectionary power remains outside the political. She represents apolitical kinship. Antigone incarnates the transition from maternal law to paternal law. She is a threshold between kinship and the state, a transition from one to another. This is not 'precisely an *Aufhebung*, for Antigone is surpassed without ever being preserved when ethical order emerges.'[16] That is, she remains excluded from the state and political.

Eternal Irony

Butler disagrees with the Hegelian reading that considers Antigone the idealized representative of kinship that is opposed to the state. It is true that this kind of opposition stabilizes Antigone and the radical ethical and political possibilities her figure opens. In *Antigone's Claim*, Butler begins by defining how we should see Antigone. First of all, Antigone does not represent a feminism that is unimplicated in the power it opposes. She is not a figure that would represent some idealized—and hierarchical and exclusionary—gender norms even if this would be in keeping with feminist discourse. Steeped in an incestuous legacy, she does not represent the normative principles of kinship. For Butler, Antigone is not a mimetic or representative figure but a textual appearance. As such, she points not to any politics of representation but to a 'political possibility that emerges when the limits of representation and representability are exposed.'[17]

Butler writes, 'her act is hardly a simple assimilation to an existing norm.'[18] I would see the political possibility in Butler's Antigone lying in three interrelated transgressions. First, the figure of Antigone transgresses the border between the political and the family. Secondly, she interrupts the kinship norms. Third, she interrupts the Oedipal law.

These three transgressions come together in Antigone's double position of being outside/inside. Her position is 'outside life as we know it' but importantly it 'is not necessarily a position outside life as it must be,' that is, she is outside the symbolic and social constraints under which 'livability is established' and from her position a critical perspective is opened from which 'the very terms of livability might be rewritten.'[19]

For Hegel, Antigone is 'the eternal irony of the community.' Butler reminds us that this irony is more profound that even Hegel thought. This is in line with Butler's general attempt to think what political agency is and could be even if it cannot be isolated from the dynamics of power. 'Prohibited from action, she nevertheless acts.'[20] Antigone not only acts, she acknowledges publicly her deed. She even compounds the illegal act through her speech, a performative speech act that consists of committing the crime (again).

Antigone speaks. She speaks in public 'in the name of politics and the law.'[21] She, Butler continues, 'cannot make her claim outside the language of the state' from which she is excluded.[22] By doing this, she must absorb the language of the state that never belongs to her. This political language cannot be disavowed since it is the condition of the possibility of Antigone's defiance. Butler sees Antigone and Creon as 'metaphorically implicated in one another ... chiasmically related.'[23] In the political sphere, Antigone speaks 'in the language of sovereignty that is the instrument of political power.'[24] Thus, her rebellion and disagreement are not pure—the purity of family or kinship—but 'scandalously impure,' since she has 'already departed from kinship.'[25] Her opposition is not a pre-political opposition against the political. Instead, she turns Creon's normative words into her dissensual speech, that is, political, juridical, and ethical words. In this sense Antigone is anti-statist but at the same time enters the sphere of politics. She does not merely enter this sphere but asserts her sovereignty against Creon's sovereignty. She sets herself up in the position of sovereignty. Therefore, she is not merely the negation of the political authority and the law but a rival authority. Even if 'negations riddle her speech,' she is not saying merely 'no.'[26]

Antigone, the daughter born from incest, brings forth the crisis of kinship given by the symbolic order as a function of language. The crucial point for her, a blind spot in many interpretations of *Antigone*, is the incest topic. Butler's main opponent is Hegel, who considered only absence of desire between the sister and the brother.

In her reading of *Antigone*, Butler links trans-historical heteronormativity and primal incest taboo together. Antigone's symbolic position in the kinship structure is incoherent. The 'kinship line from which she descends, and which she transmits, is derived from a paternal law that is already confounded by the manifestly incestuous act that is the condition of her own existence.'[27] Her brother is her father, who defines her as his son. Antigone occupies all family positions except that of the mother 'at the expense of the coherence of kinship and gender.'[28] In her family history, the stability of paternal and maternal positions is not stable and secure. Moreover, in her figure gender is displaced.

Antigone transgresses both kinship and gender norms bringing forth the precarious character of kinship and gender norms. Instead of being a failed transgression, as Hegel defined her opposition, according to Butler her rebellion exposes the kinship as a socially contingent system. She puts the hegemonic regime of representation and kinship in crisis and, at the same time, shows their transferability and re-iterability. Because the symbolic kinship structure is not an eternal truth, Antigone destabilizes the symbolic order and makes political and social transformation possible. Simultaneously, she interrupts gendered subject formation.

Could it be that even if the incest taboo is a way to establish kinship relations, that these forms of kinship may not be the only intelligible ones? Is it so that a primordial and universal law is the basis of the symbolic norms that encode kinship relations independent of socio-cultural context? Perhaps every psyche should not accept the stable and similar symbolic positions of the mother and the father regardless of contextual social norms and practices. Perhaps the universal structure of kinship and the symbolic order 'works to domesticate in advance any radical reformulation of kinship.'[29] Antigone upsets the norms and vocabulary of kinship and sexual difference that are considered the preconditions for being human. Through her interrelated words and deeds, she raises the question of what these preconditions really are.

She is entangled in terms of kinship and gender norms. Simultaneously, she is outside of these norms. Antigone does not conform totally to the symbolic law. She concludes the Oedipal drama, but she does not produce heterosexual closure for this drama. She deinstitutes heterosexuality by choosing the tomb as her bridal chamber over the marriage with Haemon. The name of the bridal chamber itself destroys the possibility of marriage and childbearing.

She thus transgresses the lines and norms of kinship. The assumed universal normality of the heterosexual monogamous family structure and the unavoidable (breaking the norms leads only to their renewal) norms of sexual difference regulating sexual exchange are interrupted. Kinship and heteronormativity are presented as a socially alterable set of arrangements. The paternal law is not beyond social norms and it does not 'constitute the condition and limit of all social alterations.'[30] Patriarchal normativity is not a trans-historical law but 'vulnerable to subversion.'[31] Antigone demonstrates that not only social and juridical norms but also kinship norms have a temporality that opens them to 'a subversion from within and to a future that cannot be fully anticipated.'[32] As a consequence, she interrupts the Oedipal law.

However, she cannot be reduced to a figure who has a representative function. She cannot quite stand for the subversion as its representative.

Going back to Butler's *Gender Trouble*, we may conclude that Antigone does not represent a new gendered way of life that might be taken as an ethical model. Rather, she is an opening up of possibilities wherein gender is displaced and alternative kinship arrangements emerge.[33]

A third transgression is the rethinking of the ethics of psychoanalysis with and contra Lacan. Butler's question is: What if Antigone instead of Oedipus were the corner stone of psychoanalysis, that is, what if psychoanalysis freed itself from the grip of Oedipal law? If so, this fundamental law would not be considered a universal formal law but social and juridical laws with variable substances. In my view, this question answers the question of the ethics of psychoanalysis. In her reading of Antigone, Honig notes that Butler sets herself against Lacan in the same way Antigone, to make her claim, sets herself against Creon. Butler borrows and reiterates Lacan's language to make her claim. She does not negate Lacanian psychoanalysis, she rearticulates it.[34]

Lévi-Straussian structural anthropology considers incest and kinship norms as, on the one hand, social norms belonging to normative world, and on the other hand, pre-social—a threshold between nature and culture—in their universality and the type of relationships on which it imposes its norms. The elementary structure of kinship emerges on the basis of linguistic set of relations (the exchange of women considered as the exchange of signs). In its totality, these relations where each term signifies only in relation to other terms, is called the symbolic. Butler argues that one cannot strictly separate the symbolic order, which sets up kinship as the function of language, and the social order, which gives rise to the social arrangements of kinship.

Butler notes the same problem is found in Lacanian psychoanalysis. Symbolic norms—the symbolic order as the law that regulates desire in the Oedipus complex derived from a primary prohibition against incest—are independent of social norms. According to Butler, for Lacan symbolic and linguistic norms are what is universal in a culture. They are irreducible to social and juridical forms and norms. However, the symbolic order that institutes and maintains kinship relations constructs the intelligible structural sphere where the social and juridical norms emerge. Hence the symbolic position is not the same as the social, cultural, or legal position. For her, the symbolic itself is 'the sedimentation of social practices,' and the symbolic order—based on universal and primordial law—cannot be strictly separated from the social order.[35]

A structuralist view considers the symbolic order, language, and kinship as institutions that are not social and alterable. For Butler, this view does not hold. Her supposed critics claim that 'it is the law,' the law beyond social and juridical laws. In *Antigone's Claim*, she answers them by arguing that this is a sign of desire for the indisputable law, the final authority, and the limit that one clings to, that is, 'a fantasy of law as insurpassable authority.'[36] Actually, the universal validity of the paternal law depends on its performativity and repetition. Moreover, for Butler there is always a gap between the symbolic—and social and juridical—norms and their obedient performance in society. The law may condition us but not determine our action, relations, positions and desires.

Oedipus refers to the curse of gender and kinship trouble which must be forgotten and resolved through heterosexual futures. The Oedipus complex establishes the heteronormative family as the trans-historical universal norm that is necessary for maintaining proper gender and kinship relations. 'The Antigonean revision of psychoanalytic theory might put into question the assumption that the incest taboo legitimates and normalizes kinship based in biological reproduction and the heterosexualization of the family.'[37]

Such is the tragic fate of Antigone, or as Butler writes, whoever 'would transgress the lines of kinship that confer intelligibility on culture.'[38] The tragic Antigone is transformed in Butler's reading towards another future. Her tragic fatality 'exceeds her life and enters the discourse of intelligibility.'[39] Antigone, not as a figure but as a textual arrangement, is an opening of, and now Butler cites Lacan, an 'aberrant, unpresented future.'[40] Even if she is 'not quite a queer hero,' Antigone seems to be, after all, a representative of those who transgress heteronormative norms and positions and are marginalized or excluded because of their non-conformity to normality. In her reading of Antigone, Butler asks what social arrangements are to be recognized as 'legitimate love' and which 'human losses can be grieved as real and consequential losses.' This she relates to the victims of AIDS and which, today, could be related to refugees who have died in exile.

In *Antigone's Claim*, Butler considers her claim to be an opening up of the future, one that is not constrained by the laws of Creon and Oedipus. As said, Antigone is not negating but also affirming. She answers 'yes' to another future, kinship, and desire. She resists the state authority, heteronormative marriage, and normative kinship ties and, at the same time, proposes new kinds of kinship forms and alternative ways to be together. Antigone presents 'the occasion for a new field of the human,' for yet-to-come love, desires, passions, pleasures, enjoyments, compassions, and ways of being-together beyond heteronormative law.[41]

Human Vulnerability

In *Precarious Love*, Butler concentrates more on suffering and constructs an ethics of lamentation. As in *Antigone*, the contemporary world has a hierarchy of corpses, deaths, and losses. There are 'losses that we are asked not to mourn.'[42] Not only the dead but also grief and lamentation are silenced by sovereign violence. Butler's Antigone points towards an alternative way of being. Antigone exemplifies 'the political risks in defying the ban against public grief during times of increased sovereign power and hegemonic national unity.'[43] She stands for equality in death and grief that does not differentiate between friend and enemy as Creon's sovereign violence does. Her lamentation refers to the human condition, which includes our mortality and dependence on others. The dependence means that we are vulnerable beings.

Honig finds it peculiar that Butler takes up two elements of Arendt's human condition, labour (repeated processes for satisfying the necessities of self-preservation and the reproduction of the species) and work (production of durable objects from tools to artworks), but not the third, action (the generation of human relationships, disclosing ourselves to others and distinguishing ourselves from others as unique beings), which expresses the ontological fact of natality. Even though action does not refer to grief, it points beyond sovereign violence as 'a non-sovereign performance that works to reconstitute communities and inaugurate new realities.'[44] Even if Antigone speaks and acts for equal lamentation, Butler ignores Antigone's action. Her lamentation stands for action, resistance, singularity, membership in community and family, solidarities beyond the friend/enemy-distinction. Butler also does not take into consideration Antigone's attempt to take up the position of sovereignty as in *Antigone's Claim*. Instead of an Antigone who struggled against the violence of the law, Butler sets on the stage of her text an Antigone who mourns the violence of the law. A 'more political and natalist Antigone' of *Antigone's Claim* is displaced 'on the behalf of a humanist and mortalist one.'[45] Through her reading of Antigone, Butler presents the ethics of mortality, vulnerability, and lamentation.

Stuart Elden disagrees with Butler's reading of Antigone. For him, Butler stumbles in political blindness. The main reason for this is that while she manages to analyze the Greek *polis* properly, she nonetheless understands it in an entirely modern way.[46] I have to agree with this. The *polis* is not the constitutional and bureaucratic modern state consisting of legal, administrative, and judicial practices and discourses. It is a definite territory, a site, and a place (*khora*) made of citizens and civic activities. As an autonomous political community, as the site of coming together beyond established walls, it is the combination of time and place, people, and activities. Thus, the *polis* is the site of citizenship, *politeia*, and the abode of history, norms, and human beings.

Butler equates too quickly the state or the existing socio-political order and the political. In his analysis of the functioning of judgment and law in *Antigone*, Julen Etxabe concludes that Antigone and Creon have competing normative languages that are not incommensurable.[47] This view would already correct Butler's conception. Hölderlin emphasized the difference between the speech of the state and the speech of Antigone. Her political position in the public sphere is defined in these few words: 'The highest characteristic of Antigone ... is elevated derision (*der erhabene Spott*).'[48]

Now, Butler opens the door to the previously mentioned humanist ethics of vulnerability that concentrates on helplessness, suffering, grief, and mortality depoliticizes the ethics of tragedy. Honig is very suspicious of this view, which she calls the 'mortalist humanism of universal voice, cry, or suffering.'[49] Tragedy makes it possible for us to identify with the suffering of others, share their mortality and pain as fellow human beings. The ontological fact is not 'the capacity of reason but vulnerability to suffering,' of which Jeremy Bentham had already reminded us.[50] For mortalist humanism, tragedy 'gets under the skin of politics to scratch the essence of the human.'[51] This humanitarian view gets tragedy wrong, since it considers tragic plays transcending political divisions and ethical disagreements. As a consequence, this kind of consensual lamentation renders political and ethical differences and disagreements subject to our common vulnerability. Honig puts it very clearly—mortalist humanism displaces 'the conflicts and divisions that are fundamental to both tragedy and politics.'[52] Instead of consensual humanism, there are diverse views that 'divide and unite us.'[53]

In addition, we could read Antigone more politically by using Jacques Rancière's distinction between the police and the political. The police refers to the established distribution of the sensible (*le partage du sensible*). It is 'a symbolic constitution of the social' that structures the spaces of society, distributes places, tasks, roles and functions, makes distinctions between private and public, labour and leisure, political and social, humans and animals, and determines boundaries between the visible and invisible, audible and non-audible, comprehensible and incomprehensible.[54]

We can read tragedy by concluding that in Thebes, Antigone's body, actions, and mourning belong to the privacy of home. In the public sphere the position reserved for her is invisibility and silence. The political (*la politique*) is an event of dissensus that brings forth the wrong and interrupts the distribution of the sensible. It is Antigone's quarrel and dispute as she disagrees with Creon's proclamation and also with the distribution of the sensible.[55] This is my interpretation. Rancière himself sees Antigone in a different light as he compares Oedipus and Antigone. For him, Oedipus represents trauma as a forgotten event that can be cured when the trauma is reactivated. This would open the possibility for politics instead of the eternal ethics of mourning, the incurable trauma, and the unnameable horrors of history. Antigone is, however, 'irreducible to any salvational knowledge' and a witness to the secret terror underlying the social order, which leads to an absolute and destructive justice.[56] Rancière is wrong here.

Another problematic issue in Butler's reading is the incestuous relationship and the kinship structure. Butler's aim is to bring the incestuous family history back into the reading of the play. Perhaps her relationship to Polynices was not so pure and without desire as Hegel would claim, but Butler does not explain what the incestuous element is and why the possible erotic desire for the living body of the brother is extended to the corpse of the brother.[57] As a consequence, Butler does not see the role death has for the figure of Antigone, especially the question of the desire for death and the constant imagery of death in the play. As Butler returns to Antigone in *Undoing Gender*, the incest becomes a question mark and death more explicit. Antigone loves her brother, 'in fact, she wants to "lie with him", and so pursues death, which she also calls her "bridal chamber" in order to be with him forever. She is the child of incest, but how does incest run through her own desire?'[58] She even affirms that Antigone's crime is not sexual and her relation to the brother is 'not overdetermined by incestuous meaning.'[59] Then again, Butler's aim is not to celebrate the incestuous practice, but discuss the more general kinship crisis.

For Butler, Antigone represents a kinship crisis. This transfers Antigone into the context of the contemporary decline of the paternal function, which does not do justice to tragedy. She repeats a Hegelian understanding of tragedy, that is, she implants her own theory into tragedy and justifies it through her reading of tragedy. She thus loses tragedy as a text, a play, and a performance. Antigone seems to be a means to address contemporary issues related to sexual difference, gender, kinship, desire, love, limits, exclusion and marginalization.[60] She turns tragedy into 'a promising political programme.'[61]

Lee Edelman further criticizes Butler's view that Antigone points towards the future. Butler ignores the fact that she is married to death. Far from transforming the symbolic law, Butler's Antigone repeats it as 'the law of repetition by which our fate is bound to ... reproductive futurism.'[62] For Edelman, she monstrously rejects all domestication to the social order, motherhood, reproduction, and the future itself in a radical anti-humanist way. Edelman speaks for Antigone's death drive, with which the queer is identified. I will come back to Antigone's 'no future'—be it Edelman's or Sex Pistols'—but even if Edelman has a point, his Antigone turns out to be an idealized subject who breaks fully out of the Oedipal law. Moreover, Edelman misunderstands Butler's Antigone in her relation to the law. She does not repeat the symbolic law but repeats it in a way that ought to be understood as a creative iteration.[63]

All things considered, even if Butler does not accept Hegel's clear opposition between the state embodied by Creon and the kinship embodied by Antigone, she does not really re-think or deconstruct the concepts of law, state, and sovereignty. She blurs the distinction, which she then assumes, and at the same time repeats the same distinction albeit in modified form where state and kinship presuppose each other.

Then again, Butler is 'worried that the return to ethics has constituted an escape from politics, and I've also worried that it has meant a certain heightening of moralism'—'Bad air!' as Nietzsche complained about Hegel.[64] Elena Loizidou sees Butler's reading of *Antigone* contributing to the 'theory of gender performativity' that has 'opened up the understanding of gender as ... an ongoing process,' which shatters and undoes our thinking gender, ethics, politics, and aesthetics.[65] Martha Nussbaum excoriates Butler as not grounding her concept of resistance upon a normative concept of justice.[66] This is precisely why justice has a political and ethical force in Butler's thinking unlike in Nussbaum's humanist-educatory scheme.

Agonistic Humanism

Honig sets an agonistic humanism against a mortalist humanism of universal suffering and grief, against a lamenting Antigone. The agonistic humanism sees in mortality, suffering, and vulnerability resources for 'enacted if contestable universality' while recognizing that 'these resources are various and opaque in their signification.'[67] Mortality, suffering, and powerlessness are not ignored, but one has to keep in mind natality, power, and desire.[68] Politics should not be reduced to the ethics of finitude.[69] Let me elaborate on this with *Furious Antigone* (*Antigona Furiosa*).

During the years of the Argentina military dictatorship, the Dirty War, around thirty thousand people disappeared. In 1977, *Madres de Plaza de Mayo* began to walk in a circle around the square in front of the Presidential Palace every Thursday to demand justice for the disappeared. They demanded the return of the corpses of their sons and daughters for burial and mourning. The mothers were condemned as terrorists.[70]

Griselda Gambrona's play *Antigona furiosa* (1986) is based on these events. Sophocles' play is repeated on the streets of Buenos Aires, the poetic language and the street slang are mixed.[71] The play begins from the end: Antigone, dressed in a white dress with a withered flower-crown, is hanging in a cage. She removes the noose from her neck to start singing Ophelia's song. 'He is dead and gone. At his head a grass-green turf.' There is a distinction between the markers of death—stone and turf—and the absence of any burial traces. Coryphaeus and Antinous who are drinking coffee at the bar laugh at her, mock her singing, and confuse her with Ophelia. She takes the crown of Coryphaeus, standing for Creon's sovereignty, and smashes it. Next, Antigone walks among the unburied corpses. She finds Polynices and throws herself on his body attempting to give him burial. 'Brother. Brother. I will be your breath. Your mouth your legs, your feet. I will cover you.' Creon did not know that 'Neither God nor justice made the law. (*She laughs.*) The living is the great sepulcher of the dead!'[72] She becomes his body, coffin, and earth. Through this becoming, she becomes to embody resistance against the dictatorship that attempts not only to torture and murder but also to annihilate all traces of the disappeared. Antigone shares this fate. No one hears her weeping. 'Drag me to the cave that will be my tomb ... I will be ... uncounted among the living and among the dead. I will disappear from the world, alive.' She, who stands with her action, is condemned to death. Antonius has not heard Teiresias' warnings: 'Then Creon will always punish you.'[73] Antigone defies the murderous rule. 'But hate rules. (*Furious.*) The rest is silence! (*She kills herself, with fury.*)'[74] Once again Antigone commits suicide. It is the ultimate act of resistance. As the curtains falls, the audience sees Antigone hanging. The beginning is repeated.

The play 'cannot change the role of Antigone, who is doomed to sacrifice herself time and again.'[75] No reconciliation seems possible. The disappeared have disappeared. They cannot forgive. The disappeared are disappeared. The mothers cannot mourn their losses. The circle goes on and on. This circular structure reminds the audience of the 'circularity and lack of closure' of violence.[76] Simultaneously, the furious resistance of Antigone violently interrupts this circle time and again. Like the *Madres*, Antigone is faithful to the ethical duty to resist the violent repression that murders and denies remembrance. Those who are supposed to remain silent give a voice to the unheard and invisible.

According to Jean Bethke Elstein, the *Madres* are daughters of Antigone. They resist state terrorism through public demonstrations that reject 'both revenge and self-sanctimony.'[77] They are contemporary Antigone, 'a feminist heroine,' who represent a social feminism centred on care.[78] Elstein falls in a double humanitarian glorification of a political action. On the one hand, she humanizes Antigone as a grieving woman, who calls 'down curses on the heads of those' who desecrated Polynices' body.[79] Antigone is a passionate and violent political subject, not a humanist lamenter. On the other hand, Elstein depoliticizes the *Madres* as she defines them as universal, immutable, and eternal mothers, whose lamentation goes back to the Greek tragedy. They were not so naïve. They strategically used their position as mothers and underscored this by wearing women's traditional clothing.[80] Their aesthetico-political gesture ironically commented on their apolitical status in Argentinian society. Like Antigone, they transgressed the traditional limitations of womanhood by transforming themselves into political subjects through their protests. Like Antigone, they acted as if they were politically equal in a patriarchal and masculine society to change the coordinates of whom are counted as political subjects. Therefore Gambaro's play presents resistance, the demands of justice and remembrance that avoids the depoliticization of Antigone, as Elstein claims. On the stage, Antigone is nothing but a furiously revolting political subject. Not unlike the *Madres*.

7

Law and Dust

I will now turn to the law of Antigone. Perhaps she is not merely a self-sacrificing martyr, a mourning sister, a feminist hero, or a moment in Hegelian dialectics. Could she transform 'her abject, victim status, as one haunted by the horror of her father's unknowing act, into a hope for the future?', as Tina Chanter asks.[1] Seamus Heaney's Antigone is neither a monstrous being nor part of a Hegelian narrative. Instead, she stands for rebellion and keeps alive the tradition of resistance by contesting absolute power, unlimited authorities, unjust laws, and arbitrary governance.[2]

Perhaps she is the very figure of the ethics tragedy as she brings forth, discloses, or incarnates the truth of law, the truth of being, or the truth of desire. How does Antigone show herself in herself, bring to light her being in a distinctive way, that is, in her strangeness?[3]

In his version of Antigone, Brecht made Antigone a strange figure who had to fight this strangeness as she had a door strapped to her back throughout the play.[4] It even seems as if she is necessarily thrown into world with the door. She could not enter the door which made her movements clumsy and strange. She is always already in the world. She is ahead of herself, that is, she is projected onto her possibilities: accompanying her refugee father, burying her brother, being towards her death. She is engaged with beings and entities, rulers and loved-ones, birds and bodies in the world. The door makes her position not only uncanny but also terrifying. There is a door which would open to the homely, but she has left it behind without no possibility of return. She does not see the past, but neither can she face the future. She is isolated in time, but at the same time, she must take full responsibility for her action.

We must listen to Antigone more closely by taking into consideration her strange figure. We hear her only if we belong to the subject matter of the speech, to the tragic conflict, and tragedy. The possibility of ethics may be considered in relation to how she comes forth as she presents her law, her being, and her desire.

Antigone—The Eternal Refugee

In Sophocles' *Antigone*, Antigone defines herself not only as good and beautiful but also as a stranger. This is so often ignored in the performances of *Antigone* and in the philosophical readings of the play. Antigone is glorified as a shining hero and the stranger does not fit well with this image. In *Oedipus at Colonos*, Antigone is presented as a stranger, as a refugee. I would insist that this is a crucial notion and the ultimate consequence of sidestepping it is to misunderstand the figure of Antigone and her position in Sophocles' plays.

Antigone is a stranger not only as a refugee in exile but also in Thebes, in her home city. In Theban political community she is always already excluded as a woman from public space and political discussions. Moreover, she goes beyond the limits of the conventional social-symbolic order and becomes symbolically dead before actually dying. I will now turn to the multiple strangeness of Antigone.

In her home (*oikos*), she is a stranger as a sister of her own father. When in exile leading her father, she was a stranger outside a safe dwelling place, a stateless person without proper legal status. Back home, she becomes a stranger as she publicly breaks the law and offends the ruler. As a woman, who has no proper place in the public sphere, she enters as a stranger this patriarchal and masculine sphere. Antigone refuses to remain silent in a society that excludes women from the political participation, even though the society remains physically dependent on them. Women's voices are excluded in advance from the public sphere. Creon's decree mimics this exclusion as he excludes the corpse of Polynices and thus ignores its origin, which requires symbolic preservation.[5] Not only is Antigone strange, so is the law she refers to. Butler considers the unwritten law as a rootless law. It cannot be written or even spoken in tragedy, since this would require a script. The script would undermine the universality of the law.[6] It would become as particular as Creon's laws.

For Lacan, 'tragic heroes are always isolated, they are always beyond established limits, always in an exposed position and, as a result, separated in one way or another from the structure.'[7] The chorus affirms Lacan's description as it lays down the political morality of the *polis* in the first stasimon just before the guards lead Antigone in: 'When he applies the laws (*nomoi*) of the earth and the justice (*dikē*) the gods have sworn to uphold he is high in the city (*hypsipolis*).' *Hypsipolis* refers both to the city and the citizen. Where law and justice rules, there the city stands proudly and people are citizens of the proud city. Or, it is the citizen who has a high position in the city.

The chorus continues, an 'outcast from the city (*apolis*) is he with whom the ignoble consorts because of his recklessness.'[8] *Apolis* refers to someone who has lost the city, an unhomely being without the city. A refugee is *apolis*. Polynices is considered *apolis*, Antigone was *apolis* in *Oedipus at Colonus*, as are all the other refugees we have discussed. Creon turns from *hypsipolis* to *apolis* during the play as he refuses to recognize the limits of his legislative power. Actually, Creon forgets his own words. At the end of *Oedipus the King*, Creon criticizes Oedipus by saying: 'Do not wish to have control in everything!'[9] Because of this Oedipus became *apolis*, now it is Creon's turn. *Hypsipolis* and *apolis* are interdependent terms, since a tyrant exiled from a city turns his position immediately from one to another. But already, *hypsipolis*, or as Heidegger translates it, *hochüberragend die Stätte*, is both within the city and beyond or over it, or in a movement between these two positions.

It seems that Antigone is *apolis* in the eyes of the chorus. She has broken the valid proclamation (*kērugma*), which marks her being with the lack of the city. However, at the same time, Antigone elevates her act to the level of a valid law (*nomos*). Simultaneously, this elevation is the essence of her crime. Hence, Antigone seems to move from *apolis* to *hypsipolis* and back again. As a tragic hero, she is always already separated from all other people in the city, from citizens, foreign residents, women and children, and slaves.[10] Given *hypsipolis/apolis*, Antigone is a strange and uncanny being about whom the chorus speaks in the first stasimon as *deinon*. Another woman, whose being is *hypsipolis/apolis* is Euripides' Medea. She seeks revenge against her unfaithful husband Jason for betraying their contract, is sent into exile (*apolis*), and in the end appears above the stage with the bodies of her children in the chariot of the sun god Helios (*hypsipolis*).

For Hölderlin, Antigone is *antitheos*, which refers to *deinon*, *Ungeheuer*, and *Unheimlich*. She 'acts in the name of the god *against* god (*gegen Gott*).'[11] *Anti* does not simply mean 'against,' but also what comes instead of something, takes its place as an equal and similar being. Antigone is both against-god and like-god. She recognizes the highest spirit as *gesetzlos*, illegal, lawless (*den Geist des Höchsten gesetzlos erkennt*).[12] Alternatively, Antigone recognizes through her illegality the highest spirit. In both cases, *gesetzlos* also refers to one who breaks away (*los*) from law (*Gesetz*) or one who escapes law's clutches and is unattached to law. Moreover, we might think that it is the law that has broken free from the *polis*. Either the essence of Antigone is *gesetzlos* or she incarnates the law that has broken loose or gotten out of hand. Perhaps, at the highest point of her crime and illegality, the law is not lacking or lost but the law itself has become wild, rebellious, and transgressive. The spirit of the wild times uproots Antigone from her homely space in the *polis* and the *oikos* to follow unwritten forces that carry her towards her death. Fury uproots Antigone from her social, moral, legal, and familial base, from everyday life in the *polis*. She is an excess in the social order, an excessive element that cannot be incorporated into the social corpus.

In tragedy, the *polis* itself becomes exposed to political and ethical questions about its correctness and justice. The tragic play presents the *polis*—and the conflict that takes place in it and shapes its existence—according to a cut that opens it. As the sun rises after the battle, the *polis* is lightened as a common (*pandēmō*) but also split community. This split is not only caused by the corpses of the opposing brothers. Antigone's first words to Ismene describes ills and miseries bequeathed by Oedipus. The sisters know 'unhappiness, ruin, disgrace, dishonor,' that is, a crystallization of the combination of mental pain, ruined fortunes, and moral shame.[13] And now a new thing, she continues, Creon has made 'a proclamation (*kērugma*)' for 'the whole body of the city (*pandēmō polei*).'[14] His proclamation seems to be public and common (*pandēmō*) belonging to all the people (*pandēmō*). By adding this order to the list of miseries, Antigone shows that it splits the community. It does not 'belong to all the people' (*pandēmō*). From the beginning of the play, there exists a tragic interruption of the community. Antigone's words equate to 'storm-swift (*aellaios*) voices,' about which the chorus in Sophocles' *Phaedra* tells. The *polis* is swept across by these voices.[15] At the same time, it is the law that Antigone passionately defends throughout tragedy. She seems to preserve jealously her idea of law and justice. As Ismene confesses before Creon, she is an accomplice and bears her share of the blame; Antigone snaps: 'justice (*dikē*) will not allow you this, since you refused and I was not your associate!'[16]

Karl Reinhardt notes that in tragedy two eccentric human essences confront each other in the centre of a demonic connection.[17] However, for him, Antigone justifies her law through the ethereal unwritten laws born of the highest canopy of heaven.[18] In German existential legal philosophy, Antigone's position in the tragic conflict is often considered *Rechtlichsein* (a mode of being that is being-correct), which may be in conflict with a *richtigen Rechtsordung* (a correct or just legal order) or which may challenge the existing political order in the name of the correct order.[19] Alternatively, we could consider Antigone as not being merely or simply a legal subject, *Sein im Recht* (a being in the law), but *Sein zum Recht* (a being towards the law), which is an existential relationship between the law and *Dasein*.[20]

The tragic conflict may be seen as a conflict between *Im-Recht-sein* (being-right) and *Im-Unrecht-sein* (being-wrong), as Erik Wolf describes the potentialities of *Dasein*.[21] Right in this sense does not take place at the level of *das Man* (inauthentic being), but in the place of an authentic *Mitsein* (being-with).[22] Thus, these terms should not be understood in moral or juridical terms but more as existential possibilities and choices open to human beings in the world.

Following Werner Maihofer, we could consider Antigone to be *Alssein* (*status civilis*) as a sister, a daughter, and a woman who has a designated position and role in the *polis*. She ought to act like all others who are in the same position. She is also *Selbstsein* (*status naturalis*) under the existential maxim demanding her to be herself in the truth of her being. As such, she protects the open without the safety net of her status as someone. She does not represent *ethos* but *ethos* is her being as she appears in the light of being. She lets being be as the opening of being through which she exists as being-right.[23]

Valid Law

The concept of law is fundamental in *Antigone*. The word *polis* occurs thirty-four times in *Antigone* making it one of the most repeated terms. In the space of the *polis*, the issues of justice (*dikē*, justice, trial and penalty, *dikaios*, just, fair, right and lawful, *nomos*, law and custom, and *orthos*, straight, upright and fair, *isos*, equal, alike and fair; words occurring fifty-five times in all) and evil (*kakē*, wickedness, vice and cowardice, and *kakos*, bad, base, evil, and cowardly; words occurring eighty-nine times in all) become the main subject of disagreement and conflict.[24]

To understand the ethics of tragedy we have to tackle the question of the law as a concept and as an essential element in the tragic conflict. Often the concept of law and its function in the play is taken for granted. The tragic conflict takes place between state or positive law based on political authority and non-state, non-positive law, that is, familial, kinship, or natural law. One is temporal, based on political power and is valid only in a particular time-space context. The other is universal and based on eternal moral principles. Accordingly, the concepts of state, the political, public space, and legitimacy are more or less stable and self-evident.

Antigone and Creon are mutually dependent. Antigone reacts to Creon's law, her decision not to give up burying her brother provokes Creon to react with the violence of the excessive sanction. Instead of opposing each other, as Hegel claims, their acts mirror one another.[25] Antigone inhabits the language of sovereignty at the very moment in which she opposes sovereign power and is excluded from its terms. 'Her words, understood as deeds, are chiasmically related to the vernacular of sovereign power, speaking in and against it, delivering and defying imperatives at the same time.'[26] According to Richard Jebb, Creon represents the duty to obey the laws of the state. On the contrary, Antigone speaks for the duty to follow the voice of conscience.[27] There is an excess of law in *Antigone*, according to Etxabe, and no neutral legal ground or institutional framework that could guarantee a correct answer. There is no 'mutually acceptable ground,' so the conflict is incommensurable.[28] What are these two laws in a tragic conflict?

Creon considers his decree prohibiting the burial of Polynices as *nomos*—a law or established custom. Is he justified in doing that? Creon does not consult the citizens of Thebes before the first announcement of his decree. This probably occurred in the battlefield as a general (*stratēgos*) or as a king after Eteocles had been killed by Polynices and the fight had ceased. If we consider it from the perspective of Athenian law, the generals (*stratēgoi*) had exceptional powers in the battlefield and they had the authority to make proclamations (*kērugmata*). The prohibition of burying Polynices is in accordance with Athenian law, which prohibits the burial of traitors in Attica, but not outside its borders. It was common practice to celebrate heroes and punish enemies and traitors. It was Polynices who decided to wage war against his native city. Even though Eteocles broke their deal about ruling in turn, this would have not been justification enough for him to first visit Theseus in Athens and then Adrastus in Argos, with whose forces he allied to attack Thebes. Moreover, the *polis* has authority to regulate funeral rites and religious activities. Creon makes his decree public by his own declaration which is repeated and transmitted by the messenger. It is a law made public. The parodos of the chorus made up of Theban elders supports Creon by declaring 'what Polynices had represented while he lived—a hideous threat to his whole community'.[29]

Creon announces his decree a second time to the assembly of the Elders, whom he has called together by a public proglamation (*koinōi kērugmati*).

Instead of submitting the decree under discussion, he merely announces it. The assembly accepts it, since it is 'your pleasure ... to do this.'[30] According to Demosthenes, law is 'a general matter of the entire community.' Another problem is that Creon announces it in special circumstances of the civil war and it concerns a particular case. However, as Aristotle avers, law is 'about general matter.'[31] The law ought to be common to all and issued by a legitimate authority. Creon's law is like the tyrant's laws that are based merely on his authority and authorship. From the perspective of a democratic audience, this is not a true law.

However, Creon presents himself as a king whose will represents the will of the people and the city and who would have taken into consideration the views of citizens. He shows civic sentiments. He seems to represent the law and defend the city and its citizens. The situation immediately after the war is insecure. Polynices' funeral could end in civic strife. The chorus accepts Creon's decree with some hesitation. They want to show their loyalty and patriotism.

Later, Creon betrays his initial position by declaring to Haemon that the city belongs to the ruler. From the position of absolute sovereign, he asks his son if it is the *polis* that will tell him what to order. He shows his fate that is immanent in his name: Creon means 'ruler.'

Creon himself dissolves his position as the absolute sovereign by hesitating during the play. Creon admits the lack in the legal authority of his decree due to the pressure from the blind prophet Teiresias, who utters the immoveable (*akinēta*) prophecy of disaster, and the chorus. He decides to bury Polynices' corpse, since it is best to obey established laws. He does not specify a penalty for the burial of Polynices, then announce it to be entombment. He condemns Antigone to death, then pardons her. Contrary to this, Lacan sees Creon as 'unyielding right to the end, demanding everything, giving up nothing, absolutely unreconciled.'[32]

Badiou sees Creon as someone who names the superego, that is, not the law but a deregulated law that returns as an excess over the place it prescribes. The superego is what gives an access to the source of the force of law, to the imperative character—'you must'—of the law that is beyond the meaning of legal norms.[33] This simplifies the figure of Creon. At the beginning of the play, he acts as a lawgiver acting on the level of the symbolic order and language. Soon, however, he is transformed into a pure force of the injunction. He becomes the name for the excess and destruction, which finally destroys his law and sovereign power.

Creon assaults the law of the gods by denying the burial. Teiresias affirms this by saying that 'the gods are no longer accepting the prayers that accompany sacrifice.'[34] Because the birds have eaten 'the fat of dead human blood' their 'well-meaning crying' do not 'come rushing here.'[35] Both altars and pits, sacrificial places for gods above and below, sky and earth, are poisoned. Creon even doubles his crime in inverted form as he sentences Antigone to be buried alive. In this double transgression Creon does not respect the normative limits, which require the dead to belong to the darkness underground and the living to the lightness on earth.

If Creon falls into a ridiculous repetition of what is, Antigone celebrates the glory of a different law that is not reduced to factuality, the political and legal state of things. Her act to defend her law is an irrevocable ethical act and Creonian rule is able to answer it only, after the argumentation fails, through violence of the sovereign power.

Let us recall that Antigone is relegated to outside the public space in which she has no right to public action or political discussion. Her proper place is a privately owned place. Her pain ought to be subjective, removed from the world of human beings and human artefacts. She is not allowed to appear in the public sphere where everybody can see and hear her. In short, appearance is denied her. She is condemned to lead, in Arendt's words, an 'uncertain, shadowy kind of existence,' and in claiming the law she is 'transformed, deprivatized and deindividualized.'[36] By talking, she claims to be among human beings (*inter hominem esse*) and thus a part of the public sphere. Her experience is communicable to all and she is recognizable to the outer world. The shared world common to all opens for her, Arendt would say.

Creon's interdiction has been from the beginning part of public speech. Antigone admits this as she speaks about how it is transmitted: 'so they say' and 'it has been announced' or 'they say' that 'Creon has proclaimed' (*kērukschant echein*).[37] Already this shows that Antigone is from the beginning a part of the public discourse and a subject in the signifying chains that takes place in Thebes.

Anne Carson's translation runs:

Creon: you knew it was against the law?
Antigone: well if you call that *law*.
Creon: I do.
Antigone: Zeus does not

Justice does not

> the dead do not
> what they call *law* did not begin
> today or yesterday.
> When they say *law* they do not
> mean a statute of today or yesterday
> they mean the unwritten eternal ordinances of the gods
> that no human being can ever outrun.[38]

Antigone demonstrates arrogant scorn towards Creon's law and its validity. In *Philosophy of Right*, Hegel writes that Antigone's law 'is there displayed as a law opposed to public law, to the law of the state. This is the supreme opposition in ethics and therefore in tragedy.'[39] Actually, Antigone defends two different ethical duties. On the one hand, all dead whether heroes or traitors are equal and owed burial rites. On the other hand, Polynices is an irreplaceable brother. She speaks both for universality and singularity. Instead of differentiating between these two positions, we should see them as simultaneous. In this situation, her ethical duty is to bury the singular brother. At the same time, she is loyal to this duty that is universal. Or, could we think that she is between two laws? The universal law of equality functions within the symbolic order. The singular law disrupts established law and at the same time turns it into a singular universal law. The tragic situation is that the law is always already split.

This explains why under other circumstances, Antigone would have never broken the law. She would have married Haemon, carried children, and given her respects to the gods of the house. Then again, she does not act randomly. She acts under a 'certain legality' that is in effect 'of the order of law, but which is not developed in any signifying chain or in anything else.'[40]

Sjöholm separates the laws of Thebes and the laws of Athens. The former is based on raw power and the decision of the absolute ruler. The latter is based on the democracy principle. The law protects political space and holds communities together. It also welcomes refugees. In *Oedipus at Colonos*, Antigone seems law-abiding. 'Father, we should share the concerns of the citizens, giving way and obeying when we must.'[41] Based on this, Sjöholm argues that Antigone dies for the law of Athens. The divine law refers to the ancient use of the concept of law that connotes borders and limits. These laws institute political space as a space of plurality and natality, new beginnings. They are superior to human laws that are decreed within this instituted political space. These laws protect human laws and the political space. Therefore, Antigone is not fighting against human law itself but the law of Creon. 'Rereading Antigone with Oedipus at Colonos, we find Antigone the refugee claiming the right to political space.'[42] Sjöholm's reading is in accordance with the Ephebic Oath that the Athenian citizens had to swear. In the oath, they promised to obey those who rule prudently, the established laws, and those laws which they may prudently establish for themselves in the future. A blind obedience was not an obligation.[43] Then again, in *Crito* Socrates convinces us that one should follow the law even if it is unjust. We should also not ignore the fact that in *Oedipus at Colonus*, Antigone defends the laws of Athens. She claims the law both in *Oedipus at Colonus* and *Antigone* by using speech and argumentation in public space. Thus, she makes a claim to be part of the public discussion about justice, values, norms, and wrongs.

Antigone receives the message of the death of her brothers in the privacy of the night. She cries out for a burial place. Instead of keeping her decision and action as a family secret, she declares publicly that she has fulfilled the funeral rituals. She receives the message and the corpse. She answers to this double sending by becoming the guardian of the burial site and by declaring unconditional loyalty to her brother as a singular being and not as either 'the empirical individual' destroyed by decomposition or 'the rational universality of the citizen, the living subject.'[44] That way she breaks through the distinction between the private and public sphere. She interrupts the Hegelian scheme that considers tragedy as a conflict between two different levels: the family takes place at the level of pure existence and the state at the level of action and deeds, as Alexandre Kojève puts it.[45] As said, Antigone presents her disagreement not in the privacy of her home but in public space. She defies Creon's decree at the very spot—the steps of the royal palace—Creon announces his proclamation a second time.

When Creon asks, 'do you admit, or do you deny, that you have done this (*tade*)?' Antigone answers, "I say that I did it and I do not deny it (*kai phemi drasai kouk aparnoumai to ne*).'[46]

She does not and will not deny her deed. This doubles her crime. First, there is the act of burial. Second, she not only admits her deed but also defies the state authority by refusing to deny it or excuse herself. The act is mimetically repeated in language, even though the primary act already took place in the symbolic order.

As long as Antigone is objectified and determined by Theban law, her being as a subject is denied. In a process of subjectivation, she becomes a political subject by nominating herself out of the void—her position as an absence from public space and discourse—as a subject. She becomes a subject 'by first declaring and then maintaining' her 'fidelity to an evanescent event which cannot itself be recognized in nor specified' by the post-battle situation in which it takes place.[47] Antigone attains visibility and simultaneously political existence through the presentation of her action. As Butler says, like Creon, 'Antigone wants her speech act to be radically and comprehensively public.'[48] Publishing her act in language is the completion of the act. As she begins to act in language, she departs from herself by performing herself through the voice of the law and the juridical and political authority that she opposes. She asserts her own sovereignty, but she does this 'through appropriating the voice of the other.'[49] I agree that Antigone swims against the flow of politics in the stream of the political. The main problem with Butler's analysis is that she equates the state with the political. Antigone 'cannot make her claim outside the language of the state.'[50] Butler admits that Antigone is not 'fully assimilated by the state.'[51] I would contest her interpretation and say that Antigone acts in the public sphere but her language is not that of the state or of the established order or of the distribution of the sensible; rather it is political language as she disagrees with the state and its laws. Even if Antigone and Creon use the same vocabulary, the signifiers have radically different connotations in the signifying chains.

Antigone uses different argumentation for different audiences she addresses. Helene Foley shows how she treats Ismene as another self by evoking familial bonds and common experiences. Before Creon, she justifies her act with social and emotional motives giving equal weight to principled responsibility and personal pain. In her final self-defence, she addresses the chorus with a lyric dialogue and attempts to involve them emotionally in sharing her values by 'more intimate and sympathetic communication.'[52] In these various discourses Antigone 'personalizes the burial issue' without generalizing her case beyond the need to act 'in this *particular* situation.'[53] It is Teiresias, not Antigone, Foley continues, 'who universalizes the issue by raising the question of burying the other slain enemies.'[54] Foley misunderstands Antigone's ethical commitment, because she holds onto the dichotomy between political/principled and personal/emotional.

We can never sufficiently emphasize that Antigone embodies an affirmative departure from these categories out of faithfulness and unfaithfulness to the private family (gods) and the public state (gods). Her act disrupts prevailing dichotomies and categories. It is an act that arises from cracks in the orderly order.

In her *Antigone Interrupted*, Honig correctly treats Antigone as 'a complex political actor engaged in struggle with Creon about the terms and sites of sovereignty.'[55] If we consider Antigone as a mad, violently passionate, self-indulgent, or totally principled subject, we miss her as a political promise. Antigone is not merely a lamenting sister admired by Hegel or a political martyr praised by dissidents. 'She *is* a lamenting sister and she *does* die for her cause but she is, more fundamentally, a political actor embroiled in burial, kinship, and *polis* politics, one who plots, conspires, and maneuvers her way in and out of trouble on behalf of the sovereign form that she considers to be hers by right.'[56] Her speech acts are political acts. She is a political subject.

The limit of the political sovereignty is measured by the power of irony. The internal enemy of the community, the woman, can burst out laughing and crying since 'she knows, in tears and in death, how to pervert the power that suppresses.'[57] The ironic positioning sets itself against what the political power produces and decrees. From the site of disagreement, the ironic rebellion proceeds to affirm its own truth. The irony is a caesura that divides both the state of things and the mastery of the speculative dialectics.

Unlike the chorus and the Thebans, Antigone disagrees publicly with Creon. This is a political act. Without any doubt or fear, she disputes his prohibition. She claims that the chorus shares her view but because of their fear of Creon, whose rule she describes as *turannis* (absolute rule of one man), they do not speak.

Antigone's definition of her position in relation to law runs like this:

> Yes, for it was not Zeus who made this proclamation (*kēruma*), nor was it Justice, who dwells with the gods below, that enacted such laws (*nomima*) among mortals. And I did not think that your proclamations (*kērugmata*) are strong enough to have power to overrule, mortal as they were, the unwritten and unfailing (*asphalē*) laws (*nomima*) of the gods.[58]

The chorus in *Oedipus the King* defines the superior laws as the 'laws whose only father is Olympus;' these laws stand 'high, generated in lofty heaven ... The mortal nature of men did not beget them, neither shall they ever be lulled to sleep by forgetfulness.'[59] Olympus refers here to *kosmos*, to the vault of the sky from where the light shines through the ether. The laws come from, according to the chorus, 'the dazzling glare of Olympus.'[60]

'For present, future, and past this law (*nomos*) shall suffice.'[61]

According to Heidegger, the law is not posited by human beings, because positive law cannot override the normative word of the gods. What determines Antigone in her being is what rules over the gods above and below. At the same time, the law as such determines the human being as the human being throughout. The law not posited by human beings slips under what sways even above the gods.[62]

Antigone sees the burial of Eteocles and other defenders of Thebes as *tōi nomōi* (correct custom). Thus, she does even not credit Creon's decree with the name 'law.' For her, it is a mere *kērugma*, a word also related to *kērux* (herald). She maintains the difference between the law and the proclamation. Antigone claims that Creon's *kērumgma*, proclamation, is not sanctioned by the gods. If she is correct, there is no conflict between civic law and divine law since the gods are integral to all laws. Heraclitus is convinced that 'all human laws are nourished by one law, the divine law.'[63] It holds sway to the extent the law itself wishes. To be a valid law, the gods must be on the side of the announced law. Mere proclamation is not enough. In the end of Aeschylus's *Eumenides*, Athena holds the court of law.

Antigone first informs Ismene about Creon's order, 'And now what is this proclamation (*kērugma*) that they say the general (*strategos*) has lately made to the whole city?'[64] Then she demands Ismene to make public her act. 'Proclaim (*kērukses*) this to all.'[65] She should proclaim it like a herald. Moreover, Antigone's use of the term implies that Ismene's proclamation of Antigone's act is at the same level as Creon's edict, a proclamation. Her decision, act and law in disagreement ruptures the hegemony of Creon's law in multiple ways.

Certain Legality

Antigone may wonder, what law? To answer this, we must consider how a 'certain legality,' 'the order of law,' 'signifying chain,' and 'anything else' are linked together. First, the brother or more precisely her relationship—not emotional or any kind of Platonic love but structural-positional—to the brother, is the point that at which these four knit together. This law is the symbolic function in every society that precedes a particular socio-political order and its positive laws and conventional moral rules. The law that Lacan speaks of is 'a horizon determined by a structural relation' that 'only exists on the basis of the language of words.'[66] Lacan sees the combination of kinship and the incest taboo as a fundamental form of the symbolic order. It is a mechanism that establishes social bonds among human beings.

Second, the 'certain legality' is also related to how we consider the concept of justice. Greek *dikē* (justice) should not be reduced to a juridical or moral concept of justice, even if it also refers to it. Reading Presocratic philosophers, Heidegger sees justice (*Gerechtigkeit*) as a metaphysical concept related to *alētheia*, truth as disclosure. Justice is order (*Fug*) and the form and structure (*Gefüge*), joint (*Fuge*), prescription (*fügen*), and destiny (*Fügung*) that destines the event of being (*Seynsfuge*).[67] This conception of justice may be too metaphysical for what comes to law in tragedy. However, it reminds us that we should not simply reduce the Greek concept of justice to its understanding in our legal culture. Justice is not merely a transcendent justice, but an immanent justice, as it cuts through the *polis* and beings in the *polis* in ordering, sanctioning, lightning, measuring, disclosing fashion. Even in its immanency, it cannot be set into spoken or written laws and rules or taken as proper to oneself or one's property. It is a measuring measure where ethics, law, politics, and philosophy—as well as being and ought—are intertwined.

We should also remember that Dike, the goddess of justice, moral order, immemorial custom, and fair judgment is both an Olympian god wandering among human beings on earth (fathered by Zeus) and a chthonic dwelling in Hades (mothered by Themis). Her sisters were Eunomia (good order) and Eirene (peace) and her main opponent was Adikia (injustice).

Third, note that Creon's law is a juridico-ritualistic repetition but Antigone's legal performative act is more singular. In Kafka's *Before the Law*, a man waits to enter the law anticipating an authoritative answer to the meaning of law.[68] By doing this, he subjects himself to the law. It is exactly this anticipation that installs authoritative force to the law. Antigone refuses to accept this kind of ritual of anticipation, thus she interrupts the law and opens herself towards another idea of the law.

Fourth, the unwritten law is *phusis*. It is what it is (*to eon*) and revealed as such in its truth (*aletheia*). It is not natural law in any ordinary legal sense (*lex naturalis* of the Roman law, St. Thomas, Hugo Grotius, or Samuel Pufendorf), participation in the world of ideas or divine reason, an essence of human being as an end, purpose or dignity, or the natural laws of causality. Antigone's unwritten law is quite different. It cannot be written and is thus unsayable either in the play or on stage. 'We must instead look for the unsayable and hence unspoken ground upon which such actual laws have a claim upon her.'⁶⁹

Antigone presents her law as a question: 'What law, you ask, is my warrant for that word?' (*tinos nomou dē tauta pros charin legō?*).⁷⁰ The law is a 'horizon determined by a structural relation.' This relation 'only exists on the basis of language of words.'⁷¹ This is her relation to the brother, who is absolutely unique and irreplaceable. This makes Antigone cry for a burial place, a site made so important for her.⁷² Since the parents are dead, she cannot have another brother. The brother is related to time. Time reminds us of mortality at the core of our being. The unrepeatability is the truth of being towards death. Moreover, the unrepeatability means that the time of the tragic conflict is unique. It cannot wait and it cannot be repeated. Her law functions under a radical lack of iterability.⁷³ Under other circumstances, she would have never (*ou gar pot*) turned against the city. If the body were her husband's, she would not have acted like this, since a husband is replaceable and under the logic of iterability. Her unique act shows 'the line of sight that defines her desire.'⁷⁴

Unwritten Laws

Antigone refers to unwritten laws, which are a set of non-positive rules, customs, traditions and assumptions. There is normally no opposition between two forms of laws; rather they complete each other.⁷⁵ We, the moderns, make too much of the fact that the law is unwritten.

We do not see the script of the unwritten law before our eyes, which makes it difficult to understand its existence and validity. A reason for this may be the fact that we privilege sight—seeing and eyes—to Augustine's *concupiscentia oculorum*. Even the law ought to be for 'the lust of the eyes: for the office of seeing.'⁷⁶ Seeing the law clearly requires sacrificing the gaze. Teiresias and Oedipus knew this. On that, Antigone is their comrade.

The unwritten law is something extremely hard and heterogeneous, like the Real, before which reason wavers. It is not reduced to established political or legal dialogue and decisions. Posited neither by divine nor human authorities, this law is 'an everlasting fire, being kindled in measures and being put out in measures.'⁷⁷ The voice of the unwritten law, despite its universality, 'speaks' only to a singular presence. This silent voice touches or haunts Antigone as simultaneously strange and intimate. She responds to this call that comes from nowhere or no one. The call of the law opens a gap between an author and an addressee, a foundation and a transgression, a legitimation and revolution. By receiving the call, Antigone is chosen as its singular addressee.

Antigone touches the limit. She has a contact and tact with the unwritten law and the unconditional border. As she touches by attempting to transgress the limit, she is exposed to limit and to the fact that there is a limit. At this moment of ultimate loyalty, she affirms the universality of her law. In her singularity, she immediately participates in the universality of the law. I will come back to the question of singularity and universality in the context of theatre truths.

In the classical period, *nomos* (pl. *nomoi*) was a common word for law, even though it sometimes referred to custom. As *nomos* was used to designate a written law, the concept of the unwritten law emerged. However, in the archaic period, *nomos* designated the rule of conduct, custom, and practice. When the Greeks started to write down laws in the seventh century, *nomos* was not considered a written law. The words *graphos* (writing), *thesmos* (ordinance), and *rhētra* (pronouncement) were used to signify positive laws. Bernard Knox writes that the law was unwritten because it 'existed even before the alphabet was invented or the *polis* organized.'[78] It has, he continues, the force of law as unfailing law even if unwritten.

Pericles praises these laws (*nomoi*): 'we render obedience ... especially to those laws which are ordained for the succour of the oppressed and those which, though unwritten, bring upon the transgressor a disgrace which all men recognize.'[79] In Plato's *Laws*, the Athenian stranger claims that unwritten laws (*agrapha nomima*) equate with ancestral customs (*patrioi nomoi*) even though the Athenians have agreed that customs should not be called laws (*nomoi*). Law and custom, even if both may be called *nomos*, must be separated.[80] In *Nichomachean Ethics*, Aristotle differentiates between written and unwritten laws. First, on a general level, there are laws that are proper to the *polis* and its people set by a designated sovereign lawgiver. The validity of human laws may be questioned by referring to the criteria of the unwritten law grounded in *phusis* (all that grows by itself). This law is common (*koinos*) to all human beings, unlike written laws. This law, which comes to light on its own and by itself, is not limited to any temporal and spatial situation. The laws of the gods ought to be compared to human laws, since different gods, who may be against each other, protect different cities. Moreover, gods are immortal because their abode is in the law. 'They "only" obey and guard it.'[81] Second, in a concrete situation, the application of a written law may be criticized based on equity. There are situations where the application of equity leads to a more just solution than applying the written law literally. It shows true justice (*dikē*) instead of what only seems to be justice.[82]

Antigone speaks of *agraphoi nomoi*, 'the unwritten and unfailing ordinances (*nomima*) of the gods.'[83] The unwritten law is something that cannot be transcribed as signifiers, turned into speech and meaning. It is empty and unbound, without designated definitions and set imperatives. Antigone's two laws are equality (of brothers) and singularity (of a brother) and she declares 'commitment to both.'[84] The law of singularity is necessarily an unwritten law. Polynices is an unreplaceable (*autodelfos*) being. He is beyond general definitions. That is, Antigone defends absolute singularity that cannot be understood with the means of articulated signifiers and language.

The unwritten law is not nothing. Instead of being a posited set of legal norms, the law is always in the state of becoming. Because of this the law is out of (legal or moral) order, a displaced and split law without presence and present validity. As such, it opens a place where the soundless and unwritten may appear. It is the figure of Antigone that incarnates what is beyond signification as she opens herself to the unwritten law. Or more properly, in and through the figure of Antigone the law attempts to actualize itself, that is, presencing itself. The unwritten law functions as tragic transport, carrying the play as it interrupts all written and spoken laws. This law leads us to the limits of legal and moral normativity, understanding and meaning, symbolic and politico-legal order. As Lacan said, the law by which she acts is not 'developed in any signifying chain.'[85] One reason for this is that she aims to bring an end to this monstrous heritage of the Laius family and the law cannot have developed as symbolic norms in and through the incestuous and violent history of the house of Laius.

Next, I turn to a paradox: in *Antigone* unwritten laws are material laws. We remember that the body of Polynices is left 'unwept for, unburied, a rich treasure house for birds as they look out for food.'[86] Instead of being covered, the corpse, 'a representation of the human at its most extremely inhuman,' is left visible.[87]

Antigone buries his body by 'sprinkling its flesh with thirsty dust and performs the necessary rites.'[88] The corpse left in the dry desert is covered by a layer of dust that does not merely veil the corpse. The thirsty dust refers to the dry burial ground's need for tears of mourning and lament.[89] It could also mean that the dust Antigone scatters turns the flesh into refreshing water. Metaphorically, together the dust and the flesh open a new beginning that brings forth memory from forgetting that the body was doomed. The dust that Antigone takes from the ground is so light that it seems to offer no protective veil. However, neither a gentle breeze nor a stormy wind blows away the burial dust. Dust becomes a border that protects the body from being mauled by birds. The dust is as light as unwritten laws, which do not have the material weight of positive laws set by the sovereign lawgiver. It is as if even the materiality of dust would violate Creon's edict. Or perhaps birds and dogs, allied with Antigone, respect the scattered dust. Perhaps, they who have eaten the morsels of the abandoned corpse are an excess of the political community belonging to the same sphere as Antigone's unwritten law.

The blinding storm, divine malady (*theyan noson*), or divine 'oi' (*göttlich Weh*) as the guards call it, is a chaos that disturbs borders, blinds the sight, and silences the speech. Antigone seems to transgress the limits of nature and humanity as she becomes part of the storm. The guards must have seen the fury, as did the chorus, in the blink of Antigone's eye. It upsets the chorus, it troubles the guards. The blink as a physical movement cuts through the storm, or perhaps as storm itself, interrupting the watchful eyes of the authority.

The dust Antigone uses to cover the corpse and the storm from where Antigone appears are the materialization of the unwritten law. Dust and storms cannot be caught and laid down permanently in writing or in any other way. Sand blows in the wind. It is almost nothing, almost immaterial, even though they are powerful forces that disturb the gaze of the established order.

'Wild is the wind,' defines Antigone's position in yet another way. Antigone is, the guard explains to Creon, 'like a wild bird round an empty nest.' She lets out 'a screech' when seeing the corpse being uncovered.[90] The chorus sees Antigone as wild and this wildness comes from Oedipus. For Lacan, 'wild' refers to 'something uncivilized, something raw,' or more precisely 'eaters of the flesh.'[91] Antigone is like the birds eating the flesh of Polynices. Antigone avoids the Hegelian universality by becoming 'interchangeable with a force of Nature, and especially the bird.'[92]

Birds in Antigone fly in the wind as threateningly as in Hitchcock's *The Birds*. They eat the flesh of Polynices' unburied corpse. They are the force of nature that transforms individuals and members of community into an organic process. Teiresias attempts to consult these birds, but the birds refuse to offer any advice. Their cries are unreadable signs. This is no surprise since Creon is the cause of the pollution that turns the sky, Antigone's dwelling place as a bird, into black vomit.

After the guards have swept away all the dust that covered Polynices' body, Antigone returns to see the corpse laid bare. She cries out bitterly with 'a sound like the piercing note of a bird when she sees her empty nest robbed of her young.'[93] We witness deep grief, pain, and the suffering of a bereaved bird/mother at the limits of language, signification, and meaning. Her voice has transformed into inhuman and senseless sounds and noise. Antigone is isolated on the other side, on the side of monstrous animality and pure *phonē*. This is how the guard, who reports the event to Creon, understands Antigone's suffering. As she cries out, she weeps and also curses those who had done the deed, after which she reburies Polynices.[94] In Hölderlin's translation, '... she howled. And cursed...'[95] The cry is transformed immediately into meaningful speech, *logos*, one that blames those who have done wrong to the dignity of the body and the burial rituals. Antigone's act is divided into two. On the one hand, her bird-like cry is a dehumanized voice. This universal voice of suffering beyond language barriers and nations calls everyone to be members of the apolitical community of humankind as mortals. On the other hand, her curses are shared in the public space of the political community. They address a wrong committed by those in power. It is a sound that has meaning in a political body.

The free flying bird that has designated trajectories is a being that cannot be caught without destroying it. It recognizes no borders or validity of laws limited to a certain enclosed and defined space of community. That is, the bird is like unwritten laws, all over the place but without a stable position in the political, legal, or material order of the *polis*. Like a bird, she acts in the desert of the real as a void. This desert is the perpetual site of beginnings. It is the site where political action begins. Antigone encounters Creon's law and authority in the political void with the bird's cry but instead of being outside the political, it is its beginning.

Dust, storm, and bird are the essences of Antigone's ethical way of being in the *polis* as an illegal defender of the law that cannot be laid down. What we have here is not merely voiceless and unuttered suffering but a materiality of unheard, unnoticed, and unrecorded law. Antigone is the law for herself (*autonomous*).[96] She knows her law from the beginning without any rational reflection or moral deliberation. Her law rises from the earth (*orgē*). The verb *orgas* refers to 'swell with desire' and 'orgasm.' Antigone's unwritten laws arises from the sky and earth showing itself in the light of the ether. These laws are her figure as dust, wind, and bird. For Antigone, the law just came to light and 'no one knows how long ago' this happened.[97]

What if Antigone begins with non-representable things and material elements, not with words? Instead of considering them to belong to the home, private and feminine spheres, these things and elements take place in the middle of the public sphere, breaking down the division between *polis* and *oikos*. Thus, the interpretation of the unwritten law as homely or resting in Antigone's soul misunderstands its public, political, and ethical meaning. It continues Creon's tradition of separating the political from family business, which he actually cannot keep separate as he, in his tyrannical *hubris*, becomes a father/uncle-king.

For Louis Althusser, language constitutes an abstraction, but he also wonders if we should be able 'to speak without words, that is, to show. This indicates the primacy of the gesture over the word, of the material trace over the sign.'[98] Perhaps we can understand the unwritten law as a gesture of wind and as the trajectory of the bird that gestures, shows, and points.

8

Uncanny Stranger

'O radiance of the sun, fairest light that ever shined before on seven-gated Thebes.'[1] The first words of the parados from *Antigone* are where Heidegger begins his reading as he returns to the play in his third Hölderlin lecture course *Hölderlin's Hymn 'The Ister'* in 1942. The chorus 'composed of old and experienced men of the city of Thebes' praises the rising sun that 'pours the most radiant light upon the city' giving 'what is unconcealed its space.'[2] The 'radiance and strength of youth' presents itself. The Greeks as the chorus witnesses are strong enough to acknowledge the equal importance of the old and the young, tradition and novelty, and 'maintain the tension between them.'[3]

The Greeks are so close—even too close—to Heidegger because they started what he understands to be the true object of philosophical research, which is 'human Dasein insofar as it is interrogated with respect to the character of its being (*Seinscharakter*).'[4] Through interpreting *Antigone* and other Greek texts, Heidegger aims at restoring the ontological impact of the Greeks and their understanding of the factical life of *Dasein*.[5] Tragedy may once again make visible the human being. The context for tragedy is Heidegger's concept of fundamental ontology (*Fundamentalontologie*), that is, philosophy that is intimately concerned with being of factical life and which mainly deals with principles of the analytic of *Dasein*.[6] Being, originally called presencing—enduring-here in unconcealment—should not be mystified even if it may be a 'riddle.'[7] Our thinking should not 'merely run after it blindly.'[8] Heidegger cannot avoid being fascinated by Antigone. She represents *Dasein* in an authentic way. She achieves her authenticity as she confronts her finitude and mortality. She stands between appearance that is given to her to appear—the radiant presence (*das Anwesen*) in which she shows herself in the integrity of her being—and a return to the darkness. Thus, she is, on the one hand, subjected to the necessities of being, and on the other hand, beyond the everyday world of *das Man*. She exists in the world of beings, meanings, and possibilities in the way that she belongs to being itself (*Sein selbst*).[9] She stands in *aletheia* (the clearing of truth), as death stands before her as the shrine of the nothing. Therefore, Antigone presents the truth that normally avoids us in our way of being in the world. She, as a consequence, rises in the radiance and honour (*kalos*) of her own being. 'The event is *the* law (*Das Ereignis das Gesetz*)' insofar as it lets Antigone be present in the gathering of mortals and in the event that joins them together as they rise into the light and clearing of truth as the guardians of the radiance of being.[10] The *polis*, as the site of beings, opens in the light of being. Immediately before the parados, the first choral song, Antigone and Ismene had met in front of the king's palace. In the prologue, resolute and determined, Antigone told Ismene of her decision to bury the body of Polynices and to disobey the decree of Creon. Antigone exists in a burst of furious anger. This encounter as well as the chorus hints that 'a darkening irrupts upon what has been lightened, a darkening that must be cleared and decided.'[11] The rising light over the *polis* is at the same time the acknowledgement of the darkness and shadows, since everything is permeated by its counter-essence. This is the setting of Heidegger's reading of *Antigone*, which turns around three Greek terms, *deinon*, *polis*, and *hestia*.

The rising radiant light of the parados corresponds to the beginning of the first stasimon (the second choral song), the so-called 'Ode of Man': 'Manifold is the uncanny (*deinon*), yet nothing / uncannier than man bestirs itself, rising up beyond him.'[12] Or, as in Hölderlin, 'Monstrous (*Ungeheuer*) are many. But nothing / More monstrous than man.'[13] Heidegger has not one but two Antigones. Heidegger cannot resist the call of Antigone. Time and again he wants to 'hear the Greek words.'[14] We have to read together, or against each other, the aforementioned Hölderlin lecture course and the earlier *Introduction to Metaphysics*, without forgetting his first Hölderlin lecture course of 1934–35.

In this 1934–35 course, *Hölderlin's Hymns 'Germania' and 'The Rhine,'* Heidegger sets out the direction of his understanding of Greek tragedy. Sophocles the poet was the first to apprehend the radiant shining of nature (*phusis*). He poetically set out a projection of being that grounds *Dasein* upon the earth and in the face of the gods. He founded this being and laid the ground of the possibility for the Greeks to settle upon their dwelling place as a historical people: 'Yet the poetic work of Sophocles named Antigone is, as a poetic work, a founding of the entire Greek *Dasein*.'[15]

In the *Introduction to Metaphysics* from 1935, Heidegger deals extensively with Greek tragedy in the context of the conflict (*polemos*) between being and appearance (*Schein, doxa*), which belongs to the immanent conflict in the process of *aletheia* (truth as disclosure). There it takes place as a conflict, on the one hand, between concealment and unconcealment, and on the other hand, in the unconcealment itself between true appearing and appearing as a semblance.

Dasein as Deinon

Heraclitus and Parmenides are his guides in understanding *polemos*, but when it comes to tragedy, he concentrates on Sophocles. Heidegger expresses his fascination with the 'Ode of Man,' which he considers a poetic projection of man as *deinon*: terrible, fearful, awful; strange; mighty, powerful, skillful, able, clever; wondrous, marvellous. The chorus directly and completely confirms the strangeness and uncanniness of the human being. Thus for Heidegger, *Dasein* is *deinon*, which he translates as *Unheimliche*, which means all the aforementioned as well as *Heim* (home), *heimisch* (familiar, homely, domestic), and *heimilich* (secret and hidden). *Unheimliche* casts us out from the homely. '*Logos* as gathering, as human self-gathering to fittingness, first transposes being-human into its essence and thus sets it into the un-canny, inasmuch as at-homeness is ruled by the seeming of the customary, the usual and the trite.'[16] Homely and unhomely are not, however, simple oppositions. There is something strange and uncanny that belongs to the domestic, something familiar that exists outside the dwelling place. Both of these inspire awe.

The human being is a terrible, creative, violent, and overpowering being that tends towards the strange and uncanny by surpassing the limits of the familiar and homely. The human being lies between two versions of *deinon*, namely *dikē* and *tekhnē*. *Tekhnē* is a form of knowledge. The human being has at his disposal the violence of technological, mechanical, and liberal knowledge and also the violence of productive forces; but he is also a being that does violence.

He uses the violence of *tekhnē* against the overwhelming power of *dikē*. He crosses seas, ploughs the soil, tames animals, subjugates nature to his control, and uses language. Language is essential to human beings and human conquest and ordering of the earth. For example, the word 'sea' in a poetic speech violently contains the being of the sea. *Tekhnē* is the violence of speaking, thinking, poeticizing, building, and creating states. It is both production and the setting of limits to being. Thus, *tekhnē* is not to be considered as technical skills, materials, and tools. Since *tekhnē* is a response to the overpowering sway of being, the tragic hero is caught up, as mentioned above, in the conflict between *tekhnē* and *dikē*. *Tekhnē* as human knowing acts against *dikē* as overpowering order. In other words, there is violence inherent in the human being's way of dwelling on the earth.

This *polemos* is a challenge that draws the human being out of his home and ordinary way of being into the unhomely. This unhomeliness is not an arbitrary situation but the essence of the human being. The first stasimon of *Antigone* shows how violent departure and wandering uproot the human being and cast him out of the familial framework, severed from the *polis*, from the historic gathering place of beings in their truth. Therefore the human being is *apolis*. This is not a result of any technical or scientific progress since the human being is the uncanny at the start. In other words, violence of language, speech, action, and passion are not accidental but a part of human existence. It breaks into the un-thought, un-said, un-seen, and un-happened and transforms them into thinking, saying, appearing and acting. It is being that forces the human being to leave behind familial paths. At the same time, being appears through the violent actions of the human being, who answers to the appeal of being. All this brings disaster upon human being. This strange *apolis* being stands in peril of *atē*, the error and terror that awaits all human achievements. Disaster is the deepest affirmation of the overpowering order, *dikē*. Here we have a 'heroic-tragic assessment of the nature of human knowing' and *tekhnē* is how this way of being can be named.[17]

The *polis* is the site which includes the gods and the temples, the priests and the thinkers, the poets and the ruler, the assembly of the people and the armed forces. Heidegger thus brings together on the same side poets/thinkers and state founders, among them Hitler, as solitary and extraordinary (*Unheimliche*) beings without state (*Stadt*) and place (*Stätte*). They are first of all creators who found (*gründen*) the state and the place.

The reading of Antigone in the *Introduction to Metaphysics* ought to be read together with the Rectoral Address Heidegger gave around two years before in May 1933.[18] In it he cites Aeschylus's *Prometheus*. Prometheus dedicated his life to thinking, *bios theorētikos*. For Heidegger, there is the amalgamation between *theoria* (contemplation), *poiēsis* (production), and the accomplishments of *praxis* (action). In his first Hölderlin lecture course, which brings tragedy and the people together, he presents the trio of founders: the poet who founds, the thinker who articulates what the poet discloses when founding the *Dasein* of the people, and the statesman who founds the state adjusted to the essence of the people.[19] There is a Platonic echo as Heidegger ends in a corporatist state under the guidance of the philosopher 'wherein each of the estates (*Stände*)... provides a distinct service to a particular people, the German *Volk*.'[20]

In *Hölderlin's Hymn 'The Ister'* Heidegger hears a resonance (*Anklang*) of Sophocles' tragedy in Hölderlin's poetry. Heidegger knits together Hölderlin and Sophocles, perhaps even the figure of Antigone, given Hölderlin's poetry is concerned with the homeliness and unhomeliness essential to being human. Hölderlin's 'hymnal poetizing' tells of 'human being's becoming homely' even if human beings are initially not at home.[21]

Hölderlin forces Heidegger to correct his view on tragedy in general and *Antigone* in particular. In 1943, he looked back on *Antigone* 'as though facing the horror of error.'[22] With regard to Heidegger's 1935 reading of *Antigone*, Clare Pearson Geiman notes that 'the potential for violence and totalitarian politics belongs inextricably to the attempt to conceive human knowing through the working of *tekhnē*.'[23]

The error concerns two issues, which are not merely to do with the ethics of (mis)reading. First, in the 1935 reading of *Antigone*, Heidegger emphasizes the conflictual relationship between *dikē* and *tekhnē*. In 1943, his focus changed to the conflict, or more properly, interplay between *hypsipolis* and *apolis*.

Second, in 1935 Heidegger emphasizes a Promethean-Oedipal hero, creative men who set to work the truth of a people. Oedipus is not only a human being who meets his downfall but 'in Oedipus we must grasp that form of Greek *Dasein* in which this *Dasein*'s fundamental passion ventures into what is wildest and most far-flung.'[24] Oedipus embodies *Dasein*, who has passion for the unveiling of being, that is, for the struggle over being itself. In 1943, the witness of being is not the leader, but Antigone. She is now *apolis* but not as a founder of the state but as a figure that resists the arbitrary reason of state power. Now, Heidegger associates *deinon* with Antigone, who herself applies this term to herself in the first encounter with Ismene, even though she speaks about how Ismene sees her.

What is now explicit—Antigone as *deinon*—had been implicit already in the 1935 lectures. Heidegger has always understood the figure of Antigone in the terms of *Unheimliche*. Antigone is *der unheimlichste Mensch*. She is the unity of the fearful, the powerful, and the inhabitual. In addition, she is the most uncanny (*Unheimlichste*), which resonates in the words *unheimisch* (unhomely) and *unheimlich* (uncanny). Hölderlin translates *deinon* as *Ungeheuer* (extraordinary). Being the supreme uncanny (*das höchste Unheimliche*) does not make Antigone a beast or an angel, a sufferer or a martyr.[25] Instead, precisely because of this she is the most human of human beings.

Tragedy is about being-unhomely and becoming-homely of the extraordinary being (*Seiende*), which is also a site where the ethics of tragedy takes place if it is to take place. If the fundamental word (*das Grundwort*) of, not only the first stasimon but Antigone the play and the figure is *deinon*, *Unheimliche*, then we have to consider the function of this fundamental word. If in the *Introduction to Metaphysics*, *deinon* and *Unheimliche* were closely related to what is powerful and awe-inspiring, now as Heidegger has turned from Nietzsche to Hölderlin, the essence of these terms is unhomeliness, even though the former definitions still ring in these terms.

Antigone demands Ismene to leave the task to her 'and to that within me that counsels the dangerous-difficult.'[26] Or in Hölderlin's version, 'Let me and my errant rashness / suffer the violent power (*Gewaltige*).'[27] For Antigone, this counsel concerns taking up 'into my own essence the uncanny (*deinon*, *Unheimliche*) that here and now appears.'[28] The uncanny is an answer to Ismene's earlier question, 'What dangerous thing is to be done? What have you in mind?'[29] The thing is to bury their brother. According to Ismene, she should not pursue the impossible, that which is to no avail. Antigone's pursuit is not just any arbitrary human action she could withdraw from since it is impossible. Antigone has decided in favour of 'her brother, namely the law of the dead, and thereby the fundamental law of the living.'[30] This—what is to no avail—is the point of departure that governs all her actions and becomes her highest task. Thus, she is the supreme uncanny.

Just before this, Ismene had defined Antigone as *deinon*, 'If you have the strength (*deinon*)!'[31] Antigone may merely ironically answer to Ismene by using her words. Or as I would claim, Antigone assimilates or affirms what Ismene sees in her. Heidegger writes that 'the unhomely is nothing that human beings themselves make but rather the converse: something that makes them into what they are and who they can be.'[32] Antigone does not passively accept *deinon* as her essence, but she takes it upon herself and properly experiences it. Ismene's and Antigone's dialogue confirms Heidegger's view.

'Antigone knows that no one can take her decision away from her and that she will not flinch in her resolve.'[33] In her terrible, powerful, and clever uncanniness, Antigone is transported by fury (Hölderlin's *Zorn*) which tears her off from the familiar anchors of the *polis* and *oikos*.

Ismene confirms this: 'Your heart is fiery in a matter that is chilling.'[34] Even if Oedipus was an interruption, he was a passive instrument of fate compared to Antigone, who is an incarnation of rebellion (*insurrection*).[35] As *deinon*, she forcibly irrupts and bursts forth from out of herself. In the first scene, Antigone has invited Ismene outside of their home (*oikos*) even if she is supposed to be within the home. She is immediately introduced as a displaced and unhomely being who has strange plans. She has already transgressed the limits of her proper place at home three times: *1)* she must have stepped beyond the threshold of the home to hear Creon's decree; *2)* she meets Ismene before the king's palace; and *3)* she declares her intention to break the law in a public space. At the same time as she is loyal to the family, she transgresses its limits.[36] She has violently left the familiar and domestic sphere and turned against the overpowering order.

The 'most uncanny' Antigone is 'utterly unhomely' and 'the most unhomely human being.'[37] Antigone experiences *deinon*. She endures and suffers it. This is, according to Heidegger, what constitutes the action in tragedy. The tragic is to be measured 'according to the truth of being as a whole and in keeping with the simplicity in which it appears.'[38] The uncanny is the fact that Antigone's point of departure is this appearing that is destined for her, but no one knows whence it has arisen. However, Antigone accommodates herself to this and consequently she is 'removed from all human possibilities.'[39] She finds herself in a conflict over the site of all beings and even steps out of this site. She who has taken the uncanny within herself is now within the unhomely like no one else.

Heart

At this moment the tragic hero cannot be without being touched by death. Dastur explains that in Greek tragedy we come 'across one of the first *representations* of the fundamentally mortal condition of humanity.'[40] Antigone is not afraid of dying. Instead she faces it with certainty as the condition of her being. We must be careful how we face her (our) death. But it is not being dead (*Tod*) but dying (*Sterben*) that constitutes her *kalos*, her 'belonging to being.'[41] Antigone's dying refers to her perpetual becoming homely, which takes place within and from out of the unhomely.

Death is, for Heidegger, 'the key phenomenon in which the specific kind of "*temporality*" belonging to human *Dasein* is to be brought into relief and explicated.'[42] Dastur affirms that we are open to the world because we have a relation to death, but it is 'in *existing* that we are witnesses of death.'[43] As Hegel recognized, language is a already a way to relate to death, since imposing names upon things is to annihilate those things in their real existence. Language, writes Maurice Blanchot quoting Hegel, 'immediately overturns what it names in order to transform it into something else.'[44] The thing that is written, negates what it represents. In Blanchot's words: 'When I speak: death speaks in me.'[45] Or, as the chorus declares in Sophocles' *Tereus*, we are 'always walking blind into tomorrow.'[46]

Antigone is the most remote from the homely, but or because of this she belongs most intimately to the homely. At the same time, a human being who considers himself to be at home as he ventures forth, skilfully conquers seas, and captures animals—he comes to nothing (*kommt er zum Nichts*), following Heidegger's translation of the words of the chorus.[47] That is, he remains unhomely as he does not come towards his essence. Homely and unhomely are not opposites but turn into each other. The essence of Antigone is an unhomely homeliness, but how to understand this in relation to two homes, *polis* and *hestia*?

The *polis* is not so much a state (*Staat*) or a city-state (*Stadtstaat*) but a spatial-temporal site (*Stätte*) or position (*Statt*) of history. 'The *polis* is the site of history, the Here, *in* which, *out of* which and *for* which history happens.'[48] It is the ground of the notion of political and the place of human beings where all roads cross. To this site belongs the gods and the temples, the priests and the thinkers, the poets and the ruler, the assembly of the people and the armed forces.

The final words of the chorus are: 'Rising high over the site, losing the site is he for whom what is not, is, always, for the sake of daring.'[49] Heidegger's interpretation of his translation of the chorus runs as follows:

> Rising high in the site of history, they also become *apolis*, without city and site, lone-some, un-canny, with no way out amidst beings as a whole, and at the same time without ordinance and limit, without structure and fittingness, because they as creators must first ground all this in each case.[50]

In Hölderlin's *Hymne 'Der Ister,'* Heidegger defines *polis* as 'the abode of human history,' the 'site of being homely (*Heimischseins*).'[51] The human being moves, *pelein*, as he seeks to return home by coming into the open. *Polis* has a polar character. Thus, *polis* is *polos*, 'the pole, the swirl (*Wirbel*) in which and around which everything turns.'[52] Once again, the human being moves—and the swirl draws them—towards the site of the homely but is simultaneously without site (*Stätte-lose*) because he is 'determined in essence by the unhomely.'[53]

Hestia (heart), mentioned by the chorus, is for Heidegger not merely 'the heart of the house,' the fire that burns, but also 'the site of being-homely,' a description he also applies to the *polis*.[54] *Polis* and *hestia* are gathering sites for human beings. Even though *hestia* is 'the middle of beings,' at the centre of the *polis* to which all beings are drawn 'Being is the heart' (*Das Sein ist der Herd*).[55] In this way, Heidegger draws circles of the homely. *Hestia* is not the same as *oikos* (household), the term which Heidegger does not use to avoid the sense of an opposition between the state and the home, the civic order and the familial religion, which would, for Heidegger, miss the whole point of tragedy. Once again, the human being moves towards the heart—and the fire that radiates, illuminates, warms and glorifies draws them—but simultaneously he is expelled from the heart of the house

As the supreme uncanny Antigone takes the burial and the law of the dead and the living as her highest task, she necessarily forfeits the site, the *polis*, but at the same time she looms and stirs over it more than anyone else. She is expelled from the heart (*hestia*) while simultaneously belonging most intimately to it. Antigone reminds me of Calantha's sister in John Ford's *The Broken Heart* (1633). Even if she has received the news of 'death, death and death,' she dances and dances. She chooses her own death in her own time with the avowal: 'They are the silent griefs which cut the heart-strings; / Let me die smiling.'

In his Rectoral Address, Heidegger praises the excellence of *bios theorētikos*, contemplative life.[56] This is the perspective from which he reads Aristotle's ethics and this reading impacts on his (im)possibility to think the ethics of tragedy. 'The ultimate possibility in which Dasein is authentic, we call *Existenz*.'[57] For the Greeks, existence is the way of being and dwelling in the world.[58] From this, one is motivated to delimit one's being in its being. So for the Greeks, existence is life persisting in pure contemplation. This is the horizon along which Heidegger understands Aristotle's definition of the human being as a speaking animal (*zoon logon echon*). His error is that he does not differentiate between Plato and Aristotle.[59]

What of Aristotle's second definition of the human being as political animal (*zoon politikon*)? Heidegger recognizes this, but for him a speaking citizen is stuck in an inauthentic way of being. What is alive in the concrete world of the *polis* and what takes place in the public sphere is for Heidegger everydayness: following habits, fashion, and immediate vogue. 'For the

Greeks'—but if we include Sophocles and Antigone or other Greek tragedies and tragic heroes, we may come to a strange conclusion. Antigone is acting as a speaking and political animal, so her speech should be counted as the idle talk of *das Man*. Instead of ethical and political disagreements, there is merely nattering and chitchat. Actually, in his reading of *Antigone*, there is no change between 1934 and 1945 in his obstinate resistance to everything in tragedy that has to do with Antigone's being with others and among others, with the human interaction of the figures in tragedy. He neglects time and again how the characters are exposed to each other, how they as singular beings come into contact, how their bodies sense the touch of other bodies and the elements of nature. Political, juridical, and ethical disagreements are relevant only in so far as they have a part in the great ontological *polemos* between being and appearance. What Heidegger presents is an ontological consensus beyond the multiplicity of singularities and the political dissensus in the time and space of the *polis*.

Moreover, we may consider Antigone's action from the viewpoint of Heidegger's lecture courses on the basic concepts of Aristotle's philosophy (summer semester 1924) and Plato's *The Sophist* (winter semester 1924–25). Aristotle's intellectual virtues are divided into lower deliberative virtues that consist of *phronēsis* (practical judgement), *tekhnē* (know-how), and *poiēsis* (production) and the higher epistemic virtues that consist of *sophia* (contemplation of ultimate principles) and *episteme* (contemplation of particular objects). Heidegger does not ignore active life and deliberative virtues. Unlike *poiēsis*, *praxis* (action), the virtue of which is *phronēsis*, is a non-instrumental activity in which means and ends are not relevant. Aristotle considers it as action for its own sake (*hou heneka*). For Heidegger this translates as: *Dasein* exists for the sake of itself. Heidegger translates the 'disclosure belonging to *praxis*, i.e. *phronēsis*, into conscience (*Gewissen*), understood in strictly ontological terms with no ethical connotation, as the intimate vision by an individual *Dasein* of its ownmost possibility of being.'[60] Even if tragedy is yet to come for Heidegger, the *praxis/phronēsis* of his 1924–25 lectures will guide his 'future description of care and of authenticity as a way of facing existence.'[61] That is, Antigone's action is understood in terms of conscience which is distanced from the ethical and from the right action of a singular being—Antigone—among the plurality of equals.

After all, by opening her mouth in the public space, Antigone herself deconstructs Heidegger's reading of tragedy that sees her as an authentic tragic hero. Speaking—which all are equally capable of, whether Antigone, women, refugees, slaves, citizens—interrupts the contemplative vision in the light of which the philosopher sees a tragic figure before her ownmost past, present, and future. Or, to save Heidegger, we should consider Antigone as a split being. She is simultaneously an authentic homely/unhomely figure of disclosure of truth and an inauthentic ethico-political everywoman of opinions. The essence of the tragic hero is divided into resolute authenticity and lapse into everydayness, and into genuine appearing and semblance. She is uncanny. Once again, the splitting in itself deconstructs the heroic paradigm, the horizon within which Heidegger contemplates the Greeks and their tragedies. Moreover, according to Critchley, *hamartia* is not a tragic flaw but 'a basic experience of human fallibility and ontological limitedness. The belief in autonomy is the moment of *hybris* that precedes tragic ruination, or *atē*.'[62] If so, we could ask with Jacques Taminiaux, what does this make of Heidegger's conception of tragedy if for him Antigone is, as a pure emblem of the endurance of being, a character without *hamartia* and *hybris*?[63] Without a combination of limitedness and a transgressive-political *hybris*, Antigone would not reveal herself as an uncanny, terrifying, and extraordinarily tragic being.[64]

The third possibility is to accept that Heidegger turns *Antigone* into an object of his contemplative gaze, that is, in order to consider tragedy as an ontological disclosure the philosopher necessarily must ignore or veil the concrete ethical and political speech and action that takes place in the *polis*. In this case, the ethical dimension—the conflict or action in tragedy, or even tragedy as a play and theatre—is passed over in silence as the real focus in the way *Antigone* functions as material for an ontological analysis of human existence and finite temporality.

After all this, how shall we take Heidegger's affirmation of tragedy of ethics? He does say: 'The tragedies of Sophocles—provided such a comparison is at all permissible—preserve the *ēthos* in their sayings more primordially than Aristotle's lectures on "ethics".'[65] However, Heidegger misreads Aristotle's *arete* and the *ēthos* in Sophocles' tragedy, thinking them as the utmost possibility of being. This view on ethics in Greek philosophy and tragedy determines his understanding of the ethics of tragedy. He must ignore *arete* as related to concrete ethical action (*praxis*) to save the ethics of tragedy as a part of the ontology of tragedy. When it comes to Aristotelian virtues, Heidegger admits that he will not follow Aristotle's *aretai*, since 'concrete development of the interpretation of Dasein' does not interest him here.[66] The way he reads Aristotle is repeated in his reading of tragedy. He insists on refusing to consider concrete action where Antigone takes responsibility upon herself. Antigone's human *praxis* and *phronesis*, a virtue related to it, must be ignored in Heidegger's ontologization of tragedy. Because of this hierarchical movement made in the name of philosophy, Heidegger misses or veils what is immanent in his saying. Being not 'interested' is not the best philosophical argument. He never became interested in it or maybe it was an interest permanently deferred. More importantly, this being-not-interested is an emergency break that prevents the possibility of the ethical to emerge in Heidegger's understanding of Greek tragedy. His fundamental ontology becomes a violent *tekhnē* against *dikē*, if we understand it less metaphysically as justice. However, as Heidegger well knows, *dikē* is a necessary part of our being.

Ethics of Being

In his Aristotle lecture course, Heidegger admitted that his reading of Aristotle's ethics proceeds with a preliminary disregard for the ethical problematic. The same seems to be true in his readings of tragedy. If Heidegger ontologized Aristotle's ethics in his Aristotle lecture course, as Francisco J. Gonzales shows, then in his reading of *Antigone* he does the same thing to tragedy, which for the Greeks was an ethical experience. Immediately I must state multiple reservations, since this is just my speculation on the Greek audience. We could bracket the ethical concerns of tragedy and appreciate Heidegger's analysis of tragedy at the ontological level. Oedipus (1935)/Antigone (1945) is a brilliant presentation of Greek *Dasein* bravely standing in the face of the overpowering order. One reason for this is that even though Heidegger once and again turns to Aristotle, whose thought is placed under the authority of Heraclitus' *phusis krupesthai philei* ('nature loves to hide') in order to penetrate the Greek comprehension of *phusis* and its relationship to *tekhnē*, he never turns to Aristotle's *Poetics* as a guide to the Western conception of art and technics.[67] *Poetics* would have taught him something about the ethics of tragedy. Perhaps Heidegger thought that thinking the ethics of tragedy may be postponed until after the ontological understanding of tragedy.[68] Tragedy of ethics is yet to come. Then again, Dastur defends ontology as occupying the major position in philosophy instead of ethics, not because she considers ethics as a supplement, but because the thinking of the truth of being as the fundamental ontology of *Dasein* 'is in itself originary ethics.'⁶⁹

However, his ontological reading of tragedy is full of concepts and conceptions that have ethical sense. We could conclude that Heidegger ontologizes ethical vocabulary. More fundamentally, I think Heidegger cannot avoid the ethical in his ontological reading of tragedy. It is an excess, an overpowering force that is immanent in Heidegger thinking of tragedy. Despite everything Heidegger does to avoid the ethical, he cannot do without its insistence.

Heidegger's reading of *Antigone* should be opened to different voices, which would produce ethical effects. As Heidegger focuses on the words of the chorus and on dialogue with it, he left Antigone aside. It is especially the figure of Antigone that in Heidegger's understanding of tragedy deconstructs it. She embodies ethical interruptions that takes place within the ontologization of tragedy. In his *Zollikoner seminar*, Heidegger's definition of ethics runs: 'To be subject to the claim that presence (*Anwesenheit*) makes is the greatest claim that a human being makes. It is what "ethics" is.'⁷⁰ The presence makes this claim to Antigone, who acts in accordance to this claim.

As I leaf through Heidegger's tragedy texts, I found various traces that could be seen as marks of the ethical if Heidegger had seen Antigone for the words of the chorus. These and many other signifiers are small portals through which Antigone's ethical being enters Heidegger's text to interrupt the ontological narrative. 'Antigone knows that no one can take her decision away from her and that she will not flinch in her resolve.'⁷¹ As a consequence, she is an 'authentic' being,⁷² who appears 'beyond what is merely habitual and every day.'⁷³ She is one of those who listens to 'what they should listen to.'⁷⁴ She 'dare[s] to take up the great and lengthy task.'⁷⁵ She takes what 'is destined for her,'⁷⁶ having a 'fundamental passion'⁷⁷ for her task. In her 'uniqueness,'⁷⁸ Antigone is 'determinate,'⁷⁹ 'steadfast.'⁸⁰ She does not 'intend evil.'⁸¹ She is one 'who truly acts,' so she appears in an 'authentic sense.'⁸² She knows 'where and between what alternatives the authentic decisions must be made.'⁸³

Based on various interruptive traces, we can say that in Heidegger's thinking of tragedy, Antigone appears as the most *deinon* human being, the strangest in her power of singularity in its resistance to the everydayness of political power, legislation, and pre-given social positions. Her strangeness is her being incommensurate with pre-given positions and social generalities concerning her condition and possibilities. Her stubborn argumentation for her law—her *phronesis*—shows how skilfully she manages *praxis* in the public sphere. She even embodies the know-how (*tekhnē*) of resistance through burial rituals and dying. In her strangeness she insists and this insistence is nothing but ethical. In this way, she presents the ethical truth that avoids us as long as we do not see anything but what is presented as legitimately visible, audible, and sensible. The condition of truth circulates through her existence and her discourses without being commensurate with social conventions and legal claims. The overpowering force of the sovereign threatens to override her absolute singularity.

All this makes Antigone an ethical figure, the strangest type, not so much in the Aristotelian sense of having a stable ethical position, but in, paradoxically, the Heideggerian sense. That is to say, her ethics is brought forth in her constant movement between *hypsipolis* and *apolis*, between homely and unhomely, from one to another and back again as she takes on the duty and responsibility, makes them her own, in her way of being-in-the-world and, hence, affirms her being. Her exposure to both other beings and existence is an integral part of her trajectory. The essence of Antigone is the same as her ethical position as movement. She is an uncanny being in an ethical relation to being.

There is another ethical dimension in Heidegger's readings of tragedies, the human condition measured by finitude. Dastur speaks about the 'kingship of finitude,' which we hear in Heidegger's reading of tragedy, but contemporary societies go wholly without recognition of this kingship so that 'there is forgetfulness of death' and thus finitude and limits.[84] This is the truth—the truth of limits—the ethics of tragedy discloses. In its immeasurability, death alone 'can give man the measure that Hölderlin had already found only in the emptiness of the heavens,' as we have already seen.[85] *Antigone* and Hölderlin's poetry come together to lead us to the heart of an ethical disclosure. 'We die in order to live,' affirms Diotima without hesitation.[86] Being thrown into the world we share with others and towards death, our fundamental position is strangeness that comprises the unfinished movement between being homely and unhomely. Anxiety and freedom are inseparable in our ethical being.

Am I squeezing out an ethics of tragedy from Heidegger's ontology of tragedy? If so, I would be falling into *hamartia* (error), like Heidegger but in reverse. There is no doubt that he has no morality in the sense of a moral theory or philosophy as a discipline. Nor does he construct a systematic set of rules and principles for human behaviour. This is not even a task of philosophy, which is 'paths – not works' as the motto of his *Gesamtausgabe* goes.[87]

Nancy claims that Heidegger sets aside ethics while it remains a continuous object of his thinking. Heidegger does not consider *ēthos* as a set of moral norms and value; and as such exterior to being. On the contrary, it refers to the truth of being and an action (*agir*) in accordance with this truth. Ethics is to be understood in the register of the action of *Dasein* that sets itself outside of itself as it ex-poses itself to sense. This is the position of ex-istence. Action (*praxis, handeln, agir*) is not an accidental characteristic of *Dasein* but related to 'a total and joint responsibility for the sense and existence.'[88]

Thinking this kind of action is original ethics, which considers the *ēthos* as the truth of being and acting in accordance with it. This *ēthos* is not exterior to being, that is, being is the ex-isting action of human *Dasein* that exposes itself to sense. This thinking does not lead to moral norms but to thinking in action, which grants sense to being. This thinking is only possible as acting.

Ethical traces are already immanent in Heidegger's thinking as an existential confrontation. In his writing on Greek tragedy, the ethical traces function as deconstructive moments—and here I will be more reserved than Nancy—deferring the closure of the ontology of tragedy or the enfoldment of ethics in Heidegger's ontological terms. I would even claim that when Heidegger writes in the *Introduction to Metaphysics*, 'Human being is *to deinotaton*, the uncanniest of the uncanny,' immanent in these words is the strangeness of a singular being as an exposure to the world for which she must take responsibility. Ethics is part of this exposure and taking responsibility, but it is never without the risk of terror (*Schrecken*) and madness (*Wahn*), error (*hamartia*), and measurelessness (*hybris*). Let me come back to Hölderlin's question that Heidegger considered as fundamental: 'What good are poets in a time of poverty?' If, as said ealier, the vocation of poets is to answer the fundamental question concerning our earthly destination, immanent to this question is the ethical that tragedy as dramatic poetry, as a play, and as theatre cannot ever avoid. This is what Heidegger has yet to learn from his own texts on tragedy. It is always already inscribed in these texts.

I have no regrets saying that if for Hegel, the tragic conflict takes place within the social, political, and legal order of the *polis* (or within the symbolic), then Heidegger radicalizes the co-ordinates of the conflict. It exceeds the limits of the pre-given order as Antigone goes to the limit and reaches beyond the borders of the social, symbolic, and normative orders. Instead of aiming at a utopian re-articulation of the existing order, as Butler would prefer to see it, Antigone becomes a radical outside of the distribution of the sensible. This is also what Lacan has in mind as he brings desire on stage.

Heidegger's thinking of being is the thinking of original ethics (*l'éthique originaire*), which must be kept separate from ethics as a moral theory. 'Heidegger's thought considered itself thoroughly as a fundamental ethics (*une éthique fondamentale*).'[89] In thinking being, original ethics is even more proper than fundamental ontology.[90]

What this means is that being gives being but instead of giving something it lets being be. *Dasein* must answer to this giving by taking responsibility for it. It has to find the right way towards being—'to let be (*laisser être*).'[91] A responsible answer does not allow *Dasein* to fall back into established meanings since *Dasein* is exposed to the sense by making sense. 'To let be' does not mean to let it be as things happen to be.[92] In its open and active relation to the fact of being, *Dasein* gives sense to being. Being as the fact of being does not precede the desire to have the sense of this fact. Being is a gift that forms a desire that this fact of being is realized as sense. Therefore, being is nothing but the gift of the desire of sense. The relation between being and *Dasein* is 'the relationship of sense (*sens*)' and giving sense to the fact of the being (*donner sens au fait d'être*).'[93] Being touches *Dasein*, and *Dasein* touches being, when *Dasein* is ex-posed to being as the opening of making sense (*faire sens*).[94] In this action, *Dasein* becomes free in its dignity. Human dignity is not an essential element. Without action, it does not make sense.

For Heidegger, the action is fundamentally thinking—and poetry— that addresses the sense of being. Without this kind of action, there would be no action at all. Thinking as an existential action is an experience of absolute responsibility for sense. Instead of creating norms and values that would restrict the possibilities of human action, thinking is an action that measures the measureless difference between the thinking of ideas, norms, and measures and the originary action that makes one think. As such, it takes full responsibility for the sense of the world. Nancy is tempted to say that 'the respect of existence is imperative,' but he immediately adds that this does not refer to setting any meaning of 'life' or 'human' or the definition of their value.[95] The imperative merely presupposes giving sense to existence as existence.[96] 'Thinking does not become action only because some effect issues from it or because it is applied. Thinking acts insofar as it thinks.'[97] In his reading of Heraclitus, Heidegger defines thinking: 'The world of thinking rests in the sobering quality of what it says. Just the same, thinking changes the world.'⁹⁸

As previously said, poetry (*Dichtung*) is thinking and as such an original action. This has been elaborated as we considered poetry. Now we can conclude that Heidegger thinks a tragic poem as an existential action. As a consequence, Heidegger's fundamental ethics is a way to understand the ethics of tragedy. Tragedy means responsibility for sense as it stands in relation to truth, that is, with the unconcealment of the facticity of being. The ethical task of tragedy is to gather, bring-forth, and disclose the world. The ethics of tragedy is related to making sense by letting the tragic world set itself in the light of its being to the tragic poem. The poetic action illuminates by naming things in their essence, which makes these things available for another kind of action.

At the very moment Heidegger considers the sense of the ethical in tragedy, he turns away from tragedy and from ethics. The Aristotelian *eudaimonia* comes 'from being present to beings *kata ten sophian*,' according to thought.⁹⁹ As a consequence, ethics is reduced to an existence in a philosophical/poetical life, 'the life that acts the essence of man.'¹⁰⁰ Another consequence is that he misses tragedy as theatre since he ignores the materiality of tragedy— actions, bodies, movements, sounds, cries, signifiers, rhythms, scenes, and sets. As he hears the thoughtful word of the tragic poem, Heidegger does not listen to the materiality of this poem.¹⁰¹

This forgetfulness is intimately related to the gesture of fundamental ontology that brushes aside the dimension of sharing the world and being-with, without which the tragic poem would not function as tragedy. Being in ek-sistence consists of 'being the there' (*être le là*), which means that *Dasein* is not to be understood in the way of an adverbial of a place (being there, être *là*) but in a way of an active transitive verb (being the there, être *le là*). Hence, *Dasein* does not name a substance but is an action sentence. However, Nancy concludes, Heidegger's ethics 'is far from putting emphasis on the "being-the-there-with-others" (*être-le-là-avec-autrui*).'¹⁰²

Even when Heidegger considers being-with, he reduces it to a historical co-belonging, to the fate of the people, which realizes itself and affirms its identity by willing its essence and destiny. He connects it to the groundedness (*Bodenständigkeit*) of the people (*Volk*) to the homeland (*Heimat*). Instead of thinking being-with as it takes place in the presentation of tragic action, he concentrates on tragedy as the affirmation of Greek destiny.

A double ignorance. The matter of tragedy and ethics (not norms and values but being-with) are brushed aside in combining fundamental ontology and original action. This is not an accidental gesture but a political choice. For Lacoue-Labarthe, this is the first political choice and as such it is 'philosophical through and through ... because it is the first choice ... [it] is a philosophical choice ... the choice of philosophy itself.'[103]

9

Unconditional Desire

Next, from phenomenology to psychoanalysis. Psychoanalysis continuously confronts the tragic, not 'the pop psychology of Oedipus complex but a reflection on the tragic' in a similar way Freud brought the petty affairs of the bourgeois family back to the Greek tragedy.[1] Freud himself spoke of Antigone 'only' when he referred to his daughter Anna Freud, who remained unmarried to become the support and inheritor of his father. Lacan drew heavily from theatre. He 'encountered the power of tragedy' to which he never ceased to refer.[2] Lacan upheld the concept of the subject central to phenomenology but radically rethought its constitution in terms of the unconscious structured like language and the irreducibility of the desiring subject configuring its own destiny. This is the terrain in which we confront Antigone, an embodiment of a stubborn hardness of an ethical subject, who does her duty, that is, she does not give up on her desire. What steps does this tragic hero becoming homely take in 'the dance between Creon and Antigone?'[3] This is a question Lacan answers in his *The Ethics of Psychoanalysis*. How are tragedy, ethics, and psychoanalysis coupled in this dance? The dance leads to neither ideal love nor the authentic independence of the dancing partners. Nor does this dance end in a Hegelian lesson of ethical life. It is a tragic dance. Tragedy 'is in the forefront of our experiences as analysts' as the key word 'catharsis' implies.[4] Lacan refers to Aristotle as he defines its place in tragedy as a means of accomplishing catharsis of the emotions of pity and fear. As previously stated, catharsis has nothing to do with biological, natural, or moral purification. Instead, it is related to desire and the relationship between tragedy and psychoanalysis. This analytic experience is an invitation to reveal the desire of the subject. For him *the* tragedy that teaches us about desire is not *Oedipus the King*, as it was for Freud, but *Antigone*. Even if Freud did not 'expressly discuss *Antigone* as tragedy, that doesn't mean to say it cannot be done at this crossroads to which I have brought you.'[5] Actually, Freud was more focused on the myth of Oedipus than the tragedy as a play and theatre.

Antigone exists in an uncanny liminal situation between two deaths and 'the central third of the play is composed of a detailed display (*apophanie*) of ... a life positioned and destined to be lived on the point of life merging with death, death intruding on the domain of life, life trespassing on death.'[6] What often goes unnoted is that Polynices shares his sister's position but in an inverted way. He is condemned to exist between two deaths: the biological death marked by the decomposition of his body and the symbolic death that is yet to come as the inscription of his name through burning rituals.

The ethics of psychoanalysis has a special importance for Lacan. As tragedy reveals desire it brings forth the ethics of desire as a central element of psychoanalysis. Lacan's reading of *Antigone* is, as Philippe van Haute claims, the place of the destining of being of psychoanalysis.[7] At this crossroads, Lacan brings to light the essence of tragedy, catharsis, desire, and the end of psychoanalysis and combines all of this into the question of ethics. To make it even more complicated, Lacan situates his ethics beyond all forms of the ethics of the good; or at least he deconstructs traditional ethics.

The first reaction is that all these various elements cannot be gathered together in an annual seminar. His theory of desire ties psychoanalysis, tragedy, and ethics together. What takes place at this crossroads (of psychoanalysis and ethics, tragedy and ethics, Lacan and Antigone, law and desire)?

What does Lacan find in *Antigone*? *Il y a d'abord Antigone* (first of all, Antigone).[8] So many have found the figure of Antigone an admirable ethical subject who opposes state power and repression. Lacan does not merely admire her. Without any hesitation, Lacan admits, 'it is Antigone herself who fascinates us,' and not just any Antigone, but Antigone 'in her unbearable splendor (*éclat insupportable*)'[9] It is not the dialogue of the play, the conflict between the state and the family, or the moralizing arguments that captivates Lacan. Rather it is Antigone, who attracts and startles us, intimidates and terrifies us. She is in short, a 'terribly voluntary victim.'[10] Her 'fascinating image' forces us to close our eyes at the very moment we look at it. The blindness effect is caused by her beauty (*kalon, éclat*), a beauty to be seen at the level of the imaginary.[11]

At this crossroads, Lacan begins his reading of *Antigone* by asking the following question: 'Is there anyone who doesn't evoke *Antigone* whenever there is a question of law that causes conflict in us even though it is presented in the name of community as a just law (*une loi juste*)?'[12] The question, of course, includes an answer and orients our passage. Antigone gets into trouble with the just law of the political community, or at least with the law the community considers as legitimate.

For Hegel, the tragic conflict is internal to the socio-symbolic order as the split of the ethical substance. Following Hegel, Lacan sees in *Antigone* a conflict between two ethical positions. This view, I would claim, directs Lacan's understanding of the whole tragedy and the position of Antigone. For Lacan, far from standing for kinship, Antigone assumes a limit-position of the instituting gesture of the symbolic order 'of the impossible zero-level of symbolization, which is why she stands for death-drive: while still alive, she is already dead with regard to the symbolic order, excluded from the socio-symbolic co-ordinates.'[13]

For Lacan, Antigone does not present the conflict between two laws but a finitude of the law. It cannot guarantee the good, pleasure, or value, even though this is what Creon, the representative of the law, speaks for as he asserts his absolute authority. His maxim to deny Polynices' burial is in accordance with Kant's principle of universality: Polynices is a traitor and traitors are never to be respected for any reason. He goes beyond this maxim. For Creon, the power of the law is unlimited. Its power reaches not only beyond the *polis* but beyond life. His law reminds one of de Sade's law, the perverse mirror image of Kant, a categorical morality that follows the universal maxim of having the right to use anyone as the instrument of one's pleasure. Creon wants to punish Polynices even after his death. He wants him to suffer eternally beyond the order of nature and culture. He wants to destroy him even as a signifier and thus erase all traces of him from the world. Like a Sadean sadist, Creon considers himself free from of any limits as he denies any lack in his being and desire.

Creon does not realize—or refuses to accept—that the 'law cannot give the good it promises, it can only give our desire for that good.'[14] For Lacan, his fault is not so much *hubris* than *hamartia*, 'error of judgment ... to promote the good [Lacan does not use the term supreme good since Plato has not yet created this mirage] of all as the law without limits, the sovereign law, the law that goes beyond or crosses the limit.'[15] In his error of judgment, Creon does not even notice that he has crossed the limit Antigone defends. The limit takes 'the form of the unwritten laws (*lois non écrites*)' of Dike.[16] Lacan even thinks that Creon transgresses the limit 'like an innocent.'[17] Creon's argumentation is in accordance with what 'Kant calls the concept, *Begriff*, of the good.'[18] For Lacan, the difference between a traitor and a defender of the country, is 'a maxim that can be given as a rule of reason with a universal validity.'[19] The tragedy is therefore against the ethics of the good.

'My life has long been dead, so as to help the dead,' mourns Antigone.[20] Tragedy is an impossible ordeal of death. She moves towards the unavoidable nothingness. For Lacan (as it was also for Heidegger) the human being is towards death. This is not all. She serves death. Antigone does not hesitate, 'I chose death!'[21] Her life is inevitable turning into death, 'a death lived by anticipation, a death that crosses over into the sphere of life, a life that moves into the realm of death.'[22] Antigone is between two deaths. She is living but already symbolically dead because her position in the community is uninhabitable, that is, there is no place for her with regard to the way the space of the *polis* is structured, divided, and distributed. She is excluded from the distribution of the sensible, or more properly, her non-position in this distribution is being non-existent, that is, without existence. The physical death is yet to come. Her punishment doubles this situation. She is buried alive in the cave to wait the coming death. Accordingly, she renews her father's faith, who was between the symbolic death as a refugee and the yet to come physical death.

The Real

The ethical trajectory of Antigone is about how she presents us desire in terms of a relation to death. Antigone presents the death drive, which is not to be understood as self-destruction. It is not without relation to Heidegger's being-towards-death and his difference between death (*Tod*) and dying (*Sterben*). Freud called what is beyond the pleasure principle the death drive to explain the compulsive repetition of traumatic or painful events. For Lacan, the death drive is not a tendency towards destruction, the moment of physical death, or inanimate homeostasis. We have to keep in mind that it is 'the signifier, as such ... [that] has brought into him the meaning of death.'[23] It is also not a version of the pleasure principle's logic of lowering tension. It is not merely one drive among other partial drives. Instead, 'every drive is virtually a death drive.'[24] It is about being driven by death, or more properly, it is the gap and hole around which drives congregate. Thus, all partial drives and their objects are repetitions of this gap which constitutes the objects of drives as object. Drives circulate around this gap. They repeatedly keep returning to it. The Thing is the gap, hole, and lack in the symbolic order. It is the Real that is not something but no-thing—always already lost, since it was never there to be lost—that is missing from the symbolic, representation, and signification. The Thing as the Real is what the signifier cannot capture, and which is expelled from reality in the process of signification. The impenetrable, impossible, and imperceptible Thing is not the goal of the subject and it will be never reached. The Thing is the (no-)thing around which representation and affects gravitate. It is not the object of desire even though it attracts desire as the impossible object cause of desire.

Massimo Recalcati explains Antigone's fidelity to the Real from the base of the Lacanian difference between reality and the Real, which is intimately linked to the ethical possibility of her as a subject. Reality is the everyday reality of the world that no one doubts, a reassuring covering for the subject. It possesses the traits of permanency and regularity as 'something repeating itself in time.'[25] Reality is the regular repetition of the sameness, where 'everything that is unavoidable returns to the same place.' As such, reality is independent of the will of the subject.[26] The Real, to which we should return to reconsider ethics, is beyond reality. It is the core of the human being. However, as an enigmatic core it is beyond symbolization and avoids an ultimate interpretation. The confrontation with the Real defamiliarizes the subject. It shatters the familial reality, conventional moral norms, and conformist notion of the self. The Real is what 'disturbs and unsettles the sphere of reality,' what 'traumatically breaks' the pattern of reality.[27] Recalcati's main point is that the Real ruptures the continuity of reality as a tear in the fabric of reality. This encounter with the Real engenders for the subject the need for ethical reassessment.

A side note on Kant: For Lacan, Kant showed the way towards Freud's notion of beyond the pleasure principle. For Kant, desire of an object was always related to pathological motives and thus excluded from the field of ethics. However, Lacan's desire is 'motivated' by the void and gap, the object cause of desire, and not by any object that could bring with it momentarily pleasure. Thus, pure desire can be understood in relation to Kantian non-pathological motives. We act not only out of respect for the moral law, but out of respect for desire in itself.

In the end of *Oedipus at Colonus*, Oedipus disappears as he goes towards the limit, towards the Thing, which is a non-place beyond the symbolic and imaginary, an absolute secret because it is without any burial signs or traces. Beyond it he comes 'to the threshold that plunges down, rooted into earth' after which he perishes among mortals. Theseus, the only one who witnesses this, holds 'his hand before his face to shade his eyes, as though some terrifying sight, which he could not bear to look on, had been presented.'[28] As the messenger tells us, Oedipus 'has left our ordinary life' as Antigone.[29] It is the loss and void around which the desire of Oedipus and Antigone revolve. It is this loss coupled with the emergence of Antigone's line of desire that Lacan follows.

Antigone's passion to bury her brother is absolute. In her inflexibility she is beyond fear and pity to the very end, unlike Creon who in the end gives in to fear. Antigone, 'a victim of her hubris,' is also beyond *atē*, which can be understood as the mayhem that leads to destruction, the divinity causing ruin, and the mental state leading to turmoil. In Lacan's reading, *atē* refers not so much to a state of things but to a direction and movement or Antigone's being between two deaths. Antigone is already dead, and she is going towards *atē* and beyond it.[30]

Antigone's Desire

This must be understood in relation to her desire. Antigone is the subject of the desire of the Other. Her desire depends on the Other and the symbolic law. The Other makes her desire possible. By her desire she is bound with the symbolic order. At the same time, she affirms that the Other and the law are lacking and desiring. There is no established good that would answer her desire. In her tragic act, she is in a position where the Other as the symbolic order is presented as incomplete and finite. In this way, her desire as a pure desire is disclosed. The subject of the law is not Creon but Antigone as a desiring subject.

Antigone reveals the line of sight that defines desire.'[31] Let us follow this line. Antigone goes beyond established limits as her act pushes her to the limits. Existing as she does between two deaths, Lacan puts words in Antigone's mouth saying 'I am dead and I desire death'.[32] Lacan writes, 'there isn't even the suggestion of a peripetia. Everything is there from the beginning; the trajectories that are set in motion have only to come crashing down one on the top of the other as best they can.'[33]

Her desire aims at no object. Her good is absolutely different from all other goods. Her desire aims *pros atan* (towards *atē*) and even *ektos atas* (beyond *atē*), that is, going beyond the limit. She is driven to the limit of *atē* by the misfortunes of the house of the Labdacids. What is *atē*? Lacan considers it irreplaceable, so he does not translate it. 'Misfortune' (*malheur*) is too weak, 'atrocious' (*atroce*) is closer, but Lacan associates it with 'the pure and simple desire of death as such' incarnated by Antigone.[34]

The desire of the Other linked to the desire of the mother that, on the one hand, brought into the world Eteocles, Polynices, Antigone, and Ismene; on the other hand, it is a criminal desire. The result of the incestuous union between mother and father is split into opposing brothers, a legitimate one and a criminal. 'There is no one to assume the crime and validity of crime apart from Antigone' and she chooses to be the guardian of the unburied criminal whose corpse has turned into a horrible and uncanny wound.[35] Antigone must sacrifice herself. However, in her final utterances, she does not lament her faith but expresses her going beyond the symbolic and the dialectic between the desire of the Other and the law, after which she leaves the stage as Oedipus does in *Oedipus at Colonus*.

Antigone appears 'as a pure and simple relationship of the human being to that of which he miraculously happens to be the bearer.'[36] What she bears is the signifying cut. She is beyond the limit of *atē*, beyond the symbolic order, but this does not mean for Lacan that she is beyond reason.[37] Yes, she is beyond conventional social order and valid law, but this does not equate with the position of non-sense. Instead, in this position another kind of rationality is functioning. This rationality does not follow the conventions of the discourse of the symbolic order. As Antigone inhabits this uncanny position, she is able to bring forth the inconsistency of the symbolic order, unveil its antagonisms and open the social and political closure of the political order to lack, fractures, and dissensus that have always already been immanent to it.

Moreover, Antigone is not without law even at the limits of the symbolic. The law by which she acts is not 'developed in any signifying chain.'[38] This shows Antigone's fidelity to the uncompromising unwritten law that, as unwritten, does not provide maxims at the level of language and signifiers. Antigone defends Polynices as an absolutely singular body—singularity itself—without any qualities among other qualities that could be articulated in language. He is absolutely singular, because he cannot be compensated with another brother, since both their father and mother are dead. Thus, Antigone keeps her eye on the body that is a horrible wound in the order of things, which is the Thing beyond signification. Antigone is directed towards a point beyond the symbolic world of signifiers and all possible meanings, to a non-place where all signification is turned into meaninglessness and all political, social, or ethical calculation lose its sense. In this way, Antigone reveals the truth of desire, which does not aim at any objects or goods that would satisfy it.[39]

Ethics does not give us the good but our desire.[40] Ethics is not the substance of Antigone's claim, a specific object or the good of the family, but her persistent clinging to the desire. Lacan wonders: 'What makes Philoctetes a hero?'[41] He went off all excited to the Trojan War even if he was not wanted: 'He was dumped on an island because he smelled so bad,' where he rotted away for ten years consumed with hate.[42] Once again, a tragic figure in exile. The answer Lacan gives to his question simple: 'Nothing more than the fact that he remains fiercely committed to his hate right to the end.'[43]

Antigone is a hero since she is, as previously said, stubbornly insistent. An uncompromising being—a Kantian in the sense that she does not take into consideration pathological motivations, like her interests, emotions, feelings, or natural attachments—she does not give up her desire. She is faithful to her desire, which takes her beyond the limits of natural and cultural orders and which makes her Antigone. Without this faithfulness she would not be what she is, one who is faithful to the lack at the core of her being. She does not betray her being as the subject of desire, which means that she does not disavow the lack. She refuses to remain silent and withdraw behind the wall of her home. Instead, she persists in performing her act and following her desire until the end. Her categorical insistence on her desire excludes her from the political and social community situating her at the level of the monstrous. She is a dangerous figure that becomes detrimental to the established legal and political order as she goes beyond the limits of the human, beyond the symbolic order and the law. Coming back to pure desire, we can now conclude that it is pure because it is purified from everything that guarantees us meaning and direction in the world. Antigone acts in the name of pure desire at the limits of the law of signifiers in their materiality, which must be separated from the law of interdiction, 'transgression is forbidden,' the norm of the neurotic.

Here we confront the question of the lack. First, there is lack in the signifier. In their materiality signifiers refer to other material signifiers and are always separated from their meaning. As lack, signifiers have to express their meaning again and again even though there is an inbuilt fundamental incapacity in them to do so definitively. These signifiers present us to other subjects, that is, other signifiers, and thus we are never fully present in the symbolic world we share with others. Second, the ultimate 'object' of desire is a lack, loss, void, and death; the Thing, whose topological place is in the Real beyond the symbolic and signifiers. This is the condition of the possibility of us having multiple subjective positions in relation to our desire, that is, even if our unconscious is structured like a language, we have the possibility to freely affirm the structure of our desire and undertake 'a risk of an ethical nature' not to give up on our desire.[44] The symbolic life 'turns around an excessive point to which it is attracted and towards which, at the same time, it keeps its distance.'[45] Without this tragic human condition that drives our excessive desire, we would not be subjects but merely unfree objects. If the Thing were filled by the Supreme Good—be it a Platonic idea, a Supreme Being or an ideological Truth—there would not be any ethics.

Desire is, Lacan states, 'the metonymy of our being,' which makes ethical acts possible.[46] Here we must be careful to understand that ethics takes place beyond the pleasure principle. Otherwise, we would merely have an ethics of the good and happiness. Antigone does not follow the function of the good (*la function du bien*).[47] As she does not give way to her desire, she is led beyond the good. Lacan comes back to the ethics of psychoanalysis in an interview aired on French television in 1973. His own question, addressed to himself, implies an answer: 'What else is the famous lowering of tension with which Freud links pleasure, other than the ethics of Aristotle?'[48] In the 1959–60 seminar he concentrated on Aristotle's ethics 'so as to strongly distinguish from it the ethics of psychoanalysis.'[49] For Lacan, ethics is beyond calculations of pleasure and pain. It is the death drive that makes possible the ethical act. Because of this, Creon is not an ethical figure. He is dominated by the pleasure principle. Antigone, by contrast, incarnates the fundamental drive. This is a rare point where Lacan and Gilles Deleuze come together, since the death drive for Deleuze is a transcendental principle—a Kantian hint that Lacan does not share—that gives repetition to Eros and which 'can be lived only through repetition.'[50]

Desire is located beyond the pleasure principle as 'eccentric, even scandalous.'[51] As already said, Antigone's desire is directed towards the Thing beyond the symbolic order. Antigone is a central knot of the speech (*la parole*), which means that she is the place where the founding words that carry forward the Labdacid family actualize themselves. At the very same moment, she completes the fate of the family. The chain of signifiers supporting the family and herself reaches the limit where the Thing beyond speech appears. She is at the border between, on the one hand, the *polis*, the symbolic order, and the law, and on the other hand, the terrifying and measureless wildness beyond reason and categories. At this moment, language and signifiers cannot ground her existence. Desire as the effect of language and the symbolic law appears so that its background is the Thing. Antigone thus reveals our truth as desiring beings.

Glimmering Crime

At the moment of the achievement of the *atē,* as she crosses an invisible line, we face 'the violent illumination' and 'the glimmer of beauty.' This effect of beauty has a blinding effect. It prevents us seeing what happens beyond, that which we cannot look at. The function of the beauty that Antigone incarnates is to open a way to our death drive, which is not psychological but 'an absolutely fundamental ontological notion' that reveals to us in a blinding flash our relationship to our own death.[52] Antigone is one who is made for desire and it 'can be posited only in … [the] beyond.'[53] Tragedy engenders the fascinating image of Antigone, her radiant burst towards whom our desire moves as she moves beyond the symbolic world. At the limits or as Rainer Maria Rilke writes in *Duino Elegies,* at 'the beginning of terror, that we are still able to bear,' her beauty appears.[54] Her beauty is what offers us the relation to the beyond, to the ultimate object of desire, the Thing as the Real, which constitutes her and our desire. The figure of Antigone forces the impossible Thing to appear momentarily in and through her. In short, as Antigone does not cede desire she is able to offer us an encounter with 'the limit in which the problematic of desire is raised.'[55] Here a sublimation takes place and the object of desire is elevated 'to the dignity of the Thing.'[56] In this way, Antigone acts like an analyst, who shows that in analysis the only measure is that we should not give up our desire. If we insist on following our desire as it appears we confront a liminal stage where our fantasy support, which functions as a defence mechanism against the Real, starts to wither away. At that point, the subject becomes the subject of its desire again. Neither tragedy nor analysis are a comfortable or a deliberative experience. As Jacques-Alain Miller makes clear, 'the praxis of analysis is a suffering, not an intellectual journey.'[57]

Then again, Antigone goes beyond these limits. Is the ethics of psychoanalysis an ethics of desire or an ethics of the Real? The ethics of desire would lead us to the limits of the symbolic and signifiers. Even though our desire is oriented towards the Real, it would stop at this limit and turn back, as a new subjective position in relation to desire would have been affirmed. This is ethics taking place at the level of signifiers. The ethics of the Real that Antigone incarnates would go—or at least attempt to go—beyond this point, beyond signifiers and their protection against the Real. Antigone stays faithful to her desire against politico-juridico-moral demands. She plugs into the death drive, which first carries her beyond the symbolic order and the sphere of moral norms, established positive law, and consensual truths, and second affirms her relationship to the absolute absence and mortality that makes her what she is as a human being. Integrity and purity, absence and death are intertwined as her ethical trajectory comes to the end.

Marc De Kesel strictly denies the possibility of the ethics of the Real, since for him ethics must operate at the level of signifiers giving space to desire. The ethics of the Real would mean that our desire is realized at the level of de Sade's sadistic fantasies. The other argument is that it would found psychoanalysis 'in the *real* state of things.'[58] I find both of these arguments problematic. First of all, the Real must not be understood as reality, as the state of things. Secondly, the Real is beyond fantasies that protect subjects from the Real. Instead, Antigone moves from fantasies and pathological motivations to the ethical that involves a creation of an ethical subject. I do not consider there to be a contradiction between these two versions of ethics. Antigone's desire is directed towards the Real and beyond the symbolic. This is the trajectory of her desire she does not give up. The ethics of desire is thus the ethics of the Real. What I would add is that Antigone is not an ethical example that orders what we should do but an incarnation of the truth of desire. All of us should confront this truth in his or her own singular, ineffable, and ungrounding way.

Here we arrive at the crossroads of ethics and aesthetics. Antigone's aesthetic quality supports or even generates her ethical value. For Lacan, 'ethics exists only insofar as it is sustained by aesthetics.'[59] Lacan does *not* deny it, on the contrary he does not cease to affirm it. His seminar on the ethics of psychoanalysis is situated 'between a Freudian ethics and a Freudian aesthetics,' which 'reveals one of the phases of the function of the ethics.[60]

Freudian aesthetics means 'the analysis of the whole economy of signifiers.'[61] It reveals to us the 'inaccessible Thing,' the Other in the internal exclusion, the extimacy (*extimité*).[62] The Thing is in relationship to art. One of the most primordial features of human creation, *tekhnē*, is a vase—the same vase Heidegger speaks of in relation to *das Ding*—a thing whose essence is the void. It is a utensil but also a signifier. In its signifying function, this fabricated signifier signifies no particular signified. It is a signifier of signifying itself. It creates the void and introduces emptiness and fullness. The vase may be filled but in its essence it is empty. For Lacoue-Labarthe, this is mimesis of an unimaginable, that is, a mimesis without model, an originary mimesis (*mimesis originaire*).[63] Lacan goes on to argue that the vase represents nothing but the existence of emptiness that is called the Thing. The 'fashioning of the signifier and the introduction of a gap or a hole in the real is identical.'[64] The human being 'fashions this signifier' in the image of the Thing and 'introduces it into the world … whereas the Thing is characterized by the fact that it is impossible for us to imagine it.'[65] The sublimation is located at this level.

Let's come back to Antigone. A work of art encircles the Thing. Lacan refers to anamorphosis, which is an image insofar as 'an infinitesimal fragment of image is produced on each surface of the cylinder.'[66] Because of this 'we see a series of screens superimposed' and in return for which 'a marvelous illusion in the form of a beautiful image of passion appears beyond the mirror, whereas something decomposed and disgusting spreads around it.'[67] Antigone is this kind of anamorphosis. Her brilliant image rises as the image of passion. Tragedy is a catharsis of the object, that is, in the purification of the object, the Thing is indicated in its ring or encirclement (*le cerne*) in a brilliant flash (*l'éclat*). In tragedy the Thing is there in both its horror and luster, the latter purifying it. It is beauty (*le Beau*) according to Lacan, and sublime, which is no less blinding.[68] Finally, Antigone is sublimated on the level of the Thing.[69] 'Antigone perpetuates, eternalizes, immortalizes that *Atē*;' these are the last words of Lacan's reading of *Antigone*.[70] This is, Lacoue-Labarthe concludes in his reading of Lacan's reading, 'the tragic (sublime) ethics, and there is, today, no other,' but this does not mean 'a justification of the aestheticizing of ethics.'[71] Tragedy investigates our possible impossible relationship to our mortality which is the essential core of the human being. As van Haute notes, in the end Antigone encounters the abysmal nothingness of human existence, which is also the end of analysis, when the subject regains the founding words which form and determine its existence. At this moment, Antigone accepts *her* fate. In this sense, both tragedy and psychoanalysis are truth events.[72] 'If there is an ethics of psychoanalysis—the question is an open one—it is to the extent that analysis in some way or another … offers something that is presented as a measure of our action.'[73]

From Lacan's perspective, the ethics of tragedy does not answer whether Antigone was a just or a criminal figure. She is beyond the definitions of good and evil. The ethical measure of her actions is her not giving up her desire and her encounter with the Thing. She is an ethical figure that touches the lack and void in the core of the human being but also in the symbolic order. No order—be it political, social, juridical, or economic—can be totally coherent and consistent, since inherent in it is the gap. Alone and betrayed by the human community, she is the martyr of desire (one could only guess, if Lacan identified himself with Antigone as the hero of psychoanalysis).[74] We can also understand her relation to desire challenging 'the idea that desire can be reduced to the symbolic structure at all—be it social, linguistic, or something else.'[75] In his seminar *Encore*, Lacan focuses explicitly upon feminine jouissance, but in his seminar on the ethics of psychoanalysis we are still on the level of desire.

Lacan's crossroads reading presupposes that he ignores Aristotle's conception of catharsis. We feel empathy for another in whom we recognize ourselves and fear someone since we are familiar with these intentions. Catharsis depends on our possibility to identify with the other. For Lacan, this kind of catharsis takes place at the level of the imaginary order, that is, in the world that is familiar to us and where we have a more or less secure position. Lacoue-Labarthe claims that Lacan transfers catharsis from the spectators of tragedy to the tragic figures. Antigone, who is purified and has no fear is the sole hero, unlike Creon.[76] The effect of catharsis is thus distinguished from Aristotelian mimesis and the purifying pleasure (*plaisir*), joy, and satisfaction (*khairō*) that we take in viewing on stage events whose sight in reality is painful and horrible.

Antigone is seen as a model and an example of the ethics of desire that would be an alternative to the classical ethics of the good. Lacan does not actually attack classical ethics but merely decentres it by decentring the classical subject of desire to uncover the desire by which the subject is unconsciously bound to the ethical order.[77] I have some problems with de Kesel's reading. We have to keep in mind Lacan's distinction between morality (acting in accordance to juridical, social, and moral laws) and ethics (acting in accordance with desire). De Kesel's reading may blur this distinction too much as he claims that Lacan does not criticize classical ethics. The radical ethics of tragedy of *Antigone*, for me, is to be understood as an arche-ethics that goes beyond the ethics of the good and moral duty. If it is related to classical ethics, it is to be understood as a precondition for it than a reactive decentring force.

Infidel Criminal Fidelity

As I understand it, the ethics of tragedy revealed in the ethics of psychoanalysis culminates in the staying faithful to desire, lack, finitude, mortality, and absence against the positions provided by the collective conventional normative order and the distribution of the sensible. The ethics of tragedy throws Antigone, the tragic figure, out of the joint and opens her towards the empty foundations of her existence, towards transcendent singularity. She is not a mourning figure of the humanism of mortality and vulnerability but a violent ethical figure who in her resistance to injustice does not give up her desire. As she faces the impossible Thing, she has had her vengeance for the wrong done by Creon's *polis* and the Labdacid house. The border between the symbolic and the Real is not just a border that separates but it also brings together the separated fields. This separating/connecting limit is where the ethics of tragedy takes place. To reach it Antigone does not betray her desire. Through the trajectory of tragedy as the trajectory of her desire, she becomes what she is. The difference between ordinary subject and the tragic hero is that the ordinary subject betrays itself or is betrayed and as a consequence of the betrayal 'sends him back to the service of the good' after which he may never again find the sense of direction. As a tragic hero, Antigone presents the ethics of psychoanalysis, which is simultaneously the ethics of tragedy even if these two are not the same thing: 'The only thing one can be guilty of is giving ground relative to one's desire.'[78]

Another way to consider the ethics of tragedy is to focus on the figure of Creon, even though for Lacan, Creon is no tragical hero because he is afraid to encounter this truth. His sole measures are established juridical, moral, and social norms, but he errs as he considers the power of his laws to be unlimited. His transgression does not mean that he would proceed towards the Thing. It takes place within the political community and its signification system. Van Haute sees Lacan's treatment of Creon as the weakest point of his reading of *Antigone*. What if Creon proceeds beyond the good of the state and family as he unconditionally insists on extending his law to the dead? In other words, what if he is unconsciously fascinated by Antigone and identifies at the imaginary level with her? He is as stubborn as Antigone. Being anxious about this, Creon attempts to protect his identity by constantly insisting that he cannot yield to Antigone, the woman, even though this identification has already happened on another level. Because he is so anxious about his identity at the imaginary level, he does not recognize at the symbolic level, at the level of the law, that by allowing Polynices' burial he would not obey Antigone but traditional law. Because Creon is so fascinated with his sovereign power, he absolutizes his authority such that his law has no more legitimacy in the *polis*. The intervention of Teiresias, who may be considered an analyst (for Lacan there is an analogy between a psychoanalyst and the blind Teiresias), brings about a change in Creon's mind. By confessing his guilt, Creon assimilates his history and gets back from Antigone to the human dimension that he lacks. Due to this, he manages to distance himself from his imaginary identification with Antigone and assimilate his proper position in the symbolic order, that is, he adopts a new subjective position. If it had not been too late, this could have opened another future.[79]

If Antigone were not the only focus, if we were fascinated not only by this figure—because of this fascination Lacan had not yet met Teiresias in himself[80]—we might see another ethics of tragedy in *Antigone*. Assuming my reading of van Haute is correct, I consider it to be very convincing and fruitful. The tragedy of ethics would set limits for those in power, whose imaginary identification with the nation, race, soil, the people, ideology, progress, has set them on the disastrous course towards absolute power and belief in unlimited law without restraints. The figure of Teiresias not merely sets limits but also opens the way towards assimilating the symbolic position in the social order, affirming the inevitable lack in this position, and recognizing the necessary hole in the sovereign power. The ethics of tragedy would be the ethics of democracy that necessarily includes the limits for political, juridical, economic, and social power. At the same time, I must say that even if this definitely is a way to conceptualize the ethics of tragedy, the arche-ethics based on the figure of Antigone is more profound. We should think this ethics that takes place safely within the symbolic order so that we at the same time focus on its background, that is the Thing, the limits of the symbolic order, the trajectory of Antigone that discloses the ethics of desire. At this point I would just refer to Lacan's words in a supplementary note to his seminar. He addresses us by saying that even if we are not aware of it or whether we like it or not, 'the latent, fundamental image of Antigone forms part of your morality.'[81]

'Desire can never be a pure transgressive force,' Yannis Stavrakis claims.[82] I disagree with this. How can pure desire be? Lacan seems to have taken some steps back from the purity of Antigone's desire after the seminar on *The Ethics of Psychoanalysis*.

In his seminar on *Anxiety*, Lacan intertwines desire and the law. They are now in a constitutive dialectic. What makes 'for the substance of the law is desire for the mother' and what makes 'desire itself normative, what situates it as desire, is the law known as the prohibition of incest.' No desire without the law —'So, desire is law.'[83] Even in perversion that seems to be a subversion of the law, desire 'is in fact truly and verily the support of a law.'[84]

Now, desire and the law, which appear to stand in a relation of antithesis—this is how he himself saw them in the case of Antigone—'are but one and the same barrier to bar our access to the Thing. *Nolens, volens*: desiring, I commit myself to the path of the law.'[85]

This seems a Hegelian resolution of the conflict. The opposition of Creon and Antigone, the law and the desire, the thesis and the antithesis is overcome in *Aufhebung*. In *The Four Fundamental Concepts of Psychoanalysis*, Lacan rethinks the concept of pure desire that was so crucial in his reading of *Antigone*. For Lacan, the desire of the subject is always already 'the desire of the Other.'[86] Thus, desire includes an alienating dimension and cannot be absolutely pure. In *Encore*, Lacan introduces a new figure for ethics, Saint Teresa, who is not a figure of pure desire or even of desire in general but defined by the concept of jouissance.[87]

Then again, here and now, we are considering Antigone's ethical act and her desire which Lacan questions in relation to his understanding of tragedy, where desire has an essential role to play. 'Do not give way on your desire!' means that we should not give up the lack that we are by attempting to fill it with idols, things, and addictions. Instead, we must hold the lack open. That is, we must have fidelity to the lack whereby the subject freely assumes responsibility for her act. Without this dimension of freely not giving up on desire and taking responsibility there is nothing ethical in the subject's position. As mentioned previously, Lacan asks: 'What makes Philoctetes a hero?' And he answers: 'Nothing more than the fact that he remains fiercely committed to his hate right to the end.'[88] This ethics of the act reminds me of the Kantian absolutist duty ethics that detests pathological motives, like pride and compassion. A move from the pathological to the ethical involves for Kant a new beginning in which the subject is reborn. This seems to be the case with Antigone's ethical act. It is certainly in conflict with Creon's ethics of 'the good for all.'[89] Antigone's ethics of desire disagrees with conventional ethics that represents the traditional values of political community, the morality of the master, which Aristotle supports as being 'created for the virtues of the master and linked to the order of powers.'[90]

As previously mentioned, Antigone embodies the Lacanian ethics of the Real, an ethics that is not grounded on any ontology but functions in reference to the Real, which resists symbolization and marks a rupture in the symbolic order. Her ethics designates fidelity to this fracture.

Slavoj Žižek continues this way of understanding Antigone's act: 'Is not Antigone the anti-Habermas par excellence? No dialogue, no attempt to convince Creon of the good reasons for her acts through rational argumentation, but just blind insistence on her right.'[91] For Žižek, Antigone embodies an effective symbolic transgression, which is a symbolic re-articulation through 'the intervention of the real of an *act*.' This transgression just occurs without an intention and a master, which surprises even the acting subject even though the act entails a renewal of the subject. On the contrary, a false transgression is merely an imaginary action of resistance that reproduces the order it was supposed to abolish.[92]

In Antigone's ethical act the death drive is an elementary form. Antigone 'effectively puts at risk her entire social existence, defying the socio-symbolic power of the city embodied in the rule of Creon.'[93] As she takes the risk to suspend the existing symbolic and legal order, she already falls into death. This death is not a symbolic death, that is, the exclusion of Antigone from the social, political, and symbolic space. Her act is an absolute and unconditional act. This ethical act is in opposition to the ethics of finitude, which faces and assumes the constitutive lack and considers those acts as evil, where the human being acts like God and surpasses the lack. True evil is not 'a finite mortal man who acts like God, but a man who disavows that divine miracles occur and reduces himself to just another finite mortal being.'[94] Antigone incarnates the ethics of a miraculous act, one that shatters our lives and we have to just come to terms with it. This is, Žižek concludes, 'how the "divine" dimension is present in our lives.'[95]

Žižek names Antigone monstrous, because of her uncompromising stand. Actually he repeats the view of the chorus, who sees Antigone as monstrous and inhuman and of Creon, who considers her 'cold' and 'inflexible.' Should we take here into consideration Lacan's warning, 'we shouldn't situate her at the level of the monstrous.'[96] Lacan differentiates between what Antigone is for the chorus and what she is for us. For us, she veils what must be 'hidden from view.' She is monstrous for the chorus and not for us because she 'goes beyond the limits of the human ... her desire aims at ... the beyond of *Atè*.'[97] Antigone is, for Lacan, measureless and terrifying like the Kantian sublime. Therefore, she is beyond *atē* and at the limits of her symbolic existence.

Anyhow, to repeat once again, she is uncompromising. Žižek further notes that her insistence on the act makes her no-longer-human and she finds herself in an uncanny position, that is, between two deaths. She is symbolically dead while biologically alive. Being symbolically dead means that she puts herself beyond the symbolic order, 'excluding herself from the community regulated by the intermediate agency of symbolic regulations.'[98] Her fidelity is to the Thing 'that disrupts the entire social edifice. From the standpoint of the ethics of *Sittlichkeit*, of the mores that regulate the intersubjective collective of the polis, her insistence is effectively "mad," disruptive, evil.'[99]

By taking the risk to act ethically—to proceed beyond the limits of society, to suspend valid law—Antigone points towards an alternative formulation of the political order. The act occurs to her and she must ethically assume it.[100] She is the model for a radical ethical action that pushes for political transformation.

Žižek attacks three forms of ethics: communitarian ethics, deconstructionist ethics (which renounces universality and reduces ethics to the acceptance of otherness), and discursive ethics (which attempts to save ethical universalism by sacrificing all substantive content).[101] Instead of answering how not to give up Antigone's pure desire in psychoanalysis, Žižek makes things problematic with his sharp distinction between the positive and negative ethical and political positions. The negative position is that of a relativist deconstructionist ethics (he more or less ignores communitarian and discursive ethics), which stresses the irreducible finitude and the structural undecidability of the social sphere.[102] Reading Antigone from the perspective of deconstructionism would lead to criticism of her ethical act as too heroic, absolutist, totalitarian, one-dimensional. She is a representative of a suicidal heroic ethics. This kind of negativity betrays the possibility of the truly transgressive act. The positive position is that of 'a miraculous event which shatters our lives.'[103] For Žižek, the Lacanian notion of the absolute and unconditional act enables us to break with the negative ethics. Antigone's ethical act is risky, unconditional, and it suspends the social and legal order. An ethical act includes a potentiality to undermine the logic of social, political and economic necessities as an intervention that radically changes the co-ordinates of the reality, that is, what is commonly considered possible and impossible.[104] The radical ethical act includes a potentiality to undermine the logic of social, political, and economic necessities as an intervention that radically changes the coordinates of reality, that is, what is commonly considered possible and impossible.[105]

Stavrakakis claims that for Žižek, Antigone's position is so inhuman that it implies 'a total neglect of the social-political world.'[106] There are two possibilities. Either we have to accept that Antigone cannot function as a model for a transformative ethico-political act. Or her act may be seen as this kind of act but in this case her radically inhuman, anti-social, and anti-political desire must be seen in a more moderate way, that is, Antigone's pure desire is brought back into the coordinates of the social and political order. It is then not a non-intentional encounter with the Real but an autonomous subjective act. Either a radical inhuman act or a radical political act, but not both. Stavrakakis offers a getaway from this dilemma. Instead of the strict opposition between negative and positive act, we should not prioritize one position and disavow the continuous interpretation between positivity and negativity. Thus, 'why not see the assumption/institutionalization of the lack in the Other not as a limit but as the condition of possibility ... in ethically assuming the radical character of an act, of relating ourselves—as divided beings—to an event.'[107] This is commitment to 'the continuous political re-inscription of the irreducible lack in the Other.'[108]

I agree with Stavrakakis that an ethical act should not be based on a hierarchical binary opposition. It has a negative element as it disagrees, destabilize, and disrupts the existing social and political order. As such, it is a rupture within the order of things. It also has a positive element as it affects the subject that acts or more properly assumes the act. The act functions as the process of subjectivation or produces a new form of subjectivity, an ethical subject. At the same time, Žižek attacks the deconstructionist tendency to avoid pure and decisive acts, strict ruptures, and finite beings acting like gods. He is not denying the lack in the subject and the Other. The divine he uses in quotation marks does not refer to some divinity, god, or miracle, which Stavrakakis calls 'religious jargon.'[109] Instead it refers to Benjamin's concept of divine violence in his 'Critique of Violence.' It amounts to a radical interruption of the existing social and legal system, a revolution or revolutionary general strike. Moreover, Žižek does not speak about an opposition between a positive and negative act but between an active ethical act and a passive and pessimist deconstructionist undecidability.[110] Therefore, Žižek's text already answers Stavrakakis's critique, but it should be re-read through this critique to understand Antigone's transgressive ethical act.

For Žižek, ethics designates fidelity to the event. To be true fidelity, another fidelity must be presumed, namely fidelity to event-ness, which is distinct from particular events. It is fidelity to the openness of the political sphere and to the constitutive impossibility of the final suture of society, community, or symbolic order. What we are speaking of here is a fidelity to the Real *qua* impossible. Antigone assumes the ethical act and at the same time designates fidelity to the event of burying her brother and following her law. Her act ruptures the social and legal order, the symbolic order. It does not suture the lack in the order or deny the lack in the socio-symbolic Other. Thus, she designates fidelity to the event-ness.[111]

10

Caesura

In June 1978, the Théâtre National de Strasbourg presented *Hölderlin— L'Antigone de Sophocles*, a play directed by Michel Deutsch and Philippe Lacoue-Labarthe based on Lacoue-Labarthe's French translation of Hölderlin's German translation of Sophocles' *Antigone*.[1] Their *Antigone* was staged twice, the space of the first production was vertical, the second horizontal. The minimalism of the stage in these productions directed the spectators to the conflict between the text and the physical presence, between words and bodies. Hence they avoided giving in to spectacular beauty, emotion, and pathos. Lacoue-Labarthe prefers the term 'scene' to 'theatre' since it refers more to the space of a sheer exposition and appearing than to the spectacle of visuality.

Lacoue-Labarthe tells that he translated from German and not from Greek, so he translated it as if the tragedy were Hölderlin's poem. The translation was accompanied by his philosophical essay, 'La césura du spéculatif.' Also, Hölderlin had accompanied his translations with philosophical notes. This shows that tragedy and philosophy belong together. No wonder Lacoue-Labarthe considers the philosophy of tragedy to be the poetics of tragedy, a commentary on Aristotle, and a theory of a tragical effect. In fact, for Aristotle mimetic performance, the presentation of tragedy, is philosophical as it includes knowledge about the human being, action, ethical dilemmas, and world. Theatre makes you think. As a result of working with *Antigone*, Lacoue-Labarthe's work begins to shift from visual presentation to the space of spacing.[2]

Sarah Kofman was in the audience of the first staging. In her text, 'L'espace de la césura,' she writes how she encountered simultaneously a performance, a translation, and an essay. She begins her text, as one begins a theatrical experience, by considering the rituals and conventions of entering the theatre and the building dedicated to the theatre. These practices are necessary for the effect of catharsis. Entering is a step beyond, since in theatre 'we are able to "forget" our everyday concerns.'[3] From Aristotle onwards philosophers have affirmed the cathartic function of theatre, but they have not seen philosophy as having a similar function or understood speculative processes and the logic of dialectics as based on the model of tragedy.

Kofman went to see the play not in the national theatre but in a disused arsenal, the ruins of a military building earmarked for demolition. Empty buildings, ramshackle roof, broken windows, charred logs—what is today so familiar among independent theatres. To reach the auditorium, she must walk up tottering stairs leaning on shaky railings. For her, entering theatre is a metaphor for our frailty, our constant threat of breaking down.

She enters the attic and immediately faces a soldier's corpse lying among the trash and waste. From the audience two women enter the stage. Antigone tells Ismene about her decision to bury her brother who is beyond the law (*hors-la-loi*). Kofman notes that in spite of everything we are in theatre, not in a theatre that is opened onto an abyss in which Antigone proceeds to be isolated in the infinite darkness of the tomb. If she had been so lucky, Kofman adds, to get a front row seat, her feet would have hung over an empty space. The place makes her feel dizzy. For Kofman, a theatre space deconstructs the classical theatre and its conventions. She undergoes a radical experience of theatre, its rituals, effects, and space being dislocated in the ruined arsenal and in the presentation of Strasbourg's *Antigone*.

Sitting among other spectators, Kofman, still feeling dizzy, witnesses how the presentation is interrupted, disrupted, and the play is displaced. The representation is broken in this threatening space, where death kicks about and one cannot survive by dialectical sublimation. 'You are in hell,' in a chthonic, mineral, and nightly world, the world of Antigone without exit.[4] Kofman feels there is no chance for an Apollonian resurrection that would fill or veil the Dionysian void. The theatre experience becomes a reminder for Kofman, whose father was murdered in a concentration camp and who herself was saved by hiding, of 'Anne Frank, all those Jewish women, who were forced to hide, to live in secrecy to survive through the hellish night.' She writes, 'the Greek tragedy translated in this way still touches you.'[5]

The play is both an ancient and a modern tragedy, which neither invents new forms nor restores Sophocles' tragedy as such. On the stage, one encounters three languages, three rhythms, three epochs. The actors are dressed in eighteenth century costumes, the chorus signs in French, the tape plays a mixture of German and Greek readings of tragedy. Kofman 'confronts an infinite distance that separates Hölderlin from the

Greeks and which also distance ourselves from Hölderlin.'[6] This double translation of tragedy expresses the untranslability that is included in all translations. This is the tragedy of separation and distance touching Hölderlin, Kofman, and us.

The crucial element of the play that touches Kofman is caesura and its effect on catharsis. Even if the cathartic idea still defines theatre and dialectics, 'for now, theatre does not produce catharsis by the means of speculation or spectacularism but by the catharsis of the speculative itself due to caesura.'[7] The theatre space, the translations, and the events on the stage causes caesura, which interrupts speculation and dialectics. Everything is designed so that there is no hope of reconciliation.

'The entrance of Theresia is a moment of caesura, the moment of the deferral of the dialectical process.'[8] At this moment a manic position is turned into a depressive one. Before his entrance, the stage was dominated by self-confident behaviour as Creon goes around as a victorious sovereign above the law and limits, setting decrees and imposing penalties. After the caesura, the mood on the stage is one of silence, separation and loneliness marked by limits, finitude, death, and human fragility. The overall view Kofman has is that the mimetic structure of tragedy no longer guarantees a return to the same since the dialectical logic is interrupted and taken apart. Kofman finishes her notes by saying that Hölderlin disentangles the work of mourning (*Trauerarbeit*) and, as a consequence, reaches the play of mourning (*Trauerspiel*). Her experience is affirmed by Lacoue-Labarthe in his essay as he concludes that Hölderlin interrupts the speculative, to which I will come back later.[9]

Deconstructing Figures

For Lacoue-Labarthe, theatre matters and is therefore critical of both Heidegger and Lacan. To understand the ethics of tragedy, we have to take this criticism seriously. The ethics of tragedy could easily remain another version of philosophical ethics if it ignored tragedy as theatre. Tragedy may be seen as divided between its orientation towards a theatrical experience—shared vision and immanent thought—and the truth, which is the task of philosophy to extract. In the latter case, philosophy is summoned to discern the truth that is encrypted in tragedy and in its figures. The inevitable result is that philosophy reads its own truths in tragedy.[10]

Lacoue-Labarthe cannot accept Heidegger's description of tragedy as follows: 'Nothing is staged or displayed theatrically, but the battle of the new gods against the old is being fought.'[11] For Heidegger, tragedy is just a place where the truth of the subject or being of beings comes forth. Lacoue-Labarthe is astonished how violently Heidegger criticizes the notion of mimesis, which repeats Plato's condemnation of mimesis even though Heidegger is against Plato in his immense admiration of tragedy. This paradox is explained by the fact that for Heidegger, Greek tragedy is not theatre, theatrical performance, production, the presentation on stage, or the *mise-en-scène*.[12] The strength of theatre is exactly this indirect presentation. It does not say directly what one should do, what the limits are, how one should measure, or what the content of ethics is. It 'presents (*montre*), it exhibits, but it does not demonstrate (*dèmontre*).'[13]

It is the figure of Antigone that interests Lacan, not tragedy itself. Moreover, Lacan avoids the theatre, or more properly, the spectacle as if mimesis would be reduced to the mere act of representation. Lacoue-Labarthe taunts: 'Like practically all philosophers, Heidegger included, Lacan disdains theatre.'[14] The chorus takes charge of the emotions and provides commentary for the spectators. But we cannot avoid the fact that tragedy is theatre.

Like Heidegger, Lacan sees Antigone—or more properly her desire—as 'a triumph of being-towards-death' as she is directed towards *das Ding* that cannot be articulated in the system of signifiers.[15] For both Lacan and Heidegger, Antigone presents the truth of the subject. Tragedy deals with the groundless nothingness of human existence. Antigone is the one who faces this nothingness so only Antigone matters in the play. The other figures are mere ornaments. By affirming the priority of Antigone and considering her as a sole tragic hero, Heidegger and Lacan risk ignoring the plot, the imitation of action, the composition of events, the exposition of interconnected deeds done, paths taken, and fates experienced; all from which, according to Aristotle, tragedy receives its form.[16]

Antigone does not merely arouse our admiration, she also fascinates us. Yet we should not be dazzled by her lustre, lest we miss tragedy. Otherwise, we are led to overemphasizing Antigone as the embodiment of pure ethics. The risk is that we absolutize ethics or turn it into the uncritical praise of a heroic ethics. Stavrakakis insists that we turn from the figure of the hero to the tragedian, Sophocles, and tragedy as a genre and social institution that stages 'again and again the suspension of the socio-symbolic order' and permits 'a thorough self-reflection on the political order of the city and its moral foundations.'[17] The writer and tragedy reproduces ethics and democratic society through aesthetical, ethical, and political acts that re-think the ethical and political premises, institutions, and practices of society.

Another risk is that we turn Antigone into a heroic figure, like the proletariat (Lenin), the worker or the soldier (Heidegger 1935–6), the superman (Nietzsche), or Oedipus (Freud). This kind of figuration may easily turn into a new mythology, into the foundation on which political mythologization is built.

What is more, blinded by the shining heroism of Antigone, we do not see other figures of tragedy. Ismene is considered an apolitical and pre-political figure, whose acts are in conformity with traditions and conventions. She seems to not question the position she has in the established distribution of the sensible. However, her disagreement with Antigone and her demands about taking responsibility for the crime challenges the position where she is thought to be condemned to silence and invisibility. Antigone, Honig writes, 'plots and conspires with her sister.'[18] If we do not see Ismene, we continue her exclusion and this turns into accepting an exclusion in the thinking of tragedy, which is a turning away from the ethical.

I have attempted to show that the ethics of tragedy cannot be reduced to the ethics of the supreme good/goods or categorical imperatives/duties. The underlying question has been the possibility of limits, measures and measurement itself in the capitalist scientific, technological, disciplinary, and managerial world that has increasingly freed itself from all limitations.

The ethics of tragedy does not offer tragic heroes as an ethical model for us to follow. We do not simple identify with, let's say, the figure of Antigone, which would ultimately mean to follow her to death. There is in tragic plays, in theatre, a force that deconstructs the logic of modelling. Instead, tragic figures show us positions that could be our own in relation to truth. Because of deconstructive distancing, this prevents imaginary identification and forces us to confront our own position through symbolic identification marked by distance, separation, and lack. Also in this sense, tragedy interrupts unlimited identification.

Antigone is 'the incarnation of the very essence of the tragedy' and a centre of it, but an '"eccentric" one—a kind of pivot, we might say, which is impossible to centre—around which gravitate, though with difficulty.'[19] To proceed in thinking of the ethical in tragedy, I concentrate on this pivotal figure that thwarts and impedes our attempts to think philosophically her position in relation to the ethics of tragedy. In other words, as we proceed in our thinking, we cannot do without recognizing that as a centre she is always already displaced and displaces us in relation to her and tragedy. Otherwise, we either turn around her lustrous figure without pause, or pause to engage in a speculative (Hegelian) resolution. Let us see if this makes any sense.

First, the Greek term *theatron* refers to a place of and for seeing, a space for appearance. Theatre is not so much a space for tragedy, where the figuration of the figure takes place, but more about the spacing of a decision, action and judgment in the proximity to the tragic conflict. The tragic presentation, or the presencing of the tragic in the spacing of tragedy, opens a space for the ethical. Hence, the ethical is a taking place in the presencing of tragedy. In other words, tragedy leaves aside all representational images and transcendental ideas of goods and values as its spacing gives space to ethics and the spacing of ethics. That is, the theatre puts at the stage an ethics.

Second, we ought to go beyond Hegel, who reduced *Antigone* to a tragic conflict between Creon and Antigone.

Even if we distance ourselves from these two equally and reciprocally antagonistic ethical orders and powers by affirming Antigone as the true figure of ethics, we may marginalize or even ignore the tragic conflict, which is the essence of tragedy.

We have to keep in mind that the mechanism of tragedy is aesthetic, and its effect is ethical. The ethical effect 'consists in a change to the way we view ethical conflicts.'[20] Christoph Menke does not consider tragedy as a conflict where the opposing parties excluded one another. Due to the aesthetic mechanism, one position asserts itself by asserting its opposite position. This co-position means that the conflict cannot be resolved, since resolving it would entail the self-dissolution of the conflicting positions.[21]

Third, only non-action can guarantee innocence. In Hegel's scheme action and innocence exclude each other. However, innocence has nothing to do with ethics. The ethical dilemma requires an answer. The answer in itself is not enough. Ethics requires action. Antigone's answer and action make her an ethical figure. So far so good, for Hegel. Her ethical act, which incorporates desire, is what disrupts and even destroys not merely Creon's regime but also the Hegelian dialectical logic. Antigone enacts limits to sovereign power and any absolute justice based on philosophical speculation. Antigone presents how an ethical act may interrupt the authority of government and philosophy.

The ethics of tragedy must recognize what Hegel taught us about tragedy: a tragic conflict and an action are essential elements of tragedy.

The third fundamental element of the ethics of tragedy is caesura.

Interruptive Silence

Let us come now back to the concept of caesura. Lacoue-Labarthe's notion 'the caesura of speculative' (*la césure du spéculatif*) refers to the speculative movement of tragedy as a work that is interrupted.[22] A caesura is the interruption of the promise of resolution, speculative dialectics and *Aufhebung*. It is related to measure and measuring.

It is worth repeating here the quote that Antigone is 'the incarnation of the very essence of the tragedy' and a centre of it, 'albeit ... an "eccentric" one—a kind of pivot, we might say, which is impossible to center.'[23]

Hölderlin was an inventor of speculative idealism, modelling it on ancient tragedy. He shared with Hegel the idea of the work of art as the sensible presentation (*Darstellung*) of an ideal content, the Absolute. The idea was based on Friedrich Schelling's *Letters on Dogmatism and Criticism*. It dictated that in its essence, tragedy is a metaphor for intellectual intuition. As discussed, tragedy reconciles reason and necessity, from which the tragic hero is liberated as he freely accepts the punishment from the crime he has not committed and thus affirms his inalienable freedom. In Lacanian vocabulary we could say this that tragedy presents the tragic hero as situated in a transmissible and transindividual symbolic structure, which depends on language that is her fate. In spite of this, the tragic hero affirms her irreducibility as she accepts the consequences when she proceeds towards the unsymbolizable Real, the void that escapes symbolic determinations.

'The theory put forward in Hölderlin ... *is*, through and through, speculative,' claims Lacoue-Labarthe, but adds that it 'dislocates *from within* the speculative.'[24] Something prohibits, immobilizes, distends, and suspends it so that it is prevented from completing itself. Lacoue-Labarthe calls this Hölderlin's movement of regression.[25] In other words, Hölderlin distances himself (*démarque*) from speculative idealism, which is both a mark (*marque*) about it and its remarking (*remarque*), that is, speculative idealism is deconstituted the moment it arises as a system.[26] Tragedy exposes a speculative affirmation and its destruction.

Empedocles was Hölderlin's attempt to write a modern tragedy, where the conflict between nature and culture would be reconciled. In the first version, Empedocles is the figure of a speculative desire. He is nostalgic for the One-Whole and wishes to escape limitations and finitude.[27] His monologue is nothing but a justification of a speculative suicide. Hölderlin failed. There were four reasons for the failure. First, Hölderlin had only an idea about tragedy based on speculative idealism. He thought that the subject and the object could be reconciled but this is possible only as an aesthetic phenomenon taking place in the art that presents the speculative unity of life, as Hölderlin wrote in a letter to Schiller on 4 September 1795.[28] Second, Empedocles was a philosopher-king (*basileus*) in a mere speculative scenario, where everything remains monology and a political-metaphysical demonstration. There was no tragic composition, plot, and conflict. It was not tragedy but a lyric drama or oratorio without music. Third, Hölderlin followed the platonic interpretation of mimesis as a dramatic dictation, so that everything is said in an indirect way from the perspective of the dramatic poet. Hölderlin's difficulty was how the infinite enthusiasm (*die unendliche Begeisterung*), which was suffocating and blasphemous, could express itself in a tragic poem. His enthusiasm resembles the *hubris*, immoderation, and transgression of a tragic hero. The poet or thinker or philosopher cannot himself become a tragic figure. Finally and perhaps this is the most dramatic fault, there was a lack of theatre in the play. Therein lies his impasse: 'How to construct a theatrical drama from the mere representation of the destiny of poetic creation?'[29]

In the second version, Hölderlin re-organizes the play so that it shows speculative desire as a fault.[30] The plot now becomes more tragic. Besides this turn to tragedy, Lacoue-Labarthe recognizes another transition. Empedocles is set on an Oedipus scenario, that is, his fault is that he publicly declare himself as divine in the front of Agrigentine people.[31] The philosophical transgression in the first version becomes a political and religious transgression in the second version. His lack of measure is considered to be the cause of the plague ravaging the city. Hence, Empedocles is exiled as *pharmakos*, as poison and cure. This amounts to a return to Sophocles. He started to write a third version, but abandoned it.[32] Instead, he wrote an essay, 'Der Grund zum Empedocles.'[33]

What was failure to Hölderlin turned out to be luck, at least for us. He turned to theatre by moving to Sophocles' *Oedipus the King* and *Antigone*. His choice came from Aristotle, who used them as examples of *tekhnē tragikē*.[34] In his dialogue with Sophocles' tragedy, Hölderlin deconstructs the speculative-tragical matrix and his own previous thought.

His work on tragedy allowed him to distance himself from the principle of reconciliation in the Absolute. In contrast to the 'optimistic' dialectic-speculative tragedy, Hölderlin considers that a tragic figure falls further the more he attempts to rise. This fate is crystallized by Latin *altus*, which means both 'high' and 'deep.' The speculative is interrupted by the caesura, *'that which in metre is called caesura (Cäsur)*, the pure word.'³⁵ To clarify what Hölderlin means, let's have a look how caesura, which in Latin means 'cutting,' functions in poetry and music. Caesura is a break or cut—a comma, a tick, two slashed lines //—in a verse where one phrase ends and the next phrase begins.

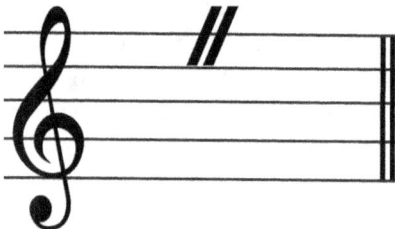

Caesura is a breath, a silent pause, a juncture. It may be silence in no time at all or a full pause. In classical Greek poetry it means a juncture between words, a natural break that separates the line in two. As an example, the opening line of *Iliad*: 'Sing, O goddess || the anger of Achilles son of Peleus (μῆνιν ἄειδε θεὰ || Πηληϊάδεω Ἀχιλῆος).'³⁶

The speculative idealism is cut. As a consequence, Hölderlin's thought can be thus considered to be radically tragic. 'The thinking of negativity allows him to articulate a way of thinking the essence of tragedy in a way that no one had done before.'³⁷ This is crucial for our understanding of the ethics of tragedy, so let us read closely Hölderlin's notes on *Antigone*. What comes next explains Hegel's icy silence in his *Phenomenology of Spirit* that came out only a year after Hölderlin's notes and translations of Sophocles. He does not mention Hölderlin, even if his understanding of tragedy, which we have dealt with, should be re-read as a comment on and rectification of Hölderlin's views. Hence, the interruption precedes the speculative reconciliation.

Hölderlin separates his translations from Hegel's theory of tragedy as he, a poet, a theoretician, and a dramatist, experienced and tested 'a new kind of dramatic writing ... which is, as he himself ... said "modern".' He even 'runs out of breath in his search for a dialectical and speculative construction,' or even a philosophical system formulation. This is because Hölderlin poses not only philosophical questions in another way, he poses the question of another way to approach questions. He thinks as a poet more than as a philosopher, which means that he is not interested in building systems but touching upon 'an absolute point of exactitude,' or having it in his sight. He does not assemble the elements of the truth of an articulated totality of tragedy. Instead of synthesis, which is the object of the philosopher, his object as a poet is synopsis. Instead of an operation demanding time and deliberation, he focuses on apprehension demanding 'the temporal space of sighting and an aiming.'[38]

Hölderlin realizes that Empedocles's desire to escape determination and the law of succession is the desire to escape finitude unto death. What Hölderlin stresses in his Sophocles translations is the ethical demand to reverse a striving form this world to the other into a striving from another world to this world.[39] The limits must be acknowledged. For Hölderlin, the lesson of tragedy is 'the affirmation of a law, which is the interdiction of transgression,' a law that sets a strict limit between the human and divine order, that is, the interdiction of divine.[40] Dastur reminds us that evil is the *hubris* of the transgression of the limits of human finitude, which leads to 'the madness of the modern man which is nothing else but the desire of absolute knowledge and domination upon earth.'[41] Hölderlin warned of this as he spoke of the categorical reversal of the human being towards the earth and the endurance of the separation. Antigone, however, attempts to transgress this law, but only through her crime a limit appears as the limit.

Hölderlin no longer attempts to make a tragic figure the hero of philosophy or make tragedy a philosophical drama. He turns away from this kind of 'persistent tradition of philosophical heroisation,' which stretches from Schelling to Heidegger via Hegel and Nietzsche, and beyond.[42]

Antitheos

Hölderlin differentiates between *Oedipus the Tyrant*, the more modern tragedy, and *Antigone*, the more Greek tragedy. This difference echoes the concepts of *atheos* (Oedipus) and *antitheos* (Antigone). Let us look first at the more Hesperian tragedy, then the Greek one.

Hölderlin now recognizes one cannot make up a tragic figure without a flaw in the sense of *nefas*, which for Hölderlin refers to *hubris*, crime. The fault of the tragic figure requires that this figure do something prohibited or even transgress the prohibition itself. If in Empedocles the fault was a fine and great 'poetico-speculative and meta-physical' fault in the infinite aspiration to the All-One, now it is fault without grandeur and it becomes a concrete fault, a 'politico-religious' fault.[43]

Also the *hamartia*, the error of appreciation, is by nature politico-religious. Oedipus makes a mistake by considering himself a king *and* a priest. The priest-king makes a mistake in his speculative desire to interpret the words of the oracle too literally. When the oracle proposed that the king should maintain good civil order and establish a severe and precise justice, he interprets these words as a demand to find the guilty person. His error is an intellectual and speculative one. In his overly absolute interpretation, he enters into a sacrificial logic that forgets the difference between earth and heaven, the limits of the sovereign king and the unlimited powers of the divine sphere.

This is our Hesperian destiny; our lot that is finitude. 'The modern *Schicksal*, the lot of the modern, is not as impressive as the Greek one, but it is, as Hölderlin stresses "more profound," because it requires that the limits between humanity and divinity should be maintained and acknowledged.'[44]

For Hölderlin this means only one thing: tyranny. Hölderlin translates the play with this decisive word in mind as *Oedipus der Tyrann* and not *Oedipus the King*. Hölderlin's translation is in line with the Greek title, *Oedipus Tyrannus*, which already constitutes a warning sign for the democratic Athenians. It was a condemnation of tyranny. Lacoue-Labarthe notes that when Hölderlin was translating the play, Napoleon Bonaparte, whom he had admired as a European republican, was increasingly showing traits of *hubris*.[45]

The fault is purified in tragedy. This is what tragedy (re)presents, 'a *katharis* of the fault.'[46] In the case of Oedipus, the catharsis lies in his slow atonement, in his quest for consciousness, wandering as an exile and finally disappearing into the horizon. He does not die consumed in flames like the Oriental Greek heroes. The word Hölderlin uses to describe the language of *Oedipus the Tyrant* is *tödtendfactisch* (fatally factual or spiritual death) for the word kills by overwhelming an enthusiastic spirit.[47] It is the death in exile at the end of *Oedipus at Colonos*. The words spoken are horrible and they kill, but they function killingly rather than causatively resulting in death.

This can be considered, as we saw in the refugee tragedies, as the modern language of refugee policy, administration, and legislation, where the words are mortifyingly factical, which leaves them to very quietly move away from the realm of the living, like Oedipus. Coming back to these tragedies, we could now ask if what is fitting for Antigone is her own native being. As tragedy teaches us, this proper being is always split and divided. As I have already said, we have to understand Antigone as a stranger, a multiple stranger. Her ethical act is her homely place that disagrees with the established public and private spheres. Even in this place she is a stranger. She has become what she is only through a voyage to a foreign place as a refugee. As you will remember, Antigone escorts her father in his exile. Experiencing the foreign makes her ownmost strong and ready in the foreign and familiar.

In the situation where the gods had withdrawn from the world, the only possibility for the Sophoclean hero was to find her/his own way of being-in-right the right way (*zurechtfinden*).[48] Now, we could say that our abode in the world, that is, our *ēthos*, is this tragic necessity to find our own way to be right and to take ethical responsibility in the world we share with others without any transcendental ideas or immanent grounds. For this perspective we could affirm Heidegger's definition of Sophocles' tragedies as preserving the *ēthos* more primordially than Aristotle's lectures on ethics. This may have an ethical sense or at least an ethical tone if we lend our ears to it. Now it is time to wonder what is the ownmost of this strange stranger. What is her *ēthos*?

Antigone is not a passive instrument of fate but an incarnation of the rebel. She embodies Apollonian fire, illegality, aorgy, and formlessness (*unförmlich*) as she rebels against Creon, who incarnates legal universality, organic laws of the *polis*, and the all too formal (*allzuförmlich*).

After Antigone has admitted that she has attempted to bury Polynices, 'I say I did it and do not deny it,' Creon asks Antigone to tell him, if she knew 'of the proclamation (*kērugma*) forbidding this (*tade*)?'[49] Antigone does not shirk her responsibility. She affirms her knowledge not only once but three times: 'I knew it; of course I knew it. It was known to all.'[50] In Hölderlin's translation she even challenges Creon by turning his questions back on him: 'I knew it. How so? It was clear.'[51] Creon is amazed at her arrogant answer: 'And yet you dared to transgress these laws (*nomoi*)?'[52] In Hölderlin, Creon answers this 'how so' with a new question: '*Was wagtest du, ein solch Gesetz zu brechen?*' (How did you dare to break this kind of law?)[53]

Her rebelliousness does not end here. She takes one even more fatal and radical step. Being the figure of *antitheos*, she turns against the gods albeit in a divine sense. She attacks the gods with derisory words and compares herself to the divine when she evokes the destiny of Niobe who once challenged the Olympian gods. She even dares to oppose not merely Creon's Zeus but also Zeus of the *polis*.

Here comes the decisive point concerning Antigone's relationship to law, and even more fundamentally, the sense of her figure in the ethics of tragedy. She answers Creon's question on how she dared to break the law (*nomos, Gesetz*) thus: 'Yes, for it was not Zeus who made this (*tade*) proclamation (*kērugma*), nor was it Justice (Dike) who lives with the gods below that established such laws (*nomoi*) among men.'[54]

First of all, she dismisses Creon's claim that his proclamation was a law, *nomos*. It was just a proclamation, *kērugma*. Second, she speaks about laws, *nomoi*, by which she means the laws of the chthonic gods. These laws do not prohibit burial rituals and they do not give any legitimation to Creon's proclamation. It is an edict without proper legitimacy. Third, it seems clear that Antigone speaks of Creon's 'law' as she defines it as law that was not given by Zeus. This (*tade*) law that prohibited the burial was not dictated by Zeus. Neither was it dictated by Dike. This law is merely Creon's proclamation without any divine legitimacy or ground.

The third point is problematic, even if Hugh Lloyd-Jones's translation seems to confirm it. Perhaps Creon hears it in this way. But 'it was not Zeus who made this' (*ou gar ti moi Zeus ēn ho kēruxas tade*) is ambiguous. We should not miss this ambiguity.

If it has already become clear in the argumentation between Antigone and Creon that Creon's law is not based on Zeus but is a proclamation dictated by Creon, why would Antigone repeat this? Hölderlin's translation of Antigone's reply to Creon is as follows. *Darum. Mein Zeus berichtete mirs nicht.* 'Because. *My* Zeus did not dictate to me.'[55] Antigone continues, '*Noch hier im Haus das Recht der Todesgötter. Die unter Menschen das Gesetz gegrenzet.*' ('Nor here in the law court of the gods of death, who under men constrains the law.')

Hölderlin's translation brings forth three crucial points.

1) A defiant Antigone claims that the lawgiver is *her* Zeus. She knows very well what the valid laws are, since she knows *her* Zeus. Antigone claims to have personal knowledge about gods and has a relationship to them. Antigone is not only speaking for divine laws but with gods themselves. She actually identifies with them. She compares her fate to that of Niobe, who 'died the saddest death ... and with her ever-weeping eyes she soaks the mountain ridges,' hence, 'very like her am I, as the god sends me to sleep.'[56] The chorus is upset: 'But she was a goddess and the child of gods, and we are mortal and the children of mortals.'[57] She makes a big issue of being—and always going to be—a virgin by which she compares herself to Pallas Athena, the virgin herself.[58] Not only god-like, she also becomes an oracle. Only Teiresias has the authority to interpret the mysterious signs of the gods and to declare what the gods want. However, Antigone goes beyond her limits as she claims to have knowledge about the god's wishes, decrees, and laws. She claims to be able to understand the sense of unwritten normative truths. She dares to speak from the same position as Teiresias as if they both share the knowledge of the unwritten truth that materializes in traces traceable only for these two seers.

2) A few lines before Antigone's defiant answer, Creon speaks explicitly of Antigone's act as *tade*: 'do you admit, or do you deny, that you have done this (*tade*)?'[59] He refers to her deed forbidden by Creon's law. What if, and against the prevailing interpretation, Antigone refers by *tade* to the same *tade* about which Creon speaks.[60] Her deed was not conditioned by Zeus. That is, it was not Zeus, who dictated the law requiring the sister to bury her brother. This is how we can understand Hölderlin's translation: Mein *Zeus berichtete mirs nicht.* Zeus did not dictate the law Antigone follows. If so, neither a human nor a divine authority would legitimate Antigone's action and the unwritten law she claims to (re)present. Therefore, Antigone's ethical act would be ungrounded and unconditional, a miraculous break that demonstrates her infidel (*her* law) fidelity (*her* Zeus).

Antigone arrogantly compares herself to gods as she dictates her own unwritten law. This law is the law of the transgressive ethical event, unwritten because it happens as her ethical act and through it. Moreover, this unwritten law is embodied in the figure of Antigone as she acts. She equals this law of the event. As Antigone says that Creon's proclamations are not 'strong enough to have power to overrule, mortal as they were, the unwritten and unfailing ordinances of the gods,' she speaks about her ordinances since she identifies—here and now—with gods.[61] She, as rebellious dust, storm, and bird materializes the law, as we have already shown. Again, she seems strange, monstrous, and unhomely.

3) The border between mortals and immortal that the chorus wishes to guard is challenged by the *Dikē*-like Antigone. Her ultimate transgression takes place on the mortal-immortal border as a border crime. Antigone advances, the chorus signs, 'to the extreme of daring,' or to uttermost and furthest space (*eskhaton*) of courage and boldness (*thrasos*).[62] She seems to transgress the border as she goes to 'the lofty altar of Justice (*Dikē*),' die Höhe des Rechts (the heights of Justice).[63] She identifies with *Dikē* or even becomes the goddess of justice (or conscience [*Gewissen*] as Hölderlin translates *Dikē*). At this moment of her infinite transgression, Antigone becomes equal to the goddess *Dikē*. The chorus cannot be without giving some credit to Antigone. It admits that she is *isotheos*, 'equal to the gods,' 'godlike' which can be said of heroes.⁶⁴

Courage, daring, and boldness; extreme, uttermost, and furthest; godlike anti-god, Athene, and Niobe—all these come together momentarily at the border. It is the time-space that is proper to Antigone, or where/when Antigone becomes what she is and has been. The stranger returns home and becomes even stranger. All this fire cannot be without leading her to *hubris*, to her *nefas*, as she is driven towards the monstrous coupling of the god and human. This is a terrible but holy crime. Her faithful infidelity is to challenge limitlessly Creon as well as the gods or the borders themselves.

At this very moment, something else *must* happen. 'Advancing to the extreme of daring, you stumbled against the lofty altar of Justice, my child!'⁶⁵ Antigone proceeds to the limits, '*Bis auf die Höhe des Rechts / Bist du, o Kind, wohl tiefgefallen* (At the threshold of Justice / she stumbles; [alternatively] at the height of Justice / she falls down).'⁶⁶ With these words, the chorus announces that the law of tragedy requires the categorical turn (*der kategorischen Umkehr*).⁶⁷ At this moment humans and gods communicate in the form of infidelity. The human being 'forgets himself and the gods and turns away, even though in a holy way, but like a traitor.'⁶⁸ At this 'extreme limit of suffering there is nothing but the conditions of time (*Zeit*) or space (*Raum*).'⁶⁹ At this very moment Antigone's limitless becoming-Dike is purified as a limitless separation. She lives wholly in time, since she is nothing but time at this moment. Both are infidel. Time because it turns categorically so that the beginning and the end cannot match. Antigone because she cannot match her starting point. The fate of Antigone seems to show that the absolute and infinite *dikē* (justice), is impossible for mortal and finite beings. Our destiny is to endure and suffer mourning for the divine, and I would add, for absolute justice.

Too often Ismene's role and words are ignored. Their argumentation in the beginning of the play is read so that Ismene is considered the embodiment of a traditional woman, whose proper place is the home and privacy. As she affirms her secondary role in the *polis*, she functions as a loudspeaker that makes Antigone's voice and presence even more heroic and more committed to the duty and the deed. Ismene affirms or doubts this by saying: 'If you have strength!'⁷⁰ Immediately after this comes one of the crucial lines in the play as Ismene continues, 'But you desire what is impossible (*amēkhanos*).'⁷¹

Law of Tragedy

The law of tragedy: Justice does not exist, or more properly, for finite beings justice is always already impossible to know, grasp, and legalize since it is always withdrawn at the very moment of its appearing. If justice is, it is merely in the constant movement of unconcealment/concealment. However, this does not mean that the tragic hero should stop the moment Ismene warns her 'to hunt for what is impossible.'[72] Quite the contrary, tragedy throws the tragic hero into the hunt for the non-negotiable, unconditional, ungraspable, hyperbolic justice beyond moral and legal norms, beyond legitimacy and legality.

In 'tragedy *justice is conflict* ... a fight between opposed parties who are prepared to act violently in its name.'[73] Peter Szondi identifies the tragic with the dialectic, which has its source in the philosophical thinking of tragedy and in the experience of the rhythm of union and dissolution.[74] If for Szondi, 'the tragic is a dialectical modality, a mode of experience, which is specifically the experience of the self-constitution and self-division of ethical life,' for Critchley it is 'a dialectical modality of negation, where things fall apart, are rent and sundered.'[75] The tragic does not necessarily allow for the 'higher reconciliation of the opposed forces that make up ethical life.'[76] Tragedy 'reveals the wounds of spirit that will not heal, but that fester and become infected.'[77]

Critchley's view is connected to the birth of tragedy, both historically and logically, as a result of certain absence and lack—the withdrawal of gods and transcendent truths. Hölderlin stresses infidelity (*treulos*) in his translation of *Antigone*. There is an infidelity between gods and human beings, or more properly, a tension between fidelity and infidelity. Antigone's transgression forces the gods to depart. This opens a social, political, and ethical space for disagreements and truth processes as well as infidelity and a new kind of fidelity. The tragic figures exist in a space between freedom and necessity, autonomy, and heteronomy. 'Action is not causally determined by necessity, nor is it free,' that is, in the 'free, volitional action there is an experience of being acted upon by ... a transgenerational curse.'[78] Tragedy 'gives us a genealogy of who we are, an account of our origins and how the curse of the past can unknowingly take shape in the present, and we don't see it and we rage when we are told what it is.'[79] Tragedy is about 'how in acting, we are acted upon, and how that being acted upon can and does convert to a certain action that takes place in our own name.'[80] Then again, the experience of being acted upon may be caused by an ethical duty and the fidelity to this duty. In fact, Antigone's fidelity is a combination of curse and duty, prophesy and fidelity, which she make her own fate. However, her transgressive *hubris* based on ethical conviction is blinded by neither curse nor anger, which she experiences because of the wrong done to her brother. She turns the curse and anger into power. Her transgression is considered impossible but through her act she converts this impossibility into a possibility of the impossible.[81]

Antigone's being-right is to be understood as this reaching towards the impossible *dikē*. In tragedy this inevitably leads her to *adikia* (injustice), which one cannot separate from *dikē*. *Dikē/adikia* is the destiny of being-right of the figure of *antitheos*. This explains also why Antigone is *hypsipolis/apolis* in the sense Heidegger gave it.

Antigone herself is the poetic accomplishment of being-in-right. Nevertheless, Hölderlin's categorical turn reminds us that finite being turns away from the infinite, from the Goddess Dike. We must suffer the withdrawal of justice and simultaneously desire impossible justice through, but also beyond, right and law. Justice hence unfolds as the finite accomplishment of the singular. One stumbles in her or his singular way from the high pedestal of Dike. The tragedy of justice is present for us only as a deconstruction of the tragedy of justice.

Even though she does not transgress the border, the god appears at this limit space and situation, which turns into a liminal stage. However, the god is present only as the figure of death. Oedipus was sent back to earth to wander in exile. Antigone as a more Greek tragic hero is annihilated. Tragedy and its words are murderous.

In a tragedy the god communicates merely as death, which is the only tragic figure of the infinity of the god. In tragedy, it is not enough that the god presents itself as the facticity of death (execution). This facticity must be turned into a word, which creates a sensible relation to the death. Antigone is confronted as a mark of the presence of death, Oedipus as the absence of death.

In the case of Antigone, the fault is the madness of enthusiasm in the monstrous (*ungeheur*) coupling with the god. Her error is to oppose *her* Zeus, 'not to that of Creon, but to the Zeus of the City, to the legal Zeus, under whose authority Creon "too formally" places himself.'[82] Her fault is to compare herself to or even identify with the divine. Her descent into the tomb reminds us of the destiny of Niobe. Niobe was turned into a stone; Antigone is to be imprisoned into stone. Antigone's fate is not to become inorganic but aorgic.

Her *hubris* is mania, a furious passion, a divine madness, the infidelity of transgression with a divine origin that transcends the common existence, and the human and divine authority. She commits the crime of crossing the border. This transgression leads to the horrible thing, the pairing of the god and the human being. Here we see that *hubris* (crime or tragic fault), and *hamartia* (error and disdain) are connected. Antigone's *nefas*, the combination of sacrilege and holy crime, is that as *antitheos* she bends with the weight of her law/desire/being—as if Brecht had materialized these ideas without weight with his heavy door attached to Antigone's back—towards and beyond the border and limit.

The terrible and monstrous thing, the coupling of god and men, becomes conceivable when this limitless fusion is purified in the limitless separation. The desire for the infinite and for divinity is presented in tragedy as finitude and separation. 'The striving from one world to the other' has to be reversed into 'a striving from another world to this one.' In *Antigone*, the catharsis takes place as the god and the human being are separated. This for Hölderlin is the issue (*Sache*) of the tragic representation—a catharsis as a purifying separation. The catharsis now takes place not among the spectators or in the tragic figures, but on the stage.

Let me add that, at the same time, the ethical catharsis interrupts the process of the figuration of the tragic hero, which hinders our identification with this interrupted figure. This is not without effects in respect of the ethical catharsis among the audience. We have to follow the trajectory of the tragic hero in a (double) movement of separation. First, we recognize and affirm the categorical turn of the hero. Second, we cannot be without a turning away from the tragic hero back to our own world. Thus, the ethical catharsis that takes place on stage is fundamental and may cause the catharsis that takes place in the audience.

Back to Hölderlin and his crucial point. To understand the ethics of tragedy as the combination of caesura and catharsis, we must listen carefully to what Hölderlin writes in one particular sentence. Everything relevant to the point of the categorical turn or reversal is already contained therein:

> The presentation of tragedy is mainly based on the monstrous—how the god and the man couple, and how natural force and the innermost of the man become without limits one in wrath—being grasped so that the boundless pairing is purified through the boundless separation.[83]

As previously stated, Antigone may have identified herself with Pallas

Athene and in fact they share the same fate at the border. Both humans and gods have to follow the law of the categorical turn. As Hölderlin writes, 'the limitless becoming one (*gränzenlose Eineswerden*) purifies itself through the limitless separation (*gränzenloses Scheiden*).'[84] A marble relief of *Pensive Athena* of around 460 BCE in the Acropolis Museum confirms the central idea of Hölderlin's understanding of tragedy (see fig. 2).[85]

In the relief, the meditative and longing, even sorrowful Goddess is standing in front of a stone stele. It may be a boundary stone for Athena's sanctuary, a catalogue of treasures or men who have fallen in battle. What is clear is that it is a boundary stone. She leans head inclined forward. The spearhead points to the border line. She cannot proceed further. Athena is forced to turn back as was Antigone. In this relief we see a double image of Athena and Antigone, both under the law of tragedy.

What tragedy presents is the catharsis of *hubris*. For Hölderlin, catharsis does not have the functional dimension it has for Aristotle. Instead it serves to purify the tragic pathos. Catharsis is transferred from the spectators to the stage. It ensues from mimesis. Lacoue-Labarthe explains that the catharsis is not an effect of the theatrical performance but an interior result of the performance itself. Tragedy (re)presents the purification of the immediate unity with god as the god's categorical turn. This is the law of tragedy. The categorical—that is, Kantian and thus unconditional—turn establishes the law, the law of critique that separates. This law appears as the gods withdraw, which is the law of withdrawal, the law of the finite and mediacy.[86] Tragedy is 'the presentation of the law.'[87]

This is what may be called Hölderlin's hyperbolic logic: the alternation of appropriation and disappropriation; the excess of presence and the excess of loss; the closer it is, the more distant it is; the more adequate, the more dissimilar; the more interior, the more exterior.[88] Here Hölderlin's 'excess of the speculative switches into the very excess of submission to finitude.'

This is a matter of catharsis, even a general theory of catharsis. This theory of catharsis distances itself from Aristotle's catharsis, which has its effect in the sphere of a spectacular relation. Moreover, it turns away from Hegelian catharsis, if there is such a thing, which takes place at the level of the destruction of tragic heroes as a way to purify conflictual separation. Hölderlin's catharsis is related to the tragic utterance or trajectory. The more tragedy is related to the speculative drive for infinite limitlessness and sameness, the more tragedy presents itself as finitude, separation, and differentiation. Tragedy 'is the catharsis of the speculative,' which is at the

Fig. 2: Pensive Athena

same time catharsis of the religious and sacrificial.[89] In this way Hölderlin signalled a caesura of the speculative process.

The gods are present in *Antigone*, but in the form of death. Antigone is *antitheos*, a counter-divine. As she confronts death, the tragic purification is violent and brutal, a Greek one. The Greek tragic word is *tödlichfactisch* (deadly-factual or actual death) for the body it seizes kills and is killed.[90] The hero is annihilated unlike Oedipus who is doomed to suffer in exile, in a living death that is the presentiment of the lack of destiny (*moira*) of all of us, our modern fatelessness (*Schicksallose*). For Hölderlin, tragedy interrupts the desire to become infinite and immortal by establishing the law of the limit that turns the tragic hero either to immediate death or back to earth to await death.

Tragedy has for Hölderlin a radical dialogical form, that is, a form of an unresolvable tragic conflict. The truth of tragedy lies not in a resolution of oppositions and disagreements, which it does not even produce, but in the conflict. Hölderlin differentiates between tragic and epic poems. In epic poetry, acts and events follow each other. In contrast, tragic poetry presents no pure sequence, since the tragic poem is 'more a matter of balance (*Gleichgewicht*) than succession (*Aufeinanderfolge*).'[91] It should not be understood as a speculative resolution of the tragic conflict. 'For the tragic transport (*der tragische Transport*) is empty and the most unbounded.'[92] The transport is incalculable and as such it differs from the calculable element in tragedy, that is, the composition of a particular play.

Here we come back to the caesura, a counter-rhythmic interpretation, a pure word. It appears in the rhythmic succession of conflicting representations, that is, the conflicting and opposing views of the tragic figures, and their constant alteration. For us, to be able to confront the whirlwind of these rhythmic changes at their crowning point, the caesura must be introduced. The caesura interrupts the change of views. The tragic transport is empty, which is to say: the purification of the transport in the unlimited separation of the unlimited pairing. What appears after the caesura is no longer the change of views but viewing itself. For Hölderlin, this empty point is the place of catharsis.

According to Hölderlin, in both *Oedipus der Tyrann* and *Antigone*, it is Teiresias whose words form the caesura. His speech turns around the play from speculative desire or divine pathos to separation and infinity. The caesura, which forms the balance of these two tragedies, appears in them in different stages.

In *Antigone*, the caesura inclines the balance towards the end since the first parts of the play consists of intensive conflicts and rhythm. It is as if the end should be protected by the caesura from the hectic beginning. This is the calculable law of tragedy.[93] The blind oracle enters led by a boy immediately after Antigone is led away once and for all. We do not see her anymore but now it has become a time to pay the price for all this. Teiresias has come to tell Creon that the birds—is Antigone among them?—are screeching in a dire and incoherent frenzy. The sacrificial rites have failed. 'And it is your will that has put this plague upon the city ... and the gods are no longer accepting the prayers.'[94]

In *Oedipus the Tyrannos* the calculable law is the opposite. The balance is inclined towards the beginning. Later events are more frantic and thus the beginning must be protected from the end.[95] Again led by a boy, Teiresias meets Oedipus. He tells, 'the man you have been looking for, that man is here!'[96]

These words are the points of caesura, which, as already said, change the rhythm of the play. Before the caesura, there is the conflictual change of representation (*der Wechsel der Vorstellung*), afterwards there is the representation (*Vorstellung*) in itself.[97] The oracle steps into the course of fate as he watches over the force of nature that wrenches the human from the sphere of life and throws him into the sphere of the dead.[98]

In the end of his notes to Oedipus, Hölderlin argues that both Oedipus in *Oedipus der Tyrann* and Haemon in *Antigone* have to go through the categorical turn.[99] Is there a mistake? What has Haemon to do with this turn? The answer is found in the notes on Antigone. 'The form of reason, which is developing here tragically, is political, more exactly republican.'[100] The republican reason is what brings balance between Antigone and Creon. It is Haemon who marks this balance and a categorical turn from tyrants and tragic heroes towards the republican form of the political. In *Rhetoric*, Aristotle refers to Haemon's argumentative speech twice. First, it is a description (*diegēsis*) of the past events, which includes arguments that answer to the expectations of the addressee.[101] Secondly, Haemon speaks to his father as if someone else—the people—were talking.[102] Hölderlin understands these hints and turns *Antigone* into a republican tragedy, while Oedipus was about tyranny.

According to Esa Kirkkopelto, the political conclusion of Hölderlin's *Antigone* is the subversion of tyranny and the republican turn, which does not remain 'merely' a double reversal of humans and gods. The patriotic turn is also presented as a real revolution and a political change. The rebellion begins when Antigone denies the tyrant's exclusive right to define laws and legitimate gods by derisively saying to him 'my Zeus.' This subversive moment runs through to modern times, when political reason means that everyone has equally their own gods.[103]

After having affirmed his loyalty to the king and the father, Haemon turns against both of these authoritative figures. He has heard citizens lamenting Antigone, disagreeing with the justification for the punishment, and considering that instead she should be praised. As Creon turns against the people by saying, 'Is the city to tell me what orders I shall give?' Haemon answers that 'there is no city that belongs to a single man'—but he feels concern for his father, who 'would be a fine ruler over a deserted city!'[104] As Creon attempts to silence him as a father, Haemon resists by continuing to speak using political and ethical vocabulary: 'I see that you are offending against justice (*dikē*)!'[105]

The echo of Haemon's words are heard in Sophocles' *Phaedra* as Theseus denounces Hippolytus' treachery, 'For no city can ever be safe in which justice and virtue are trampled underfoot, and a smooth-tongued speaker villainously takes the goad in his hands and husbands the city.'[106] Even if this is a warning against populist usurpers, who in the end will destroy justice, this functions as a reminder of the limits of sovereign power. Creon fails to measure things properly, especially his own power. As Heraclitus tells: 'The sun will not surpass his measures; if he does the Furies, ministers of justice, will find out.'[107]

Umkehr is not a historical turn in the fate of the people or Hölderlin's reversal from the classical models of art and tragedy towards his homeland.[108] His letter to Böhlendorff must be placed in the context of his Sophocles translations and work on Empedocles. The native reversal evinces the displaced character of any essential identity of the people, of the nature and native as such. First, there is a structural impossibility of a complete return to the native. Instead, the reversal is an endless journey to one's nature. The refugee tragedies present the impossible return to the displaced home. Second, the nature one attempts to reach is not so much the external nature but the inner predilection or tendency driving the people or subjects to be in their proper way, which can be reached through the process of pursuing the foreign and turning back to the native way of being. Thus, what is native to the people is not exterior or interior nature but a response to this double nature. Hölderlin, whose Böhlendorf letter is a response to Kant, denaturalizes nature as an original and stable thing. Nature is the noumenal world of the thing-in-itself, which is unknowable and inaccessible as such, and subjected to the categories of human cognition. That is, the native way of being for the Greeks or for us is not a pre-critical immediate nature but a response and reaction to the native. The access to the national is possible only by a construction. Hölderlin deconstructs the opposition between nature and art, origin and mimesis. Hence, tragedy is not an imitation of an original nature but original mimesis, a self-representation of the Athenians they constructed about themselves, their ethical nature and political community. All in all, Hölderlin situates the Greek tragedy in the mimetic tradition of aesthetic.

Thinking/Measuring

I have claimed that Hölderlin's interpretation of tragedy deconstructs the speculative interpretation of tragedy. Since we have followed Lacoue-Labarthe's interpretation of Hölderlin's interpretation, it is fair to say that for him Hölderlin does not turn away from speculative idealism. However, I would claim that he interrupts the speculative movement in tragedy more radically than Lacoue-Labarthe thinks. Then again tragedy for Hölderlin is 'after all, a catharsis of the speculative.' Separation and catharsis for Hölderlin are not part of the movement of absolute reflection but interruptions of this reflection. I would say that tragedy freed Hölderlin from speculative idealism and gave him the means to limit and set measures for speculative desire. Tragedy turned him into a thinker of limits and borders without him forgetting transgression as an essential element of tragic figures. As a consequence, Hölderlin's thinking is radically tragic unlike Hegel's or Heidegger's or Lacan's.

The human being forgets himself because he is entirely at the present moment. God forgets himself because he is nothing but time, which means that they are nothing but the Kantian conditions of time and space. The gods are unfaithful, because time turns categorically 'and the beginning and the end no longer rhyme at all; the human being because within this moment he must follow the categorical turn, and thus cannot at all equal the beginning in what follows.'[109] As Antigone proceeds to the pedestal of Dike and commits a border crime, she, first, encounters the gods and the time, second, in this encounter she is faced with the pure and empty form of time and law. Fusion and inclusion with Dike and the infinite law is impossible because of the categorical withdrawal of the gods.[110] No traces of their laws are left behind.

Antigone's transgressive ethical act has five consequences:
1) She takes the law upon herself and interrupts the circulation of the

authority and legitimacy of both human and divine laws. The destination of the law is split between a divine sending and a destined transgressive act. Hence, she makes it possible to consider the sense of justice as no longer bound, given, or complete.

2) She embodies a singular universality. Even though she is a finite being (between two deaths), she embodies a paradoxical infinity of here and now. Her transgressive aspiration defines a singular universal sense of justice and pits it against the human and divine claims of general universalism. As she commits a border crime, the sense of justice erupts and the singular universality is actualized—*my* Zeus and *my* law—as the withdrawal of gods and divine truths.

3) She exceeds the co-ordinates of the possible. She does not so much question how the possible and impossible are defined but proceeds to what is outside the calculation of (im)possibility. *Antigone* is an experience of, on the one hand, the simultaneous impossibility and necessity of the transgression, and on the other hand, the withdrawal of the gods, which opens the possibility of tragedy as a dissensual scene.

4) Antigone is the witness and guardian of the infidelity of the gods. She becomes the exponent of their infidelity. However, she needs the absence of the infidel gods. That is, she exists entirely at the moment of her transgressive act through which she becomes disloyal to the gods. To complete the withdrawal of the gods, Antigone has to turn away from the gods and their laws. In her categorical reversal and revolution, she turns away from, on the one hand, divine laws, and on the other hand, established human laws, customs, and opinions. The categorical turn springs from her rebellious ethical act. Hence, for Hölderlin, *Umkehr* does not mean merely reversal but also a revolution, which includes, on the one hand, a democratic-republican revolution, and on the other hand, a longing for an ethico-political community beyond the state.[111]

5) For Aeschylus, the limit and the border between humans and the gods remains demarcated after the border crime that exceeds this limit. However, in Sophocles' tragedies, the limit itself as the limit and the border itself as the border are in question. The Kantian law is presented as the categorical imperative devoid of divinity. Instead of being a divine law or vision of the gods, it is already the retreat of the divine: 'The law is the most proper document of such a retreat.'[112] And Sophocles' tragic is 'the most essential document of this categorical retreat (*détournement catégorique*) of the divine.'[113] Henceforth, Sophocles' tragedies are about the retreat and distancing of the divine. This is a double retreat since Antigone as *antitheos* turns away from the divine and expresses herself in the forgetting form of infidelity. At the same time, because of the combination of transgression and turn around, she commits her criminal act in a holy manner, that is, as a tragic hero.

What is more, we cannot ignore the fact that Hölderlin—in his poetry and existence—followed Antigone to the limits and to the point of transgressing borders. Zweig writes of Hölderlin's sacred frenzy, where 'the earthly, the individual, the shapely have disappeared in complete self-annihilation. Void of significance, mere Orphic melody, are his later words as they wing their way back into the ether which is their home.'[114]

The ethical moment in tragedy is centred on the caesura. The caesura is the time/space of ethical catharsis. The purification is about limits and borders, turnings, and reversals. It is a measure for the human being on the earth. Our lot is to suffer finitude and mortality; and to know this as an inevitable fact. Simultaneously, this is the pre-condition of our freedom, which makes it possible for us to challenge the limits. At the limits, at the point of reversal we appear in the truth of our being-in-the-world and being-on-the-earth.

The ethical moment is also about the measure. Tragedy does not offer any consistent system of measures or some coherent set of substantive normative criteria for us. What takes place in tragedy is measuring itself as the human being measures itself, its action, its transgression, and its limited possibilities and the possibilities of limits. Measuring—the process, the motif, the subject, and the rhythm—is the concept upon which the poetry, tragedy, and thought intersect and share themselves.

To ask what this measuring is, I come back to Hölderlin's poetry, 'In Lovely Blue…':

> But the gods,
> Ever kind in all things,
> Are rich in virtue and joy.
> Which man may imitate.
> May man look up
> From the utter hardship of his life
> And say: Let me also be
> Like these? Yes. As long as kindness lasts,
> Pure, within his heart, he may gladly measure himself
> Against the divine. Is God unknown?
> Is he manifest as the sky? This I tend

> To believe. Such is man's measure.
> Well deserving, yet poetically
> Man dwells on this earth. But the shadow
> Of the starry night is no more pure, if I may say so,
> Than man, said to be the image of God.
> Is there measure on earth? There is
> None.

The answer—'There is / None'—to the ethical question about measures does not mean that there would be no measures for the human being. Instead, the poem attempts to bring forth the truth of the grounds of measures in a situation where there exists a tension between presence and absence of grounds for measures.

Human beings always measure themselves 'with and against something heavenly.'[115] In the poem there are three different possibilities for measurement. First, seeing herself in the image of God, the human being imitates the godhead. She measures herself 'against the divine' as long as she remains pure at heart. Second, Hölderlin asks whether God is unknown or 'manifest as the sky?' (*Himmel* refers both to 'sky' and 'heaven'). Hölderlin tends to believe that the divine becomes manifest as the sky. This would be the measure of the human being. Thirdly, the human being measures herself against the heavenly (*Himmlischen*) beings, who possess 'virtue and joy.' They are the measure-givers (*das Massgebende*). 'Let me also be / Like these?' These heavenly beings—Greek gods—remain an ideal towards which human beings may aspire. However, as the question mark hints, perhaps they cannot be reached on earth.

So where or what exactly is the measure against which the human being measures herself? It is clear that the human being itself is not the measure of all things. Instead, the human being must measure herself against something that is not human—divine, godhead, heavenly beings. Heidegger answers that it is not God, sky, or even the manifestness of the sky.

> The measure consists in the way in which the god who remains unknown is revealed *as* such by the sky. God's appearance through the sky consists in a disclosing that lets us see what conceals itself, but lets us see it not by seeking to wrest what is concealed out of its concealedness, but only by guarding the concealed in its self-concealment. Thus the unknown god appears as the unknown by way of the sky's manifestness. This appearance is the measure against which man measures himself.[116]

What is unknown is thus manifested in what is present, that is, the concealed is disclosed in appearance. Hölderlin tends to believe this, as I have said, but Heidegger seems to be sure about this.

There is thus no measure on earth. Human beings or technological achievements, scientific knowledges or capital cannot offer the measure. Then again, the measure is not the known god of any religion, any divine text, or any onto-theological system. Measure is not an entity: God, sky, or human being. Instead, there may be a measure that is disclosed *as* or *like* the sky or heaven (*Himmel*).

Where does this measuring take place? Hölderlin writes: 'Such is man's measure. / Well deserving, yet poetically / Man dwells on this earth.' For Heidegger, this means that 'poetry is measuring.' Human being lives poetically, and poetry is where measuring takes place. The human being that dwells poetically seems to refer, for Heidegger, to the possibility to attain rootedness—in German soil. Not only taking into consideration Heidegger's *Black Notebooks* but so much else we know of him, this idea of rootedness seems to turn Hölderlin's poem into a racist narrative about the proper dwelling place as destiny. However, for Hölderlin, the poetical dwelling place was not any specific soil or parcel of land but unrooted spaces, the life of wandering as his personal history reveals.[117] The human being that lives poetically is a wandering being without definite borders.

What Hölderlin's poem ultimately tells us is that the measure for the human being is measuring itself. There are no given measures but the human being as a human being has to measure herself against the non-given measure. 'Such is man's measure.' This is our mode of being-in-the-world. Therefore, the human being dwells on earth measuringly. Poetry is the space where this measuring endlessly takes place.

Measure and measuring refer to setting limits. What sense does the concept of the limit have within the limitlessness of late capitalism described at the beginning of this book? Salecl reminds us that it is psychoanalysis that 'has, from its beginning, concerned itself with the logic of the limit that every speaking being must negotiate.'[118] Also Recalcati points out that psychoanalysis is possible to wake the subject from 'the sleep-like condition' (*una sorta di sonno*) of reality in which it dwells in the current era of hyperhedonism and the addiction to object consumption.[119] The selfish enjoyment may be transformed into ethical desire.

Measuring takes place in tragedy and is related to caesura and catharsis. It does not offer us rules, principles, and measures but it does offer measuring as a human condition, which is how the ethical functions in tragedy.

11

Scene

Philosophers are still as afraid as Plato to enter a theatre and see the visual appearance and not only the text, the poem or the figure. Philosophy keeps distance to theatre and, paradoxically, has always been fascinated by it. As stated, instead of a metaphysical or philosophical idea, tragedy is to be considered in its practical and material dimensions.

The performance, the presentation on stage, and the *mise-en-scène* has not been simply absent in philosophical, academic, theoretical, and aesthetic works on tragedy. It has been present in its absence. Tragedy as theatre has functioned—if it has given any thought—in the service of something considered more fundamental: sublation, absolute justice, mortality, lamentation, authentic being, desire, and so forth. Tragedy as theatre 'does not demonstrate' but 'mounts a show' and exhibits.[1] However, the philosophical reading of tragedy provides an opposite view: tragedy does not exhibit but demonstrates. The theatricality of theatre is sacrificed to affirm a more original/fundamental/sublime/absolute sphere of existence. The staging is subordinated to the narrative function of tragedy as philosophy has appropriated theatre for its purposes.[2]

The reduction of the theatricality of theatre has three historical and contemporary forms.[3] The thesis of the didactic schema claims that truth, idea, telos, human dignity, or some other supreme good is external to theatre. The semblance of the truth is prescribed from outside theatre. For this perspective, theatre is credited merely as an inauthentic character. The fundamental issue is a philosophical control of theatre and its essence exterior to the presentation. As far as this is guaranteed, theatre has a positive public effect and functions as an education. The romantic schema is opposed to this Platonic pedagogical model. Theatre is not only capable of presenting the truth. The art alone is capable of addressing and presenting the fundamental truth. It accomplishes what philosophy can only point toward. This means that theatre succeeds in transforming infinite and absolute ideas into a sensible performance. It educates, but now because it 'teaches of the power of infinity.'[4] It is *l'absolu littéraire*

('The Literary Absolute') as Lacoue-Labarthe and Nancy name their book on German romanticism.[5] The classical scheme, constructed first by Aristotle, considers the essence of theatre as mimesis. Its regime is semblance. The purpose of theatre is not the truth. It does not even claim to be about fundamental ideas. Its function is not cognitive but practical. The mimesis enables an identification and a transference, a purification and a therapy, in a word, catharsis. Theatre pertains to the ethical and 'the treatment of the affections of the soul.'[6] For theatre, the truth is inscribed in the imaginary. Or, it is 'imaginarized' and exhausted by the theatrical act.

What comes to contemporary versions of these schemas, Marxism, represents the didactic schema. For the Brechtian epic theatre, the external truth is dialectical materialism, which Brecht considers to be the foundation of revolutionary rationalism. Even if Brecht constantly searched 'for the immanent rules of a Platonic (didactic) art'—and, I would add, recognized in his search the theatricality of theatre—he did not claim that theatre would produce the truth. Instead, the performance exhibits the courage of the truth. Theatre elucidates conditions for this kind of courage. Simultaneously, it is an education against cowardice in the face of this truth. Theatre is the society of comrades of dialectics and emancipatory values. The hermeneutical scheme continues the romantic tradition. There is an intimate link between the saying of the poet and the thought of the thinker, while the poet is given priority. In the flesh of language, the poet guards the truth as a disclosure and opening out of the closure, as I have shown. The philosophical interpretation of a poem is nothing but 'the *delivery* of the poem.'[7] This is why Heidegger understands tragedy as a poem while annulling its performative aspects. Psychoanalysis is connected to the Aristotelian view. Now, theatre is considered as a space of the circulation of desire. In theatre 'the object of desire, which is beyond symbolization,' emerges 'at the very peak of an act of symbolization.'[8] It brings forth the constitutive object cause of the desire and the extimacy of this *objet petit a* to the symbolic Other. The contemporary scheme is avant-garde theatre that continues this tradition by synthesizing the didactic and romantic schemes.[9]

Reading Tragedy

The philosophical reading of tragedy considers the theatricality of tragedy as a preparatory act or a space-time that introduces and affirms the supreme principle, the heroic figure or the cathartic, moral, or theoretical lesson of tragedy. Tragedy is displaced while its theatricality is subjected to the destiny of what it represents. What is represented and said in tragedy extends its domination over the scene and saying, the mimesis of action and the trajectory of a tragic play.

Would, say, Hegel's analysis of the tragic conflict come into being without *Antigone*? Hegel could have written what he had to say about the moral life without recourse to Sophocles' tragedy. Tragedy is a mere supplement for the dialectical movement of the philosopher. The same question could be asked about any theoretical reading of tragedy. Perhaps, we should have a theatre test to measure mutilations inflicted upon the theatricality of tragedy—a measuring of the degree of the degradation of theatre.

'Yes, but.' Lacan, if you want, did not write his ethics of psychoanalysis without a vigilant reading of *Antigone*. The supplement—the theatricality—is never innocent. It haunts all theoretical readings of tragedy, even those where tragedies are used as vehicles and illustrations of philosophical argumentation. Theatricality exceeds and interrupts the mastery of the idea, since without it there would be no representation of this idea or demonstration of established meaning. What the philosophy of tragedy avoids or ignores, is always already present in tragedy. This is the excess of theatricality.

Perhaps my treatise has gone through a native turn. I hope so. A philosophical treatise of tragedy has as its starting point theoretical thinking and philosophical tradition. To learn to use this way of thinking about tragedy, we have to learn to use what is foreign to it, that is, the concreteness of tragedies in their theatricality and the equality of the aesthetic experience of these dramaturgic-scenic theatre events. Only through this concrete element can we go back to re-thinking the ethics of tragedy. There is a risk of never managing to turn back to philosophy. However, if we do not leave what is proper to philosophy, there is neither the ethics of *tragedy* nor the philosophy of *scene*. In this case, tragedy, and in more general art, remains subjected to a philosophy that uses it for its own ontological and speculative purposes.

Do I give myself over to this speculation? A philosophical treatise on the ethics of tragedy cannot avoid this possibility. Thinking includes risk. As soon as I designate certain Greek tragedies as refugee tragedies or define Antigone's law, I have measured these tragedies and conflicts by setting them in this or that position. Already, the very title of this treatise promotes a theoretical position of tragedy. It promises a proposition for the ethical dimension in tragedy. This treatise ought to be subjected to the theatre test: Is it tragedy that presents the ethical? Once again, 'yes, but.'

To think tragedy with ethics must not give in to self-sufficient ideas, structures, and ends exterior to tragedy. Thinking must resist itself as thinking. This self-resisting thinking of tragedy may construct the ethics of tragedy, not from its own premises but from the theatricality of tragedy. Thinking together with but also within tragedies. Philosophical ideas are not the problem but their mastery or their master's voice. We have to admit that tragedy exceeds its philosophical analysis, a bit like a hysteric that is never pleased with the explanations of its identity by the master supposed to know. What must be avoided is to posit the idea or/of the hero that represents itself in tragedy and comes back to itself without ever leaving its self-same essence and identity.

How to think tragedy by resisting the urge to subject tragedies to presupposed philosophical, moral, or political schemes and ideas? Heidegger gives the answer in his 1934–35 Hölderlin lectures. He defines poetry as art in its essence, 'inextricably composed of language and myth (*Sprache* and *Sage*),' which is the condition of history and the unveiling of being in terms of existence.[10] That which goes beyond *Sprache* and *Sage* and what Heidegger marginalizes or ignores is what must be thought to understand tragedy. What is excessive in tragedy is the theatricality of theatre. This supplement, however, always already functions as a deconstructive force in theoretical readings of tragedy. We have dealt with three fundamental elements of tragedy: conflict, caesura, and catharsis. All include an ethical dimension. The tragic conflict is not without conflicting ethical positions, concepts of justice, moral values or ideas about the legitimacy of law and political authority. The caesura is about ethical borders, limits, and measuring. The catharsis is an ethical one even if it may take place in different places, among spectators (refugee tragedies), in the tragic figures, in destruction of tragic figures leading to purification (Hegel), or as the tragic utterance and trajectory (Hölderlin).

To consider these ethical dimensions in tragedy, we have to think more properly the relation between the tragic text and scene. Tragedy measures without defining the measure, while this measuring runs through the tragic presentation, through mimesis, catharsis, and caesura immanent to the tragic transport. Tragedy creates a situation where we have an objective dialectic that is a tragic conflict; a subjective dialectic of disagreeing political, ethical, and legal convictions; and an absolute dialectic that introduces caesura, limits, and the duty of measuring.[11] This differs from

Hegel's dialectical conception of tragedy, which, even if it also begins from the relevance of an ethical conflict, rushes towards absolute justice as the reconciliation of the tragic conflict.

What role should we give to the texts of tragedies? Perhaps, a dramatic text is nothing if not put on the stage, since theatre cannot be reduced to the tragic poem. Aristotle takes a contrary view. For the effect of catharsis to function, it is enough to read aloud the tragic poem. Charles Segal explains this non-theatrical view by the fact that when Aristotle wrote his treatises on tragedy, tragedies had acquired 'an independent status as written texts,' which removed them from the theatricality of theatre, even though they continued to be performed.[12] Whatever, it was Aristotle, who sowed the first seeds of the disregard of the theatricality of tragedy, which came to mark a cut between the original connection between the text and theatre (the event of text/theatre) and democracy.

If we emphasize the theatrical experience that has a collective dimension which pervades 'the life of the ancient Greek community,' Aristotle's textual view cannot be justified.[13] Even if tragedy is not to be considered a common ritual, it cannot be reduced to the text. Then again, tragedy cannot be considered a tragedy without a text. Tragic poetry is an essential part of the genre of tragedy. Denis Guénoun affirms that the theatrical performance does not ignore the dramatic text, even though the essence of theatre is the scene and a *mise-en-scène*. Words are the corpus and the material that theatre intends to make its theatrical object. The theatrical event produces a visible performance from words that bring together on stage the text and the exposed body. Theatre exists in the space between linguistic and visual, voice and flesh, meaning and sensible. It requires both dimensions, physical and textual, corporeal and verbal. The audience is not witnessing a spectacle made of images and bodies but the transformation of the text into the scene, the poem into action, words into bodies. If theatre does not bring to light its unseen origin in the text and writing, it risks becoming a mere spectacle and a vacant body of images. The text in itself does not produce the theatricality of theatre. In this case, the presentation would remain a mere movement of language. The body of an actor incarnates the word. The text is actualized and embodied in the visible space of the stage. Only when the text goes beyond its textuality and is seen do words, meanings, and voices obtain a gravitational pull; only when the actor incorporates the word and closes the circle does the democratic and communal being of theatre become actualized. Only then can we speak of the scene.[14]

Badiou, for whom theatre presents 'an extraordinary space of freedom,' affirms the position of the dramatic text as open and incomplete.[15] It will be played time and again by people who are indifferent to the 'original' politico-historical context of the text. Actors and spectators change gods, values, cities, and constitutions as tragedy is repeatedly restaged. In Weber's words, the theatrical event takes place, '*come[s] to pass,*' and simultaneously '*pass[es] away.*'[16] Tragedy does not disappear since it will happen somewhere else. Out of the dislocations of its repetitions emerge 'the *singularity of the theatrical event.*'[17]

Theseus or Antigone are 'proper names of genericity' that '*can exist at any moment,*' and for us they are eternal unlike the great figures of novels, who are immortal and can exist forever but only in the text.[18] Because of the eternity latent in the texts, we may today encounter these texts as depositories of eternal tragic conflicts, actions, and figures. That is, the text is a symbolic treasure of tragedy. They have 'become *out-of-time*, but capable of becoming temporal before our very eyes.'[19] The philosophical treatise and the theatrical performance of a text is the 'encounter of the eternal in the elucidation of the instant' and both the treatise and the performance are instants of thinking.[20] The texts of tragedies confronted in this treatise are universal and may exist at any moment. As a presentation passes away, the text remains to happen somewhere else, even though always in a singular way and as an iteration. My encounter with tragedy and drama can be counted, perhaps, as a singular way to continue the incomplete re-writing or iteration of these open tragic texts actualized in theatre presentations.

The text is not-all. Neither is it nothing. Tragedy is the text and the performance of the tragic poem, a negotiation and a translation between these two phenomena through the scene. Even if we focus on the performative aesthetics, the materiality of the performance, and the interaction between spectators and performers, tragedy is not without a relation to the 'text', the meaning of which is time and again radically re-considered.[21] Without the 'text' we fall back into a naïve conception of theatre as a natural, immediate, and spontaneous happening. The purity and immediacy are not part of tragedy. For tragedy, the text is the 'thinking in interiority.'[22]

Tragic Transport

Hölderlin introduces a vital element into the philosophy of tragedy: the tragic transport. This is a step beyond those (philosophers) who hold 'theatre in contempt.'[23] The question arises: What is the theatricality of tragedy? Hölderlin requires us to consider tragedy as an assemblage of disparate components which co-produces tragedy not merely as a poem or a text but as a drama, a theatrical presentation. Gathered together, these components form a theatrical event, a performance that is an evental situation, a singular theatre event. There is no tragedy—or theatre in general—without the scene.

Hans-Thies Lehman sketches a rift between the text and the stage. 'The relation between the text and the artistic practice of theatre has never been an easy one.'[24] What is the relation between a tragic poem and a theatre performance? Does the text withdraw from the stage or dictate like a textual sovereign the conditions of the presentation? Lehman does not give much credit to the text. The 'reality of the written play is for study room, not for theatre,' which deals with, on the one hand, space and sounds, bodies and movements, lights and music, and on the other hand, with social event.[25] Lehmann advocates the post-dramatic theatre that is not based on the text as the rule or standard.[26] The literary-linguistic reality of the dramatic theatre gives way to 'the paralinguistic dimension, for voices and intonation, rhythm, speed and slowness of speech, sexual and gendered auditive information, gesture and the expressivity of body language.'[27]

It is obvious that theatre cannot be reduced to literature. Nevertheless, Greek tragedy would not exist without texts. Tragic poets and their plays competed against each other. A tragic text was not only necessary material for a tragic performance but the structural base for a tragic performance. There may have been a 'pre-dramatic' Dionysian theatre based on singing and dancing, but in Athenian democracy there was no non-textual theatre. The textual plot, the organization of the events and action, is central for tragedy. Even if the textual-dramatic narration has given way to other forms of theatrical presentations, tragedy must be confronted as a textual theatre. Tragedy is Samuel Beckett's *Endgame* or Sarah Kane's *4.48 Psychosis*. We have access to Greek tragedy only through the texts and textual fragments of tragic plays. The theatrical context in which these texts were put on the stage is extinct and we can only speculate about the ancient tragic performance. Therefore, I have concentrated on linguistic and textual material: How does this tragic material make sense and meaning? How does the ethical function in the textual structure of the play? What takes place in the tragic texture?

I could turn to Aristotle to justify this approach. His intention was to construct the theory of tragedy that considers tragedy independently of the requirements of theatrical staging. He makes this more than clear by saying that 'the potential of tragedy does not depend upon public performance and actors.'[28] The presentation on the stage is the least integral of all to the art of a poet. 'The art of the mask-maker (*skeuopoios*) carries more weight than the art of a poet as regards the elaboration of visual effects.'[29] Lyric poetry is, for Aristotle, the most important garnishing of tragedy.

I began my attempt to think the possibility of the ethical from poetry by considering how poetic saying and thinking could offer a critical and radical measuring for the current situation. As I have said, the poetry is not a moral institution that would set norms and values. It breaks up ordinary prose and 'extends the limit of the communicable and pushes back the inaccessible frontiers of *lalangue*.'[30] As a force it brings forth the possibility of an opening of truths. Poetry thus interrupts hegemonic capitalist discourse. By splitting the realism of reality, something about our dwelling may be disclosed. I could well continue with reading tragedy as poetry.

However, this is not all Aristotle had to say about tragedy. He admits that the 'spectacle is emotionally powerful.'[31] Even if for Aristotle *melopolia*—the combination of choral lyrics, music and dance; speech, voice, sound and movements—is relatively unimportant, he has to admit that the poem is necessarily connected to performative elements. Aristotle could (or would) not banish the scenic supplement.

While I have approached the ethics of tragedy by reading tragic texts, which includes *mythos* (plot), *ēthos* (figure or character), *dianoia* (thought) and *leksis* (speech), I have attempted not to fall into Aristotelian ignorance of *melopolia* (music) and *opsis* (performance). The embodiment of the text in a three-dimensional space and the pure ephemerality of the passing away of the materiality of the performance is how a tragic poem becomes a tragedy.[32] Since tragedy cannot be reduced to the text as it consists of the text and the presentation, it differs (also in its possible ethical dimension) from non-tragic poetry and epic poetry. The tragic poems are 'meant for the theatre,' which Badiou claims, 'changes everything.'[33]

I have read these tragedies aloud following Aristotle's proposition. It makes sense. Voice, movements, body, action, muscles, flesh, and rhythm come into play. The text is spatialized, and time becomes a physical issue. Even if the text does not take place on the stage, it happens in a time-space specific context. I have seen many of them in one or other form. The most faithful presentations have been those which have reinvented the tragic poems. An infidel fidelity. Those 'authentic' presentations are merely grotesque spectacles for theatre tourists.

Even if I have considered the internal engine of the ethical in tragedy, I cannot absolutely exclude the possibility of a logocentric bias to my treatise since my focus is the textual material and structure instead of the stage. However, Greek tragedy today cannot be a theatre of presence. It presents itself as the theatre of absence by which I mean the theatre of traces, which makes it possible to exist as a presentation. Avoiding the logocentric conception of tragedy may force us to pass too close the Scylla of pure actuality and self-same presence. The present in theatre is not to be considered as the self-present living theatre or 'the absolute, wholly living form which constitutes experience,' but reconstituted and always already infiltrated by trace and difference.[34] The theatrical presentation is always inhabited by textual dissemination presenting itself in the presence of the performance that presents itself infiltrated by traces. We should consider tragedy as 'an expression that cannot be subsumed in the economy of the present, but orients itself toward an eventual, utopia reception which cannot take place here and now.'[35] Tragedy consists of *pragmata*—actions, events, occurrences and happenings—which is the 'object' of the mimesis that produces these. Thus there is no tragedy outside a text.

The singularity of tragedy may be understood from the perspective of Benjamin's conception of the aura. For him, the unique existence of a theatre is its specific spatiotemporal presentation that constitutes its authenticity and authority. The aura of the theatre is its presence. The performance of a stage actor present here and now is directly presented to the public by the actor, who is able to adjust to the audience during the performance. The aura surrounding the figure 'cannot be divorced from the aura that, for living spectators, surrounds the actor who plays him.'[36]

This theatrical presence is not an immediate proximity that would make it possible to get hold of the tragic play at close range, like the reproduction of a photographic or cinematographic image that overcomes the uniqueness of things reproduced.[37] The theatrical uniqueness implies and requires a distance, where the object is inaccessible by eluding our grasp.[38] Tragedy is a shared experience, where the audience has to 'respect the performance as an integral whole,' but simultaneously it remains distinct.[39]

The uniqueness of a tragic play 'is identical to its embeddedness in the context of tradition,' which is thoroughly alive and changeable.[40] The auratic mode of existence of tragedy is never totally severed from its ritual function, but as traditions change so do functions of the art. The mystic-religious ritual ('cult value') withdraws as the democratic ritual ('exhibition value') becomes the dominant mode of life in the democratic *polis*.[41]

The 'tempo-topography' of tragedy has a polar determination. If tragedy were to accomplish a harmonious unity of the unity of the plot and the difference of the presentation, it would exist in its immediacy. Instead of this, tragedy is always elsewhere in space, elsewhere in time. The text and the signification are potentially unlimited. The action through the plot may be recollected and repeated. The presentation on the stage is finite. It has a specific space for its eventual existence. Due to this, the unity of tragedy is undermined by a difference between *synopsis* and *opsis* which is not mere difference but a difference that constitutes tragedy as a theatre. This reciprocal positioning of the text and the performance constitutes the theatrical play that presents itself to the assembled spectators in a specific time and space that, paradoxically, exceeds in its finiteness the textual infinity.

Rancière considers theatre as 'the place, where the paradigms of action are concentrated.'[42] These paradigms 'function in various manners.'[43] What happens and how does it take place? How does a cause produce an effect and who has the power for this effective kind of action? Which actions and acts have the dignity of the drama and what kind of speech is considered as art? Theatre is a place where these issues become visible and are 'carried by bodies'—it is 'a concrete space.'[44] How can we think Rancière's concrete space?

For me, it combines the cause of thinking and the method of the scene, which is made up of a figuration of signifiers, bodies, action, voices, rhythms, and truths. This theatrical event takes place as concrete theatre space, where spatialized bodies are involved in disagreement and dialogue. Lacoue-Labarthe makes two propositions. First, language is the opening of the world and the presence of beings, that is, the origin of our existence in the world. Second, language is essentially and originally dialogue or *logos dialogos*. The originality of the dialogical mimetic lexis is based on the idea of the addressee as the condition of language. This could be understood as the difference between lyric and dramatic poetry, a song and a dialogue, even though Greek tragedy included both.[45] These two (counter-)propositions are joined together by a third proposition, which Lacoue-Labarthe calls—by taking a risk, as he says—an 'arche-theatre' (*archi-théâtre*).[46]

According to Rancière, theatre should not be subjected to any general ontology.[47] Neither should it be defined as a transcendental condition of the arts. There are four reservations as—or if—we use the term 'arche-theatre.' First, it does not refer to the essence of or model for all arts. Rather, theatre is to be considered as the presupposition of arts, if we understand it as 'making a scene.'[48] Second, 'arche' does not reduce the differences between arts, the Muses. The making of a scene, or the presentation, is different in different forms of arts. The presentation makes a difference or, more fundamentally, it is the difference of differences.[49] Third, the presentation is the origin of sense. There is no absolute and essential origin, or original non-presentation. Hence, we have to speak of an original presentation, that is, mimesis as the movement of difference or '*différance*,' which signifies deferring and differing.[50] The presentation is difference as the condition of theatre. Fourth, the transcendental arche-theatre has to make itself felt, but simultaneously it has to let itself be erased so that a concrete space appears as the erasure of the transcendental 'arche.' The arche-theatre does not exist or have the status of being-present outside of its presence as the possibility of differing and self-differing concrete spaces. All in all, the arche-theatre is nothing but a base of concrete spaces and a space for theatrical events.

Lacoue-Labarthe admits that one must not forget theatre that is non-arche, 'a theatre, plain and simple.'[51] Theatre has its own dialogue, which differs from let's say an epic, philosophical, or cinematographic dialogue. Besides, not only does the dramatic dialogue make a difference between speaking beings, it also creates a split between the voice and the figure from whom it emanates. Immanent in the *dia*logue is difference as it always differs from itself. It also marks the difference between writing and speech and differs from other theatrical elements. The dramatic poem is a text and a potentiality actualized in a concrete space as a theatrical discourse, which includes not only the verbal dialogue but also non-verbal, incantatory voices, stretching vowels, stuttering consonants, twisting cries, and all other elements of the scene.

We should not subjugate the presentation, mimesis, and its scenic actualization to enunciation, speech, and dialogue.[52] Recall that the scene, *opsis*, mise-en-scène and presentation are elements of the theatricality of theatre. Theatre, as concrete spaces, consists of multiple combinations of signifiers, verses, chants, sounds, rhythms, movements, and bodies. Instead of either the general ontology or the metaphysics of theatre, which would be beyond historical, evental, and spatial contingencies, tragedy should be confronted and investigated as tragedies taking shape in, through, and as concrete theatrical spaces.⁵³ Therefore, not only do theatrical, political, philosophical, and psychoanalytical scenes differ from each other, tragedy also differs from itself, since theatre consists of the concrete spaces of presentation. There is neither body nor action as such but the becoming a space of bodies and acts. The action makes the object of mimesis, but at the same time this mimesis is the presentation of action and this presentation in itself is the method of the scene, which is not merely *tekhnê*, making a scene, but also action, *praxis*. Perhaps the action of mimesis is action in itself. The dramatic presentation, the mimesis of action, *mimesis praxeôs*, must be thought chronologically between the action, *praxis*, and the entity of the play, *drama*, between acts, *pragmata*, and dramatic actions, *dramata*. However, logically the mimesis precedes the action and the work of art.

A concrete space is a space of presentation and theatrical figuration, mimesis functioning as the figuring force. This movement is a double movement. It refers to an exhibition of figures but simultaneously a retreat of this exhibition. In tragedy, mythical-heroic figures are not figured by merely naming, fixing, or sacralizing heroic identities. Tragic figures are figured in the movement of figuration and defiguration since tragedy is always both the representation of myths and the cessation of these myths. In other words, tragedy is the spatial and temporal event in a concrete space of defiguration of mythical figures and the figuration/defiguration of tragic figures. The scene of tragedy does not take place as a space for the spectacular spectacle offered to the gaze, which would sacrifice the scene, spacing, and appearing of the fictional image and the imaginary figuration. Tragedies are the movements of scenic revolts where enunciations, embodiments, and the spacing of spaces do not merely represent heroic myths and identities. Therefore, tragedy is not the aestheticization of ethics. However, tragedy does not invoke the breakdown of the figure as some kind of beyond-figure but, as Nancy puts it, 'a movement of the cut (*coupe*), which in this cutting, traces another place of enunciation.'⁵⁴ The scene is a withdrawal from myth as a redrawing of a democratic tragedy. A concrete space as a presentation, which is also the formation of form and space, takes place time and again as 'a space of thinking' produced by 'the method of scene.'⁵⁵ Theatre: the presentation thinks in a concrete space.

Material Tragedy

There is an interplay between the material and ideal side of tragedy. The material side consists of, on the one hand, the textual element, and on the other hand, the temporal and spatial conditions of the theatre event. This substructure of tragedy functions as the means of a theatrical production including the relations of the theatrical production. The material base creates, shapes, and determines the superstructure of tragedy that consists of truths, which are to be understood not as philosophical ideas or arguments but theatre truths. The material substructure produces and reproduces these truths. At the same time, these truths maintain and influence the material base of tragedy, the means and relations of its production. The substructure produces truths, which simultaneously is an elemental part of it.

Tragedy is not the representation of truths but an encounter of the material and ideal elements both of which effects the other. Neither a figural aesthetics that defies truths nor an abstract aesthetics that defies materiality, tragedy is the combination of materiality and truths or a movement that deconstructs their difference and the border between them without abolishing their distinct features.

To think the material bases of tragedy we must consider the concept of the scene. Tragedy is about the staging of tragic presence. What matters in tragedy is the coming to presence and the presentation. More than a spectacle, tragedy as theatre is a scene producing itself. The scene is the condition of there being tragic presence at all; and this should not be read as an ontological argument.

What is the scene? A straightforward answer is the stage. I use the concept of stage to refer to an architectural space, including stage props and machinery, for the theatre performance. A theatre 'building' frames the space of the actors and the space of the spectators, as well as the borders between these two spaces even though they may be deconstructed with architectural arrangements or in the performance. A theatre experience is necessarily a spatial phenomenon, where physical, symbolic and normative architecture, the real and imaginative spaces and their interactive co-existence evoke meanings and truths.[56]

The scene is and is not the stage. The stage is *proskēnion*, where the actors present themselves and on which they enter through one of the doors. *Skēnē* was originally a shelter or an intimate place for retiring, sleeping, or drinking with friends. Later, it referred to the background of the stage. The scene opens the stage, where figures are presented, bodies move, voices are aroused, and acts are acted. The scene is something that pushes forward beings and things. The scene precedes and makes possible the stage, but also includes and reaches beyond it. However, the scene retains itself as *skēnē*, 'a light makeshift shelter ... a place of intimacy.'[57]

The scene equates with the stage. Simultaneously, it indicates the various components of the theatrical space, time, action, and their unity as a dramatic entity. The scene has a double meaning as a spatial and a temporal scene.[58] It is in the head of the spectator as in the acting of an actor. It is also in the tragic play as in the construction of the theatre 'building.'[59] It includes scenography that is not to be reduced to the stage architecture. Its temporality is both the time of the performance and the internal time of the play. As the spectators are addressed—in one way or another—they become included into the scene. As for the text, it addresses the scene as its textual-material precondition. It opens itself towards the scene or directs itself at the scene. The text is present on the stage but only in an actualized form. Tragic verses are translated into speaking bodies, who are not representatives of a tragic poem but presentations of speech and gestures, touch and movements, sound and ears, taste and odour, or as Nancy says, 'everything that is physical, or physiological, energetic, dynamic.'[60] This makes the scene.

Because the scene includes the text as its actualization on the stage, let us keep these two interconnected elements analytically distinct. The text *and* the scene make up the material base of tragedy. Understood in this way, the play institutes and constitutes the scene as the condition of the exercise of theatre. When somebody begins to act or something is put on the stage, the scene is already there.[61] The scene is both created by the play and the condition of it. The conditional is the condition as a priori. Thus the scene may be considered as the transcendental condition of the experience of theatre, which makes possible various empirical practices of spectators, actors, or the scenography.[62] The scene is the structure or the scheme of theatre while theatricality is the effectiveness of tragedy in general.[63] If theatre consists of, as Badiou argues, analytic elements (place, text, director, actor, décor, costumes and public) and dialectic elements (state, ethics, and spectator), then we can conclude that there is no theatre without the scene.[64]

The scene is not merely a space for a continuity of actions and events but also relations between 'fictive' subjects or characters on the stage. It is a spatial and temporal arrangement for the mimesis of human and non-human relations in the world. It transforms actions into the drama or dramatic actions that are causally related to each other; not merely at the level of what is seen, but also at the level of thought. The action is what we see on the stage as gestures, words, and bodily movements on the stage. The function of tragedy, however, is not reduced to physical actions or acts of saying on the stage but a network of thought dictated by fateful causality: the future is in the past.[65] As mimesis occurs at the temporal limits of the scene, it differs from *praxis*. Tragedy has a beginning (*arkhē*) and an end (*telos*) unlike *praxis*.

Aristotle considers tragedy a mimetic representation of an action, which is coherent, consistent, unified, and complete. It can be taken in a single view unlike the *epos* (epic poetry). Those producing the mimesis on the stage Aristotle calls *prattontes* ('actants' or 'actings') which is the gerund of the verb *prattein* (to act). In its substantive form *prattein* is *praxis*, 'action.'[66] Aristotle sees tragedy first of all as *praxis* represented and not as the scene. He subordinates the scene, the optical and spectacular nature of tragedy, *opsis*, to the narrative and representational function. Nor does Aristotle give much credit to a character (*ēthos*) represented through his action on the stage. For him, tragedy cannot exist without plot, but it can do without characters. This kind of predominance of the plot (*muthos*) turns tragedy into the epic poetry that Aristotle wants to distinguish from tragic poetry.

Aristotle cannot avoid acknowledging the role of the scene and the theatrical actualization of action, even though he attempts to give the theatricality of tragedy a supplementary and technical role. According to Weber, acting (*prattontes*) has a double sense: it may be applied to the acting of actors and the characters represented. The actualization of action on the stage involves a division between actors and characters. A second division takes place within the whole of the theatrical space: actors are acting before an audience to which they present the mimesis of an action. This is why a tragedy is a theatre event separated from epic poetry as a work of art.[67]

A key concept in Aristotle's thinking is *energeia* (actuality) which refers to 'being at work' (*en ergon*), where work is connected to the completion. This interrupts Aristotle's hierarchical conception of tragedy. The *muthos* cannot function as a homogeneous unit that bridges the work and being at work, the mimesis of action and its actualization, the poet and the actor, the text as a work of art and the gaze of the spectators. Moreover, *peripeteia* (an unexpected interruption that creates wonder and excitement) is connected to *anagnorisis* (an insight) requiring an actualization that brings the poetic work into the completion of recognition. The *muthos* is always already inhabited by the scene, the work by the actualization. The scene is the bursting of the text into the presence of presentation. The text explodes as it is exposed to the spatial-temporal presentation without disappearing during the force of this theatrical explosion, that is, in its coming to being as a theatre event.

The chorus is a distinctive feature of the Greek tragedy (the song of *tragōidoi* was the first meaning of tragedy). It is an elemental part in the dialogue. Unlike in Shakespearean tragedy, the chorus has an essential presence on the stage. It is involved with the fate of the protagonists and it functions as the collective and communal dimension of tragedy.[68] In 'the theater of the *polis*,' the chorus is the representative of 'the collective citizen-body.'[69] It appeals to the inherited views and norms of the community. Vernant and Vidal-Naquet differentiate between two active players who occupy the stage. The chorus is 'a collective figure played by an association of citizens' that expresses 'the feelings of spectators who make up the civic community,' and the tragic figures are 'estranged from the ordinary condition of the citizen.'[70] Their conclusion is that the chorus embodies the collective truth of the democratic city that confronts the excess of the tragic figures who die (Antigone) or undergo a transformation (Creon) while the chorus remains the same.[71]

This duality of the communal and heroic *ēthos* is problematic. There are three reasons why I beg to differ. First, the chorus does not offer an idealized voice of the *polis*. The chorus is a collective voice but its role cannot be reduced to the authoritative voice of the citizen-body expressing the ethics and values of the community. Second, by its virtue of its Doric lyricism, the language of the chorus is often a distant tongue and remote from the simple, even prosaic, speech of the tragic figures. Even if the heroes remind one of the mythical past, their speech is closer to the tongue of the democratic *polis* than the language of the chorus. Third, the chorus and the tragic hero are in consensual/dissensual dialogue.

It is wrong to consider a single model accounting for the chorus. One has to take into consideration its social and political rooting, the place from which the chorus speaks in tragedy.[72] In the fictional world of the play, the chorus was composed not of average citizens but characteristically of old men, women, foreigners, and slaves. Only three tragedies use the chorus composed of middle-aged males.[73] Then again, the old men represent tradition and experience highly appreciated in the *polis*. Moreover, the chorus was performed by a significant segment of the citizens. Even if we say that the chorus is the voice of the otherness, I do not see, like Gould does, its role as giving 'a collective expression to an alternative, even opposed, to that of the "heroic" figure.'[74] It is a simplification to claim that the chorus as the voice of the *polis* or its other is in opposition to the competing ethics of the tragic figures or to the *ēthos* of excessive heroes.

Instead of the duality between the chorus and the tragic hero, the language of the chorus is 'one among the many competing tongues of the city of words.'[75] The chorus of women, foreigners, and slaves may function as the other of both the *polis* and the tragic heroes. Through the chorus the outside is included in the public space and the collective discourse. There are not merely multiple choruses but in any one tragedy the chorus may have multiple tongues and positions. In the dialogue between the chorus and the tragic figures, both modulate each other's speech.

The collective voice of the chorus addresses and is addressed by tragic figures. What takes place on the stage is not the acts of tragic heroes but a web of relationships and collective discussion as well as disagreement concerning the ethical that involves heroic figures and the chorus. The multiple voices on the stage exceed the duality of inside/outside, community/hero, political/mythical.

The decision made by the tragic hero is not made in heroic solitude. It is, like Guénoun says, a decision before (*décision devant*) another, before the gazes, bodies, and thoughts of others. The decision and action, the courage and the truth are shown to other figures (and to the spectators). Sending these to others is to be understood as responsibility, as the responsibility of addressing and answering. The scene is to be understood as a constant opening towards multiple others.[76] The scene presents the tragic through the action, deeds, words, and fate of the tragic hero against the perspective of other tragic figures and the chorus. The scene would not be anything without the beat that spatializes and temporalizes, visualizes and 'acousticalizes.'

Rhythm and Tragedy

Rhythm (*rhytmos*) derives from the Greek verb *rheo* (to flow), but it is not merely connected with mobility, fluidity, and repetition but also to form and scheme. Rhythm produces patterns and sequences, cadences, and contours. Plato defines a song as a combination of words, melody, and rhythm. Rhythm is an order and a movement, the order in movement, which finds its way into the secret places of the soul. Plato considers rhythm to be determined by the law of numbers, hence, determined by meter and measure. In other words, rhythm, an expression of life, is a good choice of order, and the meter is a regulator of rhythm. Therefore rhythm pertains to Plato's theory of ethics and education.[77]

Rhythm organizes, structures, and unites. It functions as a periodicity and a distinctive patter of repetition and variables. It is an underlying force of the dialectics (Hegel), the absolute unifier (Schelling). Correct rhythm heals rhythmic irregularities and disorders.

Without this invisible force there is no tragedy, without flow no tragic conflicts and actions. Rhythm can be defined as the sequence of events of tragedy. It produces patterns but also movements, forces, and experiences beyond these patterns. Hence tragedies are rhythmic compositions of actions, figures, bodies, senses, corpses, convictions, loyalties, voices, cries, dialogues, music, and odes.

However, rhythm includes breaking the structure and continuity created by the rhythm itself. Poly- and counter-rhythms differentiate the structure and destroy the rhythmic coherence. Arrythmia interrupts repetition. These are rhythms belonging to the rhythmic movement. Rhythm is not a fixed form, but a dynamic flow, which should be heard and sensed as a didactic beat that discloses consensual moralities by uniting oppositions and disagreeing sounds and moments. The flow of rhythm requires interventions and irruptions, which are internal to rhythm. There is no Platonic order and movement without displacements.

During his travels, Zarathustra returns to a town he had once visited. He sees that everything is shrunk. The reason for this is the lack of rhythm. Nietzsche opposes the meter (*Takt*), the regular pattern never to be disrupted and the rule that requires submission to the rule, to rhythm that is creative and rebellious. Rhythm breaks the metric norms that organize, structure, normalize, and standardize. It is not the same as harmony. For Nietzsche, rhythm does not teach us measured morals and correct limits. Rhythm urges us to act: Let's dance![78]

The rhythm of tragedy structures. But immanent to this constructive beat is the multiplicity of unexpected vibrations that pass between actions and spectators, spatial and temporal arrangements, scenography and figures, measures and transgressions, events and turns. Rhythm brings together the configurations of tragic actors and multiple resonances between them and in their relations to themselves and their actions. The rhythms of the scene combine, harness, and force couplings. At the same time as they deform, dissipate, separate, and split. The rhythms of action and tragic heroes are combined with the rhythms of witnessing and the chorus. Rhythm is also disengaged from individual figures and events as the scene gives it an autonomous form. At the same time it produces the scene as a singular space of singularity.

In tragedy, rhythm is a measure for regular recurrences and a measuring force that organizes the unfolding of temporal and spatial, visual and acoustic phenomena on the stage. Tragic rhythmic operations include order and movement, repetition and flow as well as interruptions and displacements. The flow and vibrations do not merely constitute a tragic play but fill it with displacements, ruptures and caesuras which are immanent to the scene and as such produces the play. Rhythm is a constructive and deconstructive flow that spatializes and temporalizes the scene and the text. In this regard, Aristotle's idea of reading tragedies aloud makes more sense. Rhythm is not without relation to meaning. It signifies.

Caesura is an integral part of rhythm. It produces the flow and the beat of a tragic play, that is, rhythm not only includes but also requires caesura to become the rhythm and movement of continuity and voided beats. Actions and figures are configurations of intensities and abrupt pauses. Caesura breaks the harmonious rhythm and forces the spectators to concentrate on the events that precede and follow 'empty' moments. Moreover, caesuras are multiple, creating their own rhythm immanent to the rhythm of the scene. In Hölderlin's *Antigone*, the turn to republican political form is not only a thematic issue but takes place through and as rhythm. The caesura balances the different parts of the play.[79] Rhythm is also about the right timing, about *kairos*: when is the correct moment to act?

Rhythm precedes the figure and the visible scheme.[80] It is the precondition of the appearance of the presentation even though it is a necessary element of this very same presentation. Rhythm is also the figuration of the figure.

The wave of the beat acts on bodies on the stage and on the audience. Rhythm makes senses, bodies, and thoughts emerge during the presentation as singular places where the forces of tragic actions meet bodies. Rhythm provokes catharsis as pathos, which is a contact of rhythmically being-affected, which is structurally asymmetrical, since it has its origins in the difference between events and bodies, thoughts and voices, actions and movements, words and dance.[81] Rhythm is the form and the flow of a tragic presentation that constantly slips away from any grasp giving a spatial and temporal, ideal and material rhythm to the trajectory of tragic actions and truth procedures. Rhythm shares time, but also space, as it flows and splits, connects and displaces.

Scene as Assembly

The scene involves the assembly of the spectators. The audience becomes a part of the dialogue even though it would remain silent. Antigone's appeal is simultaneously addressed to the audience, which is capable of responding in its own way. Where there is a scene, there is an assembly of spectators, without which there would be no theatre. This is even though Aristotle considered a spectator to be an individual person, because he emphasized the ethical dimension of tragedy and the fact that tragedies presented the issue of ethical choice for individuals.[82] The scene makes possible the experience of the tragic, which, according to Gould, 'is to be lived through, perceived, and recollected collectively as well as individually.'[83] What is more, the ethical on the stage depends 'decisively on alien, or extraneous instances that, in the case of theater, are generally identified with the spectators or audiences.'[84]

I would like to emphasize that spectators are an assembly gathered together. The answering audience addressed is not a collection of individual spectators but an assembly. However the assembly that is part of the dialogue is not to be considered a consensual community with an identity. It is a singular assembly and as such it 'a *generic* public, a chance public' that 'represents humanity in its very inconsistency.'[85]

There is, however, one thing the chance audience shares. It is the presupposition of equality. Theatre presentation addresses the spectators as equally capable subjects. It is the addressing itself that is based on the presupposition of equality among the audience. Tragedy cannot do without this presupposition. When Creon interrogates Antigone or the citizens say 'no' to a refugee, those in power recognize these others as equal subjects capable of speaking and argumentation. The same applies to the audience that is addressed by words and action. Hence the scene is a space of equality.

The spatial arrangements of the ancient tragedy, an essential element of the scene, signifies in itself the condemnation of tyranny. The tragic scene itself is a democratic phenomenon taking place in an open public space. Theatre is a public assembly taking place in the space where everyone is able to see not only the play but also each other. Guénoun circles this space: the actors are part of the circle and form its closure. What is presented on the stage and what experiences are aroused among the spectators coincide. Even though the stage presents the community for the spectators, the stage and its discourse are integrated into the assembly. The space of theatre is thus the *polis* assembled together. Theatre does not do politics; it takes place in a political space. However, while the stage is part of the assembly, it is also exterior to it.[86] This coincidence and distance protects the critical distance that prevents the theatrical event from being turned into the closed community of communion. Theatre as an assembly is about the will of the community, which includes political and ethical disagreements.

Theatre—like the agora, the court, and the games—are what Honig calls public things. They do not take care only of our needs but are 'part of the "holding environment" of democratic citizenship; they furnish the world of democratic life.'[87] The scene gathers the spectators to see, experience, feel, and think together. This kind of public thing constitutes, complements, limits, thwarts and interpellates us into a democratic subjectivity.[88] Tragedy thus binds 'citizens into the complicated affective circuitries of democratic life.'[89] Theatre as a public thing and a holding environment includes an element of chance. What happens and how it takes place on the stage is not programmed or entirely rule-based. Such theatres are chance laden environments, events, and institutions, which include disagreements and the dialogue. The scene carries in itself a chance.

Rancière uses the concept of scene to describe a political space of action and speech. This can be inverted: the scene may be considered in the light of the political scene. The theatrical scene is not the theatre institution but a space and time for the exhibition of disjunction and disagreement, the conflict of arguments and interpretations, and the division of ethical reason as well as the demonstration of equality. What is ignored, silenced, or marginalized, events that are not considered as connected, unexpectedly appear on the stage as significant and connected. The scene is always the local and provisional space of political scenography that has a capacity 'to universalize the singular.'[90]

Finally, the scene includes seeing, which differs from the position of the philosopher who would observe tragedy from the distance of theory. The root word of the Greek term *theoria* (theory) is *theo* (to look/the act of seeing). *Theoria* means viewing or looking at something attentively. As a noun it refers to a sight and a spectacle. The Greek term *theatron* (theatre) has the same root word. *Theatron* is a place from which to see, a place where *theoria* is practised, which requires a spectator (*theatēs*). Theatre and theory are intimately related through seeing and observation. Both theatre and theory privilege sight and viewing, even though theatre is a space for multiple senses. One might consider the function of theory in terms of watching a tragic play from a safe (abstract) distance; seeing it as a demonstration of clear ideas. The theory of theatre should not be based on a theory that looks at theatre but on a thinking of theatre as the site of the practice of theory before watching spectators. If we activate the other meaning of the root word *theo* (to run), which designates a journey and a path, we could define theatre not merely as a spectacle but also as a path, a trajectory, a succession of events and action, bodily movements, and sound waves. It points to a trajectory of catharsis.

What is supplement for the theory, *theatron*, the scene, is to be considered as the precondition of the theoretical gaze, *theoria*. By including seeing in the scene does not give it any hierarchical superiority. The scene is the space of dwelling, thinking, and measuring.

12

Theatre Truths

After having failed in his attempts to write *Empedocles*—the repressed theatricality will always return from the cracks of the philosophical system and dialectics—Hölderlin attempted to think tragedy by translating Sophocles. We have already seen how he managed to take a step from the speculative essence of the tragic poem to tragic transport on stage, which he desperately tried to bring to language.

Jean-Jacques Rousseau writes a letter to d'Alemberto. He is worried about the nature of theatre. Placing himself at the centre of the conflict between Plato and Aristotle, he confesses to his friend that he is afraid that theatre cannot be united with morals and republican austerity. Spectacles, made for pleasure and not for utility, include infinite types of people with different morals and characters. Actresses, well, they may not be so well behaved as other women. Even good laws may not suffice to repress abuses related to theatre. And 'everything is still problematic concerning the real effects of the theatre.'[1] Reason could deal with pure passions aroused by a theatre presentation, but 'reason has no effect in theater.'[2] Because of this, the theatre does not function, Rousseau concludes in his national or cantonal aesthetics, as a self-representation of the people in the joy of solidarity and fraternity, communion itself.[3] He is right, but he admits, against his intentions, why theatre produces theatre truths. So far, so good.

Now, we can explicitly address the question of the ethical. The ethics of tragedy ought to reflect the ethics of the reading of tragedy, the question which cuts through Derrida's oeuvre.[4] A theoretical discourse about the ethics of tragedy that describes tragedy and demonstrates ethics independent of the theatricality of tragedy is a mere ethical *theory*, which is unfaithful both to the poem and the scene. To recognize the excess of the scene is not to oppose the text and the scene nor the scene and the ethical. The ethical is not to be reduced to the text. It functions in tragedy due to the material base of the text-scene. Theatre is not moral philosophy and should not be thought in the service of an ethical theory.

A theatre event is 'an event of thought,' which does not turn theatre into a theoretical or philosophical presentation.[5] The theatrical event of thought is the theatrical presentation itself, or more properly, it is what is included into the scene but as something that the scene produces. The text and the scene think to produce theatre.

This may be considered an immanent relation to tragedy, and theatre in general. This is not any kind of pure immanence. Badiou uses the term to refer to the combination of immanence and singularity.[6] Immanence refers to the fact that there is no exterior truth that the tragic scene would represent. The scene is 'rigorously coextensive with the truths that it generates.'[7] It is important to note that Badiou does not speak of the single truth or the fundamental idea, but of truths, which are always already heterogeneous truths. And *a* truth is an infinite multiplicity. Singularity indicates that these truths belong to the scene. They are given exclusively in theatre and are not reducible to other truths, be they political or scientific. The scene 'is *itself* a truth procedure.'[8] Hence, the tragic performance presents truths in and through the original mimesis of action. Rousseau and Diderot understand the work of the actor as the original mimesis. The actor is a man without properties and, more generally, he reveals the fact that there is no such thing as human nature, since 'the constitution of the humanity of man passes through a process of imitation and identification with the other,' that is, the constitution of man is an original mimesis.[9]

Theatre 'operates in the realm of *truth*.'[10] Once again, it is not my—or any philosophical—treatise that produces tragic truths. Theatre truths are truths produced by theatre itself. A theoretical treatise may expose these truths and make 'disparate truths compossible,' which is Leibniz's concept referring to a possible world, where contradicting and oppositional truths exist together.[11]

A theatre presentation is finite in space and time, limited by its completion and the framework of its presentation. Like the scene, a tragedy as a play inquires into its own finitude. A tragic play is not a finite incarnation of the infinite truth, as the romantic conception of tragedy assures. We must differentiate between tragedy as a work of art and a truth. Neither an event nor a truth, a tragic play as a work of art is a fact of tragedy as art. A tragic play is 'the subject of an artistic procedure'—and a tragic 'truth is an artistic configuration initiated' by an event.[12] Let me put this slightly differently: The scene is an event of a theatrical configuration that produces a theatrical truth.

There is no truth of this truth. The presence of tragic truths does not come from a previous presence, since they are produced by the scene that actualizes the text. Even in the tragic poem these truths are immanent to the text as potentialities to be actualized. Truths of tragedy are becoming-truths of truths without any model of the factual truth or the normative idea. These truths deconstruct the difference between description and prescription. Tragic truths are produced without ideal truths as their model and without themselves being turned into ideals. The divisions between truth and art, *phusis* and *tekhnē*, or origin and mimesis are interrupted. The production of tragic truths is an original production without ready-made models. What is produced is not the truth in itself but original truths of tragedy. What I mean is that these truths originate from theatrical production processes. The materiality of tragedy produces its original truths. These truths must be understood as original mimetic products, as results of the fashioning based on textual and scenic productive forces and their relations. In other words, these tragic truths originally and factually fictionized are not based on any philosophical, aesthetic or artist idealism or speculation but on theatrical materialism.

Concrete Tragic Situations

Badiou proposes an ethics that 'proceeds from concrete situations, rather than from an abstract right, or a spectacular Evil.'[13] The ethical hails from two concrete situations: situations presented in tragedies and the situations of theatre events. Ethics proceeds from tragedy as the text and the scene. Theatre truths in tragedy are not descriptions, facts, or scientific truths. They are ethical truths. The material base is intimately related to these ethical truths, which effects the theatrical production means and relations. Truths are cut off from the authority of the text and the author, dissected from any particular situation of the author. But this cut also combines. The text of a tragedy arrives at a scene or addresses it. At the same time, the ethical has arrived on the stage by overflowing the letters of the text. A kind of 'twofold anatomy lesson'[14] The ethics of tragedy consists of the chiasmus of these two elements, the tragic poem and the scene, each one facing the other. The scene plays a crucial part in the production of ethical truths. The scene actualizes and presents singular truths time and again. Every time the scene 'amplifies our situation in history,' which explains the gravity of the scene.[15] Two theatrical processes—textual and scenic—whose combination defines the ethics of tragedy keeps it from becoming an ideal construction or speculation. It takes place in the realm of the practical materiality of theatre.

The work of truth that would bring forth the truth of being or produce the truth in a dialectic process does not precede the interconnected pair of mimesis and presentation. Ethical truths are not to be thought as the origin and *arkhē* of tragedy, that is, the essence chronologically and logically prior to mimesis and presentation. Then again, these theatre truths are not without connection to the mimetic origin of tragedy. There is a hiatus between truths and presentation, but this hiatus is a connecting one. Due to it, singular truths produced by tragedies are simultaneously truths at the origin of tragedies. There is a paradoxical twist. The hiatus turns the products and effects to origins which are origins merely as the products of a theatrical presentation. A tragic presentation is the presentation of the law that prohibits origins and immediacy. The medium and mediacy of presentation produces and figures truths as its own origin and essence. Hence, *tekhnē* is the condition of *phusis*, which becomes the condition of *tekhnē*, but only after the fact. 'The *origin* then presupposes, indeed, a *representation*: *mimesis* or *Darstellung*.'

Anagnōrisis contains the possibility of turning out itself to be an unexpected turn, whose singularity cannot be stabilized in a prediction or a positive rule.[16] Ethical truths arise as singularities that appear in sudden shifts of events, actions, and characters. Rather than being the objects, themes, or topics these truths are the effects of events, which depend on how they are positioned with respect to actions, characters, bodies, and words, that is, how they are placed and displaced in the text and on the stage. They are recognized in their sudden, even uncanny, exposure. The appearance of these truths combine *peripeteia* with a shift from ignorance to awareness.

Tragedy attacks the defensive humanitarian didactic and moralism. It is not an institution that would represent or set moral norms, common values, or political ideologies. It is intimately linked with truths, which are not facts or Hegelian ideas that would gather singularities and pluralities into a 'self-subsistence, self-determined unity of distinct moments of becoming,' as Nancy puts it in his Hegel-reading.[17]

The Aristotelian tradition emphasizes 'organisation, framing, construction, giving form to a process which runs from a beginning to an end, with a middle in the middle.'[18] To consider tragedy in a non-Aristotelian way is not, however, to claim that the theatrical presentation would be created out of formlessness. The text gives a form but, simultaneously, the presentation figures from the scene another form. The textual and scenic forms are bound together by the moment of formlessness. This is how to understand the creative productive relations of tragedy. Ethical truths are not Hegelian ideas in which the scene gives a sensible presentation. They are instead produced by and through the theatre production. If we say that they are formless, we ought to cross out the word 'are.' They are in their formulation as the production forms them. Therefore, a tragedy takes place in and through presentation itself, which is a motion and a movement, a temporal-spatial spacing. Here tragedy touches the sublime not as a presentation without presentation but as a theatrical presentation that presents itself and as it presents itself.[19]

However, the theatre production process, which includes the aforementioned elements, can be understood from the perspective of what Lacoue-Labarthe calls fundamental mimetology. The combination of the poem and the scene produces the origin itself. The original mimesis is what makes action present on the stage and figures ethical truths. The origin is thus fictionalized and figured. The text is not the origin as it itself brings things into presence through the original mimesis—and in the theatre, it is part of mimetic productive forces. In other words, tragedy does not model itself on any pre-given form or model, since in tragedy the model is nothing but 'its own becoming-model, which makes it present as such.'[20]

If tragedy somehow addresses the question of being (*Seinsfrage*), it has to be the question of being-with (*Mitseinsfrage*). The scene has no sense without the sense of coexistence. Truths are truths between tragic figures, even co-produced truths; truths are produced through the common appearing of action (*praxis*) and character (*ethōs*). This does not mean that they would be common truths, but they have a weight not merely as thoughts in themselves but as thoughts produced by action that relates beings and things, bodies and voices on the stage.

A word of caution: the theatre should not be reduced to the question of being or being-with, which would lead to sacrificing the theatricality of the theatre for the phenomenology and/or aesthetics of theatre. Because of this, let me come back, once again, to mimesis and caesura. Lacoue-Labarthe distinguishes between a restricted and general mimesis. Restricted mimesis corresponds to the reproduction, reduplication, or copy of what is already given or established. General mimesis is *poiēsis*. It (re)produces supplements that are themselves original. Mimesis is to be understood as originary mimesis, that is, a productive and creative mimetic *tekhnē*. Therefore, the scene, and more fundamentally identity, is always torn and doubled instead of being sutured into a stable, coherent, and consistent essence.[21] The origin of theatre—an original theatre, an anterior theatre as a mimetolgy—is the scene filled with words and bodies, thoughts and actions, gazes and voices, constructions and perceptions. The theatre/scene is the presupposition of all arts, at least if we understand art as the making of a scene. The origin of tragedy—theatre, art, perhaps even philosophy—is the scene.

The scene and caesura are intimately connected. The caesura is the condition of the possibility of the presentation of the tragic. It is a 'counter-rhythmic interruption,' which organizes the rhythm, and therefore, the sense of the ensemble.[22] More specifically, the tragic caesura is the caesura of the scene, which is the origin of tragedy and theatre more generally. That is, the origin is the scene. Therefore, tragedy is the scene of a mimetological presentation interrupted by caesuras. This movement of rhythm and counter-rhythm create the sense of mimetological scenes. Therefore, the scene, caesura and mimesis are an original combination that is the precondition of the sense of tragic event.

Moreover, for Nancy, immanent to the art is the idea of singularity. It avoids theoretical generalizations. If aesthetics is an ontological 'ground' of the art, it is the ground of a plurality of arts and art works as well as the diversity of senses. Tragedy comes into being by differentiating itself from other genres—and a tragedy differs from other tragedies. Thus, a tragedy has a double singular existence. What comes to the ethical truths tragedies produce are thus necessarily singular truths. Before moving on to these theatre truths we can define the scene as a spacing that has two sides: *1)* A spacing that organizes the tragic world of actions and bodies, and *2) a* spacing that propels or throws singular truths into presence.

With these truths we come back to the grand themes of courage and justice Lacan spoke of in his first seminar.[23]

Antigone begins with a particular situation, the elements of which include acts of violence, moral and legal norms, justificatory discourses, popular conceptions, authoritarian and revolutionary words, corpses and birds, silences and cries, rituals and revolts, borders and conflicts, exiles and citizens. Antigone and Ismene as well as Haemon and Creon find themselves part of a set of a multiplicity of elements that is structured by a particular count that distinguishes these elements as the elements of the situation. As set theory asserts, the situation always includes a void or an empty set to which nothing belongs. Therefore, the foundation of the situation is a void. As a consequence, the set cannot self-ground itself and structure itself as a closed unity.[24]

The state of the situation, which is not the situation but a meta-structure of the situation, constructs a united whole by arranging and combining the counted elements together. For example, the set of Thebans includes those who are counted as the members of the *polis*. The state of the situation organizes the elements by counting them as parts of the *polis*, that is, as rulers, citizens, guards, aristocrats, seers, aliens, family members, and so forth. The state keeps elements in their designated proper places and positions. In this count, the aforementioned void exists. The meta-structure of the state that imposes an order on the situation and names its parts also manages the void by preventing it from being exposed. As women, Ismene and Antigone are the founding void of the situation. The state of the situation includes sisters but only as it excludes them from the set of elements that belongs to the *polis*. It prohibits Antigone's revelation, which is exactly how the scene presents her.[25]

This is not all, since tragedy is a sign that points 'to what is to come rather than what merely is.'[26] Antigone's act interrupts the state of the situation that counts, names, manages, controls, and excludes. Her act cuts through the representation of the law and the authority of the *polis*. Something new and unpredictable happens as she defies the valid law and the legitimate socio-political order. She, who used to be integrated into the state of the situation as a void, does not merely break the law but also presents herself as belonging equally to the *polis* and having equal capacity for political speech and argumentation. From the space of the void Antigone presents her law that interrupts the representation of state law.

In this event, she tears herself away from the position of female passivity into which the state had coerced her and articulates a singular truth of the situation. The truth is not something already present that she would *re*present, but a truth that emerges due to and through the event. Instead of verifying, she proclaims the truth at the limit of the void. This is a theatrical-evental site, which, as a part of the situation, is included in the state of the situation but not recognized by it.

The theatre event is an irreducibly singular one. It cannot be inferred from the situation and it is beyond state law. That is, the event exists only because of her intervention on the stage. Antigone proclaims the event to exist. Antigone's law begins with this event to which she shows fidelity. In her action and speech, in her resistance and revolt, she practices absolute fidelity to the event.

There are three steps in this process. First, she encounters Creon's decree and Polynices' body. Second, she declares her resistance first with words, then with action. Third, she is 'faithfully connected to the name of the event,' to Dike, to the unwritten law.[27] These moments are marked by her fidelity to her action and cause. These three interrelated moments on the stage are connected by the concepts of the subject and truths.

The ethical theatre truths in *Antigone* are *1)* courage, *2)* justice, and *3)* care. They are knotted together by ethical catharsis. Courage, which includes revolt, transgression, and confrontation with limits and borders, brings forth justice and care; which cuts through courage and justice. The knot designates what needs to be rendered 'at once to the propriety of each one and to the common impropriety of all.'[28]

Courage

The tragic hero, like Antigone, does not remain in the conventional position. Her action interrupts the community and her words constantly repudiate authoritative discourse. As discussed, she stands out in her *kalos*, beauty in the brightest light, which draws Eros to herself and at the same time Eros draws her away from the customary lawfulness.[29] At each moment of her course on the stage, Antigone affirms the excess of possibilities that may have previously been considered impossible.

Antigone, who confronts the excess of possibilities, is vulnerable like Ismene or Haemon. The considerable painful experiences and destructive misfortunes may destroy even the most flourishing life.[30] King Priam lived the most prosperous life blessed with great wisdom, political power, and children but a great misfortune changed (*metabolein*) everything. In the end, his life could not be considered a life of happiness (*eudaimonia*).[31] Antigone's life may be considered a life of happiness if we consider Aristotle's two definitions of happiness. First, activities in conformity with excellence constitute happiness. Second, a virtuous person, like Antigone, 'will not be readily dislodged from his happy state.'[32] However, the fate of her family shows that happiness is fragile. How much can sisters endure? For a tragic hero, there would be no happiness without endurance and courage.

Aber treulos / Fängt man mich nicht. (But faithless / Will they not catch me).[33] This is how Brecht's Antigone crystallizes her courageousness. Her courage—and also Haemon's as he resists his father/sovereign/judge—is the 'courage of a possibility' that she invents and defends.[34] This courage includes the acceptance of the fundamental insecurity of existence and the anxiety before the excess of possibilities of being over fixed positions and common values.

Aristotle defines courage (*andreia*) as a mean with respect to fear (*phobos*) and daring (*tharros*). Primarily, courage is concerned with death in battle since this kind of death takes place at the moment of the greatest and noblest danger. Courage requires, firstly, a display of strength and prowess, secondly, to be fearless with respect to a noble and honourable death. Courageous action can be exhibited also in situations other than war, but there must be a similarity between the purest manifestation of courage and courage in a wider sense. Aristotle defines courage in a wider sense as a confident way to face dangers and threats. A courageous person follows practical reason and this reason bids him to choose the noble act.

Antigone chooses the noble act to defend the singular-universal unwritten law, which is, as we have shown, an excess over the law, the state, the place, and the symbolic. It requires courage to choose insubordination with respect to the political and symbolic orders. She does the latter since her dedication to the unwritten law carries her towards the limits of the symbolic.

Courage is not so much the *ethōs* of Antigone or Haemon but their way of acting. The hero is defined by her courageous action. Antigone, to cite Aristotle, 'feels and acts as the occasion merits.'[35] Antigone defends her fatal decision to Ismene that 'it is honourable (*kalos*) for me to do this and die.'[36] If she would not act, her 'death will not be one of honor (*kalos*).'[37] Because she acts, she will die in the sparkle of beauty (*kalos*). Due to her ethical—honourable and beautiful—action for the noble cause, she rises in the radiance of her own being, as Lacan has showed.

Could Antigone have decided not to follow her desire and remain in her designated position as a woman? Could she have chosen Ismene's possible possibility instead of her own impossible possibility? Could Haemon have remained silent, mourned awhile, and taken his proper place in the Theban political order? The answer is 'no.' Then again, 'why not.'

The term drama is related to the verbs *prattein* and *poiein*, but also dereived from the Greek verb, *dran*, 'to do.' While *praxis* is action itself (tragedy being the mimesis of this action) and *poiesis* refers to a productive action, drama indicates the decision to do what constitutes the action, which, for its part, realizes the decision. Claire Nancy connects *dran* to the choice the tragic hero makes without any normative or justificatory guarantees.[38] Derrida's conception of the moment of decision as a madness describes well Antigone's situation in which she finds herself. The decision is not insured by normative or theoretical guarantees, by tradition, authority, orthodoxy, rule, or doctrine. It exceeds calculation and legal certainty by coming into being in an excessive space of decision without which all responsibility would be destroyed, that is, if decision is transformed into a programmable effect of determinant causes, there is no ethics.[39] Even if the yet-to-come decision captivates Antigone before her actual choice, there is a decisive moment in which she is between freedom and necessity: free to decide what must be done. Guénoun considers *dran* as being contained in the action, which makes its undivided normative heart the heartbeat of an action.[40] Antigone's and again Haemon's relation to the action is one of courageous responsibility, which comes with the decision even if it would precede the decision. To use Derrida's words, responsibility is the 'already-there of the not-yet.'[41]

I hope that I have convinced you that there is no *Moralität* of tragedy but only the *Sittlichkeit* of tragedy. Morality belongs to the realm of calculative reflection, ethics to incalculability. Ethics requires, as tragedy shows, an immediate answer, an answerable answer. In its immediacy, a situation cannot wait until the ethical has gone through the process of juridical or moral legislation or a theoretical-normative systematization. Neither can Antigone's or Haemon's ethical decision and action be postponed so that it can be justified by a consensual deliberation or a speculative dialectics. What is given in the here-and-now of the tragic situation cannot be put aside or delayed. Both Antigone and Haemon realize and actualize the fact that *something must be done*.

Ismene is in a similar situation as she decides to act by publicly standing beside Antigone and defy the sovereign. At that point, Ismene must see clearly the situation and the required action. She at once transgresses the position she is given by the Theban order as well as by Antigone. She becomes visible and claims her equal capacity to resist the unjust law.

Does fear play any role at the moment of their decisions? For Aristotle, a courageous person is fearless but not beyond fear. Even a fearless tragic hero may experience fear. Antigone, Haemon, and Ismene may have rationally evaluated that there will be fatal risks and dangers, and experience fear. However, they do not escape the object, action, or event that causes fear, since they have chosen the noble cause. They fear those things but 'will withstand them.'[42] Lacan would not deny this. Antigone stands her ground, but this is 'not a path one can take without paying the price.'[43] 'One knows what it costs to go forward in a given direction, and if one doesn't go that way, one knows why.'[44] Aristotle affirms Lacan's point by saying that a courageous person is 'as unshakeable as a human being can be.'[45]

Antigone shows no hesitation whatsoever. She does not beg or plead but dares and challenges. If there is any sadness, it is defiant. The course of the events is not a presentation of her ethical choice in the making, since her choice is made before any words are pronounced. The rest of the play is an affirmation of her faithfulness to the cause. Or in Lacan's words, Antigone 'reveals to us the line of sight that defines desire.'[46] This line of sight leads us, on the one hand, beyond the Hegelian reading of tragedy, and on the other hand, beyond the ethics of good. At the end of this line, 'We know very well that over and beyond the dialogue, over and beyond the question of family and country, over and beyond the moralizing arguments, it is Antigone herself, who fascinates us.'[47] There are other courageous figures in the play that should fascinate us.

For Lacan, the question of ethics is: Has the subject given in? This question does not concern the moral character or quality of the subject but the existence of the subject. 'To give in means to disappear. Nothing will then have taken place.'[48] The subject gets dissipated into the nonsense of the positive juridical or moral law as soon as the maxim is perverted into a form of giving in. Lacan verifies this. 'Desire, what is called desire, suffices to make life meaningless if it turns someone into a coward.'[49] Cowardice, defined by the perspective of ethics, is to give in for the sake of some good (self-interest, identity, nation, humanitarian care, the other, utility, moral values, the law, the state, the socio-political consensus). It is an ethical betrayal, and on this score, courage is at the heart of the ethical.

What Lacan avoids seeing is that this line of sight cannot be seen as the isolated figure of Antigone or the lonely figure in the poem but only as the line of sight that takes place on the stage. Lacan's courageous Antigone, who is faithful to her desire, must be rethought as part of the scene, which for Lacan is present in its absence. This is not restricted to *Antigone* but is a general problem in Lacan's understanding of Greek tragedy.

Antigone, subjected to the necessities of the world, is released from the bonds of the everyday *polis* as she achieves her authenticity by courageously confronting her finitude. She stands firmly between a return to darkness and the radiant presence, where she is exposed in the integrity of her being as the guardian of the radiance of being.[50] As death stands before her as the shrine of nothing, she stands in the clearing of truth (*aletheia*).[51] Once again, this must be understood as an ethical event (*Ereignis*) that takes place only in the tragic movement that takes place on stage as a theatrical presentation. The clearing of truth requires the presentation of the action and the event, that is, the scene, which insists on Heidegger's reading of tragedy despite his continuous attempt to deport the theatricality of tragedy from the tragic poem and his reading of the text.

Courage is what the scene carves, tears, and claws out. The scene presents courage not as the demonstration of isolated courageous figures. Courageousness functions only in interrelation with various actions, conflicts, and characters. It also functions in relation to those who have to endure terrible things from other than noble causes, like Creon who is not courageous but acts through wit, daring, and overconfidence.

Antigone becomes what she is—the figure of the tragic hero—through her action motivated by the courage to follow faithfully the noble cause. This scene presents this courage not as her *ethōs* but as her action that takes place in the context of the 'objectivity' of the tragic transport, conflict, and the destiny she makes her own. Courage is an insubordination that exceeds the pre-given place, locus, position, and law. It addresses and carries out the disorder or dissensus of the symbolic order. Courage, rather than being Antigone's attribute, is the divisible process of intrinsic existence of a tragic figure. That is, Spinoza's fortitude, a strength of mind that sustains itself from ethical truths.[52] Antigone's courage splits the symbolic order and marks the social reality with an internal division. It is 'the assumption of the real by which the place is split.'[53] The presentation of courage is activated by a tragic conflict, incarnated in the action and embodied by Antigone as well as Haemon and Ismene. We should not ignore Eurydice, who resists her subordinated position by committing suicide. Rather than being a desperate act, it shows her fortitude. Her death is to be considered an ultimate courageous act of resistance.

Hegel considers that even if a woman has a desire, she has no right to it. Haemon or Creon, who goes out of the home into civil society, have the right to their desire but 'the politico-sexual instance deprives the woman of the right to desire as well as her freedom concerning desire.'[54] Antigone's desire attacks this phallocentric conception of desire as she claims for herself the structure and trajectory of her desire and configures her own action and destiny. Consequently, she has the courage and ability to undertake the risk of an ethical action brought forth by the scene of desire.

Her courageous sisters are found in Aristophanes' political satire *Ekklesiazousai* in which woman have decided to take over Athens. They do not oppose some particular law or socio-political practice but women's unequal position in society. Dressed as men, they attend the Assembly and manage to pass a law which puts women in charge of the *polis*. An egalitarian government is set up, property is declared communal, and desire and sexual relations are democratized. As Praxagora declares: 'The poor will no longer be obliged to work; each will have all that he needs, bread, salt fish, cakes, tunics, wine, chaplets and chick-pease ... The ugliest and the most flat-nosed will be side by side with the most charming.'[55]

Justice

Courage is a process of tragic division and disagreement that allows for the advent of justice. In *Antigone*, as in the refugee tragedies, courage intrinsically refers to justice, the sense of which is not only the scission in the essence of the law or the juridical, political, and moral order but a radical change in the concepts of law, legality, and legitimacy themselves. As an ethical torsion, justice interrupts the rule of law. An unconditional attitude and radical non-compliance leads to the ultimate limits of being-in-the-world. The law Antigone follows is, for her, 'an unconditional limit or a fixed point (*point d'arrêt*).'[56] She acts and clashes against the laws of the *polis* because, as Etxabe makes clear, she is absolutely certain that her decision is right and she would not be able to be with herself if she did not carry out her intention as prescribed by her perception of the law.[57] This trajectory on the stage discloses justice. Therefore, the play presents an excess of the juridical and moral law over itself from the perspective of the ethical.

Before coming back to justice in *Antigone*, let see how Badiou sees its function in Aeschylus' and Sophocles' tragedies. Badiou presents two different Greek tragic modes. The orientation of Aeschylus' *Oresteia* trilogy is a rupture that allows for the advent of the new idea of justice to emerge. Orestes flees after the murder, which subjectivizes him through anxiety. The Erinyes, the custodians of the repetitive totality of family revenge, are the watchdogs of the super-ego persecuting Orestes. Enter Athena. She is the interruptive force. Her decree ceases the violent repetitive series and brings forth a new right. The dispute is settled by instituting a new rule, justice by numbers, that is, the majority deliberation beyond appeal. 'Athena's degree produces an egalitarian torsion from whence the new juridical coherence ... interrupts the mechanical seriality of revenge.'[58] Athena is hence the name of justice. In the beginning, Orestes was the name of anxiety, but becomes the name of courage. Even if he is devoured by anxiety, he courageously refuses to internalize the law of blood debt. Instead of 'blind fury ... he demands a discussion based on facts.'[59] Hence, justice arises from the interruption of the power of origin as the division of the one law.

If the Aeschylean mode of tragedy orients towards the contradictory advent of justice with the courage of the new, the direction of Sophoclean tragedy is an anguished quest for the super-egoic origin through reversal. Creon represents the super-ego, Antigone being the name of anxiety, the principle of the infinity of the Real. Although they are antagonistic figures, they accomplish the same process, which defines the Sophoclean subject through the combined categories of anxiety and the superego. The unity of this opposition prevails over the division of these figures. Therefore, Antigone's insurrection is a reversal, 'by which the road of the new is barred.'[60] As a consequence, the contradictory origin is returned within the framework of regulations. For Badiou, Sophocles' tragedies are about the returning quest of the near in what is remote. The truth of a patriotic proximity is so intimate that in its name the tragic figure must die to uncover this truth. Aeschylus, the other way around, stands for the remote in the near, an intimate exile.[61]

Badiou relates the difference between these two modes of tragedy to Hölderlin's preference for Sophocles. Hölderlin could not bear the exile without return, to hold on to a step once taken, as Rimbaud would say. He had to maintain the nomination of what is near. 'Exile for him never stopped being the crucifying meditation of the return.'[62] The native reversal that pretends to cure anxiety, where it takes place, is the return of the same. The reversal of exile, which is the denegation and scission of the old law, 'revokes the original in its scant reality, while restoring the real in justice.'[63]

Badiou wishes to erase the past and pass or overtake nostalgia. This is the only way to exceed 'the pregnant form of the return by the way of courage.'[64] As a result of this, Badiou misreads *Antigone*. Unlike him, I do not consider the play a dialectic between super-ego and anxiety that would continue the repetitive series that makes up the social order.

Hölderlin considered tragedy as putting into play the contradiction of the native versus the formal, the heavenly fire versus the sobriety, the holy pathos versus the gift of representation, the beautiful passion versus the perfection of the art and the *polis*. The native place is divided by an internal tragic contradiction. There is a scission in tragedy that sets the foundation of the law against the function of the law of the *polis*.[65] In other words, the original non-law of the native violence is opposed to the finitude of the closure of the Greek legal order. Hölderlin may have questioned his exile, but he did not translate *Antigone* as a tragedy where Antigone did not hold on to the step she had taken. For Hölderlin, as for Sophocles, Antigone was exiled—without return—towards justice.

Antigone is a formless rebel, who stands violently against the function of the formal law. The force of excess is an interruption of the effects of the morality and the efficacy of the legal order, an interruption of the Real in the middle of the symbolic and imaginary order. Antigone is a force that exceeds the political and familial place determined by this order. Thus, she is unhomely, and this unhomeliness or uncanniness is what is ethical. The ethical is the excess of homely (morality). Her insurrection sets the tragic conflict in motion. As she embodies the excess of the formlessness, she cannot be positioned and placed within the regulated finitude of the temporal-spatiality of the *polis*. Creon reacts to her rebellious formlessness by transforming the formal law into the formal too-muchness of the law, that is, into an excessive law, the law of the super-ego. Antigone's act is not an institutive disruption that would recompose a new order of justice. This does not mean that her action, which includes disagreeing with argumentation based on facts, would not be a disruption grounded on a courageous refusal. Her formless excess is an interruption by which a space of justice is opened as a caesura in the closure of the legal and legitimate *polis*. Even if she does not found a new idea of justice like Athena, her rebellion—the scandalous turn away from the given social and family position—coincides with the recognition of justice previously ignored by the formal sovereign (positive law) and the formal excess (the law of super-ego). In the tragic/native reversal, as Hölderlin would say, the entire form of things and laws changes without returning to their native origin. At this moment in tragedy, nature and necessity incline towards a new form as they pass into a new sense of justice.

The courage of refusal and interruption unfolds justice as a generic ethical truth in the tragedies of Aeschylus, Sophocles, as well as Euripides. These tragedies are scissions that open justice but at the same time they cannot be without being in a tension with a return to the origin of the formal rule of law. It is Hegel, who presents another mode of tragedy. In his theory or tragedy, the tragic ethical conflict constitutes the becoming of the unity of the ethical substance. It is this speculative relief of the oppositions that destroys the tragic in tragedy and thus also the ethical dimension of tragedy, where the opposition rages in the ethical.[66]

Antigone speaks in the name and in the place of the goddess of Justice. But immanent to this is a split between human and divine spheres. There is a limit, but 'the human limit is undiscoverable, always disappearing.'[67] This limit appears only through the transgression as the unwritten law is actualized. Becoming conscious of the limit does not make the law of the other (Creon) valid or the law that would reunite the elements of the ethical split absolute justice.[68] There is no calm of equality of laws even in death.

Aristotle differentiates between specific written law (defined by the people in reference to themselves) and the unwritten law (based on nature). There is 'in nature a common principle of the just and unjust that all people share.'[69] This natural law is not what Antigone defends or what I mean. Rather, justice as a theatre truth is about how tragic figures are exposed on stage to the sense of justice.

Antigone touches justice, which is a law that is not a law at the limits of the law. Justice is not a factual or normative object but something that is touched at the limits of the law. Justice is actualized as she touches the limit between the touchable positive or natural law and the untouchable justice. Justice is both untouchable and the limit that may be touched. At the same time, it is neither the representative figure of the foundation of the legal order nor the object used in legal interpretation and adjudication. The scene gives form to justice in its formation. This form that justice will take is not based on any form of law. The formation of justice has no ideal ground, since its ground is the material base of tragedy. The formation of justice is a presentation of justice based on the text and the scene. It is productive forces and relations that figure justice from an unwritten or a non-figurable law.

As you will recall, Antigone knows Zeus (*my* Zeus). She compares herself with Niobe and aims at taking the place of the goddess of Justice. She embodies the singularity of the infinite moment of the act, responsibility, and fidelity. Her ethical act holds itself withdrawn from the figuration of divine truths and common necessities, and for this reason her non-figurative ethical act is the act of truth and a desire for the sense of justice and existence. As a faithful subject turned into a subject of infidelity, she commits a transgressive act in the name of her infallible sense of justice. This sense is not the generality granted by the common human/divine order, institutions, or laws. It can only be *in* common.[70] *Antigone* is a space for the uprising of dissensual politics and ethics in spaces where the consideration of what is just is aroused. *Antigone*, as a scene, makes sense; it allows for a possibility for a new sharing of justice and being-in-common.

Haemon: what about his relation to justice? He touches justice in his own way at the border of sovereign/father law and the citizens. He brings forth justice as a democratic will of the people. It is an unwritten law since it lacks institutional inscription. It is based on the absence of legal ground. The absent ground is the place of the democratic voice of disagreement that transforms an impossible justice into the possibility of a new justice. Haemon's action presents rendering justice to Theban subjects. Justice is measuring that gives a proper measure, which is the affirmation of the equal political capacity of every subject. Justice is measuring everyone as equal in political matters. For Haemon, justice 'designates what needs to be *rendered*.'[71] This means 'returning to each existence what returns to it according to its unique, singular creation in its coexistence with all other creations.'[72] This is to be read by keeping in mind that justice does not come from outside *Antigone* but stirs inside it.

As Derrida says of Hegel's thought, innocence is an absence of action. To be like a stone. Contrary to this, 'the ethical action includes within itself the moment of the crime.'[73] The ethical action takes into account, first, one *and* another law, then one *or* another law, because it has to restrain the other law. Only after this, the law 'commands actually acting,' whether the law is at the level of consciousness or the unconscious.[74] If the opposition between two laws becomes conscious, it is for Hegel more purely ethical and in the order of universality as a law against another law 'even if the crime is committed in the name of the law of singularity.'[75] This tragic 'crime' Antigone commits is where the question of justice is addressed. The justice arises from courageous actions of Antigone and Haemon and not from the dialectical overcoming of opposing laws.

Since I just mentioned Hegel, I should remind the reader that justice in *Antigone* is not presented in Hegelian dialectical movement: a law transgressed by another law negated by justice as a synthesis of these opposing laws. Justice as a theatre truth is beyond or before any sublation movement of abolishing and elevating, negating and preserving. Justice differs radically from opposing laws instead of gathering them into the united unity of justice.

Rather than being a unified essence, justice is a theatre truth that keeps the diversity of laws and ideas of justice open both at an intra- and inter-level. Justice in *Antigone* differs from justice figured in refugee tragedies. In many of these tragedies—and here we should be careful not to consider them as the refugee tragedy but the multiplicity of tragedies that produce their singular truths—justice embodied by the actions of rulers and citizens is presented as hospitality. *Antigone* includes a passage from one justice to another. Antigone and Haemon portray different ideas of justice; and even Creon, at the moment he recognizes the limits of his power, embodies justice as the rule of law.

Care

Antigone is exposed to the world of tragic conflict and projected toward something that is beyond her designated social and familial positions. Instead of being trapped into taking care, she is committed to truths and her cause. Once again, we should not ignore Haemon. They are strangers, which refers to 'nothing other than singularity itself,' as they may ultimately disrupt the conventional way of belonging to the community.[76] A situation places a demand on Antigone, who approves this ethical duty, but it is her faithful conviction that binds her to the demand. Antigone's and Haemon's ethical acts are acts of *pistis* (faith). Faith, 'is entirely an outward act of presence (*une compuration à l'extérieur*)... like clearly turning one's face toward the manifest heavens.'[77] Their fidelity is an opening towards the sense of being-with in the socio-political community and sharing the world with human and non-human others. The glory of the faith that shines only in the tragic figure's excessive act of faith must be kept separate from the glory that shines as the halo of the saint.

However, far from being isolated figures, their transgressive actions take place in a socio-political community. Their strangeness and self-exile arise in the realm of multiple relationships in aesthetically structured worlds. The material base of Sophocles' text and the scene constructs a tragic world where appearing and co-appearing of the tragic figures take place. It is here where *Antigone*—as a text and a scene—produces care as an ethical truth.

Care should be understood in the register of the combination of friendship (*philia*) and care (*kharia*). Care consists of charities and the repayment of these charities, but also favours to others in return for their existence and being-with. *Kharia* refers to goodwill and gratitude, to an altruistic feeling that makes one do something for another. It is great if the recipient is in need of what is important and difficult to get. It is valued in the times of crisis or when the giver is the only one or the first to offer it. Those 'who stand by someone in poverty and those in exile exhibit *kharis*, even if their services are small, because of the greatness of the need.'[78]

Care is not merely goodwill or empathy but related to being friendly (*to philein*), wanting for someone what one thinks is good for the friend, not what one thinks benefits oneself. A friend loves and is loved in a mutual relationship. A friend is friendly to those who are just and with whom the same things are shared. Friends join in doing good.[79] *Philēsis*, a friendly feeling, affection, attachment and love, produces care and caring, which has the sense of being good to an other, *philēton*, for his own sake. *Philēsis* is accompanied by intensity and intimacy that may arise suddenly. It is a befriending; breathing as friends and sharing the sameness and differences as companions and comrades (*hetairoi*). What I mean here with care is centred around the same root of *phil* that connects, *-ein*, which refers to action and character, *-ēsis*, process, *-ēton*, to whom this process is directed, and *-ia*, an enduring condition.

Politike philia is friendship the circle of which includes not only citizens but also others. Political friendship is a form of public care and solidarity that binds together people, citizens, and others. Without it, there is no *homonoia* (social and political concord). *Xenia* is a quest-friendship, a friendship ritualized by customs and laws, a friendship of mythic-aristocratic heroes as well as tragic-democratic figures. It requires the provision of hospitality to suppliants—and the corpses of death brothers and bodies of exiled fathers—who are *xenoi*.[80]

All in all, care should not be understood as humanitarian empathy. It is an ethical truth related to solidarity. As a theatre truth it is not a truth of a proposition that is verified or tested, a definition of a thing or an object, but fidelity, being true to a tragic situation. The ethic of truths that I propose does not proceed from metaphysical ideas or an abstract right but from concrete situations. Antigone's or Haemon's commitment is the process of truth, 'the real process of fidelity to the event.'[81]

Antigone is *kalon*, as we have seen, because her action is done well. She acts rightly and justly, which makes her beautiful. For her, it is 'beautiful to die' for her action, because of her solidarity.[82] At this very moment, her care and solidarity come together with two other ethical truths, courage and justice. Or, as Aristotle would say, Antigone is a just figure, since she has all the virtues that affect other people. Justice is the right distribution of solidarity, caring, and hospitality. The opposite of this is *echtra* (enmity and hostility). Thus, care in *Antigone* is to be considered according to the consistency of courage and justice, that is, a scission in the *polis* and an eruption of something new. In other words, the courage of the excess is an event of justice that requires care. Justice is introduced by the effect of interruption and insurrection, but it requires two forms of care: first, loyalty to the act, second, sharing the commitment with others.

The concepts of confidence, loyalty, and faith are related to courage and justice. Loyalty is consistency, not with the legitimate system, but with the chosen action and justice declared through this action. Antigone transforms the absence of security—there is no socially valid rule that would guarantee, legalize, and legitimize her position, action, and justice—into her excessive ethical force. The courage is to affirm the excess of force of justice over the political, legal, moral, and social order that demands that one give in and follow the law; and that demands that one repeat the self-same and dissolve one's being into systemic dictates. Security would lead her into subjective impotence and betrayal of justice.

As a courageous subject, Antigone is unconditionally faithful to her decision and action. She does not betray singular truths that arise but shows loyalty to them as universal truths. The scene produces an aesthetic and ethical amplification of these truths. They are augmented on the stage, which does not inevitably require a sense of largeness. These truths become powerful ethical causes due the productive process of the scene.

Antigone's relation with Ismene and Haemon, with Creon and the chorus is a sharing of her truth. Haemon's idea of justice is already justice shared by the people, which he then shares with the father and the sovereign. The scene presents an 'active solidarity with truths,' which is shared with others, but sharing does not mean that others would accept or even tolerate these truths.[83] Tragic figures touch each other. Truths touch those figures as truths and are shared so that these truths become embodied as singular entities on stage.

Therefore, the ethics of *Antigone* is not about the absolute character of Antigone, the hero. Instead it is situational and relational. *Antigone* (and even less the refugee tragedies) is not a play that would set a tragic-heroic paradigm. Instead, it consists of a plurality of singular tragic figures acting in Thebes, the tragic world, figured and opened by the text and the scene. The scene includes not only protagonists and the chorus, but also communities, languages, corpses, burial sites, deserts, temples, altars, gods, birds, and dogs. Antigone exists by being exposed to all these other beings and things. Even a tragic conflict would not be possible without a plural singularity—no tragic action, courage, and justice without the movement of 'singularization and, therefore, its distinction from other singularities.'[84] Antigone's fidelity to her cause is also loyalty to materiality, flesh, blood, voices, and corpses as Creon speaks about universality, principles, norms, and subjects.

The sharing of the tragic world of Thebes is the law of this figured tragic world.[85] By this I mean that courage and justice are co-substantial with the reciprocal action of the figures of *Antigone*. They are exposed in their appearing and acting to exteriority, alterity, and multiplicity. This being-exposed is belongingness. Even Antigone cannot avoid 'addressing-one-another' or 'being-the-ones-with-the-others' (*être-les-uns-avec-les-autres*).[86] Her father existed by sharing the world with others as an orphan, as a king and as a refugee as he had to endure truths that were his fate.

Antigone takes place as the presentation of the in-between of plural singularities. The scene presents sharing not as a *relation* (relationship) but as a *rapport*, a relation not as a substance but as an action that happens on stage.[87] The situation is shared by figures of the play as *rapport*. This plurality is not reduced into a common unity. The unity of the Theban tragic world in the theatre event is not made of the consensual essence of community but of diversity, disparity, disagreement, opposition, and conflict. Antigone's becoming a political subject sharing the public space together with other political subjects is the configuration of a truth process that affirms ethical truths.

The scene presents Antigone and Haemon as heroic subjects, whose courageous existence is essentially being together with others, *être-avec*, 'being-with,' in which 'with' is not added to the being of the tragic hero but is originary to her being.[88] If we wish to define the mode of being of the tragic figures as being-with, then the 'with' of this being-with is reformulated through the events on stage.

Haemon defends Antigone not in the name of private *philia* (love) but in the name of reason, justice, and, democracy. He does take up their familial connection but only to note that the father, as a king, should be the defender of these. His argumentation is not as offensive as Antigone's speech. He makes reservations. He would always follow Creon if the father and the king has deliberated judgements (*gnōmas echōn chrēstes*). No marriage has priority over the good and beautiful hegemony (*sou kalōs hēgoumenou*). As the father blames him for acting in the name of a woman, Haemon says that he speaks in the name of Creon, himself, and the underworld gods (*kai theōn nerterōn*, which are exactly the same to whom Antigone had referred). Haemon's act is an ethical act as he shows unconditional solidarity to Antigone and the people. He does not merely represent citizens but is one of them. Unlike Creon, who would be a good ruler in a desert, Haemon recognizes the essential feature of the *polis*, which is a shared space of an infinite amount of finite relations with others and with oneself as an other. Haemon's position is that of being-with. The figure of Haemon brings forth the path that leads from any supposed self-immanency or being-towards-death to a political world where ethical relations with others take place.

Antigone repeatedly affirmed her solidarity to her brother with whom she shared the world. To understand this aspect of Antigone, we have to read *Antigone* together with *Oedipus at Colonos*. In the latter, both sisters show unconditional solidarity to each other and their blind father in exile. Antigone goes into exile once again to bury her brother and is consequently condemned to infinite exile. Exiled multiple times, she aims beyond the gods of myth toward the ultimate limits, towards desire and death. Perhaps, there is a conflict that is opened as a split or a rift in the figure of the tragic hero herself. This is the moment when the tragic hero faces exteriority not as an outside and strange element but as an immanent exteriority, that is, the strangeness in herself. Antigone is strange not merely because she is labelled a stranger by the established order but because she is strange. She does not give up on her desire, her authentic way of being, or her insistence to act. At the same time, in her purity she is necessarily exposed to others, to being-with, to care, which makes her exist as a double tragic hero.

In contrast to this ethical position, Creon incarnates the position of sovereign non-care. The body of Polynices is an absolutely singular body that must be taken care of in the singular situation. For Creon this body is nothing since for him bodies only have the value they have in the established normative order and distribution of the sensible. Recall the political conclusion of Hölderlin's *Antigone*, which transforms a tyranny to republicanism and brings about a revolutionary political and ethical movement that, I would say, reaches us.

This care does not end at the walls of the home. *Hestia* does not belong merely to one particular family. It should be understood as a shared heart (*hestia koine*) of the political community. Moreover, as the refugee tragedies shows, the circle of care also includes non-natives, those who flee terror and persecution to apply and request refuge. As we have seen, refugee tragedies transform ideas about oneself and others. They further transform responsibility into the materiality of bodies, voices as visible signs into refugees, and suppliants requesting solidarity into ethical acts affirming being-with. The tragic figure's existence may be grounded in its relation to being or desire but this groundless grounding forces her to identify herself with the shared world and others. Is care something that is shared under the heaven and shared even with gods? If 'sacred names are lacking,' as Hölderlin wrote, we may conclude that the divine has withdrawn from the world or has diffused itself in fragments into our discourses. In this case, even if the religious or ontotheological gods are dead or irrevocably absent, the withdrawal of gods have left traces—of withdrawal, of presence, of absence—all over. In other words, 'wherever thought comes up against the furthest extreme, the limit, against truth, or ordeal, in short wherever it thinks, it encounters something that once bore, or seems to have borne, at one time or another, a divine name.'[89] Are we now baptizing the hero's experience of the limit with a divine name and then protecting this name from idolatry? This would turn us to the ethics or pragmatics of the divine realm. This is not the case in Greek tragedy. The tragic figures have to assume the responsibility of being-with. Thus, one of the central question of *Antigone* is not how to bury Polynices and how to treat a traitor, but 'how should the polis treat others'—heroes, women, mothers, rebels, refugees, the stateless, suppliants—'in life and death?'[90]

The scene never misses the dimension of sharing. Even the deaths of Antigone, Haemon, and Eurydice are possibilities of 'the with and as the with.'[91] As Aristotle says, friendship (*philia*) is 'a kind of excellence ... very necessary for living,' and the life of happiness is a life shared with friends.[92]

Inevitably, the scene presents various limits between Antigone and Ismene, Creon and Teiresias, Eurydice and Haemon, the guards and the chorus. They are not merely separating walls but veils that may be turned inside out, veils that dance in the wind, porous fabrics that connect bodies, actions, and voices. At these limits, these figures do not separate themselves from each other but expose themselves so that they are touched by dramatic events, bodies, decisions, actions, words, cries, and thoughts. These figures are affected by these multiple touching layers and points. Thus the scene presents a necessary sharing, which has a double sense: having in common and being partitioned. In other words, in the space-time of the scene, sense and truths are produced and announced between actions and bodies. Truths can only happen between figures, falling from one figure to another as they share the tragic world in agreement and disagreement, touching and withdrawal.

The scene implies interpersonal relations and responsibilities. This interpersonal dimension of the in-between is not reduced to a common essence or identity, even though the Athenian *polis* would be praised. Co-existence in tragedy represents a certain distance from the co-essence. The senses of the common and community become critical issues in tragedies. The scene shows how the *polis* is exposed to its non-essential elements, events, or figures, which may be its political, ethical, and economic strength. Perhaps it is not an exaggeration to say that the *polis* presents itself in the production of tragedies as a space of the in-common that challenges the self-same essence. If so, the ethics of tragedy could be said to arise from the theatrical spaces and dramatic moments of the in-common interrupting the sameness of the Athenian community.

Courage, justice, and care—these are the singular ethical theatre truths of *Antigone*. This tragedy is not an exception. All tragedies have their ethical truths. As I have spoken of various tragedies, I have touched on truths that are also in the tragic poems as potentialities. For example, the granting of asylum in *The Suppliants* to those in exile is to be understood as a *singular* ethical truth of hospitability. Concepts of courage, justice, and care play an important role in these truths. However, they are not meta-truths. Singular truths cannot be subsumed to general or common truths at some higher level of abstraction and inclusiveness. There is no truth of singular truths. Perhaps they could be considered generic truths immanent to tragedies. Singular truths do not imitate them but could be unpredictable variables of these generic truths, like hospitability as a variable of care. They may be shared by Greek tragedies, but they have to be produced through and as singular truths time and again on the stage.

Singular truths are immanent truths internal to the scene. They are also universal truths. This does not repudiate their original immanency and singularity. How can one think these truths as singular-universal truths? A possibility is to claim, like Badiou, that theatre is 'a singular procedure of universalization.'[93] The universal emerges in and through the singularity of the theatre event as well as through singular truths.

Singular truths are not particular truths that may have general validity. They transcend the limits of particular orders and instances of knowledge. Antigone's action distances herself from mythological predicates, her designated position in Thebes, and particular laws. Singular truths that emerge in an incalculable way in *Antigone* and in the refugee tragedies are thus not restricted particular-general truths but truths that traverse particular limits and borders.

Singular and universal are not opposite parts of theatre production. Universal truths are not based on some transcendental constitution. Universality is not to be understood as the objective knowledge or the objective morality and legality. It is experienced only through the scene and the production of a trajectory of action, which constitute singular and universal truths. Singular truths have universality at the moment of the presentation, here and now of the scene. On the one hand, singular truths are identifiable as a procedure at work in a theatre situation in which they have universal validity. On the other hand, the scene is a singular procedure of universalization, where the universal emerges as a singularity. This kind of situated universality can be only experienced through the scene that effectuates it. The scene as the localization of a universal singularity and singular universality is the temporal-spatial event of a sudden emergence of singular-universal truths and their coming into presence as such truths.

Even though these truths may fade away as the performance ends, the scene itself has always already opened and closed as an urgent case that in itself pushes spectators to confront these truths. The time of theatre truths is a passage. Perhaps they do not disappear totally. As traces, as left-overs or surplus of the material production of truths, truths continue to live in the infinite iterations of the tragedies. They remain as potentiality in tragic poems. As traces and potentialities truths endure even if they are always already immanent truths. Catharsis may be withdrawn from the passage of time as it is a passage of these singular-universal theatre truths.

Ethical Catharsis

According to Badiou, art has a pedagogical dimension, but it teaches nothing apart from its own existence. The scene is '*encountering* this existence.'[94] This touches on Nancy's idea of the strangeness of art, which is particularly relevant in relation to theatre. The scene is beyond anticipation and it 'comes into presence on its own limit and as this limit, which borders on what is still strange.'[95]

This encounter produces a truth, which re-arranges established forms of knowledge or the distribution of the sensible in such way that this truth interrupts, pierces holes, and cuts. Because the scene always involves the element of chance, the scene may as well fail to become a truth procedure; catharsis is doomed to fail. The failure may be a double failure since catharsis has a dual function.

For Hölderlin, the trajectory of tragedy actualizes catharsis. It happens on stage. In the Aristotelian version it takes place among the spectators. These two versions can function together and by doing so even strengthen the theatre effect. Where it takes place does not matter. The nature of catharsis is ethical.

Catharsis takes place on the stage and is immanent to the presentation of the tragic action and events. That is, the scene is a spacing of ethical catharsis, which can be considered as the verification of the consequence of the events on the stage that inaugurate an open-ended transformative ethical and political process. In *Antigone*, catharsis takes place when justice as a truth emerges due to Antigone's transgressive act that provokes the separation of humans and gods at the ultimate limit.

In the spectators, *Antigone* produces effects of considerable force: 'it moves them, it transports them ... it is a living vibration.'[96] The catharsis functions through gravity, as a weight of the contact of the presentation that surges forth at the theatre. The scene and matter of tragedy *weigh* on our thought, senses, and judgement; and this is what causes the 'purification' of our ability to measure.[97] The scene 'makes it known to you that you will not be able innocently to remain *in your place*.'[98] Being a spectator is to be touched and modified. As a result, the subjective position of a spectator may go through conscious and/or unconscious transformation. Rancière considers the spectator as a subject who thinks/feels, compares and connects, agrees and disagrees as she composes her own tragic poem 'with the elements of the poem before her.'[99] The scene includes a transformative power and it may become a space of an event of transformation. It opens a vector that points towards a radical break with and the transformation of the given situation—the truth of measuring.

Catharsis knits together the text, scene, the audience, and singular and universal truths. This doubles the assembly of the spectators. On the one hand, the assembly of the spectators is part of the scene. The spectators are summoned before the tribunal of the scene and theatre truths. They gather together to make the theatre event possible. On the other hand, the theatre presentation and the effect of catharsis make the spectators products of the scene. The ethical on the stage is a provocation that may cause catharsis. The assembly of the spectators are called to become loyal friends of these truths and to take responsibility for them, to carry on. For the spectators, as long as they are part of the scene and catharsis, these truths are universal truths towards which they may continue to show loyalty.

The *pathemata* that goes through catharsis are not merely humanist emotions and empathic passions but '*painful* affects or troubles of the *pathē*,' which are contrary to pleasure and joy.[100] Fear and pity/compassion, two *pathemata*, but they may have opposite directions. Pity is related to compassion, association, and connection; fear to dissociation and disconnection. The task of ethical catharsis is not to purify these passions; it is to moderate their excess, since in themselves they are disastrous.[101]

Once again, I would like to point out that mimesis and its effect, catharsis, are not to be restricted within the boundaries of passions, emotions, and sensibilities. Catharsis has to be understood in its ethical, theoretical, and intellectual dimensions without compromising its fundamental theatricality. Mimesis and presentation includes a potentiality that the spectators carry on with these truths. Mimesis authorizes catharsis and, simultaneously, the scene denaturalizes mimesis as the natural mimetic faculty of imitation. Mimesis transports its nature by becoming an original figuration and production of events, characters, ethics, truths, and catharsis.

The categorical turn is the law of tragedy that brings together catharsis and caesura. At the same time, immanent to this turn is the law in another sense, that is, the law as the categorical imperative. The tragic figure is turned from limitless passion into a finite ethical subject, one who alone is responsible for her actions and who must show fidelity to the consequences of those actions. Does this mean that the fate of the tragic hero expresses the limits of human being and her possible actions? Yes, for a finite being it is impossible to couple with gods and infinity. No, because with the withdrawal of gods the borders also disappear, or more properly, human beings have the sole responsibility for setting limits and borders. We are not and cannot become infinite beings. It is possible to limitlessly transgress the order of things, the distribution of the sensible, or the symbolic law, but transgressive acts always already include the responsibility of taking care of limits and limitlessness, of the art of measuring.

This is what tragic catharsis is about. The categorical turn that the tragic transport presents is not a native turn back to the nature of our being (which is a product of mimesis). Instead, tragedy presents this turn as the imperative of the possibility of the impossible. Being 'purified' from the desire to couple with gods, we are left alone to act as ethical subjects without any divine or transcendental guidance. The turn leaves humans without divine intuition of their ethical judgments.[102] We have only unwritten laws, which we may imitate in an original way in our actions. Ultimately, ethical catharsis, which brings together law and transgression, limits and limitlessness, categorical turn and categorical imperative, impossibility and possibility, is a caesura in the rhythm of the life of a tragic figure. Continuity is ruptured, the beginning is not equal to what is yet to come. In the transport of *Antigone*, a counter-rhythmic cut and pause coincides with the *Umkehr*, which is not pure negativity but a revolutionary reversal that springs from Antigone's constitutive antinomy of the revolutionary act. The caesura is an interruption constitutive of transgressive human action and a tragic revolutionary turn.[103] Antigone's categorical turn brings together a revolutionary conversion and ethical catharsis.

Antigone as a theatrical performance is not politics in a strict sense. The truths of *Antigone* are new openings and the interruptions are political agendas, institutions, and ideologies. Sometimes, the scene 'requires' a political action and friendship that takes place outside the theatre. The theatre is not without the political, but it is not politics. Catharsis may bring together the tragical and the political without transforming tragedy into politics. The social, communicative, communal, and democratic aspects have always been part of tragedy and theatre, even though too often these tendencies have been philosophically and aesthetically considered secondary.[104]

Conclusion: Capitalism and Tragedy

Back to our dwelling place. I have been exposed to tragedy. I have traced how tragedies present the ethical and rejuvenate concepts such as courage, justice, and care; conflict, community, and law; measure, limit, and violence; fear, pity, and suffering; dwelling, thinking, and measuring. I have considered the function of ethics in relation to tragedy and tragedy in relation to ethics without giving an essential definition of either of these distinct yet related spheres. The ethical and the tragical touch each other due to the scene.

We live in a 'brutally capitalist' situation that affects practically everyone in the world.[1] Tragedy includes the presentation of conflicts and disagreements, but capitalism avoids the images, mimesis, and presentation of conflicts. What is the role of the theatre 'in the age of omitted images of conflict?'[2] All issues are verbalized and made visible even though 'we find hardly a sign of society's capacity to "dramatize" the uncertainty of its really founding and fundamental issues, which are after all deeply shaken.'[3]

The less there is room for rebellious acts and those grand themes we have traced, the more everything is calculated to the last fraction, as Brecht's Fatzer said.[4] There is no lack of economic, technical, technological, scientific, and security measures and statistics. Climate change and human rights violations are thoroughly analyzed and measured. In the context of limitless economic growth, potential catastrophes are only manageable risks. The more we have information and statistics, images and measures, the more we are distanced from our ability to measure; the more social media connects us, the more disjointed is the sending of a message and response. We lack the capacity for measuring, since all measures are already set, produced, standardized, and calculated. Instead of being measuring subjects, we have become measured commodities who consume spectacles. We are permanent spectators without any distance from those spectacles we constantly enjoy, like slaves in Plato's cave.

Tragedies come into existence as theatre in singular theatrical events that come to pass, pass away and, once again, take place. As such, tragedies are unfinished inquiries about truths actualized in tragic events and scenes. Tragic gravity cuts through given structures and affirms new links and sensibilities. Hence, tragedy is an interruption of the capitalist reproduction of one-dimensional discourses and images, and pathological knowledges. The configuration of tragedies 'may always be seized upon again' and 'rearticulated in the name of a new event.'[5]

According to Kierkegaard, the Greeks considered knowing as a recollection. The recollection mourns the loss of the past and has nothing to lose since it has already given up. Modern philosophy, instead, is based on a repetition, which is the same movement as recollection but in the opposite direction. A repetition is *Gjentegelsen* (again-taking) something that takes again or takes back what has been given. What has been, comes into existence as a repetition. A true repetition should also give 'back what is taken again.'[6] The conclusion following from this could be that tragedies are a constant movement of recollection and repetition in which what is recollected and repeated does not remain the same, and on that score, the movement that remodels tragedy is the movement of *différance*, that is, the movement of deferring and differing.'[7]

As Critchley speaks about a *gap* between theory and practice, he concludes that this gap 'opens *in* theater and *as* theater. Theater is always theoretical, and theory is a theater, where we are spectators on a drama that unfolds: *our* drama.'[8] The '*praxis* is internally divided or questioned by *theoria* in the space of the theater, where the empty space of the theater is a way of calling into question the spaces we inhabit and subverting the divisions that constitute social and political space.'[9]

The spectators have 'come to the theater to be *struck* by the theatre truths.'[10] These theatre truths include a revolt in the realm of the thinkable, seeable, and sensible since they set themselves against the general calculation of security and the multiplicity of particular knowledges; against the abstraction of financial exchange and the posited interests of a community; and against global management and identity politics. The spectators are response-able as part of the scene and as answerable participants in the creation of by the theatre truths. This scene summons the spectators into the immanence of the play to exceed themselves and to create their own possibilities to prevail. Subjective transformative processes are provoked. A solidarity among spectators is established.

Tragedy addresses and speaks to us, touches us as we share existence without being reduced to a common essence or a given world view. What the spectators assembled together share is not common measures but the art of measuring. Therefore, measuring is not based on any social and moral order, which would 'be valid independently of the ambiguities of the political world.'[11] The affirmative introduction of generic, singular, and universal truths that the scene produces does not give ready-made measures for the spectators but provokes the question of measuring itself. Perhaps, there is one measure that tragedy presents, 'the measure of that which humanity is capable of.'[12]

Tragedy may cultivate, on the one hand, affects and sensibilities, and on the other hand, measuring and thinking that are not subjected to instrumental rationality and capitalist discourse. Heidegger considers the destiny of European history as a technological enframing in which all that is disclosed requires an enframing that drives out other possible ways to reveal things. Planetary technology is spreading without limits and transforms nature, climate, and animals into exploitable objects and a standing reserve beyond any limits. Instead of being home everywhere, we are transformed into exiles in our dwelling place.[13] Tragedy reminds us that we should use our ability to measure to give technology a proper measure and place instead of leaving it to dominate our being and the world. Our mode of dwelling measuringly does not amount to the domination and annihilation of the planet (and hence human and non-human beings).

Tragedy is a transgressive event, where the tragic hero transgresses the borders and touches the ultimate limits to bring forth justice. Her courage calls attention to her excessive action, as Heidegger and Lacan show. Courage is not, however, limited to tragic heroes. It is for the spectators to whom the scene addresses the ethical demand to be courageous, to not give up their desire. Tragedy calls us to enjoy transgression and fear, outrage and love, shock and justice, revolt and courage, destruction and solidarity.

Tragedy is about a shared way of making sense, and the scene of resistance that produces ethical truths that interrupts the limitless capitalist ideology without ethics. The spectators share the theatre as a space of care while confronting conflict, measuring, and truths on stage. The rhythms and caesuras immanent to it are essential for ethical catharsis, since it is 'a measuring of the diverse human faculties by which the tragic figures or the spectators learn to "count time".'[14]

Tragedy has a double interruptive force: the action on stage and the assembled audience. Similarly, ethical catharsis takes place on stage as the mimesis of the action and among the audience as the theatre effect of the events on stage. Ethical catharsis is about measuring.

Catharsis 'purifies' the spectators from the mastery of pre-given measures and necessities, from the established distribution of the sensible or the state of situation. It is up to the spectators to learn to measure and to commit themselves to truth processes. The spectators are forced to take a stand 'with respect to the history of truth.'[15]

This double ethical catharsis is a transgressive purification that opens unknown possibilities and unthinkable courage. Tragedy shall not remain a mere representation of the prevailing state of things or the spectacle of an *imago mundi*. It must be a dissensual presentation of the human condition, our situation in the world.[16] In this case, it requires us 'to think where we stand, in historical time, with respect to being.'[17] It functions as 'a medium of reflection, as a metaphor, as a vehicle,' where history turns into performance to become an issue for thinking.[18] Tragedy is an excess and exception to the capitalist distribution of the sensible. As a scene it points us to the possibility of the revolutionary reversal.

The task of the philosophy of tragedy is to think the concept of the scene and to distinguish the tragic text, performance, audience, and its ethical truths conceptually from capitalist spectacles, common opinions, totalitarian necessities, and humanitarian moral codes. My treatise on the ethics of tragedy has constructed neither an ontology of tragedy nor a theory of justice. I have traced, on the one hand, the function and effects of tragedies, and on the other hand, the inscriptions of ethical truths in tragedies. 'The essence of philosophical intervention is really affirmation' and a proposal for a new framework of thought.[19] The ethics of tragedy shares this task. 'How to speak to people in such a way that they think their lives otherwise than they usually do?'[20]

Oedipus' *hubris*, to be both the legitimate king and the divine priest, may be compared with capitalist *hubris*. Oedipus, punished not by the gods but by himself, returns to lucidity as a blind refugee. The inner predilection of capitalism drives it to pursue the foreign, a limitless excess that links capital, knowledge, elements, beings, and nature limitlessly. Because of this preoccupation with infinite exploitation, we have lost touch with our native element, which is the precondition of our being-in-the-world. Tragedy tells us about taking responsibility for our actions. We have gained mastery of the excessive fire of capitalism but have forgotten to reverse to what is our native trait, that is, the measure, not as a limit but as an infinite possibility. Our freedom, our possibility to exist, results from becoming an infidel to the new god of capitalism. This means turning away from capitalist excessive passion and turning towards the realm of symbolic law and measuring, that is, we must acquire what is in our mimetic nature as limitlessly measuring subjects capable of ethical, aesthetical, political, and scientific truths without limits. However, the categorical law, which in tragedy is included in the categorical turn as an emancipatory force that includes humans and non-humans, may come too late.

At the end of Sophocles' *Tereus*, the chorus reminds us all: 'Human nature must think human thoughts, knowing this, that Zeus and no one else is the dispenser of what is to be accomplished in the future.'[21] The ethics of tragedy reminds us of our duty to think unthought thoughts and to have the courage to do the impossible. Fidelity is an ethical gravity without which the capitalist world would be left to drag us to our destruction.[22]

In Euripides' *Alcestis*, Heracles, with a large cup and wine-skin in his hands, blusters: 'Do you know the nature of our mortal life?' With a drunken gravity, he answers,

> I think not .... death is a debt all mortals must pay, and no man knows for certain whether he will still be living on the morrow. The outcome of our fortune is hidden from our eyes, and it lies beyond the scope of any teaching or craft. ... Cheer your heart, drink, regard this day's life as yours but all else as Fortune's![23]

But fortune should not be received passively. Tragedy shows we must take responsibility for it, transform it into *our* fate through ethical and political action.

Bibliography

Adkins, Arthur W. H. *Merit and Responsibility: A Study in Greek Values.* Oxford: Clarendon Press, 1960.
Aeschylus. *Agamemnon*. Translated by Herbert Weir Smyth. Cambridge: Harvard University Press, 1971.
———. *Eumenides*. Translated by Alan Shapiro and Peter Burian. Oxford: Oxford University Press, 2003.
———. *The Libation Bearers*. Translated by Hugo Lloyd-Jones. London: Duckworth, 1993.
———. *Suppliant Maidens.* Translated by Herbert Weirs Smyth. Cambridge, Mass.: Harvard University Press, 1956.
Agamben, Giorgio. *Homo Sacer: Sovereign Power and Bare Life*. Translated by Daniel Heller-Roazen. Stanford: Stanford University Press 1998.
———. 'Note luminaire sur le concept de démocratie.' In Démocratie, dans quel état? Paris: La Fabrique, 2009, 11–12.
———. *The State of Exception*. Translated by Kevin Attell. Chicago: University of Chicago Press, 2005.
Alleman, Beda. *Hölderlin und Heidegger*. Freiburg: Atlantis Verlag, Freiburg, 1954.
Althusser, Louis. *Philosophy of the Encounter: Later Writings, 1978–1987*. Translated by G. M. Goshgarin. London: Verso, 2006.
Arendt, Hannah. *The Human Condition*. Chicago: The University of Chicago Press, 1998.
Aristophanes. *The Frogs*. Translated by Benjamin Bickley Rogers. London: Heinemann 1924.
———. *Ecclesiazusae*. Translated by Eugene O'Neill, Jr. New York: Random House, 1938.
Aristotle. *Eudemian Ethics*, Translated by Anthony Kenny. New York: Oxford University Press, 2001.
———, *History of Animals*. Translated by A. L. Beck and D. M. Balme. Cambridge: Harvard University Press, 2014.
———. *Metaphysics*. Oxford: Oxford University Press, 1997.
———. *Nicomachean Ethics*, Translated by Christopher Rowe. Oxford:

Oxford University Press, 2002.
———. *Poetics*. Translated by Stephen Halliwell. London: Duckworth, 1987.
———. *The Politics*. Translated by Carnes Lord. Chicago & London: The University of Chicago Press, 1984.
———. *On Rhetoric*. Translated by George A. Kennedy, New York & Oxford: Oxford University Press, 1991.
Augustine. *Confessions*. Translated by William Watts. Cambridge, Mass.: Harvard University Press, 1979.
Aulagnier, Piera. *La violence de l'interprétation*. Paris: PUF, 1975.
Austin, Michel and Pierre Vidal-Naquet. *Économies et sociétés en Grèce ancienne*. Paris: Armand Colin, 1972.
Azoulay, Vincent. 'Repolitiser la cité grecque, trente ans aprés.' *Annales* 69/3 (2014), 689–719.
Badiou, Alain. 'Discussion.' In *Philosophy in The Present*. Translated by Peter Thomas and Alberto Toscano. Edited by Peter Engelman. Cambridge & Malden, MA: Polity, 2009, 73–104.
———. *Ethics: An Essay of the Understanding of Evil*. Translated by London: Verso, 2001.
———. *Handbook of Inaesthetics*. Translated by Alberto Toscano. Stanford: Stanford University Press, 2004.
———. *L'Etre et l'événement*. Paris: Seuil, 1988.
———. *Monde contemporain et désir de philosophie*. Reims: Cahier de Noris, 1992.
———. 'On Evil: An Interview with Badiou, Alain. Christopher Cox & Molly Whalen.' *Cabinet* 5 (Winter, 2001/2002).
———. *Polemics*. Translated by Steven Corcoran. London & New York: Verso, 2006.
———. *Rhapsody for the Theatre*. Translated by Bruno Bosteels and Martin Puchner. London & New York: Verso, 2013.
———. *Rhapsodie pour le théâtre*. Paris: Presses Universitaires de France, 2014.
———. 'Theatre and Philosophy.' In Alain Badiou, *Rhapsody for Theatre*. Translated by Bruno Bosteels with the assistance of Martin Puchner. London & New York: Verso, 2013, 93–109.
———. *Theory of the Subject*. Translated by Bruno Bosteels. London & New York: Continuum, 2009.
———. 'Thinking the Event.' In *Philosophy in Present*. Translated by Peter Thomas and Alberto Toscano. Edited by Peter Engelman. Cambridge & Malden, MA: Polity, 2009, 1–48.
———. *The True Life*. Translated by Susan Spitzer. Cambridge & Malden, MA: Polity, 2017.

Badiou, Alain with Nicolas Truong. *In Praise of Theatre*. Translated by Andrew Bielski. London: Polity, 2015.
Badiou, Alain and Élisabeth Roudinesco. *Jacques Lacan, Past and Present: A Dialogue*. Translated by Jason E. Smith. New York: Columbia University Press, 2014.
Balibar, Etienne. *La crainte des masses: politique et philosophie avant et après Marx*. Paris: Galilée, 1997.
Ballengee, Jennifer R. 'Mourning the Public Body in Sophocles' *Antigone*.' *Colloquy: Text, Theory, Critique*, 11 2006, 31–59.
Balogh, Elmer. *Political Refugees in Ancient Greece: From the Period of the Tyrants to Alexander the Great*. Johannesburg: Witwatersrand University Press, 1943.
Beaufret, Jean. *Hölderlin et Sophocle*. Brionne: Gerard Monfort, 1983.
Beckett, Samuel. *L'Innommable*. Paris: Minuit, 1953.
Benjamin, Walter. *On the Concept of History*. Translated by Harr Zohn. Selected Wirings 4, 1939–1940. Cambridge, Mass. & London: Harvard University Press, 2003, 389–400.
———. *Ursprung des Deutschen Trauerspiels*. Gesammelte Schriften I.1. Frankfurt am Main: Suhrkamp, 1963.
———. *The Work of Art in the Age of Its Reproducibility*. Third Version. Selected writings 4. Translated by Edmund Jephcott and Harry Zohn. Cambridge, MA & London: Harvard University Press, 2006, 251–83.
Bethke Elstein, Jean. 'Antigone's Daughters Reconsidered: Continuing Reflections of Women, Politics and Power.' In *Life-World and Politics: Between Modernity and Postmodernity*. Edited by Stephen K. White. West Bend, Ind: University of Notre Dame Press, 1989, 222–36.
Blanchot, Maurice. *Infinite Conversation*. Translated by Susan Hanson. Minneapolis: University of Minnesota Press, 1992.
———. 'Literature and the Right to Death.' In *The Gaze of Orpheus, and Other Literary Essays*. Translated by Lydia Davis, Paul Auster, and Robert Lamberton. New York: Station Hill Press, 1995.
Bogue, Ronald. 'The Betrayal of God.' In *Deleuze and Religion*. Edited by Mary Bryden. London & New York: Routledge, 2001, 9–29.
Brecht, Bertolt. *Antigone*. Translated by Judith Malina. New York: Applause, 1990.
———. *Electra*. Translated by E. P. Coleridge. New York: Random House, 1938.
Butler, Judith. *Antigone's Claim: Kinship Between Life and Death*. New York: Columbia University Press, 2000.
———. 'Ethical Ambivalence.' In *The Turn to Ethics*. Edited by Marjorie

Garber, Beatrice Hanssen, and Rebecca L. Walkowit. London & New York: Routledge, 2000.

———. *Gender Trouble: Feminism and the Subversion of Identity*. London & New York: Routledge, 1990.

———. *Precarious Life: The Powers of Mourning and Violence* London & New York: Verso, 2004.

———. *Undoing Gender*. London & New York: Routledge, 2004,

Cacciari, Massimo. *The Unpolitical: On the Radical Critique of Political Reason*. Translated by Massimo Verdicchio. New York: Fordham University Press, 2009.

Campbell, Scott. 'The Tragic Sense of Life in Heidegger's Readings of Antigone.' In *The Science, Politics, and Ontology of Life-Philosophy*. Edited by Scott Campbell and Paul W. Bruno. London & New York: Bloomsbury, 2013, 185–196.

Camus, Albert. 'Lecture Given in Athens on the Future of Tragedy.' In Albert Camus, *Selected Essays and Notebooks*. Translated by Philip Thody. London & New York: Penguin Books, 1970, 192–203.

Chanter, Tina. 'Antigone's Political Legacies: Abjection in Defiance of Mourning.' In *Interrogating Antigone in Postmodern Philosophy and Criticism*. Edited by S. E. Wilmer and Audrone Zukauskaite. Oxford: Oxford University Press, 2010.

Cohen, Edward E. *The Athenian Nation*. Princeton. NJ: Princeton University Press, 2000.

Crisp, Roger. 'Compassion and Beyond.' *Ethical Theory and Moral Practice* 11/3 (2008), 233–46.

Critchley, Simon. *Ethics, Politics, Subjectivity: Essays on Derrida, Levinas and Contemporary French Thought*. London & New York: Verso, 1999.

———. 'Interview with Simon Critchley: The Tragic and its Limits by John Douglas Millar.' *The White Review*, November 2012.

———. *Tragedy, the Greeks and Us*. Ebook version. New York: Pantheon Books, 2019.

———. *What We Think About When We Think About Football*. London: Profile Books, 2017.

Dastur, Françoise. *Death: An Essay on Finitude*. Translated by John Llewelyn. London: Athlone Press, 1996.

———. *Hölderlin:Le retournement natal : Tragédie et modernité & nature et poésie*. Paris: Encre Marine, 1997.

———. 'Hölderlin and the Orientalisation of Greece.' Translated by Hector Kollias, *Pli* 10 (2000), 156–73.

———. 'Tragedy and Evil: From Hölderlin to Heidegger.' In *Law and Evil:*

Philosophy, Politics, Psychoanalysis. Edited by Ari Hirvonen and Janne Porttikivi. London & New York: Routledge, 2010, 31–40.
——. 'Tragedy and Speculation.' In *Philosophy and Tragedy*. Edited by Miguel de Beistegui and Simon Sparks. London & New York: Routledge, 2000, 76–85.
De Beistegui, Miguel. *The New Heidegger*. London & New York: Continuum, 2005.
De Kesel, Marc. 'Antigone's Fart.' A paper presented at a seminar on Simon Critchley, Ghent, 27 May 2000.
——. 'There is No Ethics of the Real.' A paper delivered at the International Conference Rhetoric, Politics, Ethics. Ghent University 21–23 April 2005.
De Vries, Hent. 'Theotopographies: Nancy, Hölderlin, Heidegger.' *MLN* 109/3 (1994), 445–77.
Declerq, Frédéric, 'Lacan and the Capitalist Discourse: Its Consequences for Libidinal Enjoyment and Social Bonds.' *Psychoanalysis, Culture & Society* 11/1 (2006), 74–83.
Deleuze, Gilles. *Difference and Repetition*. Translated by Paul R. Patton. New York: Columbia University Press, 1994.
Denby, David. 'Battle of the Stereotypes.' *New York Magazine. 28 June 1982*, 52–4.
Derrida, Jacques. *Disseminations*. Translated by Barbara Johnson. Chicago: Chicago University Press, 1981.
——. 'Force de loi: Le "fondement mystique de l'autorité" / Force of Law; The "Mystical Foundation of Authority".' Translated by Mary Quaintance. *Cardozo Law Review* 11/5–6 (1990), 920–1043.
——. *Glas*. Translated by John P. Leavey Jr. and Richard Rand. Lincoln & London: University of Nebraska Press, 1996.
——. Margins of Philosophy. Translated by Alan Bass. Chicago & London: University of Chicago Press, 1982.
——. 'Heidegger's Ear: Philopolemology Geschelecht IV.' In *Reading Heidegger: Commemorations*. Edited by John Sallis. Bloomington: Indiana University Press, 1993, 163–218.
——. *Of Grammatology*. Translated by Gayatri Chakravorty Spivak. Baltimore & London: The Johns Hopkins University Press, 1976.
——. Signature Event Context. In Jacques Derrida, *Limited Inc*. Translated by Alan Bass. Evanston: Northwestern University Press, 2000.
——. 'Violence and Metaphysics.' In Jacques Derrida, *Writing and Difference*. Translated by A. Bass. Chicago: Chicago University Press, 1978.
——. *Writing and Difference*. Translated by Alan Bass. Chicago: Chicago University Press, 1978.

Diogenes Laertius, *Complete Works*. Translated by R. D. Hicks. Hastings: Delphi Classics, 2015.

Dufour, Dany-Robert. *Le Divin Marchè: La reviolution culturel libérale*. Paris: Gallimard, 2012.

Dufour, Dany-Robert. *L'individu qui vient ... après le libéralisme*. Paris: Gallimard, 2015.

Easterling, P. E. 'Weeping, Witnessing, and the Tragic Audience. Response to Segal.' In *Tragedy and the Tragic: Greek Theatre and Beyond*. Edited by M. S. Silk. Oxford: Clarendon Press, 1998, 173-181.

Edelman, Lee. *No Future: Queer Theory and the Death Drive* Durham, DC: Duke University Press, 2004.

Elden, Stuart. 'The Place of The Polis: Political Blindness of Jufith Butler's *Antigone's Claim*.' *Theory and Event* 81 (2005), http://muse.edu.

Eliot, George. 'The *Antigone* and Its Moral.' *Essays of George Eliot* London: Routledge and Kegan Paul, 1963.

——. *Felix Holt: The Radical*. Novels Vol. V. Edinburgh & London: William Blackwood and Sons, 1867.

Elytis, Odysseus. *In the Name of Luminosity and Transparency*. Translated by Nobel Foundation. Athens: Aiora, 2016.

Etxabe, Julen. *The Experience of Tragic Judgement*. London & New York: Routledge, 2012.

Euripides. *Alcestis*. Translated by David Kovacs. Cambridge: Harvard University Press, 1994.

——. Translated by E. P. Coleridge. New York: Random House, 1938.

——. *The Children of Heracles*. Translated by Mark Griffith. Chicago & London: The University of Chicago Press, 2013.

Fischer-Lichte, Erika. 'Politicizing Antigone.' In *Interrogating Antigone in Postmodern Philosophy and Criticism*. Edited by S. E. Wilmer and Audrone Zukauskaite. Oxford: Oxford University Press, 2010.

Fisher, Marx. *Capitalist Realism: Is There No Alternative?* Winchester: Zero Books, 2008.

Fletcher, Judith. 'Sophocles' Antigone and the Democratic Voice.' In *Interrogating Antigone in Postmodern Philosophy and Criticism*. Edited by S. E. Wilmer and Audrone Zukauskaite. Oxford: Oxford University Press, 2010.

Foley, Helene P. 'Antigone as Moral Agent.' In *Tragedy and the Tragic: Greek Theatre and Beyond*. Edited by M. S. Silk. Oxford: Clarendon Press, 1998, 48-73.

Freud, Sigmund. 'Psychopathic Characters on the Stage.' Standard Edition 7. Translated by James Strachey. London: Hogart Press, 1953, 305-10.

Freud, Sigmund and Joseph Breuer. *Studies in Hysteria*. Translated by Nicola Luckhurst. London: Penguin, 2004.
Froment-Meurice, Marc. *That Is to Say: Heidegger's Poetics*. Translated by Jan Plug. Stanford: Stanford University Press, 1998.
Gagarin, Michael. *Writing the Greek Law*. Cambridge: Cambridge University Press, 2008.
Gambaro, Griselda. 'Antigona furiosa.' In *Three Plays by Griselda Gambaro*. Translated by Marguerite Fetlowutz. Evanston: Northwestern University Press, 1992, 133–59.
Gatrell, Peter. *The Making of the Modern Refugee*. Oxford: Oxford University Press, 2013.
Gerdes, K. E. 'Empathy, Sympathy, and Pity.' *Journal of Social Service Research* 37/3, (2011), 230–41.
Gernet, Louis. *Droit et société dans la Grèce ancienne*. Paris: Publications de l'institut de droit romain de l'université de Paris, 1955.
Gonzales, Francisco J. 'Beyond or Beneath Good and Evil? Heidegger's Purification of Aristotle's Ethics.' In *Heidegger and the Greeks*. Edited by Drew A. Hyland and John Panteleimon Manoussakis. Bloomington & Indianapolis: Indiana University Press, 2006, 127–56.
Gould, John. 'Tragedy and Collective Experience.' In *Tragedy and the Tragic: Greek Theatre and Beyond*. Edited by M. S. Silk. Oxford: Clarendon Press, 1996, 217–243.
Gouldhill, Simon. 'Collectivity and Otherness: The Authority of the Tragic Chorus: Response to Gould.' In *Tragedy and the Tragic: Greek Theatre and Beyond*. Oxford: Clarendon Press, 1996, 244–256.
Gosetti-Ferencei, Jennifer Anna. *Heidegger, Hölderlin, and the Subject of Poetic Language: Towards a Poetics of Dasein*. New York: Fordham University Press, 2004.
Gottlob, Susanne. *Stimme und Blick*. Bielefeld: Transcript, 2002.
Gray, Benjamin. 'Citizenship as Barrier and Opportunity for Ancient Greek and Modern Refugees.' *Humanities* 7/3 (2018), accessed 1 October 2019, https://doi.org/10.3390/h7030072.
———. 'Exile, Refuge and the Greek Polis: Between Justice and Humanity.' *Journal of Refugee Studies*, 30/2 (2016), 190–219.
Griffith, Mark. 'Commentary.' In Sophocles, *Antigone*. Edited by Mark Griffith. Cambridge: Cambridge University Press, 1999, 118–355.
Gross, Linda. 'The Thing.' *Los Angeles Times 25 June 1982*.
Guénoun, Denis. *L'Exhibition des mots: Une idée politique du théâtre*. Paris: L'Aube, 1992.
———. *Hypothéses sur l'Europe: Un essai de philosophie*. Paris: Circé, 2000.

———. *Näyttämön filosofia*. Translated by Kirkkopelto, Esa. Helsinki: Like, 2007.

———. 'Qu'est qu'une scène?' In Denis Guénoun, *Philosophie de la scène*. Besançon: Les Solitaires Intempestifs, 2010, 11–24.

Hallward, Peter. 'Generic Sovereignty: The Philosophy of Alain Badiou.' *Angelaki: A Journal of the Theoretical Humanities*, 3/3 (1998), 87–111.

Haraway, Donna. 'Situated Knowledges: The Science Question in Feminism and the Privilege of Partial Perspective.' *Feminist Studies* 14/3 (1988), 575–599.

Heaney, Seamus. *The Burial at Thebes: A Version of Sophocles' Antigone*. London: Faber and Faber, 2004.

Hegel, G. W. F. *Philosophy of History*. Translated by J. Sibree. New York: Dover, 1956.

———. *Aesthetics*, Vol. I & II. Translated by T. M. Knox. Oxford: Clarendon, 1975.

———. *Phenomenology of Spirit*. Translated by A. V. Miller. Oxford: Oxford University Press, 1977.

———. *Outlines of the Philosophy of Right*. Translated by T. M. Knox. Oxford: Oxford University Press, 2008.

Heidegger, Martin. 'The Anaximander Fragment.' In *Early Greek Thinkers*. Translated by David Farrell Krell and Frank A. Capuzzi. San Francisco: Harper & Row, 1975, 13–58.

———. *Aus der Erfahrung des Denkens*. Gesamtausgabe 13 Frankfurt am Main: Klostermann, 1983.

———. *Being and Time*. Translated by John Macquarrie and Edward Robinson. Oxford & Cambridge, Mass.: Blackwell, 1995.

———. *Building Dwelling Thinking*. Translated by Albert Hofstadter. In Martin Heidegger, *Poetry, Language, Thought*. New York: Harper & Row, 1971.

———. *Elucidations of Hölderlin's Poetry*. Translated by Keith Holler. New York: Humanity Books, 2000.

———. *Frühe Schriften*. Gesamtausgabe 1. Frankfurt am Main: Vittorio Klostermann, 1978.

———. *Gelassenheit*. Pfullingen: Neske, 1985.

———. *Grundbegriffe der aristotelischen Philosophie*. Gesamtausgabe 18. Frankfurt am Main: Vittorio Klostermann, 2002.

———. *Hölderlin's Hymn 'The Ister.'* Translated by William McNeill and Julia Davis. Bloomington & Indianapolis: Indiana University Press, 1996.

———. *Hölderlin's Hymns 'Germania' and 'The Rhine.'* Translated by William McNeill and Julia Ireland. Bloomington & Indianapolis: Indiana

University Press, 2018.
——— . *Introduction to Metaphysics*. Translated by Gregor Fried and Richard Polt. New Haven & London: Yale University Press, 2000.
——— . *Letter on 'Humanism.'* Translated by Frank A. Capuzzi. In *Pathmarks*, Cambridge: Cambridge University Press, 1998, 239–76.
——— . *Nietzsche I*. Gesamtausgabe 6.1. Frankfurt am Main: Vittorio Klostermann, 1996.
——— . 'Logos.' In Martin Heidegger, *Early Greek Thinkers*. Translated by David Farrell Krell and Frank A. Capuzzi. San Francisco: Harper & Row, 1975, 59–78.
——— . *The Origin of the Work of Art*. Translated by Alfred Hofstaedter. In *Basic Writings*. San Francisco: Harper, 1993.
——— . *Parmenides*. Gesamtausgabe 54. Frankfurt am Main: Vittorio Klostermann, 1982.
——— . 'Phenomenological Interpretations in Connection with Aristotle: An Indication of the Hermeneutical Situation.' Translated by John van Buren. In Martin Heidegger, *Supplements: From the Earliest Essays to* Being and Time *and Beyond*. Albany, NY: SUNY Press, 2002, 111–45.
——— . *Plato's Sophist*. Translated by Richard Rojcewitcz and André Schuwer. Bloomington: Indiana University Press, 1997.
——— . '...Poetically Man Dwells...' In *Poetry, Language, Thought*. Translated by Albert Hofstadter. New York: Harper & Row, 1971, 211–29.
——— . *The Question Concerning Technology*. Translated by William Lovitt. In *Basic Writings*. New York: Harper & Row, 1962.
——— . 'The Self-Assertion of the German University.' Translated by K. Harries. In *Philosophical and Political Writings*. London: Continuum Press, 2003, 2–11.
——— . 'Der Spruch des Anaximander.' In *Holzwege*. Frankfurt am Main: Vittorio Klostermann, 1963, 354–7.
——— . *Unterwegs der Sprache*. Pfullingen: Neske, 1959.
——— . 'What Are Poets For?' In *Poetry, Language, Thought*. Translated by Albert Hofstadter. New York: Harper & Row, 1971, 91–142.
——— . *Zollikoner Seminare*. Frankfurt am Main: Vittorio Klostermann, 1987.
——— . *Zu Hölderlin-Griechenlandreisen*. Gesamtausgabe 75. Frankfurt am Main: Vittorio Klostermann, 2000.
Heikkilä, Martta. *At the Limits of Presentation: Coming-into-Presence and its Aesthetics Relevance in Jean-Luc Nancy's Philosophy*. Helsinki: Dissertation, Department of Aesthetic, University of Helsinki, 2007.
Heinemann, Walter. *Die Relevanz der Philosophie Heidegger, Martins für das*

Rechtsdenken. Freiburg: Universität zu Freiburg, 1970.
Heraclitus. *Fragments.* Translated by T. M. Robinson. Toronto: University of Toronto Press, 1987.
Hesiod. *Works and Days.* Translated by Apostolos N. Athanassakis. Baltimore & London: The Johns Hopkins University Press, 2004.
Hirvonen, Ari. 'Between Signifier and Jouissance—Lacan with Teresa.' In *Sexuality and Psychoanalysis: Philosophical Criticism.* Edited by Jens de Vleminck and Eran Dorfman. Leuven: Leuven University Press, 2010, 199–214.
Hölderlin, Friedrich. 'An Casimir Ulrich Böhlendorff, 4.12.1801.' Sämtliche Werke 6. Briefe 1. Stuttgart: W. Kohlhammer Verlag, 1954.
———. *Anmerkungen zur Antigonae*, Sämtliche Werke 5. Stuttgart: W. Kohlhammer, Verlag 1952, 263–72.
———. Anmerkungen zum Oedipus. Sämtliche Werke 5. Stuttgart: W. Kohlhammer Verlag, 1952, 193–202.
———. *Antigonae.* Sämtliche Werke 5. Stuttgart: W. Kohlhammer Verlag, 1952, 203-262.
———. *L'Antigone de Sophocle.* Translated by Philippe Lacoue-Labarthe. Paris: Christian Bourgois, 1998.
———. 'The Archipelago.' In Friedrich Hölderlin, *Poems and Fragments.* Translated by Michael Hamburger. London: Anvil, 2004, 272–91.
———. 'Bread and Wine.' In Friedrich Hölderlin, *Poems and Fragments.* Translated by Michael Hamburger. London: Anvil, 2004, 319–29.
———. 'Frankfurter Plan. Sämtliche Werke 4. Stuttgarter Hölderlin-Ausgabe. W. Kohlhammer Verlag, 145–8.
———. *Grund zum Empedocles.* Zweite Fassung. Sämtliche Werke 4. Stuttgart: W. Kohlhammer Verlag, 1961, 149–62.
———. *Hyperion.* Sämtliche Werke 3. Stuttgart: W, Kohlhammer Verlag, 1957.
———. *Hölderlin's Sophocles: Oedipus & Antigone.* Translated by David Constantine. Tarset: Bloodaxe Books, 2001.
———. 'Menon's Lament for Diotima.' In Friedrich Hölderlin, *Poems and Fragments.* Translated by Michael Hamburger. London: Anvil, 2004, 293–301.
———. *Oedipe le Tyran de Sophocle.* Translated by Philippe Lacoue-Labarthe. Paris: Christian Bourgois, 1998.
———. *Oedipus der Tyrann.* Sämtliche Werke 5. Stuttgart: W. Kohlhammer Verlag, 1952, 121–92.
———. 'Plan der Dritten Fassung,' Sämtliche Werke 4. Stuttgarter Hölderlin-Ausgabe. W. Kohlhammer Verlag, 163–68;

———. 'The Poet's Vocation.' In Friedrich Hölderlin, *Poems and Fragments*. Translated by Michael Hamburger London: Anvil, 2004, 233–7.
———. 'The Titans.' In Friedrich Hölderlin, *Poems and Fragments*. Translated by Michael Hamburger. London: Anvil, 2004, 629–33.
———. *Der Tod des Empedocles.* Erste Fassung. Sämtliche Werke 4. Stuttgarter Hölderlin-Ausgabe. W. Kohlhammer Verlag, 1961, 3–85.
———. *Der Tod des Empedocles.* Zweite Fassung. *Sämtliche Werke 4.* Stuttgart: W. Kohlhammer Verlag, 1961, 87–141.
———. *Der Tod des Empedocles*. Dritte Fassung. Sämtliche Werke 4. Stuttgart: W. Kohlhammer Verlag, 1961, 119–41.
Homer. *The Iliad*. Translated by Samuel Butler. The Project Gutenberg EBook, 2000.
Honig, Bonnie, *Antigone Interrupted*. Cambridge: Cambridge University Press, 2103.
———. 'Antigone's Two Laws: Greek Tragedy and the Politics of Humanism.' *New Literary History* 41/1 (2010), 1–33.
———. *Public Things: Democracy in Despair*. New York: Fordham University Press, 2017.
Hoxby, Blair. *What Was Tragedy? Theory and the Early Modern Canon*. Oxford: Oxford University Press, 2015.
Irigaray, Luce, *Ce sexe qui n'en pas un*. Paris: Les Editions Minuit, 1977.
———. *An Ethics of Sexual Difference*. Translated by Carol Burke and Gillian Gill. Ithaca: Cornell, 1993.
———. *Speculum of the Other Woman*. Translated by Gillian C. Gill. Ithaca, NY: Cornell University Press, 1985.
———. *To Be Two*. Translated by Monique M. Rhodes and Marco F. Cocito-Monoc. London & New York: Routledge, 2001.
Ismard, Paulin. *La cite des réseaux: Athènes et ses associations*. Paris: Publications de la Sorbonne, 2010.
Isocrates. *Areopagiticus*. Isocrates II. Translated by George Norlin. London: Heinemann 1928.
———. *On the Peace*. Isocrates I. Translated by George Norlin. London: Heinemann 1929.
———. *Panegyricus*. Isocrates II. Translated by George Norlin. London: Heinemann 1928.
———. *Plataicus*. Isocrates III. Translated by Larue van Hook. London: Heinemann, 1945.
Jacobs, Carol. 'Dusting Antigone,' *MLN* 111/5 (1996), 888–912.
Jarcho, Julia. *Writing and the Modern Stag: Theater beyond Drama*. Cambridge & New York: Cambridge University Press, 2017.

Jebb, Richard C. *The Antigone of Sophocles with Commentary*. Cambridge University Press, Cambridge, 1966.
Jelinek, Elfriede. *Charges The Supplicants*. Translated by Gitta Honegger. London & New York & Calcutta: Seagull Books, 2016.
Kafka, Franz. *Before the Law/Vor dem Gesetz*. A Bilingual Edition. Kindle, 2015.
Kahane, Ahuvia. 'Antigone: Lacan and the Structure of the Law: Interrogating Antigone in Postmodern Philosophy and Criticism.' *Interrogating Antigone in Postmodern Philosophy and Criticism*. Edited by S. E. Wilmer and Audrone Zukauskaite. Oxford: University of Oxford Press, 2010.
Kant, Immanuel. *Groundwork of the Metaphysics of Morals*. In *Practical Philosophy*. Translated by Mary J. Gregor. Cambridge: Cambridge University Press, 1996.
Kason Poulson, Nancy. 'In Defence of the Dead: *Antigona furiosa*, by Griselda Gambaro.' *Romance Quarterly* 59/1 (2012), 48–54.
Kelner, Martha. 'Tennis rallies behind Serena Williams after US Open sexism claim.' *The Guardian*, 9 September 2018.
Kennan, George F. American Diplomacy. Chicago: University of Chicago Press, 1951.
Kempter, Lothar. *Hölderlin und die Mythologie*. Leipzig: Münster Press, 1929.
Khatab, Rhonda. 'Ethical Consciousness in the Spirit of Tragedy: Hegel's Antigone.' *Colloquy* 11 (2006), 76–98.
Kierkegaard, Sören. *Fear and Trembling*. Translated by Howard Hong and Edna Hong. Princeton: Princeton University Press, 1983.
———. *Repetition*. Translated by Howard Hong and Edna Hong. Princeton: Princeton University Press, 1983.
Kirkkopelto, Esa. 'Comparatifs de Hölderlin.' In *Lacoue-Labarthe, Philippe: La Césure et l'impossible*. Edited by Jacques Rogozinski. Paris: Lignes, 2010, 87–109.
———. 'Denis Guénounin näyttämölliset siirtymät.' In Denis Guénoun, *Näyttämön filosofia*. Helsinki: Like, 2007, 109–33.
———. 'La question de la scène.' In *Philosophie de la scène*. Besançon: Les Solitaires Intempestifs, 2010, 115–143, 116;.
———. *Le Théâtre de l'expérience: contributions à la théorie de la scène*. Paris: Presses universitaires de Paris-Sorbonne, 2008.
Klimis, Sophie. 'Antigone et Créon à la lumière du "terrifiant/extraordinaire" (*deinotès*) de l'humanité tragique.' In *Antigone et la résistance civile*. Edited by Lambros Couloubaritsis and François Ost. Brussels: Ousia, 2004, 3–102.
Knox, Bernard. *The Heroic Temper: Studies in Sophoclean Tragedy*. Berkeley: University of California Press, 1984.

Kofman, Sarah. 'L'Espace de la césure.' *Critique* 34/379 (1978), 1143–50.
Kojève, Alexandre. Introduction à la lecture de Hegel. Lécons sur la phénoménologie de l'ésprit. Paris: Gallimard, 1997.
Kosofsky Sedgwick, Eve. 'Paranoid Reading and Reparative Reading; or You're so Paranoid, You Probably Think This Introduction is about You.' In *Novel Gazing: Queer Readings in Fiction*. Edited by Eve Kosofsky Sedgwick. Durham, DC: Duke University Press, 1997, 1–37.
———. *Touching Feeling: Affect, Pedagogy, Performativity*. Durham, DC: Duke University Press, 2003.
Kristjánsson, Kristján. 'Pity: A Mitigated Defense.' *Canadian Journal of Philosophy* 2014, 44/3–4 (2014), 343–64.
Lacan, Jacques. *L'acte psychanalytique, Séminaire XV, 1967–1968*. Paris: Ecole Lacanienne de psychanalyse.
———. *Anxiety: Seminar X, 1962–1963*. Translated by A. R. Price. Cambridge & Malden, MA: Polity Press, 2014.
———. 'Du discourse psychanalytique.' In *En Italie Lacan, 1953–1978*. Edited by G. B. Contri. Milan: La Salamandra, 1973, 32–55.
———. 'Excursus.' In *En Italie Lacan, 1953–1978*. Edited by G. B. Contri. Milan: La Salamandra, 1973, 78–97.
———. *Encore: On Feminine Sexuality, the Limits of Love and Knowledge, Seminar XX, 1972–1973*. Translated by Bruce Fink. New York & London: W. W. Norton, 1975.
———. *The Ethics of Psychoanalysis*. Seminar VII, 1959–1960. Translated by Dennis Porter. London: Routlege, 1992.
———. *The Four Fundamental Concepts of Psychoanalysis*. Seminar XI, 1964. Translated by Alan Sheridan. New York: Norton, 1981.
———. *Freud's papers on Techniques, Seminar I, 1953–1954*. Translated by John Forrester Cambridge: Cambridge University Press, 1988.
———. *The Ethics of Psychoanalysis*. Seminar VII, 1959–1960. Translated by Dennis Porter. London: Routlege, 1992.
———. *The Other Side of Psychoanalysis, Seminar XVII, 1969–1970*. Translated by Russell Grigg. New York & London: Norton, 2007.
———. 'Position of the Unconscious.' In Jacques Lacan, Écrits. Translated by Bruce Fink. New York: Norton, 2006, 701–21.
———. 'The Signification of the Phallus.' In Jacques Lacan, Écrits. Translated by Bruce Fink. New York & London: Norton, 2006, 575–84.
———. *Television*. Translated by Dennis Hollier, Rosalind Krauss and Annette Michelson. New York: Norton, 1990.
Lacoue-Labarthe, Philippe. 'L'Antigone de Hölderlin. Entretien avec Philippe Lacoue-Labarthe propos recueillis par Aliette Armel.' In *Antigone: Figures

mythiques. Edited by Aliette Armel. Paris Éditions Autrement, 2015, 105–16.

———. 'The Caesura of the Speculative.' Translated by Robert Eisenhauer. In Philippe Lacoue-Labarthe. *Typography: Mimesis, Philosophy, Politics*. Stanford: Stanford University Press, 1998, 208–35.

———. La césure du spéculatif. In Philippe Lacoue-Labarthe, *L'imitation des Modernes: Typographies 2*. Paris: Galilée, 1986, 39–69.

———. 'De l'éthique: à propos d'Antigone.' In Lacan avec les philosophes. Paris: Albin Michel, 1991, 19–36.

———. 'La forme toute oublieuse de l'infidélité.' *L'animal*, 19–20 (2008), 165–9.

———. 'De Hölderlin à Marx: mythe, imitation, tragédie.' *Labyrinthe: Actualité de la recherché*, 822 (2005). www.revuelabyrinthe.org.

———. 'Hölderlin and the Greeks.' Translated by Christopher Fynsk. In Philippe-Lacoue-Labarthe, *Typographies: Mimesis, Philosophy, Politics*. Stanford: Stanford University Press, 1998, 236–47.

———. 'Métaphrasis.' In Philippe Lacoue-Labarthe, *Métaphrasis* suivi de *Le Théatre de Hölderlin*. Paris: P.U.F., 1998, 7–42.

———. *Poetics of History: Rousseau and the Theater of Originary Mimesis*. Jeff Fort. New York: Fordham University Press, 2019.

———. *Pour n'en pas finir: Écrits sur la musique*. Paris: Christian Bourgeois, 2015.

———. 'Stagings of Mimesis: An Interview by Peter Hallward.' Translated by Jane Hiddleston. *Angelaki: Journal of the Theoretical Humanities* 8/2 (2003), 55–72.

———. 'Théâtre (ou: Opéra—ou: le simulacre—ou: le subterfuge).' In Philippe Lacoue-Labarthe, *Pour n'en pas finir. Écrits sur la musique*. Paris: Christian Bourgois, 2015, chapter IV.

———. 'Le Théâtre de Hölderlin.' In Philippe Lacoue-Labarthe, *Métaphrasis suivi de Le théâtre de Hölderlin*. Paris: P.U.F., 1998, 43–73.

———. 'Transcendence Ends in Politics.' In Philippe Lacoue-Labarthe, *Typography: Mimesis, Philosophy, Politics*. Translated by Chistopher Fynsk. Stanford: Stanford University Press, 1998, 267–300.

———. 'Typography.' In Philippe Lacoue-Labarthe, *Typography: Mimesis, Philosophy, Politics*. Cambridge, MA: Harvard University Press, 1989, 43–138.

Lacoue-Labarthe, Philippe and Jean-Luc Nancy. *The Literary Absolute: The Theory of Literature in German Romanticism*. Translated by Philippe Barnard and Cheryl Lester. Albany, NY: State University of New York Press, 1988.

———. *Le mythe Nazi.* Paris: Aube, 1991.
———. 'Scéne.' *Nouvelle Revue de Psychanalyse* 46, 1992, 73–92.
Lazarus, Sylvain. *Anthropologie du nom.* Paris: Seuil, 1996.
Lear, Jonathan. *Open Minded: Working Out the Logic of Soul.* Cambridge, Mass. & London: Harvard University Press, 1998.
Lehmann, Hans-Thies. 'From Logos to Landscape: Text in Contemporary Dramaturgy.' *Performance Research* 2/1 (1997), 55–60.
———. *Postdramatic Theatre.* Translated by Karen Jürs-Munby. London and New York: Routledge, 2006.
———. 'Word and Stage in Postdramatic Theatre.' *Contemporary Drama in English* 14, 2007, 37–54.
Leibnitz, Gottfried. *Essais de Théodicée sur la bonte de Dieu, la liberté de l'homme et l'origine du mal.* Tome I, Amsterdam: Francois Changuion, 1747.
Lenin, V. I. *The Crisis Has Matured.* Translated by Yuri Sdobnikov and George Hanna. Collected Works 26. Moscow: Progress Publishers 1972, 74–85.
Lesky, Albin, *Greek Tragedy.* Translated by H. A. Frankfurt. New York: E. Benn, 1965.
Levinas, Emmanuel. 'Apropos of Buber: Some Notes.' In Emmanuel Levinas, *Outside the Subject.* Translated by Michael B. Smith. Stanford, Cal.: Stanford University Press, 1993, 40–8.
———. *Totality and Infinity: An Essay on Exteriority.* Translated by Alphonso Lingis. Hague: Martinus Nijhoff, 1979.
Lewis, Sian. *News and Society in the Greek Polis.* Chapel Hill: The University of North Carolina Press, 1996.
Lindberg Susanna. 'Ontorythmie.' *Revue philosophique de Louvain* 108 (2010), 527–48.
———. 'Tonalités élémentaires.' In *Philippe Lacoue-Labarthe: La césure et l'Impossible.* Edited by Jacob Rogozinski. Paris: Lignes, 2010, 231–47.
Liu, Xiaobo. *June Fourth Elegies.* Translated by Jeffrey Yang. London: Jonathan Cape, 2012.
Loizidou, Elena. *Judith Butler: Ethics, Law, Politics.* London & New York: Routledge, 2007.
Longo, Oddone. 'The Theater of the Polis.' In *Nothing to Do with Dionysos? Athenian Drama in its Social Context.* Edited by J. Winkler and Froma Zeitling. Princeton: Princeton University Press, 1990, 12–19.
Loraux, Nicole. *The Children of Athens.* Translated by Caroline Levine. Princeton: Princeton University Press, 1993.
———. *The Divided City: On Memory and Forgetting in Ancient Athens.*

Translated by Corinne Pache with Jeff Fort. New York: Zone Books, 2002.
———. *The Invention of Athens: The Funeral Oration in the Classical City*. Cambridge, Mass.: Harvard University Press, 1986.
———. *The Mourning Voice: An Essay on Greek Tragedy*. Translated by Elizabeth Trapnell Rawlings. Ithaca & London: Cornell University Press, 2002.
Low, Polly. *Interstate Relations in Classical Greece: Morality and Power*. Cambridge: Cambridge University Press, 2007.
Lucas, D. W. 'Hamartia.' In Aristotle, *Poetics*. Oxford: Clarendon Press, 1968, 299–307.
Lysias. *Funeral Oration*. Translated by W. R. M. Lamb. Cambridge, Mass.: Harvard University Press, 1930.
Magun, Artemy. *The Concept of the Experience of Revolution*. Dissertation. Ann Arbor, MI: University of Michigan, 2003.
———, *Negative Revolution: Modern Political Subject and its Fate after the Cold War*. London: Bloomsbury Academic, 2013.
Maihofer, Werner. *Recht und Sein: Prolegomena zu einer Rechtsontologie*. Freiburg: Universität zu Freiburg, 1953.
Mandela, Nelson. *Long Walk to Freedom*. Philadelphia: Little, Brown, 1994.
Marx, Karl. *The Communist Manifesto*. Translated by Samuel Moore. In Karl Marx and Friedrich Engels, Selected Works. Volume I. Moscow: Progress, 1969, 98–137.
Marx, Werner. *Gibt es auf Erden ein Maß? Grundbestimmungen einer nichtmetaphysischen Ethik*. Hamburg: Felix Meiner Verlag, 1983.
———. *Towards a Phenomenological Ethics: Ethos and the Life-World*. Translated by Stefaan Heyvaert. Albany, NY: State University of New York Press, 1992.
———. *Vernunft und Welt: Zwischen Tradition und anderem Anfang*. Den Haag: Springer, 1970.
McAuley, Gay. *Space in Performance: Making Meaning in the Theatre*. Ann Arbor, MI: University of Michigan Press, 1999.
Menke, Christoph. 'The Presence of Tragedy,' *Critical Horizons* 5/1 (2004), 201–225.
Merleau-Ponty, Maurice. *The World of Perception*. Translated by Oliver Davis. London & New York: Routledge, 2008.
Miller, Jacques-Alain. 'Ethics of Psychoanalysis.' Translated by Jorge Jauregui and Marguerite Laporte. http://www.lacan.com/lacinkV1.htm.
Morin, Marie-Eve. *Jean-Luc Nancy*. Cambridge & Malden, MA: Polity, 2012.
Müller, Max. 'Die ontologische Problematik des Naturrechts.' In *Die ontologische Begründung des Rechts*. Edited by Arthur Kaufman. Darmstadt:

Wissenschaftliche Buchgesellschaft, 1965, 461–69.
Mumford, Lewis. *Technics and Civilization*. New York: Harcourt, Brace and World, 1934.
Murray, Gilbert. *Euripides and His Age*. London: Williams and Norgate, 1913.
Nancy, Claire. 'La raison dramatique.' *Po&sie* 11 (2002), 111–21.
Nancy, Jean-Luc. *L'Adoration: Déconstruction du christianisme, 2*. Paris: Galilée, 2010.
———. *After Fukushima: The Equivalence of Catastrophes*. Translated by Charlotte Mandell. New York: Fordham University Press, 2015.
———. *Being Singular Plural*. Translated by Robert D. Richardson and Anne E. O'Byrne. Stanford: Stanford University Press, 2000.
———. 'Body-Theatre.' In *Figures of Touch: Sense, Technics, Body*. Edited by Mika Elo and Miika Luoto. Helsinki: Academy of Fine Arts, 2018, 13–32.
———. 'The Calculation of the Poet.' Translated by Simon Sparks. In *The Solid Letter: Readings of Friedrich Hölderlin*. Edited by Aris Fioretos. Stanford: Stanford University Press, 1999, 45–73.
———. *Dis-enclosure—Deconstruction of Christianity*. Translated by Bettina Bergo, Gabriel and Michael B. Smith. New York: Fordham University Press, 2008.
———. 'L'"éthique originaire" de Heidegger.' In Jean-Luc Nancy, *La pensée dérobée*. Paris: Galilée, 2001, 85–113.
———. 'The Free Voice of Man.' Translated by Richard Stamp. In Philippe Lacoue-Labarthe and Jean-Luc Nancy, *Retreating the Political*. London & New York: Routledge, 1997, 32–54.
———. *The Gravity of Thought*. Translated by François Raffoul and Gregory Recco. New York: Humanity Books, 1997.
———. *L' "il y a" du rapport sexuel*. Paris: Galilée, 2001.
———. *The Inoperative Community*. Translated by Peter Connor. Minneapolis: University of Minneapolis Press, 2006.
———. *Noli me tangere: On the Raising of the Body*. Translated by Sarah Clift, Pascale-Anne Brault and Michael Naas. New York: Fordham University Press, 2008.
———. *The Sense of the World*. Translated by Jeffrey S. Librett. Minneapolis: University of Minnesota Press, 1997.
———. *The Speculative Remark: One of Hegel's Bons Mots*. Translated by Céline Surpenant. Stanford: Stanford University Press, 2001.
———. 'The Sublime Offering.' Translated by Jeffrey S. Librett. In *Of the Sublime: Presence in Question*. Edited by Jean-François Courtine and Jean-Luc Nancy. Albany: SUNY Press, 1993, 36–8.
Nancy, Jean-Luc and Philippe Lacoue-Labarthe. 'Le "retrait" du politique.' In

Jacob Rogozinski, et. al. *Le Retrait du politique* Paris: Galilée, 1983.
Nietzsche, Friedrich. *The Birth of Tragedy.* Translated by Ronal Speirs. Cambridge: Cambridge University Press, 1999.
——. *Gay Science.* Translated by Walter Kaufmann. New York: Random House, 1974.
——. *Thus Spoke Zarathustra.* Translated by Graham Parkes. Oxford: Oxford University Press, 2005.
Nonet, Philippe. 'Antigone's Law.' *Law, Culture and the Humanities*, 2 (2006), 314–35.
Noren, Lars. *En dramatikers dagbok 2000–2001.* Stockholm: Bonnier, 2009.
Nussbaum, Martha. 'Compassion: The Basic Social Emotion.' *Social Philosophy and Policy* 13/1 (1996), 27–58.
——. 'The Professor of Parody: The Hip Defeatism of Butler, Judith.' *New Republic* 22 February 1999, https://newrepublic.com/article/150687/professor-parody; see Loizidou, *Butler, Judith,* 157– 63.
——. *Upheavals of Thought.* Cambridge: Cambridge University Press, 2001.
Nägele, Rainer. *Reading after Freud: Essays on Goethe, Hölderlin, Habermas, Nietzsche, Brecht, Celan and Freud* New York: Columbia University Press.
——. *Theater, Theory, Speculation: Walter Benjamin and the Scenes of Modernity.* Baltimore, Md.: Johns Hopkins University Press, 1991.
O'Neill, Onora. *Towards Justice and Virtue.* Cambridge: Cambridge University Press, 1996.
Otfried Müller, Karl. *Geschichte der griechischen Literatur bis auf das Zeitalter Alexanders.* Band 2. Stuttgart: Verlag von Albert Heitz, 1876.
Pearson Geiman, Clare. 'Heidegger's Antigones.' In *A Companion to Heidegger's* Introduction to Metaphysics. Edited by Richard Polt and Gregory Fried. New Haven, CT: Yale University Press, 2001.
Pearson, Giles. 'Courage and Temperance.' In *The Cambridge Companion to Aristotle's Nicomachean Ethics.* Edited by Ronald Polansky. New York: Cambridge University Press, 2014, 110–34.
Plato. *Phaedrus,* Translated by R. Hackforth. Cambridge: Cambridge University Press, 2018.
——. *Republic.* Translated by H. D. P. Lee. London & New York: Penguin, 2017.
——. *Timaeus.* Translated by A. E. Taylor. London: Routledge, 2014.
Price, M. E. *Rethinking Asylum: History, Purpose, and Limits* Cambridge: Cambridge University Press, 2009.
Rancière, Jacques. *Aesthetics and Its Discontents.* Translated by Steven Corcoran. Cambridge & Malden, MA: Polity Press, 2009.
——. *Disagreement: Politics and Philosophy.* Translated by Julie Rose.

Minneapolis & London: University of Minneapolis Press, 1999.
———. 'Dissenting Words: A Conversation with Jacques Rancière,' *Diacritics* 113 2000.
———. *The Emancipated Spectator*. Translated by Grefory Elliot. London & New York: Verso, 2009.
———. *La haine de la démocratie*. Paris: La Fabrique, 2005.
———. *Malais dans l'esthétique*. Paris: Galilée, 2004.
———. *La méthode de la scène*. Paris: Lignes, 2018.
———. *The Politics of Aesthetics*. Translated by Gabriel Rockhill. London & New York: Continuum 2006.
———. 'A Precarious Dialogue: Maria Kakogianni and Jacques Rancière.' Translated by Olivia Lucca Fraser. *Radical Philosophy* 181 2013, 18–25.
———. 'Ten Thesis of Politics.' In Jacques Rancière, *Dissensus: On Politics and Aesthetics*. Translated by Steven Corcoran. London & New York: Continuum 2010, 27–44.
Rancière, Jacques (avec Adnen Jdey). *La méthode de la scène*. Paris: Lignes, 2018.
Recalcati, Massimo. 'Il sonno della realtà e il trauma del reale.' In *Bentornata realtà: Il nuovo realismo in discussione*. Edited by Mario De Caro and Maurizio Ferraris. Turin: Einaudi, 2012, 193–206.
Reed, Valerie. 'Bringing Antigone Home?' *Comparative Literary Studies*, 45/3 (2008), 316–40.
Reinhardt, Karl. *Sophocles*. Frankfurt am Main: Vittorio Klostermann, 1976.
Ricoeur, Paul. *The Symbolism of Evil*. Translated by Emerson Buchanan. New York: Harper & Row, 1967.
Rilke, Rainer Maria. *Das Buch von der Armut und vom Tode*. Gesammelte Werke, Band II Leipzig: Insel Verlag, 1927.
Rousseau. Jean-Jacques. *Letter to Alembert and Writings for the Theater*. Collected Writings 10. Translated by Allan Bloom, Charles Butterworth, and Christopher Kelly. Hanover: University of New England, 2004.
Rubinstein, Lene. 'Immigration and Refugee Crisis in Fourth-Century Greece: An Athenian Perspective.' *The European Legacy* 23/1–2 (2018), 5–24.
Salecl, Renata. 'Society of Choice.' *Differences* 20/1 (2009), 157–80.
Santanen, Sami. 'Dimensions of Touch.' In *Figures of Touch: Sense, Technics, Body*. Edited by Mika Elo and Miika Luoto. Helsinki: Academy of Fine Arts, 2018, 213–309.
———. 'Mimesis ja teatterinautinto.' In *Mikä mimesis? Philippe Lacoue-Labarthen filosofinen teatteri*. Edited by Ari Hirvonen and Susanna Lindberg. Helsinki: Tutkijaliitto, 2009, 130–60.
Savage, Robert. 'The Precedence of Citation: On Brecht's *The Antigone of*

Sophocles.' Colloquy: Text, Theory, Critique 11(2006), 99–126.
Schelling, F. W. J. *The Unconditional in Human Knowledge: Four Early Essays 1794–1796*. Translated by Fritz Marti. Lewisburg: Bucknell University Press, 1980.
——— . *The Philosophy of Art*. Translated by Douglas W. Scott. Minneapolis: University of Minnesota Press, 1989.
Schmitt-Pantel, Pauline. 'Collective Activities and the Political in the Greek City.' In *The Greek City: From Homer to Alexander*. Edited by Oswyn Murray and Simon Price. Oxford: Clarendon Press, 1990, 199–214.
Seery, John E. 'Acclaim for Antigone's Claim Reclaimed.' In Judith *Butler's Precarious Politics: Critical Encounters*. Edited by Terrell Carver and Samuel A. Chambers. London & New York: Routledge, 2008, 62–76.
Segal, Charles. 'Catharsis, Audience, and Closure in Greek Tragedy.' In *Tragedy and the Tragic: Greek Theatre and Beyond*. Edited by M. S. Silk. Oxford: Clarendon Press, 1998, 149–172.
Sjöholm, Cecilia. *The Antigone Complex: Ethics and the Invention of Feminine Desire*. Stanford: Stanford University Press, 2004.
——— . 'Naked Life: Arendt and the Exile at Colonus.' In *Interrogating Antigone in Postmodern Philosophy and Criticism*. Edited by S. E. Wilmer and Audrone Zukauskaite. Oxford: University of Oxford Press, 2010. DOI: 10.1093/acprof:oso/9780199559213.001.0001.
Sophocles. *Antigone*. Translated by Richard Jebb. Cambridge, Mass.: Cambridge University Press, 1891.
——— . *Antigone*. Translated by Hugh Lloyd-Jones. Cambridge, Mass.: Harvard University Press, 1998.
——— . *Antigone*. Translated by Mark Griffin. Cambridge, Mass.: Cambridge University Press, 1999.
——— . *Antigone*. Translated by Anne Carson. London: Oberon Books, 2015.
——— . *Electra*. Translated by Hugh Lloyd-Jones. Cambridge, Mass.: Harvard University Press, 1994.
——— . *Oedipus at Colonus*. Translated by Hugh Lloyd-Jones. Cambridge, Mass.: Harvard University Press, 1998.
——— . *Oedipus Tyrannus*, Translated by Hugh Lloyd-Jones. Cambridge, Mass.: Harvard University Press, 1997.
——— . *Phaedra*. Selected Fragmentary Plays I. Translated by Alan H. Sommerstein, David Fitzpatrick and Thomas Talboy. Oxford: Oxbow Books, 2006.
——— . *Tereus*. Selected Fragmentary Plays I. Translated by Alan H. Sommerstein, David Fitzpatrick and Thomas Talboy. Oxford: Oxbow Books, 2006.

Spargo, Clifton R. 'The Apolitics of Antigone's Lament from Sophocles to Ariel Dorfman.' *Mosaic: A Journal for the Interdisciplinary Study of Literature* 41/3 (2008), 117–135.

Spencer, Alan. 'John Carpenter's The Thing.' *Starlog* 64 (1982), 67–69.

Stallings, A. E. 'After a Greek Proverb.' In *Futures*. Poetry of the Greek Crisis. Edited by Theodoros Chiotis. London: Penned in the Margins, 2015, 15–16.

Stavrakakis, Yannis. *In Traversing the Fantasy: Critical Responses to Slavoj Žižek*. Edited by Geoff Boucher, Jason Glynos, and Matthew Sharpe. Aldershot: Ashgate, 2005, 171–182.

Steadman, Geoffrey. Sophocles' Antigone. Greek Text with Facing Vocabulary and Commentary. 2015. https://geoffreysteadman.files.wordpress.com/2015/06/antigone-23june15w.pdf.

Steinbock, Bernd. *Social Memory in Athenian Public Discourse: Uses and Meanings of the Past*. Ann Arbor: The University of Michigan Press, 2013.

Steiner, George. *The Death of Tragedy*. Newburyport: Open Road Media, 2013.

Szondi, Peter. *An Essay on the Tragic*. Translated by Paul Fleming. Stanford: Stanford University Press, 2002.

——— . *Hölderlin Studien: Mit einem Traktat über philologische Erkenntnis*. Frankfurt am Main: Suhrkamp,1967.

Taminiaux, Jacques. 'Antigone dans l'histoire de la philosophie.' In Antigone et la résistance civile. Edited by Lambros Couloubaritsis and François Ost. Brussels: Ousia, 2004, 9–39.

——— . 'The Platonic Roots of Heidegger's Political Thought.' *European Journal of Political Theory* 6/1 (2007), 11–29.

Taylor, Diana. *Disappearing Acts: Spectacles of Gender and Nationalism in Argentina's 'Dirty War.'* Durham, NC: Duke University Press, 1997.

Taylor, Markland. 'The Children of Herakles.' *Variety* 14 January 2003.

Thucydides. *The History of Peloponnesian War*. Translated by Charles Foster Smith. London: William Heineman, 1919.

Tomšič, Samo. *The Capitalist Unconscious: Marx and Lacan*. London & New York: Verso, 2015.

Tosaki, Eiichi. *Mondrian's Philosophy of Visual Rhythm: Phenomenology, Wittgenstein, and Eastern Thought*. Dordrecht: Springer, 2017.

Van Haute, Philippe. 'Antigone, heldin van de psychoanalyse? Lacans lectuur van Antigone.' In *De God van denkers en dichters*. Opstellen voor Samuel IJsseling. Edited by Egdius Berns, Paul Moyaert and Paul van Tongeren. Boom: Amsterdam, 1997, 172–191.

——— . 'Antigone, psykoanalyysin sankaritar.' Translated by Janne Kurki.

Tiede & edistys 3 (2003).
Vanheule, Stijn. 'Capitalist Discourse, Subjectivity and Lacanian Psychoanalysis,' *Frontiers in Psychology* 7 (2016), 1–46. http://doi.org/10.3389/fpsyg.2016.01948.
Varoufakis, Yannis. *And the Weak Suffer What They Must?* London: The Bodley Head, 2016.
Vernant, Jean-Pierre. *Les origins de la pensée grecques* Paris: Presses universitaires de France, 1962.
——— . *Tragedy and Myth in Ancient Greece.* Brighton: Harvester Press, 1981.
Vernant, Jean-Pierre and Pierre Vidal-Naquet. *Myth and Tragedy in Ancient Greece.* Translated by Janet Lloyd. New York: Zone Books, 1988.
Vives, Jean-Michel. 'Catharsis: Psychoanalysis and the Theatre.' Translated by Andrew Weller. *The International Journal of Psychoanalysis* 92 (2011), 1009–27.
Vlassopoulos, Kostas. 'Beyond and Below the Polis: Networks, Associations, and the Writing of Greek History.' *Mediterranean Historical Review* 22/1 (2007), 11–22.
——— . 'Free Spaces: Identity, Experience and Democracy in Classical Athens.' *Classical Quarterly* 57/1 (2007), 33–52.
——— . *Unthinking the Greek Polis.* Cambridge: Cambridge University Press, 2007.
Wannamaker, Annette. 'Memory Also Makes a Chain: The Performance of Absence in Griselda Gambaro's *Antigona furiosa*.' *The Journal of the Midwest Modern Language Association* 33/3 (2001), 73–85.
Weber, Max. 'Science as Vocation.' In Max Weber, *Essays in Sociology.* Oxford & New York: Oxford University Press, 1946.
Weber, Samuel. *Theatricality as Medium.* New York: Fordham University Press, 2004.
Werner, Laura. *The Restless Love of Thinking: The Concept of Liebe in Hegel's Philosophy.* Helsinki: A Dissertation, 2007.
Weil, Simone. 'Human Personality.' In Simone Weil, *An Anthology.* Translated by R. Reese. New York: Grove Press, 1986, 49–78.
——— . '*The Iliad*, or the Poem of Force,' *Politics,* November 1945. https://archive.org/stream/SimoneWeilAndThePoemOfForce/Simone%20Weil.%20HOMER.%20The%20Poem%20of%20Force_djvu.txt.
Weinfield, Henry. '"Is there A Measure on Earth": Hölderlin's Poem "In lovely Blueness" in Light of Heidegger's Essay "Poetically Man Dwells".' *Journal of Philosophy: A Cross-Disciplinary Inquiry,* 613 (2010), 54–61.
White, Stephen. *Ethos of a Late-Modern Citizen.* Cambridge, MA: Harvard University Press, 2009.

Wolf, Erik. *Rechtsphilosophische Studien.* Ausgewählte Schriften I. Frankfurt am Main: Vittorio Klostermann, 1972.

Xenophon. *Hellenica.* Xenophon 1. Translated by Carleton L. Brownson. London: William Heinemann, 1918.

Žižek, Slavoj. *Did Somebody Say Totalitarianism? Five Interventions in the Mis(use) of a Notion.* London & New York: Verso, 2009.

———. 'From Democracy to Divine Violence.' In *Democracy in What State?* Edited by Giorgio Agamben et al. New York: Columbia University Press, 2011.

———. 'From "Passionate Attachments" to Dis-Identification.' *Umbra* 1 (1998), 3–17.

———. 'Philosophy is not a Dialogue.' In *Philosophy in Present.* Translated by Peter Thomas and Alberto Toscano. Edited by Peter Engelman. Cambridge & Malden, MA: Polity, 2009, 49–72.

———. *The Plague of Fantasies.* London & New York: Verso, 1997.

———. 'The Real of Sexual Difference.' In *Reading Seminar XX: Lacan's Major Work on Love, Knowledge, and Feminine Sexuality.* Edited by Suzanne Barnard and Bruce Fink. Albany, NY: State University of New York Press, 2002, 57–75.

———. *The Ticklish Subject: The Absent Centre of Political Ontology.* London & New York: Verso, 1999.

———. *Violence: Six Sideways Reflections.* London: Profile Books, 2008.

———. *Welcome to the Desert of the Real.* London & New York: Verso, 2002.

Zupančič, Alenka, *What is Sex?* Cambridge, Mass. & London: The MIT Press, 2017.

Zweig, Stefan. *The Struggle with the Daemon: Hölderlin, Kleist, Nietzsche.* Translated by Eden and Cedar Paul. Lexington, Mass.: Plunkett Lake Press, 2012.

Notes

Introduction

1. David Denby, 'Battle of the Stereotypes,' *New York Magazine*, 28 June 1982, 52–54.
2. Linda Gross, 'The Thing,' *Los Angeles Times*, 25 June 1982.
3. Alan, Spencer, 'John Carpenter's The Thing,' *Starlog* 64 (1982), 69.
4. Mark Fisher, *Capitalist Realism: Is There No Alternative?* (Winchester: Zero Books, 2008), 6, 8.
5. Fisher, Capitalist Realism, 54.
6. George F. Kennan, *American Diplomacy* (Chicago: University of Chicago Press, 1951), 17.
7. We never know whether Childs is the Thing or not. In *The Thing* commentary, Carpenter himself says that he has no idea who's a Thing and who's not.
8. V. I. Lenin, *The Crisis has Matured*, trans. Yuri Sdobnikov and George Hanna, Collected Works, Volume 26 (Moscow: Progress Publishers 1972), 74–85.
9. Karl Marx, 'The Communist Manifesto,' in *Selected Works*, Karl Marx and Friedrich Engels, Volume 1 (Moscow: Progress, 1969).
10. Jacques Rancière, 'A Precarious Dialogue. Maria Kakogianni and Jacques Rancière,' trans. Olivia Lucca Fraser, *Radical Philosophy* 181 (2013), 20.
11. Rancière, 'A Precarious Dialogue,' 19.
12. Rancière, 'A Precarious Dialogue,' 19.
13. Rancière, 'A Precarious Dialogue,' 19.
14. Jacques Rancière, *The Politics of Aesthetics*, trans. Gabriel Rockhill (London & New York: Continuum 2006), 12.
15. Jacques Rancière, 'Ten Thesis of Politics,' in *Dissensus: On Politics and Aesthetics*, trans. Steven Corcoran (London & New York: Continuum 2010), 36.
16. Gottfried Leibnitz, *Essais de Théodicée sur la bonte de Dieu, la liberté de l'homme et l'origine du mal*. Tome I, (Amsterdam: Francois Changuion, 1747), 97.
17. Giorgio Agamben, *The State of Exception*, trans. Kevin Attell (Chicago: University of Chicago Press, 2005), 14.
18. Rancière, 'A Precarious Dialogue,' 19.

19. Jean-Luc Nancy and Philippe Lacoue-Labarthe, 'Le "retrait" du politique,' in *Le Retrait du politique*, eds. Jacob Rogozinski, et. al. (Paris: Galilée, 1983), 192.
20. Slavoj Žižek, *Violence: Six Sideways reflections* (London: Profile Books, 2008), 11.
21. Jacques Rancière, *Disagreemen: Politics and Philosophy*, trans. Julie Rose (Minneapolis: University of Minnesota Press, 1999), 113.
22. Slavoj Žižek, 'From Democracy to Divine Violence,' in *Democracy in What State?* (Columbia University Press 2011), 101.
23. Giorgio Agamben, 'Note luminaire sur le concept de démocratie,' in *Démocratie, dans quel état?* (Paris: La Fabrique, 2009) 11–12.
24. Jacques Rancière, 'Dissenting Words. A Conversation with Jacques Rancière,' *Diacritics* 113 (2000), 125.
25. Jacques Rancière, *La haine de la démocratie* (Paris: La Fabrique, 2005), 78.
26. Simone Weil, '*The Iliad*, or the Poem of Force,' *Politics* November (1945), accessed 1 September 2019, https://archive.org/stream/SimoneWeilAndThePoemOfForce/Simone%20Weil.%20HOMER.%20The%20Poem%20of%20Force_djvu.txt.
27. Walter Benjamin, *On the Concept of History*, trans. Harr Zohn, Selected Writings 4, 1939–1940 (Cambridge, Mass. & London: Harvard University Press, 2003), 392.
28. Etienne Balibar, *La crainte des masses: politique et philosophie avant et après Marx* (Paris: Galilée, 1997).
29. Stijn Vanheule, 'Capitalist Discourse, Subjectivity and Lacanian Psychoanalysis,' *Frontiers in Psychology* 7 (2016), http://doi.org/10.3389/fpsyg.2016.01948.
30. Lacan presented his discourse theory in his Seminar XVII (1969–70). It includes four discourses: the discourse of the master, the discourse of the hysteric, the discourse of the university, and the discourse of the analyst. Every determination of the subject depends on these discourses. They determine the identity of the subject, its affects, thoughts, and enjoyments. The basic discourse is one of the master based on the master/slave dialectic. The master signifier represents the subject for all other signifiers. Jacques Lacan, *The Other Side of Psychoanalysis, Seminar XVII, 1969–1970*, trans. Russell Grigg (New York & London: Norton, 2007.)
31. Samo Tomšič, *The Capitalist Unconscious: Marx and Lacan* (London & New York: Verso, 2015), 220.
32. Vanheule, 'Capitalist Discourse,' 17–19.
33. Jacques Lacan, 'Excursus,' in *En Italie Lacan 1953–1978*, ed. G. B.

Contri (Milan: La Salamandra, 1973), 97, my translation.

34. Jacques Lacan, 'Du discourse psychanalytique,' in *En Italie Lacan 1953-1978*, ed. G. B. Contri (Milan: La Salamandra, 1973); see also Tomšič, *The Capitalist Unconscious*; Vanheule, 'Capitalist Discourse,' 2.

35. Frédéric Declerq, 'Lacan and the Capitalist Discourse: Its Consequences for Libidinal Enjoyment and Social Bonds. Psychoanalysis,' *Psychoanalysis, Culture & Society* 11/1 (2006), 74–83.

36. Renata Salecl, 'Society of Choice,' *Differences* 20/1 (2009), 159.

37. Salecl, 'Society of Choice,' 161.

38. Lacan, 'Du discourse psychanalytique,' 48.

39. Eve Kosofsky Sedgwick, 'Paranoid Reading and Reparative Reading; or You're so Paranoid, You Probably Think This Introduction is about You,' in *Novel Gazing: Queer Readings in Fiction*, ed. Eve Kosofsky Sedgwick (Durham, DC: Duke University Press, 1997), 6–7; see also Eve Kosofsky Sedgwick, *Touching Feeling: Affect, Pedagogy, Performativity* (Durham, DC: Duke University Press, 2003).

40. Sedgwick, 'Paranoid Reading and Reparative Reading,' 8.

41. Donna Haraway, 'Situated Knowledges: The Science Question in Feminism and the Privilege of Partial Perspective,' *Feminist Studies* 14/3 (1988), 582.

42. Sedgwick, 'Paranoid Reading and Reparative Reading,' 23.

43. The plan was to save finance institutions while ensuring that the weakest citizens of the weakest nations pay the price of the mistakes of finance capitalism. Yannis Varoufakis, *And the Weak Suffer What They Must?* (London: The Bodley Head, 2016), 13.

44. Thucydides, *The History of Peloponnesian War*, trans. Charles Foster Smith (London: William Heineman, 1919),

45. Sophocles, *Antigone*, trans. Hugh Lloyd-Jones (Cambridge, Mass.: Haravrd University Press, 1998), 332–4. See also Sophocles, *Antigone*, trans. Richard Jebb (Cambridge: Cambridge University Press, 1891).

46. Friedrich Hölderlin, *Antigonae*, Sämtliche Werke 5 (Stuttgart: W. Kohlhammer, 1952), 219. My translation. See also Friedrich Hölderlin, *Hölderlin's Sophocles: Oedipus & Antigone*, trans. David Constatantine (Tarset: Bloodaxe Books, 2001).

47. Cecilia Sjöholm, *The Antigone Complex: Ethics and Invention of Female Desire* (Stanford University Press, 2004), 69.

48. Lewis Mumford, *Technics and Civilization* (New York: Harcourt, Brace and World, 1934), 156–8.

49. Sophocles, *Antigone*, trans. Anne Carson (London: Oberon Books, 2015), 364.

50. Maurice Merleau-Ponty, *The World of Perception*, trans. Oliver Davis (London & New York: Routledge, 2008), 43. The explicit aim of Google's medical company Calico is to take on aging itself using a big-data approach. Biotechnology, regenerative medicine, nanotechnology, organ creation using 3D printers, nanobots correcting DNA replication, and molecular manufacturing are the future means of life production. Cryonics, where a body or head is suspended in liquid nitrogen, or sending a 'human being' into virtual reality relieves us from our corpses.

51. Friedrich Hölderlin, 'Anmerkungen zum Oedipus,' Sämtliche Werke 5 (Stuttgart: W. Kohlhammer, 1952), 201. My translation.

52. Martin Heidegger, 'What Are Poets For?', in *Poetry, Language, Thought*, trans. Albert Hofstadter (New York: Harper & Row, 1971), 125.

53. Françoise Dastur, *Death: An Essay on Finitude*, trans. John Llewelyn (London & Atlantic Highlands, NJ: Athlone, 1996), 70.

54. Rainer Maria Rilke, *Das Buch von der Armut und vom Tode*, Gesammelte Werke, Band II (Leipzig: Insel Verlag, 1927), 273.

55. Plato, *Timaeus*, trans. A. E. Taylor (London: Routledge, 2014), 22c.

56. Alain Badiou, *Ethics: An Essay of the Understanding of Evil*, trans. Peter Hallwood (London: Verso, 2001), 56.

57. Jacques Lacan, *The Ethics of Psychoanalysis, Seminar VII, 1959–1960*, trans. Dennis Porter (London: Routledge, 1992), 36. Translation modified.

58. Lacan, *The Ethics of Psychoanalysis*, 23. Translation modified.

59. Lacan, *The Ethics of Psychoanalysis*, 23.

60. Dany-Robert Dufour, *Le Divin Marchè: La reviolution culturel libérale* (Paris: Gallimard, 2012).

61. Lacan, *The Ethics of Psychoanalysis*, 11.

62. Immanuel Kant, *Groundwork of the Metaphysics of Morals*, in *Practical Philosophy*, trans. Mary J. Gregor (Cambridge: Cambridge University Press, 1996), 57.

63. Onora O'Neill, *Towards Justice and Virtue* (Cambridge: Cambridge University Press, 1996), 5.

64. Jacques Lacan, *Encore: On Feminine Sexuality, the Limits of Love and Knowledge, Seminar XX, 1972–1973*, trans. Bruce Fink (New York & London: W. W. Norton, 1975), 1.

65. Philippe Lacoue-Labarthe, 'De l'éthique: à propos d'Antigone,' in *Lacan avec les philosophes* (Paris: Albin Michel, 1991), 21.

66. Lacoue-Labarthe, 'De l'éthique,' 22.

67. Lacan, *The Ethics of Psychoanalysis*, 133; Lacoue-Labarthe, 'De l'éthique,' 22.

68. Lacan, *The Ethics of Psychoanalysis*, 231, 237; Lacoue-Labarthe, 'De

l'éthique,' 23.

69. Lacan, *The Ethics of Psychoanalysis*, 230; Lacoue-Labarthe, 'De l'éthique,' 23.

70. Lacan, *The Ethics of Psychoanalysis*, 234; Lacoue-Labarthe, 'De l'éthique,' 24.

71. Lacan, *The Ethics of Psychoanalysis*, 232; Lacoue-Labarthe, 'De l'éthique,' 24.

72. Jacques Lacan, *Freud's papers on Techniques, Seminar I, 1953–1954*, trans. John Forrester (Cambridge: Cambridge University Press, 1988), 199.

73. I have translated Heidegger's *Sein* as 'being.' I prefer the lowercase 'b' even though it is often with the uppercase 'B.' The capital 'B' is taken from the German way of capitalizing nouns. In English, this may essentialize *Sein* too much. For Heidegger, *Sein* is not an abstract noun. It is derived from the infinitive of the verb *sein*, 'to be.' *Sein* should be understood as a tension between a noun and a transitive verb, as a verbal noun, 'being' and 'to be,' that is, as 'the to be'. (Jean-Luc Nancy, *Being Singular Plural*, trans. Robert D. Richardson and Anne E. O'Byrne [Stanford: Stanford University Press, 2000], 28.) Moreover, it would be meddling to translate *Sein* sometimes with the uppercase 'B' ('Being'), sometimes with the lowercase 'b' ('being-in-the-world,' 'being-with,' etc.). If the context does not make clear the difference between *Sein* and *Seiende*, I will use 'a being' or plural 'beings' for *Seiende*.

74. Werner Marx, *Towards a Phenomenological Ethics*, trans. Stefaan Heyvaert (Albany, NY: State University of New York Press, 1992), 67.

75. Philippe Lacoue-Labarthe, 'Stagings of Mimesis: An Interview by Peter Hallward,' trans. Jane Hiddleston. *Angelaki: Journal of the Theoretical Humanities* 8/2 (2003), 68.

76. Badiou, *Ethics*, 3.

77. Slavoj Zizek, 'Philosophy is not a Dialogue,' in *Philosophy in the Present*, ed. Peter Engelman (Cambridge & Malden, MA: Polity, 2009) 72; Alain Badiou, 'Thinking the Event, in *Philosophy in the Present* (Cambridge & Malden, MA: Polity, 2009), 44.

78. Alain Badiou, *Polemics*, trans. Steven Corcoran (London & New York: Verso, 2006), 231.

79. Badiou, *Ethics*, 86.

80. Lacan, *The Ethics of Psychoanalysis*, 2.

81. Alain Badiou and Élisabeth Roudinesco, *Jacques Lacan: Past and Present: A Dialogue*, trans. Jason E. Smith (New York: Columbia University Press, 2014), 33.

82. Badiou and Roudinesco, *Jacques Lacan*, 33.

83. See Sylvain Lazarus, *Anthropologie du nom* (Paris: Seuil, 1996).

84. Samuel Beckett, *L'Innommable* (Paris: Minuit, 1953), 261.
85. Badiou and Roudinesco, *Jacques Lacan*, 24.

Chapter One

1. Friedrich Hölderlin, 'Bread and Wine,' in *Poems and Fragments*, trans Michael Hamburger (London: Anvil, 2004), 327. Translation modified.
2. Odysseus Elytis, *In the Name of Luminosity and Transparency*, trans. Nobel Foundation (Athens: Aiora, 2016), 30–1.
3. Hölderlin, 'Bread and Wine,' 327.
4. Hölderlin, 'Bread and Wine,' 327.
5. Hölderlin, 'Bread and Wine,' 325. Translation modified.
6. Hölderlin, 'Bread and Wine,' 329.
7. Hölderlin, 'Bread and Wine,' 327. Translation modified.
8. Heidegger, 'What are Poets For?', 94.
9. Martin Heidegger, 'What are Poets For?', 94.
10. Friedrich Hölderlin, 'The Titans,' in *Poems and Fragments*, 631.
11. Martin Heidegger, *Elucidations of Hölderlin's Poetry*, trans. Keith Hoeller (New York: Humanity Books, 2000), 224.
12. Friedrich Hölderlin, 'The Poet's Vocation,' in *Poems and Fragments*, 233.
13. Stefan Zweig, *The Struggle with the Daemon: Hölderlin, Kleist, Nietzsche*, trans. Eden and Cedar Paul (Lexington, Mass.: Plunkett Lake Press, 2012), 35.
14. Zweig, *The Struggle with the Daemon*, 35.
15. Heidegger, *Elucidations of Hölderlin's Poetry*, 223–4.
16. Heidegger, *Elucidations of Hölderlin's Poetry*, 224.
17. Hölderlin, 'The Titans,' 629.
18. Martin Heidegger, *Zu Hölderlin—Griechenlandreisen*, Gesamtausgabe 75 (Frankfurt am Main: Vittorio Klostermann, 2000), 39.
19. Martin Heidegger, '… Poetically Man Dwells …,' in *Poetry, Language, Thought*, trans. Albert Hofstadter (New York: Harper & Row, 1971), 228.
20. Heidegger, 'Poetically Man Dwells,' 229.
21. Lacoue-Labarthe, 'Stagings of Mimesis,' 70, 66.
22. Lacoue-Labarthe, 'Stagings of Mimesis,' 66.
23. Martin Heidegger, *Aus der Erfahrung des Denkens*, Gesamtausgabe 13 (Frankfurt am Main: Klostermann, 1983), 11.
24. Zweig, *The Struggle with the Daemon*, 35.
25. Jean-Luc Nancy, *The Inoperative Community*, trans. Peter Connor (Minneapolis: University of Minneapolis Press, 2006), 114.

26. Nancy, *The Inoperative Community*, 123.
27. Nancy, *The Inoperative Community*, 124.
28. Hent de Vries, 'Theotopographies: Nancy, Hölderlin, Heidegger,' *MLN* 109/3 (1994), 456.
29. Nancy, *The Inoperative Community*, 126.
30. Nancy, *The Inoperative Community*, 124.
31. Nancy, *The Inoperative Community*, 131.
32. Jacques Derrida, 'Violence and Metaphysics,' in *Writing and Difference*, trans. A. Bass (Chicago: Chicago University Press, 1978), 146.
33. See Martin Heidegger, *Gelassenheit* (Pfullingen: Neske, 1985), 30.
34. Jacques Derrida, 'Heidegger's Ear: Philopolemology (Geschelecht IV),' in *Reading Heidegger: Commemorations*, ed. John Sallis (Bloomington: Indiana University Press, 1993), 167.
35. Jean-Luc Nancy, *Dis-enclosure—Deconstruction of Christianity*, trans. Bettina Bergo, Gabriel and Michael B. Smith (New York: Fordham University Press, 2008), 157.
36. Nancy, *The Inoperative Community*, 121.
37. Zweig, *The Struggle with the Daemon*, 36.
38. See Rainer Nägele, *Reading after Freud: Essays on Goethe, Hölderlin, Habermas, Nietzsche, Brecht, Celan and Freud* (New York: Columbia University Press, 1987), 51–65.
39. Nancy, *The Inoperative Community*, 131.
40. Nancy, *The Inoperative Community*, 125.
41. Nancy, *The Inoperative Community*, 115.
42. Lacoue-Labarthe, Stagings of Mimesis, 67.
43. Lacoue-Labarthe, Stagings of Mimesis, 67.
44. Philippe Lacoue-Labarthe, 'Typography,' in *Typography: Mimesis, Philosophy, Politics* (Cambridge, MA: Harvard University Press, 1989), 137.
45. Xiaobo Liu. *June Fourth Elegies*, trans. Jeffrey Yang (London: Jonathan Cape, 2012).
46. Hölderlin, 'Bread and Wine.'
47. Zweig, *The Struggle with the Daemon*, 36.
48. Aristophanes, *The Frogs*, trans. Benjamin Bickley Rogers (London: Heinemann, 1924), 1008–10.

Chapter Two

1. Friedrich Hölderlin, 'The Archipelago,' in *Poems and Fragments*, trans. Michael Hamburger (London: Anvil, 2004), 277.

2. Hölderlin, 'The Archipelago,' 277.
3. Hölderlin, 'The Archipelago,' 277. Translation modified.
4. Hölderlin, 'The Archipelago,' 277.
5. Friedrich Hölderlin, 'Menon's Lament for Diotima,' in *Poems and Fragments*, trans. Michael Hamburger (London: Anvil, 2004), 297.
6. Albert Camus, 'Lecture Given in Athens on the Future of Tragedy,' in *Selected Essays and Notebooks*, trans. Philip Thody (London & New York: Penguin Books, 1970), 192.
7. Camus, 'Lecture Given in Athens on the Future of Tragedy,' 194.
8. George Steiner, *The Death of Tragedy* (Newburyport: Open Road Media, 2013).
9. See Friedrich Nietzsche, *The Birth of Tragedy*, trans. Ronald Speirs (Cambridge: Cambridge University Press, 1999); Friedrich Nietzsche, *Gay Science*, trans. Waltder Kaufmann (New York: Rasndom House, 1974).
10. Max Weber, 'Science as Vocation,' in Max Weber, *Essays in Sociology* (Oxford & New York: Oxford University Press, 1946), 148.
11. A. E. Stallings, 'After a Greek Proverb,' in *Futures: Poetry of the Greek Crisis*, ed. Theodoros Chiotis (London: Penned in the Margins, 2015), 15.
12. Simon Critchley, 'Interview with Simon Critchley: The Tragic and its Limits by John Douglas Millar.' *The White Review*, November 2012, accessed 1 September 2019, http://www.thewhitereview.org/feature/interview-with-simon-critchley-the-tragic-and-its-limits-2/.
13. See Philippe Lacoue-Labarthe and Jean-Luc Nancy, *Le mythe Nazi* (Paris: Aube, 1991).
14. Simon Critchley, *Ethics, Politics, Subjectivity: Essays on Derrida, Levinas and Contemporary French Thought* (London & New York: Verso, 1999), 231.
15. The King was determined to introduce politically liberal Prussia, which would combine the legal order and the ethical community rooted in the family.
16. Cited in Erika Fischer-Lichte, 'Politicizing Antigone,' in *Interrogating Antigone in Postmodern Philosophy and Criticism*, eds. S. E. Wilmer and Audrone Zukauskaite (Oxford: Oxford University Press, 2010), doi:10.1093/acprof:oso/9780199559213.001.0001.
17. Robert Savage, 'The Precedence of Citation: On Brecht's *The Antigone of Sophocles*,' *Colloquy: Text, Theory, Critique*, 11 (2006), 119–20.
18. Lars Noren, *En dramatikers dagbok 2000–2001* (Stockholm: Bonnier, 2009), 25 August 2001.
19. Jacques Derrida, 'Signature Event Context,' in *Limited Inc*, trans. Alan Bass (Evanston: Northwestern University Press, 2000), 7.
20. Jean-Luc Nancy, *After Fukushima: The Equivalence of Catastrophes*, trans. Charlotte Mandell (New York: Fordham University Press, 2015), 38–39.

21. Jean-Luc Nancy, *The Gravity of Thought*, trans. François Raffoul and Gregory Recco, (New York: Humanity Books, 1997), 53–5.
22. Jean-Luc Nancy, *Being Singular Plural*, trans. Robert D. Richardson and Anne E. O'Byrne (Stanford: Stanford University Press, 2000), 171.
23. Nancy, *Being Singular Plural*, 172.
24. Sören Kierkegaard, *Fear and Trembling*, trans. Howard Hoing and Edna Hong (Princeton: Princeton University Press, 1983), 54.
25. Christoph Menke, 'The Presence of Tragedy,' *Critical Horizons* 5/1, (2004), 201–25, 207.
26. Jean-Pierre Vernant, *Tragedy and Myth in Ancient Greece* (Brighton: Harvester Press, 1981), 9.
27. Vernant, *Tragedy and Myth in Ancient Greece*, 9–10.
28. Oddone Longo, 'The Theater of the Polis,' in *Nothing to Do with Dionysos? Athenian Drama in its Social Context*, eds. J. Winkler and Froma Zeitling (Princeton: Princeton University Press, 1990), 12–19, 15.
29. Reiner Nägele, *Theater, Theory, Speculation: Walter Benjamin and the Scenes of Modernity* (Baltimore, Md.: Johns Hopkins University Press, 1991), 165.
30. Alain Badiou, *Rhapsody for the Theatre*, trans. Bruno Bosteels and Martin Puchner (London & New York: Verso, 2013), 93.
31. Philippe Lacoue-Labarthe, 'Théâtre (ou: Opéra—ou: le simulacre—ou: le subterfuge),' in *Pour n'en pas finir: Écrits sur la musique* (Paris: Christian Bourgois, 2015), IV.9.
32. Simon Critchley, *Tragedy, the Greeks and Us*, Ebook version (New York: Pantheon Books, 2019), 61.1.
33. Critchley, *Tragedy, the Greeks and Us*, 61.4.
34. I use the term 'a tragic figure' instead of 'a tragic character' to emphasize that 'a tragic *ēthos*' is not a stable being or a pre-given essence but more being-in-the-world-of-tragedy as a verbal noun, that is, a figure that is always already in the process of the figuration of a figure.
35. Critchley, *Tragedy, the Greeks and Us*, 61.5.
36. Lacoue-Labarthe, 'Stagings of Mimesis,' 59.
37. Critchley, 'Interview with Simon Critchley.'
38. Critchley, 'Interview with Simon Critchley.'
39. Critchley, *Ethics, Politics, Subjectivity*, 225.
40. Critchley, *Ethics, Politics, Subjectivity*, 225.
41. Critchley, *Ethics, Politics, Subjectivity*, 225.
42. Marc De Kesel, 'Antigone's Fart,' paper presented at a seminar on Simon Critchley, Ghent, 27 May 2000.
43. Menke, The Presence of Tragedy, 212.

44. Menke, The Presence of Tragedy, 212.
45. Jean-Pierre Vernant, *Les origins de la pensée grecques* (Paris: Presses Universitaires de France, 1962).
46. Walter Benjamin, *Ursprung des Deutschen Trauerspiels*, Gesammelte Schriften I.1 (Frankfurt am Main: Suhrkamp, 1963), 294–6. For Benjamin, Florens Christian Rang's views on the connection of the tragedy and the trial were important. In a letter dated on 28 January 1924, Rang wrote to Benjamin about the dialogue in the theatre and the legal process, which originally refers to the correct circulation of the stars (*Rechtslauf*). An ecstatic word in the dialogue means that the extraordinary (*Ausserordentlichkeit*) overpowers the ordinary (*Ordentlichkeit*) and the higher law (*Recht*) arises from proof of the living speech.
47. Louis Gernet, *Droit et société dans la Grèce ancienne* (Paris: Publications de l'institut de droit romain de l'université de Paris, 1955), 63.
48. Nicole Loraux, *The Divided City: On Memory and Forgetting in Ancient Athens*, trans. Corinne Pache with Jeff Fort (New York: Zone Books, 2002), 230–5.
49. Loraux, *The Divided City*, 60.
50. Loraux, *The Divided City*, 94.
51. Loraux, *The Divided City*, 61.
52. Loraux, *The Divided City*, 55, 57.
53. Loraux, *The Divided City*, 15.
54. Homer, *Iliad*, trans. Samuel Butler (The Project Gutenberg EBook, 2000) 19.65.
55. Loraux, *The Divided City*, 97.
56. Nicole Loraux, *The Mourning Voice: An Essay on Greek Tragedy*, trans. Elizabeth Trapnell Rawlings (Ithaca & London: Cornell University Press), 2002, 82.
57. Loraux, *The Divided City*, 61, 96–98.
58. Vernant, *The Origins of Greek Tragedy*, 48.
59. Loraux, *The Mourning Voice*, 81.
60. Loraux, *The Divided City*, 96.
61. Cited in Loraux, *The Divided City*, 117.
62. Heraclitus, *Fragments*, trans. T. M. Robinson (Toronto: University of Toronto Press, 1987), fragment 8.
63. Vernant, *The Origins of the Greek Tragedy*, 45.
64. Heraclitus, *Fragments*, fragment, 80.
65. Jean-Luc Nancy, 'The Free Voice of Man,' trans. Richar Stamp, in Philippe Lacoue-Labarthe and Jean-Luc Nancy, *Retreating the Political* (London & New York: Routledge, 1997), 34.
66. Savage, 'The Precedence of Citation,' 112.

67. J. W. Goethe, 'A Letter of 6 June 1824 to Chancellor Müller,' cited in Albin Lesky, *Greek Tragedy*, trans. H. A. Frankfort (New York: E. Benn, 1965), 8.
68. Noren, *En dramatikers* dagbok, 25 August 2001.
69. Aeschylus, *Agamemnon*, trans. Herbert Weir Smyth (Cambridge: Harvard University Press, 1971), 160.
70. Friedrich Hölderlin, 'An Casimir Ulrich Böhlendorff' (undated) in *Sämtliche Werke 6, Briefe 1*, Stuttgarter Hölderlin-Ausgabe, ed. Friedrich Beissner (Stuttgart: W. Kohlhammer Verlag, 1954), 433.
71. Friedrich Hölderlin, 'An Casimir Ulrich Böhlendorff 4 Dec. 1801,' in *Sämtliche Werke 6, Briefe 1*, 425. My translation.
72. See Philippe Lacoue-Labarthe, 'Hölderlin and the Greeks,' in *Typographies: Mimesis, Philosophy, Politics*, trans. Christopher Fynsk (Stanford: Stanford University Press, 1998), 244.
73. Martin Heidegger, *Elucidations of Hölderlin's Poetry*, trans. Keith Holler (New York: Humanity Books, 2000), 112–13.
74. The organic refers to the principle of art and organization, the difference between various parts and elements. The aorgic, as an opposite of the organic, refers, not to the inorganic, but to wild and coarse, to nature in its infinite oneness without organization and form.
75. Friedrich Hölderlin, 'Anmerkungen zur Antigonae,' Sämtliche Werke 5 (Stuttgart: W. Kohlhammer, 1952), 271. My translation; Jean Beaufret, *Hölderlin et Sophocle* (Brionne: Gerard Monfort, 1983), 10–11.
76. Beaufret, *Hölderlin et Sophocles*, 19. My translation.
77. Beaufret, *Hölderlin et Sophocles*, 20. My translation.
78. Hölderlin, 'Anmerkungen zum Oedipus,' 202. My translation,
79. Beda Allemann, *Hölderlin und Heidegger* (Atlantis Verlag, Freiburg, 1954), 13–34.
80. Jennifer Anna Gosetti-Ferencei, *Heidegger, Hölderlin, and the Subject of Poetic Languages: Toward a Poetics of Dasein* (New York: Fordham Unibversity Press, 2004), 11.
81. Beaufret, *Hölderlin et Sophocle*, 12–13.
82. Hölderlin, 'An Casimir Ulrich Böhlendorff 4 Dec. 1801,' 425–6.
83. Heidegger, *Elucidations of Hölderlin's Poetry*, 112.
84. Hölderlin, 'An Casimir Ulrich Böhlendorff 4 Dec. 1801,' 426.
85. Hölderlin, 'An Casimir Ulrich Böhlendorff 4 Dec. 1801,' 426.
86. Lacoue-Labarthe, 'Hölderlin and the Greeks,' 242.
87. Massimo Cacciari, *The Unpolitical: On the Radical Critique of Political Reason*, trans. Massimo Verdicchio (New York: Fordham University Press, 2009), 59.

Chapter Three

1. Elfriede Jelinek, *Charges (The Supplicants)*, trans. Gitta Honegger (London & New York & Calcutta: Seagull Books, 2016), 26.
2. Jelinek, *Charges*, 13.
3. Jelinek, *Charges*, 32.
4. Jelinek, *Charges*, 47.
5. Jelinek, *Charges*, 15.
6. Jelinek, *Charges*, 25, 11.
7. Jelinek, *Charges*, 22.
8. Jelinek, *Charges*, 50.
9. Aeschylus, *Suppliant Maidens*, trans. Herbert Weirs Smyth (Cambridge, Mass.: Harvard University Press, 1956), 5, 74.
10. Benjamin Gray, 'Exile, Refuge and the Greek Polis: Between Justice and Humanity.' *Journal of Refugee* Studies, 30/2 (2016), 194.
11. Aristotle, *The Politics*, trans. Carnes Lord (Chicago & London: The University of Chicago Press, 1984), 1275b 36–37.
12. Gray, 'Exile, Refuge and the Greek Polis,' 197. A *metoikon* had to pay the migrant tax and to find a citizen sponsor, otherwise he risked being sold into slavery.
13. Edward E. Cohen, *The Athenian Nation* (Princeton, NJ: Princeton University Press, 2000), 17.
14. Sophocles, *Tereus*, in *Sophocles: Selected Fragmentary Plays I*, trans. Alan H. Sommerstein, David Fitzpatrick, and Thomas Talboy (Oxford: Oxbow Books, 2006), 163, 180.
15. Sophocles, *Tereus*, 163, 180.
16. Euripides, *The Children of Heracles*, trans. Mark Griffith (Chicago: The University of Chicago Press, 2013), 15–16.
17. Euripides, *The Children of Heracles*, 31.
18. Euripides, *The Children of Heracles*, 57–8.
19. See Giorgio Agamben, *Homo Sacer: Sovereign Power and Bare Life*, trans. Daniel Heller-Roazen (Stanford: Stanford University Press 1998).
20. M. E. Price, *Rethinking Asylum: History, Purpose, and Limits* (Cambridge: Cambridge University Press, 2009), 26–31; Gray, 'Exile, Refuge and the Greek Polis,' 213.
21. Xenophon, *Hellenica*, trans. Carleton L. Brownson (London: William Heinemann, 1918), 2.3.52–3.
22. Euripides, *The Children of Heracles*, 107–108.

23. Euripides, *The Children of Heracles*, 248–249, 260.
24. Euripides, *The Children of Heracles*, 423.
25. Euripides, *The Children of Heracles*, 109.
26. Euripides, *The Children of Heracles*, 427–430.
27. Aristophanes, *The Frogs*, 949–52.
28. Aristophanes, *The Frogs*, 959.
29. Euripides, *The Children of Heracles*, 319.
30. Euripides, *The Children of Heracles*, 266.
31. Euripides, *The Children of Heracles*, 329–30.
32. Euripides, *The Children of Heracles*, 168, 199–201.
33. Euripides, *The Children of Heracles*, 345.
34. Lysias, *Funeral Oration*, trans. W. R. M. Lamb (Cambridge, Mass.: Harvard University Press, 1930), 2.11–12.
35. Gilbert Murray, *Euripides and His Age* (London: Williams and Norgate, 1913), 91; see also Elemér Balogh, *Political Refugees in Ancient Greece: From the Period of the Tyrants to Alexander the Great* (Johannesburg: Witwatersrand University Press, 1943).
36. Markland Taylor, 'The Children of Herakles.' *Variety*, 14 January 2003.
37. Bernd Steinbock, *Social Memory in Athenian Public Discourse, Uses and Meanings of the Past* (Ann Arbor: The University of Michigan Press, 2013), 179–80.
38. Aeschylus, *The Suppliant Maidens*, 69–73.
39. Aeschylus, *The Suppliant Maidens*, 78.
40. Aeschylus, *The Suppliant Maidens*, 84–5.
41. Aeschylus, *The Suppliant Maidens*, 963–5.
42. Aeschylus, *The Suppliant Maidens*, 963.
43. Aeschylus, *The Suppliant Maidens*, 963–5.
44. Vincent Azoulay, 'Repolitiser la cité grecque, trente ans aprés.' *Annales* 69/3 (2014).
45. Aristotle, *The Politics*, 1275b 16–19.
46. Azoulay, 'Repolitiser la cité grecque.'
47. Pauline Schmitt-Pantel, 'Collective Activities and the Political in the Greek City,' in *The Greek City: From Homer to Alexander*, eds. Oswyn Murray and Simon Price (Oxford: Clarendon Press, 1990), 203.
48. Isocrates, *Areopagiticus*, Isocrates II, trans. George Norlin (London: Heinemann 1928), 7.15.
49. Kostas Vlassopoulos, 'Free Spaces: Identity, Experience and Democracy in Classical Athens,' *Classical Quarterly* 57/1 (2007), 39, 51; Sian Lewis, *News and Society in the Greek Polis* (Chapel Hill: The University of North Carolina Press, 1996), 14–15.

50. Rancère, *Disagreement*, 8, 23–29.
51. Kostas Vlassopoulos, 'Beyond and Below the Polis: Networks, Associations, and the Writing of Greek History.' *Mediterranean Historical Review* 22/1 (2007).
52. Aristotle, *Nicomachean Ethics*, trans. Christopher Rowe (Oxford: Oxford University Press, 2002), 1160a9–10.
53. Benjamin Gray, 'Citizenship as Barrier and Opportunity for Ancient Greek and Modern Refugees.' *Humanities* 7/3 (2018), https://doi.org/10.3390/h7030072.
54. Kostas Vlassopoulos, *Unthinking the Greek Polis* (Cambridge: Cambridge University Press, 2007); Paulin Ismard, *La cite des réseaux: Athènes et ses associations* (Paris: Publications de la Sorbonne, 2010).
55. Gray, 'Exile, Refuge and the Greek Polis,' 203; Peter Gatrell, *The Making of the Modern Refugee* (Oxford: Oxford University Press, 2013).
56. John Gould, 'Tragedy and Collective Experience,' in *Tragedy and the Tragic: Greek Theatre and Beyond*, ed. M. S. Silk (Oxford: Clarendon Press, 1996), 221.
57. Gould, 'Tragedy and Collective Experience,' 221.
58. Gould, 'Tragedy and Collective Experience,' 220–1.
59. Gould, 'Tragedy and Collective Experience,' 224.
60. Aeschylus, *Suppliant Maidens*, 1071.
61. Aeschylus, *Suppliant Maidens*, 1060.
62. Aeschylus, *Suppliant Maidens*, 1061.
63. Beaufret, *Hölderlin et Sophocle*, 22.
64. Susanne Gottlob, *Stimme und Blick* (Bielefeld: Transcript, 2002), 9–19.
65. Friedrich Hölderlin, *Oedipus der Tyrann*, Sämtliche Werke 5 (Stuttgart: W. Kohlhammer, 1952), 184. My translation.
66. Gottlob, *Stimme und Blick*, 18.
67. Cecilia Sjöholm, 'Naked Life: Arendt and the Exile at Colonus.'
68. Sophocles, *Oedipus at Colonus*, trans. Hugh Lloyd-Jones (Cambridge, Mass.: Harvard University Press, 1998), 183–184.
69. Sophocles, *Oedipus Tyrannus*, trans. Hugh Lloyd-Jones (Cambridge, Mass.: Harvard University Press, 1997) 658–9, 661.
70. Françoise Dastur, *Death: An Essay on Finitude*, trans. John Llewelyn (London: Athlone Press, 1996), 17.
71. Sjöholm, 'Naked Life: Arendt and the Exile at Colonus.'
72. Agamben, *Homo Sacer*, 181.
73. Some groups of refugees were granted specific rights and privileges by the Athenian assembly that went far beyond merely a safe residence, but Oedipus was honoured with citizenship. Likewise, the exiled Plataeans, the close allies of

Athens, were granted citizenship as they had to flee their destroyed city near the beginning of the Peloponnesian war.

74. Sophocles, *Oedipus at Colonus*, 1472–3.
75. Sophocles, *Oedipus at Colonus*, 1475.
76. Alain Badiou and Élisabeth Roudinesco, *Jacques Lacan, Past and Present: A Dialogue*, trans. Jason E. Smith (New York: Columbia University Press), 2014, 55.
77. Jean-Pierre Vernant and Pierre Vidal-Naquet, *Myth and Tragedy in Ancient Greece*, trans. Janet Lloyd (New York: Zone Books, 1988), 33.
78. Sophocles, *Tereus*, 165.
79. Sophocles, *Tereus*, 165.
80. Sophocles, *Tereus*, 165.
81. Sophocles, *Tereus*, 165, 185.
82. Sophocles, *Tereus*, 167.
83. Isocrates, *On the Peace*. Isocrates I, trans. George Norlin (London: Heinemann 1929), 8.138–9.
84. Isocrates, *Panegyricus*. Isocrates II, trans. George Norlin (London: Heinemann 1928), 4.51–2.
85. Isocrates, *Panegyricus*, 4.50.
86. Gray, 'Exile, Refuge and the Greek Polis,' 199–201; Polly Low, *Interstate Relations in Classical Greece: Morality and Power* (Cambridge: Cambridge University Press, 2007), 177–186.
87. Isocrates, *Plataicus*. Isocrates III, trans. Larue van Hook (London: Heinemann, 1945), 14.52–7.
88. Diogenes Laertius, *Complete Works*, trans. R.D. Hicks (Hastings: Delphi Classics, 2015), 6.49, 63, 93.
89. Lene Rubinstein, 'Immigration and Refugee Crisis in Fourth-Century Greece: An Athenian Perspective,' *The European Legacy* 23/1–2, 2018, 6–7.
90. Isocrates, *On the Peace*, Isocrates I, trans. George Norlin (London: Heinemann 1929), 8.139.
91. Michel Austin and Pierre Vidal-Naquet, *Économies et sociétés en Grèce ancienne* (Paris: Armand Colin, 1972), 118.
92. Rubinstein, 'Immigration and Refugee Crisis in Fourth-Century Greece,' 16.
93. Aeschylus, *Eumenides*, trans. Alan Shapiro and Peter Burian (Oxford: Oxford University Press, 2003), 850. Translation modified.
94. Aeschylus, *Eumenides*, 908. Translation modified.
95. Nicole Loraux, *The Children of Athens*, trans. Caroline Levine (Princeton: Princeton University Press, 1993), 137–8.
96. Euripides, *Electra*, trans. E. P. Coleridge (New York: Random House.

1938), 71.
97. Euripides, *Electra*, 131–133.
98. Sophocles, *Electra*, trans. Hugh Lloyd-Jones (Cambridge, Mass.: Harvard University Press, 1994), 78–9.
99. Sophocles, *Electra*, 70–1.
100. Sophocles, *Electra*, 1506.
101. Aeschylus, *The Libation Bearers*, trans. Hugo Lloyd-Jones (London: Duckworth, 1993), 988.
102. Aeschylus, *The Libation Bearers*, 1041–2. Translation modified.
103. Aeschylus, *The Libation Bearers*, 1062.
104. Aeschylus, *The Libation Bearers*, 1064.
105. Aeschylus, *Eumenides*, 477.
106. Aeschylus, *Eumenides*, 876.
107. Aeschylus, *Eumenides*, 884–894.
108. Aeschylus, *Eumenides*, 851–5. Translation modified.
109. Aeschylus, *Eumenides*, 994.
110. Aeschylus, *Eumenides*, 1022.
111. Aeschylus, *Eumenides*, 992, 1016–17.
112. Euripides, *The Children of Heracles*, 14–15.
113. Bertolt Brecht, *Antigone*, trans. Judith Malina (New York: Applause, 1990), 33.
114. Brecht, *Antigone*, 47–48.
115. Euripides, *The Children of Heracles*, 100–104.
116. Euripides, *The Children of Heracles*, 260.
117. Euripides, *The Children of Heracles*, 329–30.
118. Aristotle, *Nicomachean Ethics*, 1155a 22–3.
119. Aristotle, *Nicomachean Ethics*, 1155a 15.
120. Aristotle, *Nicomachean Ethics*, 1155a 20–1.
121. Aristotle, *Nicomachean Ethics*, 1155a 21, 30–1.
122. Aristotle, *Nicomachean Ethics*, 1157b 28–9.
123. Aristotle, *Nicomachean Ethics*, 1157b 27.
124. Lacoue-Labarthe, 'Stagings of Mimesis,' 70.
125. Emmanuel Levinas, *Totality and Infinity: An Essay on Exteriority*, trans. Alphonso Lingis (Hague: Martinus Nijhoff, 1979), 298.
126. Emmanuel Levinas, 'Apropos of Buber: Some Notes,' in Emmanuel Levinas, *Outside the Subject*, trans. Micheal B. Smith (Stanford, Cal.: Stanford University Press, 1993), 47.
127. George Eliot, *Felix Holt: The Radical*, Novels Vol. V (Edinburgh & London: William Blackwood and Sons, 1867), 8.
128. Simone Weil, 'Human Personality,' in *An Anthology*, trans. R. Reese.

(New York: Grove Press, 1986), 52.

129. Charles Segal, 'Catharsis, Audience, and Closure in Greek Tragedy,' in Silk, *Tragedy and the Tragic,*' 149; see also Stephen White, *Ethos of a Late-Modern Citizen* (Cambridge, MA: Harvard University Press), 2009.

130. Homer, *Iliad*, 24.507–25.

131. Judith Butler, *Precarious Life: The Powers of Mourning and Violence* (London & New York: Verso, 2004), 43, 30–2.

132. Loraux, The Mourning Voice, 87.

133. Loraux, The Mourning Voice, 89.

134. Loraux, The Mourning Voice, 89.

135. Loraux, The Mourning Voice, 89.

136. Loraux, The Mourning Voice, 26.

137. Bonnie Honig, *Antigone Interrupted* (Cambridge: Cambridge University Press), 26.

138. Bonnie Honig, 'Antigone's Two Laws: Greek Tragedy and the Politics of Humanism,' *New Literary History* 41/1 (2010), 8.

139. See Aristotle, *Nicomachean Ethics*, 1155a 20–1.

140. Jean-Luc Nancy, *The Sense of the World*, trans. Jeffrey S. Librett (Minneapolis: University of Minnesota Press, 1997), 143.

Chapter Four

1. Critchley brings together spectators in the football game and the theatre. Simon Critchley, *What We Think About When We Think About Football*, 64.

2. Aristotle, *Poetics*, trans. Stephen Halliwell (London: Duckworth, 1987), 1449b 24–6. Translation modified.

3. Aristotle, *Poetics*, 1459a 21.

4. Philippe Lacoue-Labarthe, 'Hölderlin's Theatre.'

5. See Sami Santanen, 'Mimesis ja teatterinautinto,' in *Mikä mimesis? Philippe Lacoue-Labarthen filosofinen teatteri*, eds. Ari Hirvonen and Susanna Lindberg (Helsinki: Tutkijaliitto, 2009), 132.

6. Aristotle, *Poetics*, 1449b 25.

7. Santanen, 'Mimesis ja teatterinautinto,' 132–34; Philippe Lacoue-Labarthe and Jean-Luc Nancy, 'Scéne,' *Nouvelle Revue de Psychanalyse* 46, 1992.

8. Aristotle, *Poetics*, 1462a 10–1462b 19.

9. Jonathan Lear, *Open Minded: Working Out the Logic of Soul* (Cambridge, Mass. & London: Harvard University Press, 1998), 208–9.

10. Aristotle, *On Rhetoric*, trans. George A. Kennedy (New York & Oxford: Oxford University Press, 1991), 1382a.

11. Aristotle, *On Rhetoric*, 1385b.
12. Martha Nussbaum, 'Compassion: The Basic Social Emotion.' *Social Philosophy and Policy* 13/1 (1996), 37.
13. Aristotle, *On Rhetoric*, 1386a 20–4.
14. Martha Nussbaum, *Upheavals of Thought* (Cambridge: Cambridge University Press, 2001), 301.
15. K. E. Gerdes, 'Empathy, Sympathy, and Pity,' *Journal of Social Service Research* 37/3 (2011), 230-1, 233; Kristján Kristjánsson, 'Pity: A Mitigated Defence,' *Canadian Journal of Philosophy* 44/3–4 (2014), 355–7.
16. Segal, 'Catharsis,' 164.
17. Aristotle, *On Rhetoric*, 1385a.
18. Aristotle, *On Rhetoric*, 1385b 32–33.
19. Aristotle, *On Rhetoric*, 1385b 16–23.
20. Aristotle, *Nicomachean Ethics*, 1105b 26–7.
21. Roger Crisp, 'Compassion and Beyond,' *Ethical Theory and Moral Practice* 11/3 (2008), 242.
22. Aristotle, *Nicomachean Ethics*, 1105b 28.
23. Aristotle, *History of Animals*, trans. A. L. Beck and D. M. Balme (Cambridge: Harvard University Press, 2014), 582b 1–21.
24. Lear, *Open Minded*, 193–194,
25. Lear, *Open Minded*, 195.
26. See Jonathan Lear, who rejects the cognitivist understanding of catharsis. Lear, *Open Minded*, 200–6.
27. Aristotle, *Politics*, 1460b 13–15.
28. See Piera Aulagnier, *La violence de l'interprétation* (Paris: PUF, 1975).
29. Samuel Weber, *Theatricality as Medium* (New York: Fordham University Press, 2004), 294; see also 281.
30. Werner Marx, *Towards a Phenomenological Ethics: Ethos and the Life-World*, trans. Stefaan Heyvaert (Albany, NY: State University of New York Press, 1992), 44.
31. Werner Marx, *Gibt es auf Erden ein Maß? Grundbestimmungen einer nichtmetaphysischen Ethik* (Hamburg: Felix Meiner Verlag, 1983), 12; Werner Marx, *Vernunft und Welt: Zwischen Tradition und anderem Anfang*. Den Haag: Springer, 1970).
32. Marx, *Gibt es auf Erden ein Maß?*, xvii.
33. Werner Marx, *Gibt es auf Erden ein Maß?*, 4.
34. Werner Marx, *Gibt es auf Erden ein Maß?*; see also Marx, *Towards a Phenomenological Ethics*, 43–67.
35. Sigmund Freud and Joseph Breuer, *Studies in Hysteria*, trans. Nicola Luckhurst (London: Penguin, 2004), 25–30.

36. Sigmund Freud, 'Psychopathic Characters on the Stage,' Standard Edition 7, trans. James Strachey (Hogart Press, 1953), 309.
37. Freud, 'Psychopathic Characters on the Stage,' 305.
38. Freud, 'Psychopathic Characters on the Stage,' 305.
39. Lacan, *The Ethics of Psychoanalysis*, 323.
40. Jean-Michel Vives, 'Catharsis: Psychoanalysis and the Theatre,' trans. Andrew Weller, *The International Journal of Psychoanalysis* 92 (2011), 1025.
41. Vives, Catharsis, 1017.
42. Vives, Catharsis, 1017.
43. Vives, Catharsis, 1017; see also 1014–21.
44. Lacan, *The Ethics of Psychoanalysis*, 244.
45. Lacan, *The Ethics of Psychoanalysis*, 323.
46. Lacan, *The Ethics of Psychoanalysis*, 323.
47. Lacan, *The Ethics of Psychoanalysis*, 323.
48. Lacan, *The Ethics of Psychoanalysis*, 323.
49. Aristotle, *Poetics*. 1456a 20. Translation modified.
50. Aristotle, *Poetics*, 1452a 1–6.
51. Aristotle, *On Rhetoric*, 1371a 31–1371b 1.
52. Weber, *Theatricality as Medium*, 255–6, 261.
53. Aristotle, *Poetics* 1453a 2. Translation modified.
54. Aristotle, *Poetics* 1453a 3–8. Translation modified.
55. Aristotle, *Poetics* 1456a 21. Translation modified.

Chapter Five

1. George Eliot, 'The *Antigone* and Its Moral,' in *Essays of George Eliot* (London: Routledge and Kegan Paul, 1963) 261.
2. Eliot, 'The *Antigone* and Its Moral,' 262.
3. Eliot, 'The *Antigone* and Its Moral,' 263.
4. J. W. Goethe, 'Letter of 6 June 1824 to Charles Müller,' cited in Sarah Dewar-Watson, *Tragedy* (Hampshire: Palgrave MacMillan, 2014), 81.
5. Fischer-Lichte, 'Politicizing Antigone.'
6. See Fischer-Lichte, 'Politicizing Antigone.'
7. Sophocles, *Antigone*, 1064–76.
8. Sophocles, *Antigone*, 1067.
9. D. W. Lucas, 'Hamartia,' in Aristotle, *Poetics* (Oxford: Clarendon Press, 1968), 307.
10. Antigone, *Sophocles*, 1090. Translation modified.
11. Antigone, *Sophocles*, 1098–102. Translation modified.

12. Antigone, *Sophocles*, 1111–14. Translation modified.
13. Sophocles, *Antigone*, 1257–60.
14. Euripides, *The Children of Heracles*, 423–4.
15. I am tempted to compare Creon and the chorus to the chair umpire and radio announcer in the 2018 US Open women's tennis finale. In an on-court tirade Serena Williams publicly criticized the umpire's decisions. The radio announcer described Williams's protests as 'hysterical' and a 'meltdown.' In the background, we could hear Williams's voice saying, 'I understand why you made that call, but it's unfair.' Later, she explained that there is a double standard in tennis for men and women. And she is fighting for the future rights of women players. Billy Jean King, a former world No 1, said that when 'a woman is emotional, she's "hysterical" and she's penalized for it' but when a man does the same, he's "outspoken".' Martha Kelner, 'Tennis rallies behind Serena Williams after US Open sexism claim,' *The Guardian*, 9 September 2018.
16. Plato, *Phaedrus*, trans. R. Hackforth (Cambridge: Cambridge University Press, 2018), 250D.
17. Plato, *Phaedrus*, 265A.
18. Sophocles, *Antigone*, 72.
19. Sophocles, *Antigone*, 97.
20. Simone Weil, *Intimations of Christianity*, 10.
21. Lucas, 'Hybris,' 306.
22. Lucas, 'Hybris,' 306.
23. Sophocles, *Antigone*, 71–2. Translation modified.
24. Nelson Mandela, *Long Walk to Freedom* (Philadelphia: Little, Brown, 1994), 451.
25. Sophocles, *Antigone*, 381–2.
26. Sophocles, *Antigone*, 791–9.
27. Sophocles, *Antigone*, 791–9.
28. Sophocles, *Antigone*, 853–6.
29. Sophocles, *Antigone*, 639–680.
30. Jennifer R. Ballengee, 'Mourning the Public Body in Sophocles' *Antigone*,' *Colloquy: Text, Theory, Critique*, 11 (2006), 44.
31. Ballengee, Mourning the Public Body in Sophocles,' *Antigone*, 41.
32. Honig, *Antigone Interrupted*, 98.
33. Nicole Loraux, *The Invention of Athens: The Funeral Oration in the Classical City* (Cambridge, Mass.: Harvard University Press), 1986.
34. Loraux, *The Invention of Athens*, 63.
35. Sophocles, *Antigone*, 935. See Honig, *Antigone Interrupted*, 109; about mourning 95–120.
36. Honig, *Antigone Interrupted*, 120.

37. Eliot, 'The *Antigone* and Its Moral,' 264.
38. Eliot, 'The *Antigone* and Its Moral,' 264.
39. Eliot, 'The *Antigone* and Its Moral,' 265.
40. Eliot, 'The *Antigone* and Its Moral,' 264.
41. G. W. F. Hegel, *Phenomenology of Spirit*, trans. A. V. Miller (Oxford: Oxford University Press, 1977), 282.
42. Aristotle, *Poetics*, 1450b 8–10.
43. Peter Szondi, *An Essay on the Tragic*, trans. Paul Fleming (Stanford: Stanford University Press, 2002), 1.
44. F. W. J. Schelling, *The Unconditional in Human Knowledge: Four Early Essays (1794–1796)*, trans. Fritz Marti (Lewisburg: Bucknell University Press, 1980), 193.
45. Paul Ricoeur explains that fate 'must first feel the resistance of freedom, rebound (so to speak) from the hardness of the hero, and finally crush him before the pre-eminently tragic emotion;' fear, can be born. Paul Ricoeur, *The Symbolism of Evil*, trans. Emerson Buchanan (New York: Harper & Row, 1967), 218.
46. F. W. J. Schelling, *The Philosophy of Art*, trans. Douglas W. Scott (Minneapolis: University of Minnesota Press, 1989), 256; Blair Hoxby, *What Was Tragedy? Theory and the Early Modern Canon* (Oxford: Oxford University Press), 2015, 16.
47. Schelling, *Philosophy of Art*, 251.
48. Schelling, *Philosophy of Art*, 251.
49. Hegel, *Phenomenology of Spirit*, 284.
50. Hegel, *Phenomenology of Spirit*, 284.
51. Hegel, *Phenomenology of Spirit*, 275.
52. Hegel, Phenomenology of Spirit, 268.
53. Hegel, *Phenomenology of Spirit*, 270–1.
54. Hegel, *Phenomenology of Spirit*, 270.
55. Hegel, *Phenomenology of Spirit*, 280.
56. Hegel, *Phenomenology of Spirit*, 280.
57. Seen Arthur W. H. Adkins, *Merit and Responsibility: A Study in Greek Values* (Oxford: Clarendon Press, 1960).
58. G. W. F. Hegel, Philosophy of History, trans. J. Sibree (New York: Dover, 1956), 252.
59. Hegel, *Philosophy of History*, 253.
60. Hegel, *Philosophy of History*, 253.
61. Hegel, *Philosophy of Right*, trans. T.M. Knox (Oxford: Oxford University Press, 2008), 168–9..
62. Hegel, *Phenomenology of Spirit*, 274. Translation modified.
63. Hegel, *Phenomenology of Spirit*, 275.

64. Hegel, *Phenomenology of Spirit*, 275.
65. Laura Werner, *The Restless Love of Thinking: The Concept of Liebe in Hegel's Philosophy* (Helsinki: A Dissertation, 2007), 119–23.
66. Thucydides, The History of Peloponnesian War, 6.30–32, 6.24.3, 6.13.1.
67. Hegel, *Phenomenology of Spirit*, 280.
68. Hegel, *Phenomenology of Spirit*, 288.
69. Hegel, *Phenomenology of Spirit*, 288.
70. Hegel, *Phenomenology of Spirit*, 282.
71. Rhonda Khatab, 'Ethical Consciousness in the Spirit of Tragedy: Hegel's *Antigone*I,' Colloquy 11 (2006), 79–83.
72. Hegel, *Outlines of the Philosophy of Right*, 228.
73. Hegel, *Phenomenology of Spirit*, 276.
74. Werner, *The Restless Love of Thinking*, 122.
75. Hegel, *Phenomenology of Spirit*, 288. Translation modified.
76. Hegel, *Phenomenology of Spirit*, 288.
77. Hegel, *Phenomenology of Spirit*, 288.
78. Hegel, *Phenomenology of Spirit*, 276.
79. Hegel, *Phenomenology of Spirit*, 280.
80. G. W. F. Hegel, *Aesthetics*, Vol. I, trans. T. M. Knox (Oxford: Clarendon, 1975), 204.
81. Hegel, *Phenomenology of Spirit*, 287.
82. Hegel, *Phenomenology of Spirit*, 374.
83. Hegel, *Phenomenology of Spirit*, 282.
84. Hegel, *Phenomenology of Spirit*, 284.
85. Hegel, *Phenomenology of Spirit*, 284.
86. G. W. F. Hegel, *Aesthetics II*, trans. T.M. Knox (Oxford: Clarendon, 1975), 1216.
87. See Philippe Lacoue-Labarthe, 'The Caesura of the Speculative,' in *Typography: Mimesis, Philosophy, Politics,* trans. Robert Eisenhauer, (Stanford: Stannford University Press, 1998), 208–35, 208–9.

Chapter Six

1. Hegel, *Phenomenology of Spirit*, 268; 274.
2. Khatab, 'Ethical Consciousness in the Spirit of Tragedy,' 86.
3. Lacan, *The Ethics of Psychoanalysis*, 236.
4. Jacques Derrida, *Glas*, trans. John P. Leavey Jr. and Richard Rand (Lincoln & London: University of Nebraska Press, 1996), 162.

5. Khatab, 'Ethical Consciousness in the Spirit of Tragedy,' 86, see also 87–9.
6. Luce Irigaray, *An Ethics of Sexual Difference*, trans. Carol Burke and Gillian Gill (Ithaca: Cornell, 1993), 119.
7. Luce Irigaray, *Speculum of the Other Woman*, trans. Gillian C. Gill (Ithaca, NY: Cornell University Press, 1985), 217.
8. Luce Irigaray, *To Be Two*, trans. Monique M. Rhodes and Marco F. Cocito-Monoc (London & New York: Routledge, 2001), 78–79.
9. Irigaray, *To Be Two*, 77.
10. Irigaray, *To Be Two*, 80.
11. Irigaray, *To Be Two*, 80.
12. Irigaray, *Speculum of the Other Woman*, 215.
13. Irigaray, *To Be Two*, 81.
14. Luce Irigaray, *Ce sexe qui n'en pas un* (Paris: Les Editions Minuit, 1977), 76.
15. Irigaray, *Speculum of the Other Woman*, 70.
16. Judith Butler, *Antigone's Claim: Kinship Between Life and Death* (New York: Columbia University Press, 2000).
17. Butler, *Antigone's Claim*, 2.
18. Butler, *Antigone's Claim*, 82.
19. Butler, *Antigone's Claim*, 55.
20. Butler, *Antigone's Claim*, 82.
21. Butler, *Antigone's Claim*, 5.
22. Butler, *Antigone's Claim*, 28.
23. Butler, *Antigone's Claim*, 6.
24. Butler, *Antigone's Claim*, 27.
25. Butler, *Antigone's Claim*, 5–6.
26. Butler, *Antigone's Claim*, 68.
27. Butler, *Antigone's Claim*, 72.
28. Butler, *Antigone's Claim*, 72.
29. Butler, *Antigone's Claim*, 71.
30. Butler, *Antigone's Claim*, 75.
31. Butler, *Antigone's Claim*, 55.
32. Butler, *Antigone's Claim*, 21.
33. Judith Butler, *Gender Trouble: Feminism and the Subversion of Identity* (London & New York: Routledge, 1990).
34. Honig, *Antigone Interrupted*, 49–50.
35. Butler, *Antigone's Claim*, 19.
36. Butler, *Antigone's Claim*, 30.
37. Butler, *Antigone's Claim*, 66.

38. Butler, *Antigone's Claim*, 72.
39. Butler, *Antigone's Claim*, 82.
40. Butler, *Antigone's Claim*, 82.
41. Butler, *Antigone's Claim*, 82.
42. Judith Butler, *Precarious Life: The Powers of Mourning and Violence* (London: Verso, 2004), 46.
43. Judith Butler, *Precarious Love*, 46.
44. Honig, *Antigone Interrupted*, 43–44.
45. Honig, *Antigone Interrupted*, 45, see also 49.
46. Stuart Elden, 'The Place of The Polis: Political Blindness of Judith Butler's *Antigone's Claim*,' *Theory and Event* 8/1 (2005), https://doi:10.1353/tae.2005.0008.
47. Julen Etxabe, *The Experience of Tragic Judgement* (London & New York: Routledge, 2012), 69–70.
48. Friedrich Hölderlin, 'Anmerkungen zur Antigonae,' 267. My translation.
49. Honig, *Antigone Interrupted*, 26.
50. Honig, 'Antigone's Two Laws,' 1.
51. Honig, 'Antigone's Two Laws,' 3.
52. Honig, 'Antigone's Two Laws,' 2.
53. Honig, 'Antigone's Two Laws,' 4.
54. Jacques Rancière, 'Ten Thesis of Politics,' in Jacques Rancière, *Dissensus : On Politics and Aesthetics*, trans. Steven Corcoran (London & New York: Continuum, 2010), 36.
55. Rancière, *Disagreement*.
56. Jacques Rancière, *Aesthetics and Its Discontents*, trans. Steven Corcoran (Cambridge & Malden, MA: Polity Press, 2009), 113–14.
57. John E. Seery, 'Acclaim for Antigone's Claim Reclaimed,' in *Judith Butler's Precarious Politics: Critical Encounters*, eds. Terrell Carver and Samuel A. Chambers (London & New York: Routledge, 2008), 68.
58. Judith Butler, *Undoing Gender* (London & New York: Routledge, 2004), 169.
59. Butler, *Undoing Gender*, 166.
60. Seery, 'Acclaim for Antigone's Claim Reclaimed,' 70.
61. Seery, 'Acclaim for Antigone's Claim Reclaimed,' 71.
62. Lee Edelman, *No Future: Queer Theory and the Death Drive* (Durham, DC: Duke University Press, 2004), 105.
63. Honig, *Antigone Interrupted*, 218, see also 50–3.
64. Judith Butler, 'Ethical Ambivalence,' in *The Turn to Ethics*, eds. Marjorie Garber, Beatrice Hanssen and Rebecca L. Walkowitz (London & New York: Routledge, 2000), 14.

65. Elena Loizidou, *Judith Butler: Ethics, Law, Politics* (London & New York: Routledge, 2007), 166.

66. Martha Nussbaum, 'The Professor of Parody: The Hip Defeatism of Judith Butler,' *New Republic*, 22 February 1999, accessed 1 September 2019, https://newrepublic.com/article/150687/professor-parody; see Loizidou, *Judith Butler*, 157– 163.

67. Honig, *Antigone Interrupted*, 19.

68. Honig, *Antigone Interrupted*, 19.

69. Honig mentions as a third theoretical conception of tragedy the perspective of the death-drive anti-humanism of desiring monstrousness where Antigone is seen as a heroic solitary conscience in her fight against arbitrary powers. I will come to this when dealing with Heidegger's Antigone. Honig, *Antigone Interrupted*, 19.

70. Three founders of the movement—Azucena Villaflor, Esther Careaga and María Eugenia Bianco—were kidnapped, tortured, and murdered.

71. Nancy Kason Poulson, 'In Defence of the Dead: *Antigona furiosa*, by Griselda Gambaro.' *Romance Quarterly* 59/1 (2012), 48–54.

72. Griselda Gambaro, 'Antigona furiosa,' in *Three Plays by Griselda Gambaro*, trans. Marguerite Fetlowutz (Evanston: Northwestern University Press, 1992), 141–2.

73. Griselda Gambaro, 'Antigona furiosa,' 158.

74. Griselda Gambaro, 'Antigona furiosa,' 159.

75. Diana Taylor, *Disappearing Acts: Spectacles of Gender and Nationalism in Argentina's 'Dirty War'* (Durham, NC: Duke University Press, 1997), 222; see Honig, *Antigone Interrupted*, 40–1.

76. Annette Wannamaker, 'Memory Also Makes a Chain: The Performance of Absence in Griselda Gambaro's *Antigona furiosa*,' *The Journal of the Midwest Modern Language Association* 33/3 (2001), 77.

77. Jean Bethke Elstein, 'Antigone's Daughters Reconsidered: Continuing Reflections of Women, Politics and Power,' in *Life-World and Politics: Between Modernity and Postmodernity*, ed. Stephen K. White (West Bend, Ind.; Universtity of Notre Dame Press, 1989), 233.

78. Elstein, 'Antigone's Daughters Reconsidered.'

79. Sophocles, *Antigone*, 427–8, 476–7.

80. Honig, *Antigone Interrupted*, 39–40; Clifton R. Spargo, 'The Apolitics of Antigone's Lament (From Sophocles to Ariel Dorfman),' *Mosaic: A Journal for the Interdisciplinary Study of Literature* 41/3 (2008), 130.

Chapter Seven

1. Tina Chanter, 'Antigone's Political Legacies. Abjection in Defiance of Mourning,' in in S. E. Wilmer *Interrogating Antigone.*
2. Seamus Heaney, *The Burial at Thebes: A Version of Sophocles' Antigone* (London: Faber and Faber, 2004).
3. See Martin Heidegger, *Being and Time*, trans. John Macquarrie and Edward Robinson (Oxford & Cambridge, Mass.: Blackwell, 1995), 58.
4. Brecht, *Antigone.*
5. Chanter, 'Antigone's Political Legacies.'
6. Butler, *Antigone's Claim*, 2000, 38.
7. Lacan, *The Ethics of Psychoanalysis*, 271.
8. Sophocles, *Antigone*, 368–372,
9. Sophocles, *Oedipus Tyrannus*, 1523.
10. Walter Benjamin, *Ursprung des Deutschen Trauerspiels*, Gesammelete Schriften I.1 (Suhrkamp, Frankfurt am Main, 1963), 285–6.
11. Hölderlin, 'Anmerkungen zur Antigonae,' 268. My translation.
12. Hölderlin, 'Anmerkungen zur Antigonae,' 268. My translation.
13. Sophocles, *Antigone*, 4–5. Translation modified.
14. Sophocles, *Antigone*, 7–8. Translation modified.
15. Sophocles, *Phaedra*, in *Selected Fragmentary Plays I*, trans. Alan H. Sommerstein, David Fitzpatrick, and Thomas Talboy (Oxford: Oxbow Books, 2006), 291.
16. Sophocles, *Antigone*, 538–9.
17. Karl Reinhardt, *Sophocles* (Frankfurt am Main: Vittorio Klostermann, 1976), 73.
18. Reinhardt, *Sophocles*, 86.
19. Max Müller, 'Die ontologische Problematik des Naturrechts,' in *Die ontologische Begründung des Rechts*, ed. Arthur Kaufman (Darmstadt: Wissenschaftliche Buchgesellschaft, 1965), 465–6.
20. Walter Heinemann, *Die Relevanz der Philosophie Martin Heideggers für das Rechtsdenken* (Freiburg: Universität zu Freiburg, 1970).
21. Erik Wolf, *Rechtsphilosophische Studien: Ausgewählte Schriften I* (Frankfurt am Main: Vittorio Klostermann, 1972), 72–3.
22. Wolf, *Rechtsphilosophische Studien*, 72.
23. Werner Maihofer, *Recht und Sein: Prolegomena zu einer Rechtsontologie* (Freiburg: Universität zu Freiburg, 1953), 112–13, 123.
24. Geoffrey Steadman, *Sophocles' Antigone: Greek Text with Facing Vocabulary and Commentary* (Geoffrey Steadman, 2015), xv–xviii, accessed

1 September 2019, https://geoffreysteadman.files.wordpress.com/2015/06/antigone-23june15w.pdf.

25. Butler, *Antigone's Claim*, 10.
26. Butler, *Antigone's Claim*, 28.
27. Richard C. Jebb, *The Antigone of Sophocles with Commentary* (Cambridge University Press, Cambridge, 1966), s.xvii–xviii.
28. Etxabe, The Experience of Tragic Judgement, 88, 69.
29. Mark Griffith, 'Commentary,' in Sophocles, *Antigone*, ed. Mark Griffith (Cambridge: Cambridge University Press, 1999), 139.
30. Sophocles, *Antigone*, 211.
31. Aristotle, *Politics*, 1137b 11–14, 27–9.
32. Jacques Lacan, *The Ethics of Psychoanalysis*, 342.
33. See Alain Badiou, *Theory of the Subject*, trans. Bruno Bosteels (London & New York: Continuum, 2009).
34. Sophocles, *Antigone*, 1120.
35. Hölderlin, *Antigonae*, 102. My translation.
36. Hannah Arendt, *The Human Condition* (Chicago: The University of Chicago Press, 1998), 50.
37. Sophocles, *Antigone*, 22–32.
38. Sophocles, *Antigone* (Anne Carson), 444–55.
39. Hegel, Outlines of the Philosophy of Right, 169.
40. Jacques Lacan, *The Ethics of Psychoanalysis*, 278.
41. Sophocles, *Oedipus at Colonus*, 171–2.
42. Sjöholm, 'Naked Life.'
43. Judith Fletcher, 'Sophocles' Antigone and the Democratic Voice,' in S. E. Wilmer *'Interrogating Antigone.'*
44. Derrida, *Glas*, 143.
45. Alexandre Kojève, *Introduction à la lecture de Hegel: Léçons sur la phénoménologie de l'ésprit* (Paris: Gallimard, 1997), 105.
46. Sophocles, *Antigone*, 442–3.
47. Peter Hallward, 'Generic Sovereignty: The Philosophy of Alain Badiou,' *Angelaki: A Journal of the Theoretical Humanities*, 3/3 (1998), 87.
48. Butler, *Antigone's Claim*, 28.
49. Butler, *Antigone's Claim*, 11.
50. Butler, *Antigone's Claim*, 28.
51. Butler, *Antigone's Claim*, 28.
52. Helene P. Foley, 'Antigone as Moral Agent,' in *Tragedy and the Tragic: Greek Theatre and Beyond*, ed. M. S. Silk (Oxford: Clarendon Press, 1998), 53.
53. Foley, 'Antigone as Moral Agent,' 52.
54. Foley, 'Antigone as Moral Agent,' 52.

55. Honig, *Antigone Interrupted*, xii.
56. Honig, *Antigone Interrupted*, 20.
57. Derrida, *Glas*, 187.
58. Sophocles, *Antigone*, 450–5.
59. Sophocles, *Oedipus Tyrannus*, 865–7.
60. Sophocles, *Antigone*, 609.
61. Sophocles, *Antigone*, 613.
62. Martin Heidegger, *Hölderlin's Hymn 'The Ister,'* trans. William McNeill and Julia Davis (Bloomington & Indianapolis: Indiana University Press, 1996).
63. Heraclitus, *Fragments*, fragment 114.
64. Sophocles, *Antigone*, 7–8.
65. Sophocles, *Antigone*, 87.
66. Lacan, *The Ethics of Psychoanalysis*, 278.
67. Martin Heidegger, 'Der Spruch des Anaximander,' in *Holzwege* (Frankfurt am Main: Vittorio Klostermann, 1963), 354–7; Martin Heidegger, *Nietzsche I*, Gesamtausgabe 6.1 (Frankfurt am Main: Vittorio Klostermann, 1996), 168; Martin Heidegger, *Parmenides*, Gesamtausgabe 54 (Frankfurt am Main: Vittorio Klostermann, 1982), 54.
68. Franz Kafka, *Before the Law/Vor dem Gesetz*, a bilingual edition (Kindle, 2015).
69. Phillippe Nonet, 'Antigone's Law,' *Law, Culture and the Humanities* 2 (2006), 324.
70. Sophocles, *Antigone*.
71. Lacan *The Ethics of Psychoanalysis*, 278.
72. Derrida, *Glas*, 164.
73. See Ahuvia Kahane, 'Antigone: Lacan and the Structure of the Law,' in S. E. Wilmer *'Interrogating Antigone.'*
74. Lacan, *The Ethics of Psychoanalysis*, 247.
75. Fletcher, 'Sophocles' Antigone and the Democratic Voice.'
76. St. Augustine, *Confessions*, Vol. I, trans. William Watts (Cambridge, Mass.: Harvard University Press, 1979), 177.
77. Heraclitus, *Fragments*, fragment 30.
78. Bernard Knox, *The Heroic Temper: Studies in Sophoclean Tragedy* (Berkeley: University of California Press, 1984), 97.
79. Thucydides, *The History of Peloponnesian War*, II.37.3.
80. Michael Gagarin, *Writing the Greek Law* (Cambridge: Cambridge University Press, 2008).
81. Phillippe Nonet, 'Antigone's Law,' *Law, Culture and the Humanities*, 2 (2006), 321.
82. Aristotle, *Nicomachean Ethics*, 1137b 1–35.

83. Sophocles, *Antigone*, 454–5.
84. Honig, *Antigone Interrupted*, 193.
85. Lacan, *The Ethics of Psychoanalysis*, 278.
86. Sophocles, *Antigone*, 26–30.
87. Jennifer R. Ballengee, 'Mourning the Public Body in Sophocles' *Antigone*,' *Colloquy: Text, Theory, Critique*, 11 (2006), 37.
88. Sophocles, *Antigone*, 247.
89. Griffith, 'Commentary,' 167–8.
90. Sophocles, Antigone, 427-427.
91. Lacan, The Ethics of Psychoanalysis, 263.
92. Carol Jacobs, 'Dusting Antigone,' *MLN* 111/5 (1996), 903–8.
93. Sophocles, *Antigone*, 424–5.
94. Sophocles, *Antigone*, 424–5.
95. Hölderlin, *Antigonae*, 83. My translation.
96. Sophocles, *Antigone*, 821.
97. Sophocles, *Antigone*, 457.
98. Louis Althusser, *Philosophy of the Encounter: Later Writings, 1978–1987*, trans. G. M. Goshgarin (London: Verso, 2006), 265.

Chapter Eight

1. Sophocles, *Antigone*, 100–1. Translation modified.
2. Heidegger, *Hölderlin's Hymn 'The Ister,'* 51–2.
3. Heidegger, *Hölderlin's Hymn 'The Ister,'* 51.
4. Martin Heidegger, 'Phenomenological Interpretations in Connection with Aristotle: An Indication of the Hermeneutical Situation,' trans. John van Buren, in *Supplements: From the Earliest Essays to* Being and Time *and Beyond* (Albany, NY: SUNY Press, 2002), 113.
5. Jacques Taminiaux, 'The Platonic Roots of Heidegger's Political Thought,' *European Journal of Political Theory* 6/1 (2007), 16.
6. Taminaux, 'The Platonic Roots of Heidegger's Political Thought,' 16, 18.
7. Martin Heidegger, 'The Anaximander Fragment,' in *Early Greek Thinkers*, trans. David Farrell Krell and Frank A. Capuzzi (San Francisco: Harper & Row, 1975), 58.
8. Martin Heidegger, 'Logos,' in *Early Greek Thinkers*, trans. David Farrell Krell and Frank A. Capuzzi (San Francisco: Harper & Row, 1975), 78.
9. Heidegger, *Hölderlin's Hymn 'The Ister,'* 150.
10. Heidegger, *Unterwegs der Sprache* (Pfullingen: Neske, 1959), 259.

11. Heidegger, *Hölderlin's Hymn 'The Ister,'* 52.
12. Martin Heidegger, *Introduction to Metaphysics*, trans. Gregor Fried and Richard Polt (New Haven & London: Yale University Press, 2000), 170.
13. Hölderlin, *Antigonae*, 219. My translation.
14. Heidegger, *Introduction to Metaphysics*, 163.
15. Martin Heidegger, *Hölderlin's Hymns 'Germania' and 'The Rhine,'* trans. William McNeill and Julia Ireland (Bloomington & Indianapolis: Indiana University Press, 2018), 197.
16. Heidegger, *Introduction to Metaphysics*, 188.
17. Clare Pearson Geiman, 'Heidegger's Antigones,' in *A Companion to Heidegger's Introduction to Metaphysics*, eds. Richard Polt and Gregory Fried (New Haven, CT: Yale University Press, 2001), 161.
18. Martin Heidegger, 'The Self-Assertion of the German University,' trans. K. Harries, in *Philosophical and Political Writings* (London: Continuum Press, 2003), 2–11.
19. Heidegger, *Hölderlin's Hymns 'Germania' and 'The Rhine,'* 29, 108, 126–7.
20. Taminiaux, 'The Platonic Roots of Heidegger's Political Thought,' 14.
21. Heidegger, *Hölderlin's Hymn 'The Ister,'* 51, 55.
22. Marc Froment-Meurice, *That Is to Say: Heidegger's Poetics*, trans. Jan Plug (Stanford: Stanford University Press. 1998), 127.
23. Geiman, 'Heidegger's Antigones,' 162; see also Scott Campbell, 'The Tragic Sense of Life in Heidegger's Readings of Antigone,' in *The Science, Politics, and Ontology of Life-Philosophy*, eds. Scott Campbell and Paul W. Bruno (London & New York: Bloomsbury, 2013), 86–188.
24. Heidegger, *Introduction to Metaphysics*, 117.
25. Heidegger, *Hölderlin's Hymn 'The Ister,'* 102.
26. Heidegger, *Hölderlin's Hymn 'The Ister,'* 102. Translation modified.
27. Hölderlin, Antigonae, 209. My translation.
28. Heidegger, *Hölderlin's Hymn 'The Ister,'* 103.
29. Sophocles, *Antigone*, 42.
30. Heidegger, *Hölderlin's Hymn 'The Ister,'* 101.
31. Sophocles, *Antigone*, 90.
32. Heidegger, *Hölderlin's Hymn 'The Ister,'* 103.
33. Heidegger, *Hölderlin's Hymn 'The Ister,'* 102.
34. Sophocles, *Antigone*, 88.
35. Françoise Dastur, *Hölderlin, Le retournement natal: Tragédie et modernité & nature et poésie* (Paris: Encre Marine, 1997), 87.
36. Valerie Reed, 'Bringing Antigone Home?', *Comparative Literary Studies*, 45/3 (2008), 319.

37. Heidegger, *Hölderlin's Hymn 'The Ister,'* 103–4.
38. Heidegger, *Hölderlin's Hymn 'The Ister,'* 103.
39. Heidegger, *Hölderlin's Hymn 'The Ister,'* 103.
40. Françoise Dastur, *Death: An Essay on Finitude*, trans. John Llewelyn (London: Athlone Press, 1996), 14.
41. Heidegger, *Hölderlin's Hymn 'The Ister,'* 104.
42. Martin Heidegger, 'Phenomenological Interpretations in Connection with Aristotle,' 119.
43. Dastur, *Death*, 81.
44. Maurice Blanchot, *Infinite Conversation*, trans. Susan Hanson (Minneapolis: University of Minnesota Press, 1992), 35.
45. Maurice Blanchot, 'Literature and the right to death,' in *The gaze of Orpheus, and Other Literary Essays*, trans. Lydia Davis, Paul Auster, and Robert Lamberton (New York: Station Hill Press, 1981), 43.
46. Sophocles, *Tereus*, in Selected Fragmentary Plays I, trans. Alan H. Sommerstein, David Fitzpatrick, and Thomas Talboy (Oxford: Oxbow Books, 2006), 167.
47. Heidegger, *Hölderlin's Hymn 'The Ister,'* 73.
48. Heidegger, *Introduction to Metaphysics*, 170.
49. Heidegger, *Introduction to Metaphysics*, 164.
50. Heidegger, *Introduction to Metaphysics*, 170.
51. Heidegger, *Hölderlin's Hymn 'The Ister,'* 82.
52. Heidegger, *Hölderlin's Hymn 'The Ister,'* 81.
53. Heidegger, *Hölderlin's Hymn 'The Ister,'* 86.
54. Heidegger, *Hölderlin's Hymn 'The Ister,'* 105.
55. Heidegger, *Hölderlin's Hymn 'The Ister,'* 112.
56. Heidegger, 'The Self-Assertion of the German University.'
57. Martin Heidegger, *Grundbegriffe der aristotelischen Philosophie*, Gesamtausgabe 18 (Frankfurt am Main: Vittorio Klostermann, 2002), 44.
58. Heidegger, *Grundbegriffe der aristotelischen Philosophie*, 44.
59. Taminiaux, 'The Platonic Roots of Heidegger's Political Thought,' 18.
60. Taminiaux, 'The Platonic Roots of Heidegger's Political Thought,' 19. Translation modified.
61. Taminiaux, 'The Platonic Roots of Heidegger's Political Thought,' 19.
62. Critchley, *Tragedy, the Greeks and Us*, 8.10.
63. Jacques Taminiaux, Antigone dans l'histoire de la philosophie, in *Antigone et la résistance civile,*' eds. Lambros Couloubaritsis and François Ost (Brussels: Ousia, 2004) 9–39.
64. Sophie Klimis, 'Antigone et Créon à la lumière du 'terrifian/extraordinaire' (deinotès) de l'humanité tragique,' in *Antigone et la résistance civile*, eds.

Lambros Couloubaritsis and François Ost (Brussels: Ousia, 2004), 89.
65. Martin Heidegger, *Letter on Humanism*, trans. Frank A. Capuzzi, in *Basic Writings* (New York: Harper & Row, 1977), 269.
66. Heidegger, *Grundbegriffe der aristotelischen Philosophie*, 103.
67. Philippe Lacoue-Labarthe, *Poetics of History: Rousseau and the Theater of Originary Mimesis*, trans. Jeff Fort (New York: Fordham University Press, 2019), 13–14.
68. See Francisco J. Gonzales, 'Beyond or Beneath Good and Evil? Heidegger's Purification of Aristotle's Ethics,' in *Heidegger and the Greeks*, eds. Drew A. Hyland and John Panteleimon Manoussakis (Bloomington & Indianapolis: Indiana University Press, 2006), 149–50.
69. Françoise Dastur, 'Tragedy and Evil: From Hölderlin to Heidegger,' in *Law and Evil: Philosophy, Politics, Psychoanalysis*, eds. Ari Hirvonen and Janne Porttikivi (London & New York: Routledge, 2010).
70. Martin Heidegger, *Zollikoner Seminare* (Frankfurt am Main: Vittorio Klostermann, 1987), 273.
71. Heidegger, *Hölderlin's Hymn 'The Ister,'* 102.
72. Heidegger, *Introduction to Metaphysics*, 137–8.
73. Heidegger, *Hölderlin's Hymns 'Germania' and 'The Rhine,'* 161.
74. Heidegger, *Introduction to Metaphysics*, 143.
75. Heidegger, *Introduction to Metaphysics*, 137–138.
76. Heidegger, *Hölderlin's Hymn 'Ister,'* 103.
77. Heidegger, *Introduction to Metaphysics*, 117.
78. Heidegger, *Hölderlin's Hymns 'Germania' and 'The Rhein,'* 127.
79. Heidegger, *Hölderlin's Hymns 'Germania' and 'The Rhein,'* 126.
80. Heidegger, *Hölderlin's Hymns 'Germania' and 'The Rhein,'* 197.
81. Heidegger, *Introduction to Metaphysics*, 130.
82. Heidegger, *Introduction to Metaphysics*, 140.
83. Heidegger, *Introduction to Metaphysics*, 159.
84. Dastur, *Death*, 84.
85. Dastur, *Death*, 83.
86. Hölderlin, *Hyperion*. Sämtliche Werke 3 (Stuttgart: Kohlhammer 1957), 148.
87. Martin Heidegger, *Frühe Schriften*, Gesamtausgabe 1 (Frankfurt am Main: Vittorio Klostermann, 1978), unnumbered page. Even though Heidegger's growing interest in Hölderlin distances him from the idea of *Führerprinzip*, according to which the leader represents the will of the people (*Volkswillen*), we cannot avoid taking into consideration his sympathizing with National Socialism, his silence about the Holocaust, and his *Schwarze Hefte*, the personal and political thought journal containing controversial statements including anti-Semitic

content.

88. Jean-Luc Nancy, 'L "éthique originaire" de Heidegger,' in *La pensée dérobée*, (Paris: Galilée, 2001, 95).
89. Nancy, 'L "éthique originaire" de Heidegger,' 88.
90. Nancy, 'L "éthique originaire" de Heidegger,' 113.
91. Nancy, 'L "éthique originaire" de Heidegger,' 112. My translation.
92. Nancy, 'L "éthique originaire" de Heidegger,' 112.
93. Nancy, 'L "éthique originaire" de Heidegger,' 89. My Translation.
94. Nancy, 'L "éthique originaire" de Heidegger,' 92.
95. Nancy, 'L "éthique originaire" de Heidegger,' 98. My Translation.
96. Nancy, 'L "éthique originaire" de Heidegger,' 98.
97. Heidegger, *Letter on Humanism*, 239.
98. Martin Heidegger, 'Logos,' in *Early Greek Thinkers*, trans. David Farrell Krell and Frank A. Capuzzi (San Francisco: Harper & Row, 1975), 78.
99. Martin Heidegger, *Plato's Sophist*, trans. Richard Rojcewicz and André Schuwer (Bloomington: Indiana University Press, 1997), 120.
100. Miguel de Beistegui, *The New Heidegger* (London & New York: Continuum, 2005), 27.
101. Marie-Eve Morin, *Jean-Luc Nancy* (Cambridge & Malden, MA: Polity Press, 2012), 144.
102. Jean-Luc Nancy, 'L'éthique originaire' de Heidegger,' 111. My translation.
103. Philippe Lacoue-Labarthe, 'Transcendence Ends in Politics,' in *Typography: Mimesis, Philosophy, Politics*, trans. Chistopher Fynsk (Stanford: Stanford University Press, 1998), 286.

Chapter Nine

1. Élisabeth Roudinesco in Alain Badiou and Élisabeth Roudinesco, *Jacques Lacan: Past and Present: A Dialogue*, trans. Jason E. Smith (New York: Columbia University Press, 2014), 35.
2. Alain Badiou in Badiou and Roudinesco, *Jacques Lacan: Past and Present*, 34.
3. Lacan, *The Ethics of Psychoanalysis*, 320.
4. Lacan, *The Ethics of Psychoanalysis*, 243.
5. Lacan, *The Ethics of Psychoanalysis*, 243.
6. Lacan, *The Ethics of Psychoanalysis*, 248. Translation modified.
7. Philippe Van Haute, 'Antigone, heldin van de psychoanalyse? Lacans lectuur van Antigone,' in *De God van denkers en dichters. Opstellen voor Samuel*

IJsseling, eds. Egdius Berns, Paul Moyaert and Paul van Tongeren (Boom: Amsterdam, 1997).
8. Lacan, *The Ethics of Psychoanalysis*, 250.
9. Lacan, *The Ethics of Psychoanalysis*, 247.
10. Lacan, *The Ethics of Psychoanalysis*, 247. Translation modified.
11. Lacan considers catharsis as the purgation of the imaginary. Paradoxically, this catharsis takes place through a specific image, the image of beauty that is not a reassuring and the comforting image that would provide support for an imaginary identification. Instead, it is a blinding image, which points towards ultimate limits, and beyond representation and meaning. This image creates both a barrier and a pointer pointing beyond identities, discourses, meanings, and coordinates that sustain human existence.
12. Lacan, *The Ethics of Psychoanalysis*, 243. Translation modified.
13. Slavoj Žižek, *Welcome to the Desert of the Real* (London & New York: Verso, 2002), 99.
14. De Kesel, 'Antigone's Fart,' 3.
15. Lacan, *The Ethics of Psychoanalysis*, 259.
16. Lacan, *The Ethics of Psychoanalysis*, 259. Translation modified.
17. Lacan, *The Ethics of Psychoanalysis*, 259. Translation modified.
18. Lacan, *The Ethics of Psychoanalysis*, 259. Translation modified.
19. Lacan, *The Ethics of Psychoanalysis*; 259.
20. Sophocles, *Antigone*, 559–60.
21. Sophocles, *Antigone*, 555.
22. Lacan, *The Ethics of Psychoanalysis*, 248.
23. Jacques Lacan, 'Position of the Unconscious,' in Écrits, trans. Bruce Fink (New York: Norton, 2006), 719.
24. Lacan, 'Position of the Unconscious,' 719.
25. Massimo Recalcati, 'Il sonno della realtà e il trauma del reale,' in *Bentornata realtà: Il nuovo realismo in discussion*, eds. Mario De Caro and Maurizio Ferraris (Turin: Einaudi, 2012), 193.
26. Recalcati, 'Il sonno della realtà e il trauma del reale,' 197.
27. Recalcati, 'Il sonno della realtà e il trauma del reale,' 193.
28. Sophocles, *Oedipus at Colonus*, trans. Hugh Lloyd-Jones, (Cambridge, Mass. & London: Harvard University Press, 1998), 1590–654.
29. Sophocles, *Oedipus at Colonus*, 1584.
30. Lacoue-Labarthe, 'De l'éthique: à propos d'Antigone,' 27.
31. Lacan, *The Ethics of Psychoanalysis*, 247.
32. Lacan, *The Ethics of Psychoanalysis*, 281.
33. Lacan, *The Ethics of Psychoanalysis*, 271.
34. Lacan, *The Ethics of Psychoanalysis*, 282.

35. Lacan, *The Ethics of Psychoanalysis*, 283.
36. Lacan, *The Ethics of Psychoanalysis* 282.
37. Chanter, 'Antigone's Political Legacies.'
38. Lacan, *The Ethics of Psychoanalysis*, 278.
39. See Philippe van Haute, 'Antigone, psykoanalyysin sankaritar,' trans. Janne Kurki, *Tiede & edistys* 3 (2003), 196; see Van Haute, 'Antigone, heldin van de psychoanalyse?'. My translation.
40. De Kesel, 'Antigone's Fart,' 3.
41. Lacan, *The Ethics of Psychoanalysis*, 320.
42. Lacan, *The Ethics of Psychoanalysis*, 320.
43. Lacan, *The Ethics of Psychoanalysis*,, 320.
44. Alain Badiou in Badiou and Roudinesco, *Jacques Lacan: Past and Present*, 33.
45. Marc De Kesel, 'There is No Ethics of the Real,' a paper delivered at the International Conference Rhetoric, Politics, Ethics (Ghent University, 21–3 April 2005), 9.
46. Lacan, *The Ethics of Psychoanalysis*, 321.
47. Lacan, *The Ethics of Psychoanalysis*, 218–230.
48. Jacques Lacan, *Television*, trans. Dennis Hollier, Rosalind Krauss, and Annette Michelson (New York: Norton, 1990), 19.
49. Lacan, *Television*, 19–20.
50. Gilles Deleuze, *Difference and Repetition*, trans. Paul R. Patton (New York: Columbia University Press, 1994), 16; Alenka Zupančič, *What is Sex?* (Cambridge, Mass. & London: The MIT Press, 2017), 111.
51. Jacques Lacan, 'The Signification of the Phallus,' in Écrits, trans. Bruce Fink (New York & London: Norton, 2006), 579.
52. Lacan, *The Ethics of Psychoanalysis*, 127.
53. Jacques Lacan, *The Four Fundamental Concepts of Psychoanalysis, Seminar XI*, trans. Alan Sheridan (New York: Norton, 1981), 276.
54. De Kesel, 'There Is No Ethics of the Real,' 11. It is surprising that Lacan does not refer to this.
55. Lacan, *The Ethics of Psychoanalysis*, 300.
56. Lacan, *The Ethics of Psychoanalysis*, 112.
57. Jacques-Alain Miller, trans. Jorge Jauregui and Marguerite Laport, 'Ethics in Psychoanalysis,' *Lacanian Ink* 5 (Winter 1992), 13–27.
58. De Kesel, 'There Is No Ethics of the Real,' 16.
59. Lacoue-Labarthe, 'De l'éthique: à propos d'Antigone,' 31.
60. Lacan, *The Ethics of Psychoanalysis*, 159.
61. Lacan, *The Ethics of Psychoanalysis*, 159.
62. Lacan, *The Ethics of Psychoanalysis*. Translation modified.

63. Lacoue-Labarthe, 'De l'éthique: à propos d'Antigone,' 32.
64. Lacan, *The Ethics of Psychoanalysis*, 120.
65. Lacan *The Ethics of Psychoanalysis*, 125.
66. Lacan, *The Ethics of Psychoanalysis*, 273.
67. Lacan, *The Ethics of Psychoanalysis*, 273.
68. Lacoue-Labarthe, 'De l'éthique: à propos d'Antigone,' 35.
69. Lacoue-Labarthe, 'De l'éthique: à propos d'Antigone,' 34.
70. Lacan, *The Ethics of Psychoanalysis*, 283.
71. Lacoue-Labarthe, 'De l'éthique: à propos d'Antigone,' 36.
72. van Haute, 'Antigone, psykoanalyysin sankaritar,' 199. My translation.
73. Lacan, *The Ethics of Psychoanalysis*, 311.
74. van Haute, 'Antigone, psykoanalyysin sankaritar,' 202. My translation.
75. Cecilia Sjöholm, *The Antigone Complex: Ethics and the Invention of Feminine Desire* (Stanford, CAL: Stanford University Press, 2004), 83.
76. Lacoue-Labarthe, 'De l'éthique: à propos d'Antigone,' 29–30.
77. De Kesel, 'Antigone's Fart,' 4.
78. Lacan, *The Ethics of Psychoanalysis*, 321.
79. van Haute, 'Antigone, psykoanalyysin sankaritar,' 204–5. My translation.
80. van Haute, 'Antigone, psykoanalyysin sankaritar,' 206. My translation.
81. Lacan, *The Ethics of Psychoanalysis*, 284.
82. Yannis Stavrakakis, 'The Lure of Antigone: Aporias of an Ethics of the Political,' in *Traversing the Fantasy: Critical Responses to Slavoj Žižek*, eds. Geoff Boucher, Jason Glynos, and Matthew Sharpe. (Aldershot: Ashgate, 2005), 175. According to him, in consumer culture, there is a displacement of full satisfaction from a product to another, from a fantasy to another and with its cumulative metonymic effect desire guarantees the reproduction of the market economy.
83. Jacques Lacan, *Anxiety, Seminar X, 1962–1963*, trans. A. R. Price (Cambridge & Malden, MA: Polity Press, 2014), 150.
84. Lacan, *Anxiety*, 150.
85. Lacan, *Anxiety*, 81. Translation modified.
86. Jacques Lacan, *The Four Fundamental Concepts of Psychoanalysis. Seminar XI*, trans. Alan Sheridan (New York: Norton, 1981), 38.
87. Jacques Lacan, *Encore: Seminar XX, 1972–1973*, trans. Bruce Fink (New York & London: W. W. Norton, 1975); see Ari Hirvonen, 'Between Signifier and Jouissance—Lacan with Teresa,' in *Sexuality and Psychoanalysis: Philosophical Criticism*, eds. Jens de Vleminck and Eran Dorfman (Leuven: Leuven University Press, 2010), 199–214.
88. Lacan, *The Ethics of Psychoanalysis*, 321.
89. Lacan, *The Ethics of Psychoanalysis*, 258.

90. Lacan, *The Ethics of Psychoanalysis* 315.

91. Slavoj Žižek, 'The Real of Sexual Difference,' in *Reading Seminar XX: Lacan's Major Work on Love, Knowledge, and Feminine Sexuality*, eds. Suzanne Barnard and Bruce Fink (Albany, NY: State University of New York Press, 2002), 68; Slavoj Žižek, *The Plague of Fantasies* (London & New York: Verso, 1997), 274.

92. Jacques Lacan, *L'acte psychanalytique, Séminaire XV, 1967–1968* (Paris: Ecole Lacanienne de psychanalyse), 29.11.1967.

93. Slavoj Žižek, 'From "Passionate Attachments" to Dis-Identification,' *Umbra* 1 (1998), 6.

94. Žižek, 'From "Passionate Attachments" to Dis-Identification,' 17.

95. Žižek, 'From "Passionate Attachments" to Dis-Identification,' 17.

96. Lacan, *The Ethics of Psychoanalysis*, 263.

97. Lacan, *The Ethics of Psychoanalysis*, 263.

98. Žižek, 'The Real of Sexual Difference,' 70.

99. Žižek, 'The Real of Sexual Difference,' 67.

100. Lacan, L'acte psychanalitique, 21.2.1968.

101. Slavoj Žižek, *The Plaque of Fantasies* (London & New York: Verso, 1997), 273.

102. Slavoj Žižek, *Did Somebody Say Totalitarianism? Five Inteventions in the Mis(use) of a Notion*. (London & New York: Verso, 2009), 6.

103. Slavoj Žižek, *The Ticklish Subject: The Absent Centre of Political Ontology* (London & New York: Verso, 1999), 376.

104. Slavoj Žižek, *Did Someone Say Totalitarianism? Five Interventions in the (Mis)use of a Notion* (London & New York: Verso, 2011), 167.

105. Slavoj Žižek, *Did Someone Say Totalitarianism? Five Interventions in the (Mis)use of a Notion* (London & New York: Verso, 2011), 167.

106. Stavrakakis, 'The Lure of Antigone,' 5.

107. Stavrakakis, 'The Lure of Antigone,' 14.

108. Stavrakakis, 'The Lure of Antigone,' 16.

109. Stavrakakis, 'The Lure of Antigone,' 13.

110. Žižek, *The Ticklish Subject*, 376.

111. Žižek, *The Plague of Fantasies*, 214–15.

Chapter Ten

1. Hölderlin, *L'Antigone de Sophocle*, trans. Philippe Lacoue-Labarthe (Paris: Christian Bourgois, 1998); see also Hölderlin, *OEdipe le Tyran de Sophocle*, trans. Philippe Lacoue-Labarthe (Paris: Christian Bourgois, 1998).

2. Philippe Lacoue-Labarthe, *L'Imitation des modernes*, 9.

3. Sarah Kofman, 'L'Espace de la césure,' *Critique* 34/379 (1978), 1143.
4. Kofman, 'L'Espace de la césure,' 1146.
5. Kofman, 'L'Espace de la césure,' 1146.
6. Kofman, 'L'Espace de la césure,' 1147.
7. Kofman, 'L'Espace de la césure,' 1145.
8. Kofman, 'L'Espace de la césure,' 1150.
9. Philippe Lacoue-Labarthe, 'La césure du spéculatif,' in Philippe Lacoue-Labarthe, *L'imitation des modernes: Typographies 2* (Paris: Galilée, 1986); Philippe Lacoue-Labarthe, 'The Caesura of Speculative,' in Philippe Lacoue-Labarthe, *Typographies*; see also Philippe Lacoue-Labarthe, 'La forme toute oublieuse de l'infidélité,' *L'animal* 19–20 (2008), 169.
10. Jacques Rancière, *Malais dans l'esthétique* (Paris: Galilée, 2004), 107–8.
11. Martin Heidegger, *The Origin of the Work of Art*, in *Basic Writings*, trans. Alfred Hofstaedter (San Francisco: Harper, 1993), 168.
12. Lacoue-Labarthe, 'Stagings of Mimesis,' 57.
13. Lacoue-Labarthe, 'Stagings of Mimesis,' 59. Translation modified.
14. Lacoue-Labarthe, 'De l'ethique,' 30.
15. Lacan, *The Ethics of Psychoanalysis*, 313.
16. Aristotle, *Poetics*. 1450a15–1450a23.
17. Stavrakakis, 'The Lure of Antigone,' 17.
18. Honig, *Antigone Interrupted*, 152.
19. Lacoue-Labarthe, 'The Caesura of Speculative,' 220.
20. Menke, 'The Presence of Tragedy,' 216.
21. Menke, 'The Presence of Tragedy,' 217.
22. Lacoue-Labarthe, 'The Caesura of Speculative,' 208.
23. Lacoue-Labarthe, 'The Caesura of Speculative,' 220.
24. Lacoue-Labarthe, 'The Caesura of the Speculative,' 226–7.
25. Lacoue-Labarthe, 'The Caesura of the Speculative,' 226–7.
26. Esa Kirkkopelto, 'Comparatifs de Hölderlin,' in *Philippe Lacoue-Labarthe: La Césure et l'impossible*, ed. Jacob Rogozinski (Paris: Lignes, 2010), 89; Lacoue-Labarthe, *L'imitation des modernes*, 43.
27. Friedrich Hölderlin, *Der Tod des Empedocle*, Erste Fassung, Sämtliche Werke 4, Stuttgarter Hölderlin-Ausgabe, ed. Friedrich Bessner (Stuttgart: W. Kohlhammer Verlag, 1961).
28. Friedrich Hölderlin, *Briefe I*, Sämtliche Werke 6, Stuttgarter Hölderlin/Ausgabe, ed. Friedrich Bessner (Stuttgart: W. Kohlhammer Verlag, 1954), 181.
29. Lacoue-Labarthe, 'Hölderlin's Theatre,' 120; see also Lacoue-Labarthe, 'The Caesura of the Speculative,' 228–9.
30. Hölderlin, *Der Tod des Empedocle*.
31. Lacoue-Labarthe, 'The Caesura of the Speculative,' 228.

32. Hölderlin, *Der Tod des Empedocles*; see also Friedrich Hölderlin, 'Plan der Dritten Fassung'; Friedrich Hölderlin, 'Frankfurter Plan.'
33. Friedrich Hölderlin, *Grund zum Empedocles*, Zweite Fassung, Sämtliche Werke 4, Stuttgarter Hölderlin/Ausgabe, ed. Friedrich Bessner (Stuttgart: W. Kohlhammer Verlag, 1961).
34. Lacoue-Labarthe, 'Hölderlin's Theatre,' 121.
35. Hölderlin, 'Anmerkungen zum Oedipus,' 196.
36. Homer, *Iliad*, 1.1.
37. Lacoue-Labarthe, 'Stagings of Mimesis,' 63.
38. Jean-Luc Nancy, 'The Calculation of the Poet,' in *The Solid Letter: Readings of Friedrich Hölderlin*, ed. by Aris Fioretos. trans. Simon Sparks (Stanford: Stanford University Press, 1999), 45.
39. See Dastur, 'Tragedy and Evil.'
40. Philippe Lacoue-Labarthe, 'L'Antigone de Hölderlin: Entretien avec Philippe Lacoue-Labarthe propos recueillis par Aliette Armel,' in *Antigon: Figures mythiques*, ed. Aliette Armel (Paris Éditions Autrement, 2015), 114.
41. Dastur, 'Tragedy and Evil: From Hölderlin to Heidegger.'
42. Lacoue-Labarthe, 'Hölderlin's Theatre,' 121.
43. Lacoue-Labarthe, 'Hölderlin's Theatre,' 123.
44. François Dastur, 'Tragedy and Speculation,' in *Philosophy and Tragedy*, eds. Miguel de Beistegui and Simon Sparks (London & New York: Routledge, 2000), 84.
45. Philippe Lacoue-Labarthe, 'De Hölderlin à Marx: mythe, imitation, tragédie,' *Labyrinthe* 22 (2005), accessed 1 October 2019, http://journals.openedition.org/labyrinthe/1484.
46. Lacoue-Labarthe, 'Hölderlin's Theatre,' 123.
47. Hölderlin, 'Anmerkungen zur Antigonae,' 269. My translation.
48. Reinhardt, *Sophokles*, 10–13.
49. Sophocles, *Antigone*, 443, 446–7.
50. Sophocles, *Antigone*, 443.
51. Hölderlin, *Antigonae*, 223. My translation.
52. Sophocles, *Antigone*, 449.
53. Hölderlin, *Antigonae* 223. My translation.
54. Sophocles, *Antigone*, 450–3.
55. Hölderlin, *Antigonae*, 223. My translation.
56. Sophocles, *Antigone*, 823–33.
57. Sophocles, *Antigone*, 834–5.
58. Hesiod, *Works and Days*, trans. Apostolos N. Athanassakis (Baltimore & London: The Johns Hopkins University Press, 2004), II.212–24.
59. Sophocles, *Antigone*, 442.

60. See Heidegger, *Hölderlin's Hymne 'Der Ister,'* 145.
61. Sophocles, *Antigone*, 453–5.
62. Sophocles, *Antigone*, 853.
63. Sophocles, *Antigone*, 854; Hölderlin, *Antigonae*, 241.
64. Sophocles, *Antigone*, 837.
65. Sophocles, *Antigone*, 853–855.
66. Hölderlin, *Antigonae*, 241. My translation.
67. Hölderlin, 'Anmerkungen zur Antigonae,' 202.
68. Hölderlin, 'Anmerkungen zum Oedipus,' 202. My translation.
69. Hölderlin, 'Anmerkungen zum Oedipus,' 202. My translation.
70. Sophocles, *Antigone*, 90. Translation modified.
71. Sophocles, *Antigone*, 90. Translation modified.
72. Sophocles, *Antigone*, 90. Translation modified.
73. Critchley, *Tragedy, the Greeks and Us*, 6.2.
74. Peter Szondi, *An Essay on the Tragic*, trans. Paul Fleming (Stanford CA: Stanford University Press, 2002); see Critchley, *Tragedy, the Greeks and Us*, 17.1.
75. Critchley, *Tragedy, the Greeks and Us*, 17.8.
76. Critchley, *Tragedy, the Greeks and Us*, 17.8.
77. Critchley, *Tragedy, the Greeks and Us*, 60.1.
78. Critchley, *Tragedy, the Greeks and Us*, 60.1.
79. Critchley, *Tragedy, the Greeks and Us*, 60.11.
80. Critchley, *Tragedy, the Greeks and Us*, 60.1.
81. For Hölderlin, Oedipus' despotism stems from his own choice of a tyrannical tone instead of the unavoidable curse.
82. Beistegui and Sparks, *Philosophy and Tragedy*, 123.
83. '*Die Darstellung des Tragischen beruht vorzüglich darauf, daß das Ungeheure, wie der Gott und Mensch sich paart, und gränzenlos die Naturmacht des Menschen Innerstes im Zorn Eins wird, dadurch sich begreift, daß das gränzenlose Eineswerden durch gränzenloses Scheiden sich reinigt.*' Hölderlin, 'Anmerkungen zum Oedipus,' 201. My translation.
84. Hölderlin, 'Anmerkungen zum Oedipus,' 201. My translation.
85. *Pensive Athena* (around 460, Acr. 695). The Acropolis Museum, Photography Socratis Mavrommatis.
86. Philippe Lacoue-Labarthe, 'Métaphrasis,' in Philippe Lacoue-Labarthe, *Métaphrasis* suivi de *Le Théatre de Hölderlin* (Paris: P.U.F., 1998), 18–19, 23–6, 38–9.
87. Lacoue-Labarthe, 'La forme toute oublieuse de l'infidélité,' 167.
88. Lacoue-Labarthe, 'The Caesura of the Speculative,' 231.
89. Lacoue-Labarthe, 'The Caesura of the Speculative,' 233.
90. Hölderlin, 'Anmerkungen zur Antigonae,' 270.

91. Hölderlin, 'Anmerkungen zum Oedipus,' 196.
92. Hölderlin, 'Anmerkungen zum Oedipus,' 196.
93. Hölderlin, 'Anmerkungen zum Oedipus,' 196; Hölderlin, 'Anmerkungen zur Antigonae,' 265–6.
94. Sophocles, *Antigone*, 998–1132.
95. Hölderlin, 'Anmerkungen zum Oedipus,' 196; Hölderlin, 'Anmerkungen zur Antigonae,' 265–6.
96. Sophocles, *Oedipus Tyrannus*, 44762.
97. Hölderlin, 'Anmerkungen zum Oedipus,' 196. My translation.
98. Hölderlin, 'Anmerkungen zum Oedipus,' 197.
99. Hölderlin, 'Anmerkungen zum Oedipus,' 202.
100. Hölderlin, 'Anmerkungen zum Oedipus,' 272. My translation.
101. Aristotle, *Rhetoric*, 1417b 20.
102. Aristotle, *Rhetoric*, 1418b 32–3.
103. Esa Kirkkopelto, 'Comparatifs de Hölderlin,' in Jacob Rogozinski, *Philippe Lacoue-Labarthe: La Césure et l'impossible* (Paris: Lignes, 2010), 107.
104. Sophocles, *Antigone*, 734, 737, 739.
105. Sophocles, *Antigone*, 743.
106. Sophocles, *Phaedra*, 297.
107. Heraclitus, *Fragments*, trans. Dennis Sweet (Lanham & London: University Press of America, 1995), F94.
108. Peter Szondi, *Hölderlin Studien: Mit einem Traktat über philologische Erkenntnis* (Frankfurt am Main: Suhrkamp, 1967), 110. For the historical turn, see Lothar Kempter, *Hölderlin und die Mythologie* (Leipzig: Münster Press, 1929), 66–73.
109. Hölderlin, 'Anmerkungen zum Oedipus,' 202.
110. Beda Allemann , *Hölderlin und Heidegger* (Atlantis Verlag, Freiburg, 1954), 13–34.
111. Jennifer Anna Gosetti-Ferencei, *Heidegger, Hölderlin, and the Subject of Poetic Languages: Toward a Poetics of Dasein* (New York: Fordham Unibversity Press, 2004), 11.
112. Beaufret, *Hölderlin et Sophocles*, 19. My translation.
113. Beaufret, *Hölderlin et Sophocles*, 20. My translation.
114. Zweig, *The Struggle with the Daemon*, 70.
115. Heidegger, Poetry, Language, Thought, 221.
116. Heidegger, 'Poetically Man Dwells,' 223.
117. c.f. Henry Weinfield, '"Is there A Measure on Earth": Hölderlin's Poem "In lovely Blueness" in the Light of Heidegger's Essay "Poetically Man Dwells"' *Journal of Philosophy: A Cross-Disciplinary Inquiry*, 6/13 (2010), 54–61, 60.
118. Renata Salecl, 'Society of Choice,' *Differences* 20/1 (2009), 166.

119. Recalcati, 'Il sonno della realtà e il trauma del reale,' 196.

Chapter Eleven

1. Lacoue-Labarthe, 'Stagings of Mimesis,' 59.
2. Weber, *Theatricality as Medium*, 2.
3. Alain Badiou, 'Theatre and Philosophy,' in Alain Badiou, *Rhapsody for Theatre*, 92–109; Alain Badiou, *Handbook of Inaesthetics*, trans. Alberto Toscano (Stanford: Stanford University Press, 2004), 2–7.
4. Badiou, *Handbook of Inaesthetics*, 3.
5. Philippe Lacoue-Labarthe and Jean-Luc Nancy, *The Literary Absolute: The Theory of Literature in German Romanticism*, trans. Philippe Barnard and Cheryl Lester (Albany, NY: State University of New York Press, 1988).
6. Badiou, *Handbook of Inaesthetics*, 3.
7. Badiou, *Handbook of Inaesthetics*, 7.
8. Badiou, *Handbook of Inaesthetics*, 7.
9. Badiou, *Handbook of Inaesthetics*, 8. Badiou ignores not only the Japanese Noh-theatre but also various forms of new theatre from the theatre of images to the concrete theatre, from the theatre of scenography to post-humanist theatre and beyond, which challenges his categorization.
10. Philippe Lacoue-Labarthe, *Poetics of History: Rousseau and the Theater of Originary Mimesis*, trans. Jeff Fort (New York: Fordham University Press, 2019), 9.
11. See Badiou, *Rhapsody for Theatre*, 72.
12. Segal, 'Catharsis,' 157.
13. Segal, 'Catharsis,' 157.
14. Denis Guénoun, *L'Exhibition des mots: Une idée (politique) du théâtre* (Paris: L'Aube, 1992).
15. Alain Badiou, *Rhapsody for the Theatre*, trans. Bruno Bosteels and Martin Puchner (London & New York: Verso, 2013), 164.
16. Weber, *Theatricality as Medium*, 7.
17. Weber, *Theatricality as Medium*, 7.
18. Badiou, *Rhapsody for the Theatre*, 71.
19. Badiou, *Rhapsody for the Theatre*, 75.
20. Badiou, *Rhapsody for the Theatre*, 78.
21. Hans-Thies Lehmann, *Postdramatic Theatre*, trans. Karen Jürs-Munby (London and New York: Routledge, 2006).
22. Sylvain Lazarus, *Anthropologie du nom* (Paris: Seuil, 1996); Badiou,

Rhapsody for the Theatre, 45. [My translation.]

23. Hans-Thiels Lehmann, 'Word and Stage in Postdramatic Theatre,' in *Contemporary Drama in English* 14 (2007); see Lacoue-Labarthe, 'De l'éthique: à propos d'Antigone.'

24. Lehmann, 'Word and Stage in Postdramatic Theatre,' 38.

25. Lehmann, 'Word and Stage in Postdramatic Theatre,' 38–54, 38.

26. Hans-Thies Lehmann, 'From Logos to Landscape: Text in Contemporary Dramaturgy.' *Performance Research* 2/1 (1997) 55.

27. Lehmann, 'Word and Stage in Postdramatic Theatre,' 38–54, 38.

28. Aristotle, *Poetics*, 1450b 18–19.

29. Aristotle, *Poetics*, 1450b 19–21. Translation modified.

30. Badiou, *Theory of the Subject*, 159.

31. Aristotle, *Poetics*, 1450b 18.

32. See Julia Jarcho, *Writing and the Modern Stage: Theater beyond Drama* (Cambridge & New York: Cambridge University Press, 2017), 202.

33. Badiou, *Theory of the Subject*, 161.

34. Jacques Derrida, *Writing and Difference*, trans. Alan Bass (Chicago: Chicago University Press, 1978,) 212.

35. Jarcho, *Writing and the Modern Stage*, 199.

36. Walter Benjamin, *The Work of Art in the Age of Its Reproducibility: Selected Writings 4*, trans. Edmund Jephcott and Harry Zohn (Cambridge, MA & London: Harvard University Press, 2006), 260.

37. Benjamin, *The Work of Art in the Age of Its Reproducibility*, 105.

38. Benjamin, *The Work of Art in the Age of Its Reproducibility*, 259.

39. Benjamin, *The Work of Art in the Age of Its Reproducibility*, 259.

40. Benjamin, *The Work of Art in the Age of Its Reproducibility*, 105.

41. Benjamin, *The Work of Art in the Age of Its Reproducibility*, 106.

42. Jacques Rancière (with Adnen Jdey), *La méthode de la scène* (Paris: Lignes, 2018), 48. My translation.

43. Rancière, *La méthode de la scène*, 37. My translation.

44. Rancière, *La méthode de la scène*, 48. My translation.

45. In Ancient Greece, lyric referred to poetry sung in accompaniment to the lyre (*lyra*). The metre of the rhythmic structure of lyric poetry was freer than epic poetry, the metre of which was always the hexameter. Greek dramatic poetry included both lyric metres, sung usually by the chorus, and the iambic trimetre and the trochaic tetrametre, spoken usually by actors, even though there were crossovers. Thus, lyric was divided into the choral song and the monody. In the choral song, verses were assembled into strophes, which were based on the triadic system, where the identical strophe and anti-strophe were followed by the epode, the strophe with a diverging structure. However, this division was not a strict one,

at least before Plato's time. German idealism would present this as a dialectic, where an objective thesis (epic narrative) is followed by a subjective antithesis (non-narrative lyric poetry) ending with a synthesis (dramatic narrative).

46. Lacoue-Labarthe in Lacoue-Labarthe and Nancy, *Scéne*, 99. My translation.

47. Rancière, *La méthode de la scène*, 45, 76.

48. Lacoue-Labarthe in Lacoue-Labarthe and Nancy, *Scéne*, 99, 92. My translation.

49. See Nancy in Lacoue-Labarthe and Nancy, *Scéne*, 104–106.

50. c.f. Jacques Derrida, *Of Grammatology*, trans. Gayatri Chakravorty Spivak (Baltimore & London: The Johns Hopkins University Press, 1976), 60.

51. Lacoue-Labarthe, in Lacoue-Labarthe and Nancy, *Scéne*, 93. My translation.

52. Aristotle does not condemn mise-en-scène but announces the principle of the sobriety of art and theatre. Actually, Aristotle says that the tragic poetry is to be judged in relation to tragedy both as purely poetry and as theatre presentation. Lacoue-Labarthe in Lacoue-Labarthe and Nancy, *Scéne*, 20; Aristotle, *Poetics*, 1449a8.

53. C.f. Rancière, *La méthode de la scène*, 76.

54. On the matter of scene, Nancy sees a divergence between himself and Lacoue-Labarthe, who stresses the effacement of the figure and the cessation of the myth. Lacoue-Labarthe shares Aristotle's distrust of *opsis*, since theatre is not essentially an art of vision, figuration, and figured fictions of identity but an appearance and spacing. For Nancy, the interruption of myth is not simple cessation but a cutting movement. Nancy sees their difference in a paradoxical light since, as we have shown, Lacoue-Labarthe had practiced mise-en-scène, whilst Nancy had had little interest in theatrical shows. Nancy in Lacoue-Labarthe and Nancy, *Scéne*, 13; Lacoue-Labarthe in Lacoue-Labarthe and Nancy, *Scène*, 27–8. My translation.

55. Guénoun, *Actions et acteurs*, 93. My translation; Rancière, *La méthode de la scène*.

56. Gay McAuley, *Space in Performance: Making Meaning in the Theatre* (Ann Arbor, MI: University of Michigan Press, 1999.)

57. Jean-Luc Nancy, 'Body-Theatre,' in *Figures of Touch: Sense, Technics, Body*, eds. Mika Elo and Miika Luoto (Helsinki: Academy of Fine Arts, 2018), 24.

58. Denis Guénoun, 'Qu'est qu'une scène?' In *Philosophie de la scène* (Besançon: Les Solitaires Intempestifs, 2010), 18.

59. Esa Kirkkopelto, *Le Théâtre de l'expérience: contributions à la théorie de la scène* (Paris: Presses universitaires de Paris-Sorbonne, 2008), 38.

60. Nancy, 'Body-Theatre,' 30.

61. Kirkkopelto, *Le Théâtre de l'expérience*, 36.
62. Denis Guénoun, 'Qu'est qu'une scène?', 12.
63. Esa Kirkkopelto, 'La question de la scène,' in *Philosophie de la scène* (Besançon: Les Solitaires Intempestifs, 2010), 116; Weber, *Theatricality as Medium*, 6.
64. Badiou, *Rhapsody of Theatre*, 14.
65. Denis Guénoun, *Näyttämön filosofia*, trans. Esa Kirkkopelto (Helsinki: Like, 2007), 91, 99.
66. Weber, *Theatricality as Medium*, 257.
67. c.f. Weber, *Theatricality as Medium*, 259.
68. Karl Otfried Müller, *Geschichte der griechischen Literatur bis auf das Zeitalter Alexanders*, Band 2 (Stuttgart: Verlag von Albert Heitz, 1876), 23.
69. Oddone Longo, 'The Theater of the *Polis*,' in *Nothing to do with Dionysus? Athenian Drama in its Social Context*, eds. John J. Winkler and Froma Zeitlin (Princeton, NJ: Princeton University Press, 1990), 17.
70. Vernant and Vidal-Naquet, *Myth and Tragedy in Ancient Greece*, 312, 24, 34.
71. Vernant and Vidal-Naquet, *Myth and Tragedy in Ancient Greece*, 311–312 (Vidal-Naquet).
72. Simon Goldhill, 'Collectivity and Otherness: The Authority of the Tragic Chorus: Response to Gould.' In M. S. Silk, *Tragedy and the Tragic: Greek Theatre and Beyond* (Oxford: Clarendon Press, 1996), 247; see Gould, 'Tragedy and Collective Experience.'
73. Gould, 'Tragedy and Collective Experience,' 220.
74. Gould, 'Tragedy and Collective Experience,' 225.
75. Goldhill, 252.
76. Guénoun, *Näyttämön filosofia*, 83–6.
77. Plato, *Republic*, trans. H. D. P. Lee (London & New York: Penguin, 2017); Eiichi Tosaki, *Mondrian's Philosophy of Visual Rhythm: Phenomenology, Wittgenstein, and Eastern Thought* (Dordrecht: Springer, 2017), 149–50.
78. See Friedrich Nietzsche, *Thus Spoke Zarathustra*, trans. Graham Parkes (Oxford: Oxford University Press, 2005.)
79. Kirkkopelto, 'Comparatifs de Hölderlin,' 107–8.
80. Philippe Lacoue-Labarthe, *Pour n'en pas finir : Écrits sur la musique* (Paris: Christian Bourgeois, 2015), 147. On Lacoue-Labarthe's contribution to the philosophy of music, see Susanna Lindberg, 'Ontorythmie,' *Revue philosophique de Louvain* 108 (2010), 527–48 and Susanna Lindberg, 'Tonalités élémentaires,' in *Philippe Lacoue-Labarthe: La césure et l'Impossible*, ed. Jacob Rogozinski (Paris: Lignes, 2010).
81. Sami Santanen, 'Dimensions of Touch,' in *Figures of Touc: Sense,*

Technics, Body, ed. Mika Elo and Miika Luoto (Helsinki: Academy of Fine Arts, 2018), 218.

82. P. E. Easterling, 'Weeping, Witnessing, and the Tragic Audience. Response to Segal,' in *Tragedy and the Tragic, Greek Theatre and Beyond*, ed. M. S. Silk (Oxford: Clarendon Press, 1996), 173–81.

83. Gould, 'Tragedy and Collective Experience,' 233.

84. Weber, *Theatricality as Medium*, 43.

85. Badiou, *Handbook of Inaesthetics*, 74.

86. Denis Guénoun, *L'Exhibition des mots*.

87. Bonnie Honig, *Public Things: Democracy in Despair* (New York: Fordham University Press, 2017), xx. 'The holding environment' refers to D. W. Winnicott's peformative product and postulate of transitional activity.

88. Honig, *Public Things: Democracy in Despair*, 5.

89. Honig, *Public Things: Democracy in Despair*, 7.

90. Jacques Rancière, *La méthode de la scène* (Paris: Lignes, 2018), 23.

Chapter Twelve

1. Jean-Jacques Rousseau, *Letter to Alembert and Writings for the Theater*, Collected Writings *10*, trans. Allan Bloom, Charles Butterworth, and Christopher Kelly (Hanover: University Press of New England, 2004), 261.

2. Rousseau, *Letter to Alembert and Writings for the Theater*, 265.

3. Lacoue-Labarthe, *Poetics of History*, 79..

4. See Jacques Derrida, *Disseminations*, trans. Barbara Johnson (Chicago: Chicago University Press, 1981).

5. Badiou, *Handbook of Inaesthetics*, 72.

6. Badiou, 'Theatre and Philosophy,' 101.

7. Badiou, *The Handbook of Inaesthetics*, 9.

8. Badiou, *The Handbook of Inaesthetics*, 9.

9. Lacoue-Labarthe, 'Stagings of Mimesis,' 62.

10. Alain Badiou, 'Theatre and Philosophy,' in Alain Badiou, *Rhapsody for Theatre*, trans. Bruno Bosteels with the assistance of Martin Puchner (London & New York: Verso, 2013), 106.

11. Badiou, *The Handbook of Inaesthetics*, 14.

12. Badiou, *The Handbook of Inaesthetics*, 12.

13. Alain Badiou, Christopher Cox, and Molly Whalen, 'On Evil: An Interview with Alain Badiou,' *Cabinet* 5, Winter, (2001/2002).

14. Derrida, *Glas*, 45.

15. Badiou, 'Theatre and Philosophy,' 103.

16. Weber, *Theatricality as Medium*, 264.
17. Jean-Luc Nancy, *The Speculative Remark (One of Hegel's Bons Mots)*, trans. Céline Surpenant (Stanford: Stanford University Press, 2001), 32.
18. Lehmann, 'Word and Stage in Postdramatic Theatre,' 45.
19. Jean-Luc Nancy, 'The Sublime Offering,' in *Of the Sublime: Presence in Question*, eds. Jean-François Courtine and Jean-Luc Nancy, trans. Jeffrey S. Librett (Albany: SUNY Press, 1993), 36-8.
20. Martta Heikkilä, *At the Limits of Presentation: Coming-into-Presence and its Aesthetic Relevance in Jean-Luc Nancy's Philosophy* (Helsinki: Dissertation, Department of Aesthetic, University of Helsinki, 2007), 302.
21. Françoise Dastur, 'Hölderlin and the Orientalisation of Greece,' trans. Hector Kollias, *Pli* 10 (2000), 173.
22. Philippe Lacoue-Labarthe, 'Le Théâtre de Hölderlin,' in Philippe Lacoue-Labarthe, *Métaphrasis suivi de Le théâtre de Hölderlin* (Paris: P.U.F., 1998), 73.
23. Jacques Lacan, *Freud's papers on Techniques, Seminar I, 1953-1954*, trans. John Forrester (Cambridge: Cambridge University Press, 1988), 199.
24. Alain Badiou, *L'Etre et l'événement* (Paris: Seuil, 1988), 68-9.
25. In the capitalist situation, the proletariat is the invisible productive base. Today, refugees make the excluded void. Badiou, *L'Etre et l'événement*; see also Hallward, 'Generic Sovereignty,' 89-96.
26. Alain Badiou, *The True Life*, trans. Susan Spitzer (Cambridge & Malden, MA: Polity, 2017), 42.
27. Badiou, *L'Etre et l'événement*, 431.
28. Nancy, *Being Singular Plural*, 188.
29. Plato, *Phaedrus*, 250D, 265A.
30. Aristotle, *Metaphysics* (Oxford: Oxford University Press, 1997), 1022b 19-20.
31. Aristotle, *Nicomachean Ethics*, 1100a 4-9.
32. Aristotle, *Nicomachean Ethics*, 1101a 9-11.
33. Brecht, *Antigone*, 18. Translation modified.
34. Badiou, 'Theatre and Philosophy,' 107.
35. Aristotle, *Nicomachean Ethics*, 1115b 20.
36. Sophocles, *Antigone*, 72.
37. Sophocles, *Antigone*, 97.
38. Claire Nancy, 'La raison dramatique,' *Po&sie* 11 (2002), 114.
39. Jacques Derrida, 'Force de loi: Le "fondement mystique de l'autorité" / Force of Law; The "Mystical Foundation of Authority",' trans. Mary Quaintance. *Cardozo Law Review* 11/5-6 (1990) 920-1043.
40. Guénoun, *Näyttämön filosofia*, 78-79.

41. Derrida, *Glas*, 218.
42. Aristotle, *Nicomachean Ethics*, 1115b 12–13; Aristotle, *Eudemian Ethics*, trans. Anthony Kenny (New York: Oxford University Press, 2001), 1228b 26–27; see Giles Pearson, 'Courage and Temperance,' in *The Cambridge Companion to Aristotle's Nicomachean Ethics*, ed. Ronald Polansky (New York: Cambridge University Press, 2014), 110–13.
43. Lacan, *The Ethics of Psychoanalysis*, 323.
44. Lacan, *The Ethics of Psychoanalysis*, 323.
45. Aristotle, *Nicomachean Ethics*, 1115b 11–12.
46. Lacan, *The Ethics of Psychoanalysis*, 247.
47. Lacan, *The Ethics of Psychoanalysis*, 247.
48. Badiou, *Theory of the Subject*, 311.
49. Lacan, *Ecrits*, 782/660.
50. Martin Heidegger, *Unterwegs der Sprache* (Pfullingen: Neske, 1959), 259.
51. Heidegger, *Hölderlin's Hymne 'Der Ister,'* 150.
52. Badiou, *Theory of the Subject*, 158–160.
53. Badiou, *Theory of the Subject*, 160.
54. Derrida, *Glas*, 164.
55. Aristophanes. *Ecclesiazusae*, trans. Eugene O'Neill, Jr (New York: Random House, 1938), 605–13.
56. Alain Badiou, *Monde contemporain et désir de philosophie* (Reims: Cahier de Noris, 1992), 21.
57. Etxabe, *The Experience of Tragic Judgement*, 88, 167.
58. Badiou, *Theory of the Subject*, 165.
59. Badiou, *Theory of the Subject*, 166.
60. Badiou, *Theory of the Subject*, 162.
61. Badiou, *Theory of the Subject*, 168.
62. Badiou, *Theory of the Subject*, 168.
63. Badiou, *Theory of the Subject*, 168.
64. Badiou, *Theory of the Subject*, 168.
65. Badiou, *Theory of the Subject*, 161–62.
66. Derrida, *Glas*, 169.
67. Derrida, *Glas*, 170.
68. See Derrida, *Glas*, 172.
69. Aristotle, *On Rhetoric*, 1373b2.
70. Nancy, 'Politics and Beyond,' 97, 104.
71. Nancy, *Being Singular Plural*, 186.
72. Nancy, *Being Singular Plural*, 187.
73. Derrida, *Glas*, 171.

74. Derrida, *Glas*, 171.
75. Derrida, *Glas*, 173.
76. Nancy, *Being Singular Plural*, 8.
77. Jean-Luc Nancy, *The Inoperative Community*, 140; Jean-Luc Nancy, *Noli me tangere: On the Raising of the Body*, trans. Sarah Clift, Pascale-Anne Brault and Michael Naas (New York: Fordham University Press, 2008), 83.
78. Aristotle, *On Rhetoric*, 1358a.
79. Aristotle, *On Rhetoric*, 1381a–1381b.
80. Aristotle, *Nicomachean Ethics*, 1155a–1156a.
81. Badiou, *Ethics*, 42.
82. Sophocles, *Antigone*, 71–2.
83. Alain Badiou with Nicolas Truong, *In Praise of Theatre*, trans. Andrew Bielski (London: Polity, 2015), 42.
84. Nancy, *Being Singular Plural*, 32.
85. Nancy, *Being Singular Plural*, 185.
86. Nancy, *Being Singular Plural*, xvi.
87. Jean-Luc Nancy, *L' 'il y a' du rapport sexuel* (Paris: Galilée, 2001), 16.
88. Nancy, *Being Singular Plural*, 35. In *The Sense of the World*, Nancy makes a difference between 'being-with' and 'being-together.' Being-with refers to the place of love and truth, being-together to the place of the political and sense. Here, I do not make this difference. See also, Marie-Eve Morin, *Jean-Luc Nancy* (Cambridge & Malden, MA: Polity, 2012), 103–5.
89. Nancy, *The Inoperative Community*, 112.
90. Honig, *Antigone Interrupted*, 193.
91. Nancy, *Being Singular Plural*, 90.
92. Aristotle, *Nicomachean Ethics*, 1155a 5.
93. Alain Badiou, 'Thinking the Event,' in *Philosophy in the Present*, ed. Peter Engelman, trans. Peter Thomas and Alberto Toscano (Cambridge & Malden, MA: Polity, 2009), 32.
94. Badiou, *The Handbook of Inaesthetics*, 9.
95. Heikkilä, *At the Limits of Presentation*, 300.
96. Badiou, *In Praise of Theatre*, 25.
97. Nancy, *The Gravity of Thought*, 76–79; Nancy, *The Sense of the World*, 61.
98. Badiou, *Rhapsody for the Theatre*, 23.
99. Jacques Rancière, *The Emancipated Spectator*, trans. Gregory Elliot (London & New York: Verso, 2009), 13.
100. Philippe Lacoue-Labarthe, *Poetics of History: Rousseau and the Theater of Originary Mimesis*, trans. Jeff Fort (New York: Fodham University Press, 2019), 43.

101. Lacoue-Labarthe, *Poetics of History*, 28.

102. Ronald Bogue, 'The Betrayal of God,' in *Deleuze and Religion*, ed. Mary Bryden (London & New York: Routledge, 2001), 19.

103. Artemy Magun, *The Concept and the Experience of Revolution* (University of Michigan), 137; see also Artemy Magun, *Negative Revolution: Modern Political Subject and its Fate After the Cold War* (London: Bloomsbury Academic, 2013)

104. Lehmann, 'Word and Stage in Postdramatic Theatre,' 43.

Conclusion

1. Alain Badiou, *Rhapsodie pour le théâtre* (Paris: Presses Universitaires de France, 2014), 7.
2. Lehmann, *Postdramatic Theatre*, 183.
3. Lehmann, *Postdramatic Theatre*, 183.
4. See Lehmann, *Postdramatic Theatre*, 178.
5. Badiou, *The Handbook of Inaesthetics*, 14.
6. Soren Kierkegaard, *Repetition*, trans. Howard Hong and Edna Hong (Princeton: Princeton University Press, 1983), 131–33.
7. Jacques Derrida, Margins of Philosophy, trans. Alan Bass (Chicago & London: University of Chicago Press, 1982), 1–28.
8. Critchley, Tragedy, the Greeks and Us, 1.6.
9. Critchley, Tragedy, the Greeks and Us, 1.6.
10. Badiou, *Handbook of Inaesthetics*, 77.
11. Lehmann, *Postdramatic Theatre*, 177.
12. Badiou, *In Praise of Theatre*, 57.
13. The essence of technology is fundamentally enframing (*Ge-stell*), which designates how beings and entities are gathered together (the prefix *Ge* denotes 'gathering' and 'collection,' the root word *stellen* refers to 'to place' and 'to put'). The enframing describes an all-encompassing view of technology and a mode of human existence. This is our destiny, but there may be an alternative beginning. However, Heidegger does not declare the destruction of modern calculative thinking, abstract rationality, and technology. Martin Heidegger, *The Question Concerning Technology*, trans. William Lovitt, in *Basic Writings* (New York: Harper & Row, 1962); Martin Heidegger, *Building Dwelling Thinking*, trans. Albert Hofstadter, in *Poetry, Language, Thought*.
14. Fynsk, 'Reading the Poetics,' 246.
15. Badiou, *Rhapsody for Theatre*, 85.
16. Denis Guénoun, *Hypothéses sur l'Europe: Un essai de philosophie* (Paris: Circé, 2000), 60–1.

17. Badiou, *Rhapsody for Theatre*, 85.
18. Esa Kirkkopelto, 'Denis Guénounin näyttämölliset siirtymät,' in Denis Guénoun, *Näyttämön filosofia* (Helsinki: Like, 2007), 118.
19. See Alain Badiou, 'Discussion,' in Engelman, *Philosophy in the Present*, 81.
20. Badiou, *In Praise of Theatre*, 27.
21. Sophocles, *Tereus*, 171.
22. Lacoue-Labarthe, 'De l'éthique,' 24; Lacan, *The Ethics of Psychoanalysis*, 232.
23. Euripides, *Alcestis*, trans. David Kovacs (Cambridge: Harvard University Press, 1994), 780–90.

www.ingramcontent.com/pod-product-compliance
Lightning Source LLC
Chambersburg PA
CBHW071725080526
44588CB00013B/1904